Tourism and Hospitality in Conflict-Ridden Destinations

T0341115

Tourism and Hospitality in Conflict-Ridden Destinations provides insight into the various types of current and post-conflict destinations worldwide and the steps that might be taken to transform them into future tourist destinations.

Through both a conceptual and demonstrative approach, this book examines the steps destination management organizations as well as destination marketers need to take in order to improve their image in the eye of potential tourists. It also questions the extent to which tourism can alter the image of a destination and the possible destination marketing strategies that can be undertaken.

Analysis of a wide selection of international case studies in countries ranging from Palestine to Myanmar to Northern Ireland provides a thorough and far-reaching academic study. Written by an international and multidisciplinary team of leading academics, this book will be of great interest to students, researchers and academics in the tourism as well as development studies disciplines.

Rami K. Isaac is currently a Senior Lecturer in tourism teaching at Breda University of Applied Sciences in the Netherlands. He is also an assistant professor at Bethlehem University, Palestine.

Erdinç Çakmak teaches courses on destination management, contemporary marketing, context related research techniques and international fieldwork at both graduate and undergraduate programmes at Breda University in the Netherlands.

Richard Butler is currently an Emeritus Professor in the Business School at the University of Strathclyde, UK.

Contemporary Geographies of Leisure, Tourism and Mobility
Series Editor: C. Michael Hall
Professor at the Department of Management, College of Business and Economics, University of Canterbury, Christchurch, New Zealand

The aim of this series is to explore and communicate the intersections and relationships between leisure, tourism and human mobility within the social sciences.

It will incorporate both traditional and new perspectives on leisure and tourism from contemporary geography, e.g. notions of identity, representation and culture, while also providing for perspectives from cognate areas such as anthropology, cultural studies, gastronomy and food studies, marketing, policy studies and political economy, regional and urban planning, and sociology, within the development of an integrated field of leisure and tourism studies.

Also, increasingly, tourism and leisure are regarded as steps in a continuum of human mobility. Inclusion of mobility in the series offers the prospect to examine the relationship between tourism and migration, the sojourner, educational travel, and second home and retirement travel phenomena.

The series comprises two strands:

Routledge Studies in Contemporary Geographies of Leisure, Tourism and Mobility is a forum for innovative new research intended for research students and academics, and the titles will be available in hardback only.

Contemporary Geographies of Leisure, Tourism and Mobility aims to address the needs of students and academics, and the titles will be published in hardback and paperback. Titles include:

Resilient Destinations
Governance Strategies in the Transition towards Sustainability in Tourism
Edited by Jarkko Saarinen and Alison M. Gill

Tourism and Hospitality in Conflict-Ridden Destinations
Edited by Rami K. Isaac, Erdinç Çakmak and Richard Butler

For more information about this series, please visit: www.routledge.com/Contemporary-Geographies-of-Leisure-Tourism-and-Mobility/book-series/SE0522

Tourism and Hospitality in Conflict-Ridden Destinations

Edited by
Rami K. Isaac, Erdinç Çakmak
and Richard Butler

LONDON AND NEW YORK

First published 2019 by Routledge

2 Park Square, Milton Park, Abingdon, Oxon OX14 4RN
605 Third Avenue, New York, NY 10017

Routledge is an imprint of the Taylor & Francis Group, an informa business

First issued in paperback 2022

Publisher's Note

The publisher has gone to great lengths to ensure the quality of this reprint but points out that some imperfections in the original copies may be apparent.

British Library Cataloguing-in-Publication Data
A catalogue record for this book is available from the British Library

Library of Congress Cataloging-in-Publication Data
Names: Isaac, Rami K., author.
Title: Tourism and hospitality in conflict-ridden destinations / Rami Isaac, Erdinç Çakmak and Richard Butler.
Description: New York : Routledge, 2019. | Includes bibliographical references and index.
Identifiers: LCCN 2018057711 (print) | LCCN 2019006235 (ebook) | ISBN 9780429463235 (eBook) | ISBN 9781138615212 | ISBN 9781138615212 (Hardback : alk. paper) | ISBN 9780429463235 (Ebook)
Subjects: LCSH: Tourism—Political aspects.
Classification: LCC G155.A1 (ebook) | LCC G155.A1 I82 2019 (print) | DDC 338.4/791—dc23
LC record available at https://lccn.loc.gov/2018057711

ISBN: 978-1-138-61521-2 (hbk)
ISBN: 978-1-03-233845-3 (pbk)
DOI: 10.4324/9780429463235

Typeset in Times New Roman
by Apex CoVantage, LLC

Dedicated to our wives, Liga, Ömür and Margaret.

Contents

Figures

Tables

Contributors

Hazel Andrews, Liverpool John Moores University, UK

Raymond Boland, Breda University of Applied Sciences, The Netherlands

Stephen W. Boyd, Ulster University, Northern Ireland

Richard Butler, Emeritus Professor, Strathclyde University, Glasgow and Visiting Professor, Breda University of Applied Sciences, The Netherlands

Erdinç Çakmak, Breda University of Applied Sciences, The Netherlands

Farai Chigora, University of KwaZulu-Natal, Graduate School of Business, South Africa

Anna Farmaki, Cyprus University of Technology, Cyprus

Laura Gorlero, independent researcher

Nicole Haeusler, Honorary Professorship, University of Sustainable Development, Germany

Rami K. Isaac, Breda University of Applied Sciences, The Netherlands

Jamil Khader, Bethlehem University, Palestine

Maximiliano E. Korstanje, University of Palermo, Buenos Aires Argentina

Frauke Kraas, University of Cologne, Germany

Joram Ndlovu, University of KwaZulu-Natal, School of Social Sciences, Howard College, South Africa

Naef J. Patrick, University of Genève, Switzerland

Girish Prayag, University of Canterbury, New Zealand

Tazayian Sayira, independent researcher

Zin Mar Than, University of Cologne, Germany

Dallen J. Timothy, Arizona State University, USA

Rodanthi Tzanelli, University of Leeds, UK

Anne Marie Van Broeck, KU Leuven, Belgium and Institución Universitaria Colegio Mayor de Antioquia, Colombia

Nicholas Wise, Liverpool John Moores University, UK

Acknowledgements

The editors have a number of acknowledgements they would like to make that have contributed to the development of this volume. We would like first to thank all contributors to this book. We very much appreciate their efforts, time, assistance, understanding and patience at times with our requests for details and adjustments. Their breadth of viewpoints and their stimulating and detailed knowledge of their very different subject matter has provided us with unique and wide-ranging perspectives on the topics which are the subject of this edited volume. We also would like thank the staff at Routledge for their patience and support throughout the preparation of the book proposal and submission of the manuscript, and in particular Emma Travis and Lydia Kessell for their continued encouragement and support.

1   Introduction

Rami K. Isaac, Erdinç Çakmak
and Richard Butler

The investigation of tourism in (post) conflict destinations is a newly emerging sub-field of tourism studies (Alvarez & Campo, 2014, 2011; Çakmak & Isaac, 2012, 2016; Novelli, Morgan, & Nibigira, 2012; Morgan, Pritchard, & Pride, 2011). During recent years, tourism has proved to be more than a resilient industry; it has been framed as part of the process of resiliency in post disaster-contexts (Korstanje & Ivanov, 2012). However, the distribution of produced knowledge, along with the rise of more macabre forms of tourism such as conflict tourism and disaster tourism, leads us to consider that the emergence of conflict and post-conflict management and marketing is needed.

Whether a destination is landlocked, remote or has an unsettled history, unless visitors believe that it is worth visiting, it will not become a tourism destination. Many studies have focused on eminent tourism destinations. Fewer, however, have considered conflict-ridden regions, which have much larger problems to overcome in order to be able to accomplish success in appealing to tourists and attracting visitors. Stressing the great importance of destination marketing and management and their programmes, various studies (Buhalis, 2000; Faulkner, 1997; Fyall, Garrod, & Wang, 2012) within the tourism marketing and management contexts have demanded the extension of the current level of knowledge on destination management and marketing in conflict-ridden destinations.

Lisle (2000, p. 93) argues that entanglements between conflict and tourism 'disrupt and resist the prevailing images of safety and danger that attempt to hold them apart.' Studying these complex interconnections 'prevents the hegemonic discourses of global security from completing itself, stabilizing its boundaries and securing a totalized presence' (Lisle, 2000, p. 93). These hegemonic discourses create a separation between socio-political conflicts and tourism through recurrent reminders of the necessity of safety, and security in tourism (Hall, Timothy, & Duval, 2003).

A conflict, war or fight is a complex mismatch between two or more opposing parties. In some cases, it is seen in a linear form and the involves parties are visible. However, in the last three decades, we have been observing the emergence of multifaceted conflicts wherein the objectives are often diverse, with some hidden, invisible parties. The bulk of regional conflicts are located in the 'emerging regions' (Cohen & Cohen, 2015). The Heidelberg Institute for International

Conflict, for example, has observed 414 conflicts worldwide (HIIK, 2015). Tourism in these conflict-ridden destinations is not considered as the primary concern, and potentially the ruling regimes primarily restrict tourists from accessing such areas, largely on the grounds that the circumstances make it unsafe for tourists.

Despite the numerous political dimensions of tourism, the interconnections between politics and tourism are still insufficiently examined (Hall, 1994; Butler & Suntikul, 2010). Matthews (1978) and Richter (1983) were the first authors to address the importance of the relationship between politics and tourism. Some dimensions of the tourism-politics relationship have been tackled mostly from economic, business and managerial perspectives, for instance: political risk analysis in tourism development (Poirier, 1997), political crisis management (Elliott, 1997), politics and the public sector's management of tourism (Sönmez, 1998; Sönmez & Graefe, 1998), tourism planning and development in political border destinations (Timothy, 2001), political marketing of destinations (Beirman, 2002), the impacts of terrorism on tourist motivation and demand (Bhattarai, Conway, & Shrestha, 2005; Henderson, 2007). Much less research has examined the problems and implications of tourism and hospitality in conflict-ridden destinations.

It is important to question what steps and actions destination management organizations (DMOs), as well as destination marketers, need to do to improve their image in the eye of potential tourists. Related to this are the issues of what the role and power of tourism in changing the image of a destination should be, and what actions need to be taken in terms of possible destination marketing strategies and planning. Tourists who visit destinations in conflict areas may well like to be able to form a judgement about those societies and their memories through interacting with locals and residents who are experiencing the daily life of conflict (Çakmak & Isaac, 2012; Isaac & Ashworth, 2012). Politically oriented tourists (Brin, 2006), conflict tourists (Warner, 1999), danger-zone tourists (Adams, 2001) and war tourists (Pitts, 1996; Smith, 1996) are considered types of 'dark tourists' who travel 'to places made interesting for reasons of political dispute' (Warner, 1999, p. 137). Within an increasingly complex socio-political environment, further investigations of the connections between conflicts and danger in tourism can lead to understanding the 'greater politicization of tourism' (Butler & Suntikul, 2010, p. 1). Socio-political conflicts and violence manifest themselves in different contexts such as civil or international wars, bombings, coups, terrorism attacks, assassinations, riots and revolutions (Hall & O'Sullivan, 1996; Neumayer, 2004). These forms of social and political instability are considered to be incompatible with the planning, development and management of viable and prosperous tourism (Araña & León, 2008; Causevic & Lynch, 2013; Paraskevas & Arendell, 2007; Sönmez, 1998). To date, there has been no book dedicated to exploring the significance of destination management and marketing in conflict-ridden destinations.

In this edited volume, the focus will be on the various types of conflict-ridden destinations and their contextual issues, as well as on the current and post-conflict-ridden destinations worldwide, and the steps that might be taken to turn them into valid tourist destinations.

Structure of the book

The book is an edited volume subdivided into three main thematic sections, with introductory and concluding sections. The editors have written the introductory and concluding chapters, which set the tone for the volume and synthesize the common elements and themes in the chapters. Each of the three thematic sections consists of a collection of chapters written specifically for this book. Part I examines the contemporary issues in tourism and hospitality in conflict-ridden destinations by providing a macro-level overview as well as conceptual perspectives. In Chapter 2, Butler proposes a conceptual model for examining tourists who are motivated by the appeal of thrill-seeking and excitement by placing conflict zone tourists' visitation within a three-fold framework relating to the timing of the visit and the stage of conflict being experienced at the chosen destination. He argues that seeking a 'flow' experience lies behind the majority of visits during the conflict stage, but that the motivations of such participants vary according to the stage of conflict and also, importantly, personal characteristics of the tourist involved. This is followed by Chapter 3 by Timothy, who examines the intertwined concepts of border conflicts and territorial claims and how these affect tourism development. The core relationship between tourism and border conflict and territoriality includes conflict as a deterrent, tourism growth in spite of conflict, conflict as attraction, tourism as a catalyst for peace, tourism as a cause of hostility, tourism as a propaganda tool and tourism as a legal justification for territorial claims. This chapter draws on two case studies in South Asia and Southeast Asia. First, the border region of Jammu and Kashmir – which is hotly contested between India and Pakistan, as well as China –in which tourism has been rather successful, particularly in certain areas on the Indian side of the ceasefire line. He discusses the limitations and opportunities presented by this South Asian situation in relation to the border of India and Pakistan, and the disputed Kashmir area. Second, the chapter examines the concepts of sovereignty and territorial conflict as it pertains to the contested South China Sea and shows how tourism is being used as a political propaganda. Isaac, in Chapter 4, examines the issues of how Dutch customers have reacted to increases in threat levels, both real and perceived, for selected tourist destinations, and explores the role of the tour operators in their own destination choices. The findings of the research study reveal that all those surveyed consider travel safety and security increasingly important. Those respondents over the age of 40 are especially concerned about security matters and more likely to rely on and put their trust in tour operators for information. In terms of changes in destination choice (as a reaction to security issues), over-40s are much more likely to do so than those under 40. Respondents over the age of 40 expect tour operators to be the 'guardians of their safety,' and believe that tour operators should offer, where appropriate, practical information concerning destination security in higher risk countries. Building destination resilience through community and organizational resilience is further explored in Chapter 5, as Prayag argues that destination resilience can be conceptualized through the lenses of community and organizational resilience. Regardless of how researchers conceptualize destination resilience, two key underlying aspects are the vulnerability and coping capacity of the destination to external stressors. In post-conflict destinations, these stressors are often exacerbated by the socio-cultural and political environments. Prayag proposes a model of destination resilience, based on vulnerability and coping capacity, grounded in linkages between community and organizational resilience. It is argued that the resilience of organizations feeds into the resilience of communities; and in turn, both contribute to destination resilience. Organization resilience is very much dependent on the resilience of employees while the resilience of communities is dependent on both the resilience of individuals as well as that of organizations.

Part II deals with tourism and hospitality in conflict situations. This section provides case studies and destinations that are in conflict-ridden locations, and examines how tourism is developing in the context of political and social instable regions. It reveals that there are some niche markets which are heading to destinations not *despite* conflict, but *because* of conflict. In Chapter 6, Tzanelli and Korstanje explore the emergence of morbid fantasy 'terror camps' in Israel and the West Bank (Palestine) as new forms of dark military tourism. Centreing on scenarios of apprehending and killing fictional terrorists, who resemble Palestinian Arabs, the activity provides global tourists a chance to play the role of Israeli Defense Forces (IDF) soldiers in dramatic situations. Such staging consolidates the withdrawal of the empathic gaze from cross-cultural encounters in a highly sensitive political context. By producing an atmosphere of trivialized consumption of the macabre, which binds terror and darkness to racial politics, such activities recast 'edgework' as touring the world safely, uncritically and with impunity. Rather in contrast, In Chapter 7, Haeusler and colleagues examine tourism as a tool for peace in Myanmar. This chapter describes how informal, facilitated meetings during the initial phase of the case study on tourism and peace have provided a platform for previously rival stakeholders to convene and work towards a common goal: the development of tourism in a post-conflict/ceasefire area in Kayin State, Myanmar. The rationale behind this approach is the perception that economic development and the identification of income-generating opportunities that benefit the local population in particular are prerequisites to supporting and consolidating the peace-building process. The chapter closes with a summary of key lessons that can hopefully be applied in the future in other post-conflict areas of Myanmar. Chapter 8, by Sayira and Andrews, debates how conflicts impact tourism in a destination under crisis. It is based on ongoing research about Chilas, a small town and neighbouring valley in Gilgit-Baltistan, north Pakistan. Despite many scenic and historic attractions, Chilas has yet to reach its full tourism potential. This chapter outlines the conflicts and crises that have affected Chilas and explores the development and aid tools that have been introduced to the area in an attempt to foster development, prevent outward migration and bring more educational opportunities to women. However, the lack of community involvement has led to resistance towards proposed development plans, which in turn has led to further internal conflict in the area, although it is hoped that with persistence the projects that have been initiated will give greater voice to the marginalized residents. Chapter 9, by Ndlovu and Chigora, deals with Zimbabwe as a case study and examines the impact of economic instability on the destination's image. The global financial recession of 2008, negative publicity and the general internal political conflict exacerbated these conditions. Notable challenges include a hyper-inflationary environment, violent elections and human rights abuses. Consequently, Zimbabwe's negative image resulted in a massive decline in tourist arrivals, low occupancies recorded in hotels, and closure of businesses. The chapter draws on practical experiences of branding and rebranding a destination in order to disassociate itself from its negative past and other socio-economic ills. The aim is to demonstrate the extent to which a destination brand could address issues about brand association, perception, image and positioning and the chapter examines the marketing strategies and policies used during a conflict. Khader, in Chapter 10, presents a case study of one of the hottest tourist destinations in Bethlehem, Palestine – namely, Banksy's Walled Off Hotel – in the context of two forms of alternative tourism that have not received much attention in the literature about Palestinian tourism: dystopian dark tourism and pop-culture tourism. Khader argues that Banksy's Walled Off Hotel constitutes a heterotopic countersite that 'represents, contests, and inverts' other material and physical sites, temporalities and discursive regimes with which it is linked through unexpected shocking, jarring, and disturbing juxtapositions. The interest in the Walled Off 'heterotopia' can also be attributed to Banksy's international brand name and the vigorous international Banksy fan subculture. The discussion concludes that the Walled Off heterotopia does not simply register aspects of the dystopian realities in Palestine, but also inscribes a utopian dimension that universalizes the Palestinian struggle for freedom, by linking it to the struggles of other disposable communities around the world. Çakmak and Gorlero, in Chapter 11, examine the impacts of a social negative event on a European urban destination. They interrogate the economic, social and cultural impacts of the far-right political movement Patriotic Europeans Against the Islamisation of the West (PEGIDA), on Dresden, which is suffering from a social conflict among its residents. The social conflict is examined through ethnographic narrative accounts of stakeholders in Dresden with the aim to assess the stakeholders' positions and roles in this conflict. The resulting stories reveal the intrinsic relation between social movement and conflict. The chapter identifies social tension, community polarization and discrimination of minorities experienced as the consequences of social conflict triggered by PEGIDA's activities in Dresden, closing with recommendations for policy on social conflict resolution and destination governance.

Part III deals with tourism and hospitality in post-conflict destinations and how destinations deal with such post-conflict regarding management, marketing and branding conflict narratives in post-conflict destinations. This section reviews locations which have emerged from conflict and are now engaging in tourism. It illustrates how destinations have overcome the negative image of conflict and the physical problems relating to infrastructure and access, as well as difficulties in the political and financial areas and representations of tourism in the context of post-conflict destinations. Chapter 12 focuses on contrasting case studies in

Colombia, Bosnia-Herzegovina and Croatia. Patrick analyzes the role of tourism, and in particular some related discourses and representations, in the construction of peace. Although public authorities and international organizations often present tourism as a tool that helps enhance peace, in this chapter, research demonstrates that the reality in the field is often much more complex. Soon after armed conflicts are over, some countries and regions experience a rapid growth in tourism, and the sector can offer promising business opportunities for recovering communities, including former war actors (e.g. soldiers, fixers, guerrillas, narco-traffickers) as well as the victims. Moreover, tourism can also provide them with a platform for disseminating specific discourses and representations of the war. Thus, while tourism stakeholders generally aim to detach the country's image from the previous violence in order to attract visitors and foreign investors, the heritage and memory associated with the conflict are nevertheless elements mobilized in the tourism sector. Based on an analysis of the practices of what are conceived here as 'memorial entrepreneurs,' this chapter shows that different and sometimes competing actors contribute to building these 'touristscapes,' using conflicting narratives and representations. Van Broeck, in Chapter 13, focuses on Medellín and Colombia, employing (participant) observations, web analyses, interviews and conversations with different stakeholders in Moravia, a 'transformed' neighbourhood in Medellín, still associated with poverty and (past) violence, and analyzes the recent tourism development. At present, mainly external tour operators are bringing in tourists, but the local community is becoming more and more involved. The chapter shows how the elements of incipient 'Phoenix tourism' are present, and the problems it is facing. Chapter 14, by Wise, focuses on narrations of Sarajevo's landscape and memories of war as presented in newspaper content and promotional websites framed around experiences of being in the destination, to link narratives with critical observational reflection and interpretation. The analysis is framed around three sections: landscapes frozen in the 1990s, touring the tunnel of survival and roses of remembrance. Interpretations and discussion of the content and observations are guided by theories of landscape, memory and representations of destinations post-conflict. The conclusion discusses the notion of fading memory in relation to how other destinations have moved beyond memories and imaginations of war, as it is now more than 20 years since the conflict and siege of Sarajevo. Boland, in Chapter 15, analyzes the current (2018) campaign approach to Bangkok street food by the authorities there as an aid to understanding the wider, deeper conflict about modernization. Social and economic change in all societies produces conflict, and winners and losers. The current campaign by the authorities in Bangkok to regulate street food there exposes this deeper conflict in a clear manner. This conflict is located in differing visions of the city: one preferring a modernized, planned Bangkok, and the other seeking to preserve a more open flexible space. Economic and political interests also conflict on this issue. This conflict in Bangkok provides an interesting issue for urban and Thai tourism, too, as street food is widely seen as an attraction for the city, so tourism can play a role in preserving this heritage. This may be seen as a supporting force for the street food vendors, but it can also freeze locations in some arbitrarily set time and negatively impact on the dynamism and creativity that made the city attractive in the first place. Boyd, in Chapter 16, proposes a model of post-conflict tourism development based on a set of key attributes whereby a more safe and secure environment and a positive perception of the destination take priority over other important attributes for successful tourism development such as an accessible and attractive destination, along with a professional and highly qualified workforce. He applies this to a case study of tourism in Northern Ireland, which saw almost three decades of violence, instability and unrest. He argues that the most recognizable development of tourism connected back to the conflict era through the development of dark tourism in the form of visitation to the murals that had been part of Northern Ireland society pre-conflict. Communities expressed their heritage, identity and their politics through the murals, and peace allowed for the outside world to come and gaze on them. They formed a key element of what Boyd refers to as the Phoenix phase of post-conflict tourism. A lasting peace and a destination perceived in more positive terms over time allowed the government to make significant investments in new tourism plan, and develop products to appeal to new market niches which allowed the industry to build on an extant cultural heritage base that had survived the conflict era. Boyd refers to this as post-conflict development 'normalcy' phase where private sector investment would accompany public sector initiatives to create conditions against which tourism development would start to resemble the type of development found in destinations that had been free of conflict, and where Northern Ireland had a competitive advantage in the areas of heritage, sport, film and events. Farmaki, in Chapter 17, explores visitor-host encounters within post-conflict destinations. Drawing insights from the context of Cyprus, which has been divided since 1974 following prolonged tensions and conflict between the island's Greek Cypriot and Turkish Cypriot communities, the chapter discusses a range of encounters occurring within post-conflict settings ranging from commercial-based to social ones. It appears that an interplay of factors emanating from the socio-political environment in Cyprus conditions the relationship(s) between visitors and the host community in a politically uncertain setting. Little attention has previously been paid to the nature of the encounters between visitors and the visited community, which can be of considerable relevance. Examination of the visitor-host encounters in countries affected by prolonged conflict are characterized by fragility and political uncertainty, and the conclusions may be insightful on the conditions under which tourism might contribute to peace.

In the concluding chapter by the editors, there is a review of the issues discussed in the volume and an exploration of possible future perspectives on tourism and hospitality in conflict-ridden destinations.

References

Adams, K. M. (2001). Danger-zone tourism: Prospects and problems for tourism in tumultuous times. In T. T. C. Chang & K. C. Ho (Eds.), *Interconnected worlds: Tourism in Southeast Asia* (pp. 265–281). Oxford: Pergamon.

Alvarez, M. D., & Campo, S. (2011). Controllable versus uncontrollable information sources: Effects on the image of Turkey. *International Journal of Tourism Research*, *13*, 310–323.

Alvarez, M. D., & Campo, S. (2014). The influence of political conflicts on country image and intention to visit: A study of Israel's image. *Tourism Management*, *40*, 70–78.

Araña, J. E., & León, C. J. (2008). The impact of terrorism on tourism demand. *Annals of Tourism Research*, *35*(2), 299–315.

Beirman, D. (2002). Marketing of tourism destinations during a prolonged crisis: Israel and the Middle East. *Journal of Vacation Marketing*, *8*(2), 167–176.

Bhattarai, K., Conway, D., & Shrestha, N. (2005). Tourism, terrorism and turmoil in Nepal. *Annals of Tourism Research*, *32*(3), 669–688.

Buhalis, D. (2000). Marketing the competitive destination of the future. *Tourism Management*, *21*(1), 97–116.

Butler, R., & Suntikul, W. (Eds.). (2010). *Tourism & political change*. Oxford: Goodfellow Publishers Ltd.

Brin, E. (2006). Politically-oriented tourism in Jerusalem. *Tourist Studies*, *6*(3), 215–243.

Çakmak, E., & Isaac, R. K. (2012). Image analysis of Bethlehem: What can destination marketers learn from their visitors' blogs? *Journal of Marketing & Destination Management*, *1*(1–2), 124–133.

Çakmak, E., & Isaac, R. K. (2016). Drawing tourism to conflict-ridden destinations. *Journal of Marketing & Destination Management*, *4*(5), 291–293.

Causevic, S., & Lynch, P. (2013). Political (in)stability and its influence on tourism development. *Tourism Management*, *34*, 145–157.

Cohen, E., & Cohen, S. A. (2015). Tourism mobilities from emerging world regions: A response to commentaries. *Current Issues in Tourism*, *18*(1), 68–69.

Elliott, J. (1997). *Tourism: Politics and public sector management*. London: Routledge.

Faulkner, B. (1997). A model for the evaluation of national tourism destination marketing programs. *Journal of Travel Research*, *3*, 23–32.

Fyall, A., Garrod, B., & Wang, Y. (2012). Destination collaboration: A critical review of theoretical approaches to a multi-dimensional phenomenon. *Journal of Destination Marketing & Management*, *1*(1–2), 10–26.

Hall, C. M. (1994). *Tourism and politics: Policy, power, and place*. Chichester: Wiley.

Hall, C. M., & O'Sullivan, V. (1996). Tourism, political stability and violence. In A. Pizam & Y. Mansfeld (Eds.), *Tourism, crime, and international security issues* (pp. 105–121). Chichester: Wiley.

Hall, C. M., Timothy, D. J., & Duval, D. T. (Eds.). (2003). *Safety and security in tourism: Relationships, management, and marketing*. Binghamton, NY: Haworth.

Heidelberg Institute for International Conflict Research (HIIK). (2015). Conflict barometer. *HIIK* website. Retrieved 19 October 2016, from www.hiik.de/en/konfliktbarometer/

Henderson, J. C. (2007). *Tourism crises: Causes, consequences and management*. Amsterdam, The Netherlands: Butterworth-Heinemann.

Isaac, R. K., & Ashworth, G. (2012). Moving from pilgrimage to "dark" tourism: Leveraging tourism in Palestine. *Tourism, Culture and Communication*, *11*, 149–164.

Korstanje, M. E., & Ivanov, H. S. (2012), Tourism as a form of new psychological resilience: The inception of dark tourism. *CULTUR – Revista de Cultura e Turismo*, *6*(4), 56–71.

Lisle, D. (2000). Consuming danger: Reimagining the war/tourism divide. *Alternatives: Global, Local, Political*, *25*(1), 91–116.

Matthews, H. G. (1978). *International tourism: A political and social analysis*. Cambridge, MA: Schenkman.

Morgan, N., Pritchard, A., & Pride, R. (2011). *Destination brands: Managing place reputation* (3rd ed.). London: Butterworth-Heinemann.

Novelli, M., Morgan, N., & Nibigira, C. (2012). Tourism in a post-conflict situation of fragility. *Annals of Tourism Research*, *39*(3), 1446–1469.

Neumayer, E. (2004). The impact of political violence on tourism: Dynamic cross national estimation. *Journal of Conflict Resolution*, *48*(2), 259–281.

Paraskevas, A., & Arendell, B. (2007). A strategic framework for terrorism prevention and mitigation in tourism destinations. *Tourism Management*, *28*(6), 1560–1573.

Pitts, W. J. (1996). Uprising in Chiapas, Mexico: Zapata lives – tourism falters. In A. Pizam & Y. Mansfeld (Eds.), *Tourism, crime, and international security issues* (pp. 215–227). Chichester: Wiley.

Poirier, R. A. (1997). Political risk analysis and tourism. *Annals of Tourism Research*, *24*(3), 675–686.

Richter, L. K. (1983). Tourism politics and political science: A case of not so benign neglect. *Annals of Tourism Research*, *10*(3), 313–335.

Smith, V. L. (1996). War and its tourist attractions. In A. Pizam & Y. Mansfeld (Eds.), *Tourism, crime, and international security issues* (pp. 247–264). Chichester: Wiley.

Sönmez, S. F. (1998). Tourism, terrorism, and political instability. *Annals of Tourism Research*, *25*(2), 416–456.

Sönmez, S. F., & Graefe, A. R. (1998). Influence of terrorism risk on foreign tourism decisions. *Annals of Tourism Research*, *25*(1), 112–144.

Timothy, D. J. (2001). *Tourism and political boundaries*. London: Routledge.

Warner, J. (1999). North Cyprus: Tourism and the challenge of non-recognition. *Journal of Sustainable Tourism*, *7*(2), 128–145.

Part I

Contemporary issues in tourism and hospitality in conflict-ridden destinations

2 Tourism and conflict

A framework for examining risk versus satisfaction

Richard Butler

Introduction

The world has experienced conflict – both between humans, and between humans and other species – since time immemorial. The evidence of such conflicts is present and visible in many parts of the world, and over the past two millennia, at least, have become items of interest for travellers. In some cases, sites of past conflicts have been preserved and interpreted, sometimes in ways which cause problems for some modern-day visitors. The popularization of conflict sites has been characterized as 'dark tourism' (Lennon & Foley, 2000), implying that the motivations for visiting such sites relates to a desire to experience evidence of tragedy and horror, although that motivation may be inappropriate to assign to many visitors to these sites, as discussed later in this chapter. It is argued here that the motivations to visit sites (Isaac & Çakmak, 2014) and zones of conflict vary not only with the individual visitor, but also with the characteristic of the timing of the conflict involved: whether the visitor is going before a conflict, during a conflict, or after a conflict.

It is suggested, therefore, that tourist visitation to zones of conflict can be sub-divided on the basis of the relative stage of conflict development and the nature of the conflict (as defined earlier in this volume) in the destination zones. There are three proposed stages – pre-conflict, during conflict and post-conflict – and within this broad subdivision, there are a number of conditional forces and motivations that also influence the pattern and motivation of visitors. These elements are portrayed in Table 2.1. In reality, all tourism falls into one of these categories, mostly into the first and last of the three stages, as tourists may visit a destination which never experiences conflict (and is therefore theoretically 'pre-conflict') or visit a destination after a conflict which occurred many years, even centuries before, but is still technically 'post-conflict'. For the purposes of discussion in this chapter, we will take 'pre-conflict' to mean a situation prior to an anticipated or threatened outbreak of conflict, where the risk is apparent to potential tourists, such as the former Yugoslavia in the 1970s. 'Post-conflict' can be taken to include countries in which the evidence of previous conflict is still apparent and may be included in the list of attractions of the destination, e.g. the Demilitarized Zone in Korea or the Cu Chi caves in Vietnam. 'During conflict' is, as the term implies, a destination

Table 2.1 Stages and types of conflict zones

PRE-CONFLICT		DURING CONFLICT		POST-CONFLICT	
Conflict Unlikely	Conflict Anticipated	Internal conflict Civil war Terrorism Illegal acts Independence	External conflict Invasion Border dispute	Immediately after conflict	Long past Conflict

in which some form of conflict is ongoing, such as Israel and Palestine, Syria, or Afghanistan, whether the conflict be war between countries or internal conflict in terms of terrorism or independence struggles. In the context of this chapter, the important characteristic is that the potential, existing or recent incidence of conflict in a destination is almost inevitably going to be a factor in the decision to visit that location, whether it be in terms of consideration of personal security, the pursuit of thrills and risk (Sharifpour, Walters, & Ritchie, 2013; Wolff & Larsen, 2017), or the desire for a unique and perhaps prestige-creating experience.

Pre-conflict tourism

Conflict is not always predictable, particularly in terms of the opening of hostilities between protagonists, and in some cases, tourists anticipating visiting a peaceful destination may get an unpleasant surprise if conflict breaks out while they are present. In many cases, however, portending conflict may be fairly obvious and visitors to such locations may be prepared to take their chances of exiting the destination before conflict begins. Travellers to Germany in the late 1930s, for example, must have been increasingly aware that the Nazi regime was likely to commence military action in the relatively near future. The displays of militarism at the 1936 Olympics demonstrated the degree of war readiness of the regime, but the attractions of Germany, and undoubtedly to some visitors, the attraction of the Nazi ideology, made travel there at that time appealing, and access to and within Germany was relatively easy. Similarly, travel to the former Yugoslavia had increased steadily from the 1960s as that country offered a relatively cheap pseudo Mediterranean holiday (the Adriatic substituting for its larger neighbouring sea) for northern European travellers, with the added advantage to some of a friendly 'communist' experience, although the anticipated break-up of the country after the death of Tito was frequently discussed as being both imminent and inevitable (Gosar, 2005). There are a number of potential motivations for visiting such locations. One may be the idea of supporting a particular ideology or way of life (e.g. Germany 1930s); another might be the lower cost of such locations compared to a similar experience in conventional holiday destinations (Yugoslavia 1970s). A third might be a sense of obligation, inspired or driven by religious commitments, to visit locations before such access might be denied because of conflict, a consideration acknowledged by some visitors to Israel and Palestine (Brin, 2006; Fuchs & Reichel, 2006; Isaac, 2018).

This motivation to visit a location before such visits become impossible, in this context because of conflict, also could be related to what is currently termed 'last chance tourism' (Lemelin, Dawson, & Stewart, 2012), whereby tourists visit specific features, locations, environments and wildlife before the opportunity disappears, often because of potential destruction or extinction of the specific attraction(s). The tourists visiting mountain gorillas in Rwanda or other near extinct species of animals and birds are one form of this type of tourism. Visitors to historic sites such as the now destroyed Palmyra in Syria before the full impact of ISIS's actions took place also fit this pattern. As Weaver and Lawton (2007) have pointed out, however, such tourism does not necessarily cease once the key attraction has disappeared, as people will travel to see where something was that is now no more. The island state of Mauritius still markets the long extinct dodo, although one assumes not many tourists visit the island expecting to see the bird. Conflict can take many forms, as noted earlier, and may not involve violence or active hostility but rather conflict over differing viewpoints; for example, over access to specific sites. One such case is that of Uluru (formerly known as Ayers Rock) in central Australia, which has long been a tourist attraction and is an iconic element in the tourism promotion of Australia. The local aboriginal residents of the area regard Uluru as sacred and oppose the climbing of the monolith by tourists, although their opposition has been verbal and not physical (King, 2015). In 2019, tourists will be banned from climbing the rock as aboriginal requests have been accepted by the national park authority, thus the 'last chance tourism' opportunity to scale the rock is fast approaching. One may possibly expect verbal conflicts when tourists are finally prevented from climbing, and some doubtless will feel aggrieved at having made the long journey there only to be deprived of their 'Facebook' or 'Instagram' moment and inevitable selfies on the summit. (This writer fully supports the decision to 'close' Uluru, but understands such attitudes, having scaled it himself in 1992.)

One should also note that visiting zones of conflict in a pre-conflict stage may be entirely coincidental and accidental, in that tourists did not anticipate conflict occurring and simply chose the particular destination for what we may call 'conventional' reasons. The most recent and tragic example is probably that of those tourists, mostly from the UK, who were visiting Sousse beach resort in Tunisia in 2015, at that time seen as not being a conflict zone (although some tourists had been attacked earlier in Tunis) when they became victims of terrorism. An earlier example, although with not as catastrophic an outcome, will have been visitors to the former East Germany and the Russian Sector of Berlin, who were caught up on the wrong side of the quickly erected Berlin Wall in 1961.

During-conflict tourism

Visits to conflict zones will have a different set of motivations, although some may be shared with tourists to pre-conflict sites. The earliest example of deliberate travel to conflict zones is probably that of the Crusaders (O'Gorman, 2013), and while their visits were hardly pleasurable, there is no doubt that great satisfaction was obtained from doing what was seen as 'the Lord's work,' namely, gaining and securing the Holy Lands around Jerusalem from the 'heathen' – and if death occurred, where better and for what better cause? Thus, religious faith, fervour and fanaticism drove thousands of travellers towards Jerusalem from across Europe in the 12th to the 14th centuries, bringing with them conflict as they travelled for the purpose of religious supremacy and conquest.

While the literature is unanimous in stressing that tourism does not normally exist in conflict zones and that peace, or the absence of conflict, is a general pre-requisite for successful tourism, it is clear that there is a small amount of tourism to zones of conflict where the participants are quite aware that conflict is taking place at those locations (Adam, 2015; George, 2003). Ladarman (2013) notes several specific examples of deliberate tourist visitation to conflict zones, both individual and in group contexts, with Iraq, Afghanistan and Vietnam being relatively recent examples cited. It is possible to divide such travel into two subgroups, one being tourism in conflict zones despite the presence of conflict, the other being tourism to such zones because of the presence of conflict (Isaac & Ashworth, 2012). In the former case, tourists may have decided that the attraction(s) within the troubled location is (are) so great that the risk of being involved in the conflict is worth taking (Floyd, Gibson, Pennington-Gray, & Thapa, 2004). The reasons for such a decision may be personal, such as a commitment to visit a person, family or friend whom it may not be possible to visit later, perhaps because of their health or age. Another may be the example noted earlier as last chance tourism, visiting somewhere such as Palmyra before it was destroyed by ISIS, or a site of religious significance if someone had a desperate urge to see the specific feature for work or belief reasons and decided the risk was worth taking. The case of the mountain gorillas in Democratic Republic of Congo is a similar situation, where it is clear that armed militias control parts of the national park that is the home of the gorillas and have captured tourists and executed park rangers recently. Yet tourists still visit the area, presumably hoping or calculating that their party will avoid trouble and the sighting of the nearly extinct species is a great enough reward, both in terms of personal satisfaction and the acquisition of prestige and esteem from friends and contacts.

There are also those who chose to visit zones of conflict precisely because there is such conflict occurring. Quite what the primary motivation in such cases is remains somewhat of a mystery, and a contradiction between security and risk. One can speculate that the need or desire for excitement and thrills is one major cause. Csikszentmihályi (1990) has argued that the great satisfaction obtained from a 'flow experience' is related to excitement, challenge and thrill. The same motivation causes a skier to ski off-piste or to tackle a 'black' run which is at the limit of their ability or even beyond, for the challenge of doing something which may bring great reward in exchange for taking great risk; thus, experiencing the sense of 'flow' and the adrenaline rush that often accompanies this. Many extreme activities such as mountaineering, spelunking, sky diving or swimming with sharks require the same acceptance of risk in exchange for experience as visiting a zone of conflict during conflict. Most sensible and skilled participants in the mentioned activities, however, normally minimize the level of risk through preparation, training, skill, following advice and avoiding unnecessary hazards. Such may not be possible for all tourists in conflict zones during conflict, as such situations are normally highly dynamic and unpredictable. Not surprisingly, therefore, numbers of tourists in such situations are small and often regarded as foolhardy for ignoring governmental advice on not visiting certain locations, and for possibly putting others, who may have to try to rescue them, in danger also.

Post-conflict tourism

In many areas, post-conflict tourism may be the dominant form of tourism in that the evidence of past conflicts is widespread and popular. Castles and other fortifications, battlefield sites, ruins of cities and other features and even places whose names are famous for former conflicts are all highly popular and visited by vast numbers of tourists. Edinburgh Castle, is one of the most popular tourist sites in Scotland, if not the most popular; the Normandy beaches of D-Day in the Second World War are annually visited by tourists from around the world, as are the cemeteries of the First World War (Winter, 2011). The walled towns of Dubrovnik and York, the battlefield of Waterloo and the many monuments to battles, treaties and death all attract large numbers of visitors, not all of whom are 'dark tourists.' Dark tourism is, however, very much a part of post-conflict tourism; almost all of the events commemorated by such tourists relate to the horrors of war and conflict, both military and civil. The most vivid examples, perhaps, are those related to the Holocaust, in Europe in the form of the death camps and other memorials there (Winter 2009) and elsewhere, and at the 'Killing Fields' in Cambodia (Isaac & Çakmark, 2016). Most recently perhaps (June 2018 at the time of writing) has been the reminder that the Demilitarized Zone (DMZ) between North and South Korea, a vivid example of an as-yet-unended war, is itself a major tourist attraction to visitors to and residents of South Korea. Being only 50 kilometres from Seoul, the capital, bus tours to the DMZ can be expected to increase in popularity because of the current détente between the West and North Korea. One might argue that in many respects visiting historic features dating from centuries ago is hardly 'dark tourism' – or even related directly to conflict today – as such sites and artefacts are items of interest, curiosity and fascination and do not necessarily stir up thoughts of conflict in the minds of the visitors.

One can expect more recent conflicts, however, to disturb as well as provide satisfaction of varying sorts to modern visitors (Sönmez & Graefe, 1998). Many visitors to Holocaust memorials will have a personal involvement and linkage, as will those at war graves from the First and Second World Wars (Isaac, Narwiin, van Liemont, & Gridnevskiv, 2019). Visitors to RAF Coningsby in England to see the Lancaster, Spitfires and Hurricanes of the Battle of Britain Memorial Flight will include some who flew those planes, as well as their immediate descendents. In the same way, visitors to the Cu Chi Caves in Vietnam (Lema & Agrusa, 2013), the Leda and other crossings in Cyprus (Jacobsen, Musyck, Orphanides, & Webster, 2010), the Mostar bridge in Serbia, memorials in the Falkland Islands and most recently Afghanistan, Iran and Syria, will include visitors who have personal and/or family connections to those locations (Causevic & Linch, 2007). Tourism by members of a diaspora is common form of travel, belonging to the broad category of Visiting Friends and Relations (VFR) tourism. Israel is probably the best example of the attraction of a 'homeland' to a widely scattered group of peoples (Jews), with visitors coming in considerable numbers annually despite outbreaks of hostilities between Israel and particularly the Palestinian dispossessed, and also some of its more belligerent neighbours. Krakover (2013) notes the importance of Jewish visitors to Israel coming in support of the state and its existence, with a sense of obligation as well as religious zeal and familial ties. These feelings would appear to be strong enough to ignore the outbreaks of hostilities in Israel, and Krakover (2005, p. 193) concluded that 'the long-term trend of demand for tourism in Israel appears to overwhelmingly override disturbances caused by wars and terrorist actions.' As Farmaki (Chapter 17, this volume) has shown in the case of Cyprus, people who left their homes because of conflict and settled elsewhere often have the desire to return – even if only temporarily – to their former places of residence. In the case of Lebanon, which experienced civil war and conflict between 1975 and 1990, there was considerable emigration (to North America, Europe and Australia in particular) during that period, but following the end of conflict, some emigrants returned to live in Lebanon, and over the next two decades, many descendants and family members of those emigrants returned on visits to Lebanon, primarily to visit family and friends and their homeland (Butler & Hajar, 2005). What may be termed 'diaspora tourism' (illustrated by the Birthright Israel and Know Thy Heritage movements in the context of Israel and Palestine) is clearly related to emigration, which in turn is often the result of conflict or forcible evacuation driven by economic or ethnic cleansing motives.

Discussion

Travel to destinations which have experienced conflict, are currently experiencing it or are anticipating experiencing it in the near future is clearly driven by many often inter-related motives (Karl & Schmude, 2017). For some travellers, the conflict element may be irrelevant, with the participants either ignorant of the situation and the prevailing risks, or driven by the desire for thrills and excitement. In other cases, the journey may have much more of the nature of a pilgrimage, to visit places and features which they visited at the time of conflict, or which were visited by family and friends, some of whom may have died there. Visits to the trenches of the First World War in Flanders, the landing beaches of Normandy and the prisoner of war sites and death camps in Germany and Asia are often described as pilgrimages. The first formal pilgrimage following the First World War was one to Flanders, which took place in 1928 when 11,000 veterans and war widows visited the Somme and Ypres, and this event was duplicated in the summer of 2018, entitled the 'Great Pilgrimage 90,' organized by the Royal British Legion (as was the original trip in 1928). In contrast, as discussed elsewhere in this volume, some destinations are turning aspects of conflict into tourist attractions (Chapter 16). The example of the Walled Off Hotel in Bethlehem (Chapter 10) is one of a formal commercial operation, but it is common for tourists in Cambodia, Laos and Vietnam to be offered the opportunity to fire weapons ranging from hand guns and rifles to rocket launchers in rural areas, thus 'playing' at war (Butler personal correspondence). Thus, Ladarman's (2013) comment on 'tourism and the martial fascination' is still not only valid but alive and well in some post-conflict zones.

How much of such tourism falls within the category of dark tourism is difficult to say. The whole concept of dark tourism itself is complex, with some elements undoubtedly being focused on horror and suffering, while at the other extreme, there may be little sympathy for curiosity or empathy for war-like attitudes, and a more personal interest in appreciating the cost and suffering involved in the many conflicts. As Stone (2006) has argued, there are degrees of dark tourism, and Butler and Suntikul (2013, p. 292) proposed a continuum of war-tourism attitudes from 'Dark' to 'Heritage (Personal).' In their volume on tourism to places of horror and atrocity, Ashworth and Hartmann (2005, pp. 181–182) asked the question 'Are tourists attracted to sites of atrocity and war – or deterred?' and commented that 'In the eyes of the (young) beholder atrocity is no longer a deterrent but becomes essentially a curiosity and attraction,' reflecting the conclusions of Dann (2005), who discussed the influence of the media on what he termed 'The children of the dark.'

It would appear, from the ever-increasing numbers of tourists in general, and tourists to places and features associated with conflict in particular, that the fascination with the evidence of conflict is likely to continue to increase. While there are now no living military survivors of the First World War, visits to the sites of the horrendous battlefields of that conflict increase steadily and are increasingly involving school trips (Miles, 2016) to the 'Warscape' (Janssen-Verbeke & George, 2013) of Flanders and its neighbours. While similar sites do not exist for the Second World War or the Korean War, the official memorials and war grave sites still exert a powerful attraction for visitors and new memorials and 'experiences' are constantly being created and offered to the touring public. Some are portrayed as memorials and tributes for the dead, others as experiences for the living, and in so doing are essentially perpetuating a pattern that has existed for centuries. Spectators flocked to Waterloo for the battle there in 1815, and to the early battles of the American Civil War, and re-enactments of the latter and other battles such as those from the English Civil War are popular tourist attractions today at the same or proximal sites (Daniels, Dieke, & Barrow, 2013).

As Poria, Butler, and Airey (2004) noted, the motivations of tourists to visit heritage sites of all types – indeed, to visit almost any destination – are crucial to understanding why tourists go to such places. Visits to conflict heritage, past, current or likely future may be no different from visits to other heritage attractions. It should not be classified as 'dark' without the motivations of the providers/managers of such sites and of the visitors to those sites being fully understood. Some tourists will be visiting those sites with what many may consider inappropriate or antagonistic motives, or behave inappropriately when visiting conflict sites, while others may be driven by a highly personal sense of loss or sympathy for the victims. Whether any visits to conflict-related sites aid or prevent the outbreak of conflict is impossible to say, just as it remains impossible to argue convincingly whether tourism has any effect on peace or conflict in reality (Wintersteiner & Wohlmuther, 2013). The possible development of international tourism resorts in North Korea may take place, following the meeting of the leaders of the USA and North Korea; indeed, winter sports resorts for an international market have already been developed in North Korea, but with little indication of permanent success, either economically or politically. The real value of such developments in reducing conflict and turning the war-torn Korean Peninsula into another Asian tourist mecca is uncertain and unproven. However, as long as post-(old) conflict tourism increases at the expense of pre-conflict and during-conflict tourism, then tourism in general and the world as a whole may enjoy the experience much more.

Table 2.1 conceptualizes the relationship between stages and types of conflict zones. Each of the three major categories (pre-, during and post-) are subdivided into two sub-categories. In the case of pre-conflict zones, this division is between those zones in which no conflict is anticipated, possibly because of a long period of peace and stability, as in much of Western Europe, North America and Australasia, or areas in which governance appears stable and there is little, if any, sign of internal division or external threat. Anticipated conflict refers to regions (states, parts of states or even particular settlements) where there is an ongoing risk of conflict in the form of violence and harm to life and property, such as the likelihood of civil war or invasion, or a high risk of terrorism. Parts of Africa, the Middle East and Asia fall into this category, along with specific regions in South America (Kozak, Crotts, & Law, 2007). In this day and age, one has to acknowledge that even previously 'safe' and conflict-free locations such as London, Manchester, Paris, Brussels and Berlin in Europe, and Ottawa, New York and Boston in North America, have experienced conflict in the form of terrorism, and some potential tourists may now view those cities as falling into an unsafe category and could consider them as being in any of the three conflict categories because of the possibility of future terrorism returning there.

The during-conflict period has more subdivisions, first into internal and external, relating to where the conflict is originating. Internal conflicts include civil war as in South Sudan, and terrorism as in Afghanistan and Iraq, along with independence struggles such as in Syria and until recently in South Sudan and East Timor. There is also internal conflict between legal and illegal forces, as currently is being experienced in parts of Mexico relating to drugs, and as has been the case in Colombia (see Chapter 13, this volume), where both drugs and political issues were involved. The term 'external conflicts' refers to invasion, as in Yemen, or border disputes as occurs intermittently between India and Pakistan over Kashmir. Inevitably intrastate conflicts are often characterized by external intervention at some stage, as seen in Yemen, Syria and Iraq.

Finally, post-conflict can be divided into conflicts which occurred before the current generation, e.g. earlier than the First World War, and then those which can be remembered and were experienced by participants still alive today. In the second case, memory, personal heritage and loss, commemoration and nostalgia may be motivations for visiting destinations in that stage, but the elements of risk, challenge, excitement and thrill will not be motivations for visits. The area between post-conflict and pre-conflict is really a stage in which conflict is an irrelevancy, either not being anticipated or having happened so long ago as to also be meaningless in terms of perceptions of security and risk by present-day potential tourists.

Figure 2.1 illustrates an unending loop of stages, some of which are difficult to define, not least because many conflicts are highly dynamic and participants and territories involved, as well as alliances and external interventions, frequently

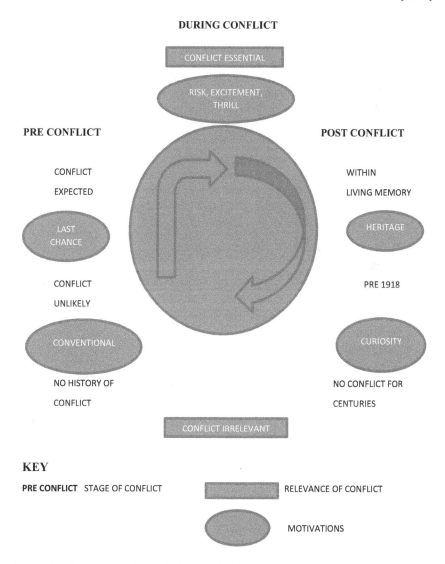

Figure 2.1 Framework of pre-, during and post-conflict

change. Thus, visitors may be caught up in such a dynamic situation, with the result being that while intending to visit an area before any anticipated conflict, they may find themselves in a zone in which conflict has broken out and is suddenly occurring. That such an occurrence may take place might also be part of the attraction (thrill and excitement of possible risk) of visiting pre-conflict zones where conflict is thought to be likely in the near future.

Conclusion

The decision to visit a zone of conflict – before such a state, during conflict or after conflict – will be made by potential visitors in the light of their motivations for such a visit. It has been argued above that the stage of conflict, pre-, during or post-, is important in that decision-making process, as the motivations for visiting will range from personal desires for excitement and risk to those of memory and personal heritage. The markets for such forms of tourism will also vary with the stage of conflict, and also – one can assume – by demographic and personality characteristics, as well factors relating to family history and geographical location (Mitchell & Vassos, 1997; Reisinger & Mavando, 2006). The links between visiting zones of conflict and 'dark tourism' are certainly present, but are far from being the dominant or only relationship and influence in the visitation of such destinations. In some cases, the 'dark' element is marketed as being a major attraction, but equally, more personal and lighter motives, even if associated with a sense of loss or obligation, along with basic human curiosity, probably explain the presence of the vast majority of visitors to such sites.

References

Adam, I. (2015). Backpacker's risk perceptions and risk reduction strategies in Ghana. *Tourism Management*, *49*, 99–108.

Ashworth, G. J., & Hartmann, R. (Eds.). (2005). *Horror and human tragedy revisited: The management of sites of atrocities for tourism*. New York, NY: Cognizant.

Brin, E. (2006). Politically-oriented tourism in Jerusalem. *Tourist Studies*, *6*(3), 215–243.

Butler, R. W., & Hajar, R. (2005). After the war: Ethnic tourism to Lebanon. In G. Ashworth & R. Hartmann (Eds.), *Horror and human tragedy revisited the management of sites of atrocities for tourism* (pp. 211–223). New York, NY: Cognizant Communication Corporation.

Butler, R. W., & Suntikul, W. (2013). *Tourism and war*. London: Routledge.

Causevic, S., & Linch, P. (2007). Hospitality as a human phenomenon: Host – guest relationships in a post-conflict setting. *Tourism and Hospitality Planning & Development*, *6*(2), 121–132.

Csikszentmihályi, M. (1990). *Flow: The psychology of optimal experience*. New York, NY: Harper & Row.

Daniels, M., Dieke, P., & Barrow, M. (2013). Civil war tourism: Perspectives from Manassa National Battlefield Park. In R. W. Butler & W. Suntikul (Eds.), *Tourism and war* (pp. 232–244). London: Routledge.

Dann, G. M. S. (2005). Children of the dark. In G. Ashworth & R. Hartmann (Eds.), *Horror and human tragedy revisited the management of sites of atrocities for tourism* (pp. 233–252). New York, NY: Cognizant Communication Corporation.

Floyd, M. F., Gibson, H., Pennington-Gray, L., & Thapa, B. (2004). The effects of risk perceptions on intensions to travel in the aftermath of September 11, 2001. *Journal of Travel and Tourism Marketing, 15*(2–3), 19–38.

Fuchs, G., & Reichel, A. (2006). Tourist destination risk perception: The case of Israel. *Journal of Hospitality & Leisure Marketing, 14*(2), 83–108.

George, R. (2003). Tourists' perceptions of safety and security while visiting Cape Town. *Tourism Management, 24*(3), 575–585.

Gosar, A. (2005). The recovery and the transition of tourism to the market economy in Southeastern Europe. In G. Ashworth & R. Hartmann (Eds.), *Horror and human tragedy revisited the management of sites of atrocities for tourism* (pp. 195–210). New York, NY: Cognizant Communication Corporation.

Isaac, R. J., & Çakmak, E. (2014). Understanding visitor's motivation at sites of death and disaster: The case of former transit camp Westerbork, the Netherlands. *Current Issues in Tourism, 17*(2), 164–179.

Isaac, R. K. (2018). Religious tourism in Palestine: Challenges and opportunities. In R. Butler and W. Suntikul (Eds.), *Tourism and religion* (pp. 143–160). Clevedon: Channel View Publications.

Isaac, R. K., & Ashworth, G. J. (2012). Moving from pilgrimage to "dark" tourism: Leveraging tourism in Palestine. *Tourism, Culture and Communication, 11*(3), 149–164.

Isaac, R. K., & Cakmark, E. (2016). Understanding the motivations and emotions of visitors at Tuol Sleng Genocide Prison Museum (S-21) in Phnom Penh, Cambodia. *International Journal of Tourism Cities, 2*(3), 232–247.

Isaac, R. K., Narwiin, J., van Liemont, A., & Gridnevskiv, K. (2019). Understanding Dutch visitors' motivations to concentration camp memorials. *Current Issues in Tourism, 22:*7, 747–762.

Jacobsen, D., Musyck, B., Orphanides, S., & Webster, C. (2010). The opening of the leda crossing in Nicosia: Social and economic consequences. In R. W. Butler & W. Suntikul (Eds.), *Tourism and political change* (pp. 199–207). Oxford: Goodfellow Publishers Ltd.

Janssen-Verbeke, M., & George, W. (2013). Reflections on the Great War centenary: From warscapes to memoryscapes in 100 years. In R. W. Butler & W. Suntikul (Eds.), *Tourism and war* (pp. 273–287). London: Routledge.

Karl, M., & Schmude, J. (2017). Understanding the role of risk perception in destination choice: A literature review and synthesis. *Tourism, 65*(2), 138–155.

King, J. (2015). Indigenous tourism: The most ancient of journeys. In R. W. Butler & W. Suntikul (Eds.), *Tourism and religion* (pp. 14–17). Bristol: Channelview Publications Ltd.

Kozak, M., Crotts, J. C., & Law, R. (2007). The impact of the perception of risk on international travelers. *International Journal of Tourism Research, 9*(4), 233–242.

Krakover, S. (2005). Estimating the effect of atrocious events on the flow of tourists to Israel. In G. Ashworth & R. Hartmann (Eds.), *Horror and human tragedy revisited the management of sites of atrocities for tourism* (pp. 183–194). New York, NY: Cognizant Communication Corporation.

Krakover, S. (2013). Developing tourism alongside threats of wars and atrocities: The case of Israel. In R. W. Butler & W. Suntikul (Eds.), *Tourism and war* (pp. 132–142). London: Routledge.

Ladarman, S. (2013). From the Vietnam War to the "war on terror": Tourism and the martial fascination. In R. W. Butler & W. Suntikul (Eds.), *Tourism and war* (pp. 26–36). London: Routledge.

Lema, J., & Agrusa, J. (2013). Revisiting the war landscape of Vietnam. In R. W. Butler & W. Suntikul (Eds.), *Tourism and war* (pp. 245–253). London: Routledge.

Lemelin, H., Jackie Dawson, J., & Stewart, E. J. (2012). *Last chance tourism adapting tourism opportunities in a changing world.* London: Routledge.

Lennon, J. J., & Foley, M. (2000). *Dark tourism.* London: Casssell.

Miles, S. (2016). *The Western front landscape, tourism and heritage.* Barnsley: Pen and Sword Books Ltd.

Mitchell, V., & Vassos, V. (1997). Perceived risk and risk reduction in holiday purchases: A cross-cultural and gender analysis. *Journal of European Marketing, 6*(3), 47–80.

O'Gorman, K. (2013). The Crusades, the Knights Templar, and Hospitaller: A combination of religion, war, pilgrimage and tourism enablers. In R. W. Butler & W. Suntikul (Eds.), *Tourism and war* (pp. 39–48). London: Routledge.

Poria, Y., Butler, R. W., & Airey, D. (2004). Links between tourists, heritage, and reasons for visiting heritage sites. *Journal of Travel Research, 43*(1), 19–28.

Reisinger, Y., & Mavando, F. (2006). Cultural differences in travel risk perception. *Journal of Travel and Tourism Marketing, 20*(1), 13–31.

Sharifpour, M., Walters, G., & Ritchie, B. W. (2013). The mediating role of sensation seeking on the relationship between risk perceptions and travel behavior. *Tourism Analysis, 18*(5), 543–557.

Sönmez, S. F., & Graefe, A. R. (1998). Determining future travel behavior from past travel experience and perceptions of risk and safety. *Journal of Travel Research, 37*(4), 171–177.

Stone, P. (2006). A dark tourism spectrum: Towards a typology of death and macabre related tourist sites, attractions. *Tourisma An Interdisciplinary Journal, 54*(2), 145–160.

Weaver, D. B., & Lawton, L. J. (2007). "Just because it's gone doesn't mean it isn't there anymore": Planning for attraction residuality *Tourism Management, 28*(1), 108–117.

Winter, C. (2009). Tourism, social memory and the Great War. *Annals of Tourism Research, 36*(4), 607–626.

Winter, C. (2011). First World War cemeteries: Insights from visitor books. *Tourism Geographies, 13*(3), 462–479.

Wintersteiner, W., & Wohlmuther, C. (2013). Peace sensitive tourism: How tourism can contribute to peace. In W. Wintersteiner & C. Wohlmuther (Eds.), *International handbook on tourism and peace* (pp. 31–62). Klagenfurt: DRAVA.

Wolff, K., & Larsen, S. (2017). A taxonomy of terror – about the effect of different kinds of terror on risk perceptions. *Scandinavian Journal of Hospitality and Tourism, 17*(2), 111–128.

3 Tourism, border disputes and claims to territorial sovereignty

Dallen J. Timothy

Introduction

Tourism is inherently a political phenomenon. In most parts of the world, those who govern states also control their tourism sectors through legal mechanisms, policies, plans and initiatives that reflect their ideological and development priorities. Likewise, the stories told by heritage interpreters are frequently determined, or at least heavily influenced, by the predominant national narratives and the ways in which the parties in power decide how the past should be interpreted (Zhao & Timothy, 2017). Tourism is also commonly used to spread propaganda, to shore up nationalistic support within a domestic context, to punish rogue states by withholding tourism through embargos, to disempower certain sectors of the population and to create a nationwide amnesia about past injustices (Kim, Timothy, & Han, 2007).

Beyond state manipulation of heritage and other forms of tourism, there is an inherent relationship between tourism and geopolitical conflicts worldwide. Most of these conflicts centre on territorial disputes and religious contestations. There are several ways in which tourism relates to geopolitical tensions. This chapter examines a few of these; namely, conflict as a deterrent to tourism, tourism during times and in places of hostilities, tourism as a potential tool for peace-building, conflict as a tourist attraction, tourism as a cause of contention, tourism as a propaganda tool and tourism as an instrument for asserting territorial sovereignty in areas of discord. Several of these concepts are examined in the India-Pakistan border area, as well as the disputed islands of the South China Sea.

Tourism, territoriality and zones of conflict

Territorial conflicts abound, and every place has been affected by them at some time in history. Although almost all land portions of the earth are universally accepted as integral parts of sovereign states, currently more than 130 territorial disputes worldwide involve two or more claimant states wrangling over land, coral atolls, subterranean resources, continental shelves or ocean waters (Allcock, 1992; Brunet-Jailly, 2015). Manifestations of these disagreements range from dormant situations where discord rarely appears in legal proceedings or conflict on the ground, to constant states of warfare with armed clashes.

There are several relationships between tourism and territorial conflict (But-ler & Suntikul, 2013), although only a few are outlined in this chapter. The most evident relationship is conflict as a deterrent to travel and tourism develop-ment. Thousands of examples abound of places whose tourism industries have all but disappeared because of territorial conflict-based tensions. In this case, active confrontations destroy natural and cultural landscapes, and they some-times target archaeological sites and other important national icons for inten-tional destruction. Tourism always faces challenges in areas of military control and active fighting, and such conditions deter would-be tourists from visiting. Contentious borders and ceasefire lines erect real barriers as they usually either prevent crossings altogether or they become filter mechanisms that are difficult to cross (Timothy, 2001).

A second connection is conflict as a tourist attraction (Fyall, Prideaux, & Timothy, 2006; Isaac, 2009). Active conflicts or their tangible remains can both function as a tourist attraction. Some people travel to witness a famous dispute for themselves, to satisfy their curiosity about a conflict that has received global notoriety. This is a high-risk form of travel and is usually undertaken by only the most ardent enthusiasts. A unique tourism niche in areas of conflict is known as solidarity tourism, or justice tourism. Its main thrust is people travelling in a show of support for one side or the other in a belligerent relationship (Higgins-Desbiolles, 2008; Isaac, 2010, 2017; Kassis, Solomon, & Higgins-Desbiolles, 2016). Visiting sites of military clashes and belligerence may also be 'dark' in character and considered a form of dark tourism and heritage tourism.

A third crossover between tourism and discord is tourism as a catalyst for peace-building. While this view has an abundance of critics who suggest peace must come before tourism can flourish, many observers suggest that tourism has the potential to create a greater understanding between peoples through exposure to different ways of thinking and dissimilar cultures, thereby contributing to more amicable relations (Moufakkir & Kelly, 2010).

Fourth, tourism may also be the cause, or partial cause, of international skir-mishes and disagreements, especially regarding territorial claims where lucrative tourism resources are located in the areas in question. One of the best examples of this is the Preah Vihear temple complex at the border of Thailand and Cambodia. The two countries have battled, physically and legally, over this prime real estate for decades. While the International Court of Justice has ruled that the entire site is Cambodian, Thailand claims ownership of the territory surrounding it. The value of tourism at such an impressive ancient site is part of the reason for the frequent armed standoffs and border closures in the area (Ngoun, 2016; Timothy, 2013). Similarly, some of the underlying concerns in the Japan-Russia impasse over the Kuril Islands relate to their tourism value (Simmons, 2006), as are the issues in the Southern Patagonia Ice Field dispute between Argentina and Chile (Brunet-Jailly, 2015).

Fifth, tourism is often used as a mechanism for state propaganda during times of crisis and in localities of conflict to reinforce national solidarity and loyalty for the cause (Kim et al., 2007). Visits to war memorials, the heroification of martyrs and nationalists, and using visits to show a state's benevolence are common manifestations of this phenomenon.

Finally, related to the fifth point previously stated, tourism is sometimes used as an apparatus to legally justify a country's claims to contested territories. According to international law, states can grow physically and acquire additional sovereign territory in several different ways, including long-term possession, land exchanges, geophysical accretion, conquest and annexation, and through subjugation of *terra nullius*, or the occupation and absorption of what the occupying force deems to be unoccupied land (Boucher, 2016; Murphy, 1990; Timothy, 2010). The doctrine of *terra nullius* was the foundation upon which the European colonial land grabs from the 16th to the 20th centuries were based, and the credo upon which many territorial claims continue today.

Traditionally, countries have needed to demonstrate certain conditions for their declared sovereign ownership over territory acquired through *terra nullius* to be recognized. These include that the new acquisition must be able to support human life and livelihoods; there should be a documented history of consistent, long-term occupation by the claimant state; and the responsibilities of national administrations must be exercised (e.g. postal services, law enforcement, infrastructure development, etc.) (Glassner & Fahrer, 2004; Murphy, 1990; Timothy, 2010, 2013). States involved in territorial claims and squabbles typically use military occupation as proof of possession, as well as a means of defending their claims. However, they also sometimes utilize tourism as a mechanism for claiming rights over lands they seized through conquest or through entitlements of *terra nullius*. According to the claimant states, tourism satisfies the legal requirements of supporting human habitation, a history of occupation and the exercise of state functions and responsibilities. There are several examples of states employing tourism to affirm their claims to disputed territories, but the Antarctic territories are probably the best examples of this anywhere in the world (Timothy, 2010).

Tourism is considered a way not only to assert claims of sovereignty, but also to build social support among nationals for the state's territorial claim (Chubb, 2017). On the international stage, tourism is frequently manipulated to demonstrate peace and to showcase a country's benevolence. It may also be used to reduce the incidents of armed conflict owing to the presence of international guests 'because if you have foreigners from different countries all over the world in that place, it decreases the chance of any other people taking rash actions against you' (Collin Koh, security specialist quoted in Jennings, 2018).

The Pakistan-India border dispute

British colonial rule in South Asia ended in 1947 with the independence of Pakistan and India. Divided largely along religious lines, Pakistan was populated primarily by Muslims and India mostly by Hindus. The nearly 600 princely states in British India were allowed to choose whether to merge with India or Pakistan, or remain independent. Jammu and Kashmir was ruled by a Hindu maharaja, while most of the population were Muslims. To appease the population, the maharaja opted to remain independent (Paul, 2005; Schofield, 2000).

Pakistan desired to possess the region and sent in armed Muslim guerrillas to overtake or divide the region along religious lines. Responding to the assault, the prince decided to unite Jammu and Kashmir with India, much to the chagrin of Pakistan and the principality's majority population. This resulted in a war, which lasted until the end of 1948 (Schofield, 2000; Wirsing, 1998). Several armed skirmishes and wars have ensued since 1948 between India and Pakistan, and India and China (Liu, 1994; Mehra, 2007). In 1971, the Line of Control (LoC) between the two countries was established. Today, Pakistan controls large parts of the region. The Indian-controlled area is known as Jammu and Kashmir, and China controls the Aksai Chin area.

Armed conflicts continue today with a constant threat of militant attacks, cross-border shootings and outright warfare. The Kashmir conflict is one of the longest and bloodiest struggles today, and is in one of the most dangerous regions of the world. It has soured relationships between the two neighbours, which frequently manifests along other parts of the border (Aftab, 2014) and within their common border policies, travel restrictions and visa regimes (Timothy, 2003).

In recognition of the needs of conflict zone residents, the two governments have been willing to compromise slightly. Some local cross-LoC roads and bus services have been established in the past few decades, although these are extremely fragile and tend to be interrupted or cancelled at random or when conflicts flare. These services were established specifically for use by local 'tourists' only, particularly for Kashmiris who have relatives on the other side of the LoC, as well as local traders and truck drivers. Long and arduous vetting processes prevent many locals from crossing the line. Entry permits can take between 6 and 18 months to be approved, and even then, crossings are not guaranteed (Malik, 2013). Non-local Pakistanis and Indians, as well as foreign tourists, are not permitted to cross or approach the LoC at any location.

There are only a few other points of entry on the India-Pakistan border, with the Wagah crossing being the busiest port and only locale where foreign tourists are permitted to cross. Since 1947, few cross-border transportation options have emerged. In 1999, a Delhi-Lahore bus service was established and may be used by foreigners, Indians and Pakistanis (Malik, 2013). However, it is difficult for Indians to acquire Pakistani visas, and vice versa. With regard to one another, neither India nor Pakistan adheres to the edicts of the South Asian Association for Regional Cooperation's (SAARC) Visa Exemption Scheme, which allows certain people to travel freely within the SAARC region (Aftab, 2014). The visa process is cumbersome, costly and time-consuming. If granted at all, Indian visas for Pakistanis and Pakistani visas for Indians restrict which cities they can visit and which airports they can use. This remains one of the biggest challenges to cross-border tourism (Rasul & Manandhar, 2009). Foreign tourists with proper Indian and Pakistani visas may come and go, except in disputed Kashmir.

Several of the relationships between conflict and tourism are manifested in this region. First is the notion of conflict as a barrier to travel and tourism development. Despite the region's vast assets and tourism potential, tourism is extremely elastic and is severely affected by local violence (Ahmad & Hussain, 2011; Chauhan & Khanna, 2009; Dar, 2014; Evans, 2005). Like other places of conflict, Kashmir's wars and insurgencies have tainted the region's tourism image (Islam, 2014; Sharma, Sharma, & Waris, 2012). Several studies show that the ebb and flow of tourism is directly connected to the number of fatalities in the conflict (Chauhan & Khanna, 2009; Islam, 2014; Soundararajan & Rajan, 2006).

There is relatively little evidence that this conflict itself is a tourist attraction, although it might be if conditions were different. For example, foreigners, as well as Pakistani and Indian tourists, are not generally permitted near the LoC. Beyond Kashmir, however, the official border itself is somewhat of an attraction, particularly at the main crossing at Wagah and Attari. Each evening, after border administrators have finished their daily duties, soldiers perform a provocative and meticulously choreographed military exercise with two official purposes and one unofficial aim: to close the frontier gate for the night, to demonstrate a competitive expression of power and intimidation, and to provide entertainment for onlookers. While satisfying official requirements, the spectacle has become a well-known tourist attraction that draws thousands of people each year to both sides of the border from nearby Lahore (Pakistan) and Amritsar (India) (Chaturvedi, 2002; Chhabra, 2018; Jeychandran, 2016; Kalra & Purewal, 1999; Timothy, 2001). The touristic attention the ceremony receives has in effect turned an otherwise contentious boundary into a permissible source of amusement despite its 'choreography of symbolic violence' (van Schendel, 2007, p. 44).

In the 1980s, tourism emerged as a leading industry on the Indian-controlled side of Kashmir. It became popular for several reasons. One was a growing Western interest in Buddhism as a spiritual philosophy (Hall, 2006; Nyaupane, 2009), and certain parts of the region (e.g. Ladakh) were known to be home to some of the purest forms of Buddhism in the world (Aggarwal, 2004; Michaud, 1991). In the past three decades, the world also began to witness patterns of 'new tourism,' or tourism beyond the ordinary and well-trodden mass tourist itineraries, which saw people travelling to less developed and out-of-the-ordinary sorts of destinations (Aggarwal, 2004). With the economic promise of this changing taste for isolated and faraway localities, India decided to open up increasingly fragile and sensitive areas for tourism, including Kashmir (Equations Team, 2013). Kashmir remains one of the least tourism-touched regions of world with extraordinary scenery and a general abundance of nature and culture (Raina, 2002; Sharma et al., 2012; Singh, 2017). However, it is increasingly becoming a much sought after destination despite the international conflict for which it is best known (Malik & Bhat, 2015).

Despite its many assets, security remains an important concern among tourists who visit (Singh, 2014). The most visited and safest part of the region is Ladakh, which has seen tourism grow in recent decades. Besides its vast natural and cultural resources, Ladakh lies a distance from the LoC, which adds layers of security that have allowed tourism to flourish (Malik, 2013). The areas nearest the LoC are far less developed and, as noted earlier, most non-residents are not permitted to enter the Kashmir Valley or approach the LoC.

While there is little evidence that tourism has been or is currently being used as a catalyst for growing more peaceful relationships between the two states, many commentators have suggested that it could play that important role (e.g. Aftab, 2014; Haq & Medhekar, 2013; Malik, 2013). Several scholars have recognized that the shared history, culture, religion, food and language form a solid foundation upon which cross-border tourism-based goodwill could be developed (Aftab, 2014; Chauhan & Khanna, 2009; Haq & Medhekar, 2013). According to these observers, more things unite the people than divide them, and cross-border tourism would allow members of both societies to visit one another and dispel inaccurate negative stereotypes of people on the other side.

The South China Sea

Another conflicted area is the islets, shoals and waterways of the South China Sea (SCS). The area is comprised of three groups of small islands and rocky outcrops: the Spratly Islands, the Paracel Islands and Scarborough Shoal. Most of these 'islands' are small sandbanks, tiny reefs, diminutive rocky outcrops and a handful of small islands, the majority of which are not capable of supporting human habitation.

The Paracel Islands include more than 130 islets and outcrops equidistance from the coasts of Vietnam and Hainan Island, China. Vietnam, China and Taiwan actively dispute sovereignty over this small archipelago, although China has controlled the Paracels since 1974 (Amer, 2014; Raine, 2017). Comprised of more than 100 small rocks, islets, shoals, cays and atolls, the Spratly Islands are the southernmost contested area in the region. China, Taiwan and Vietnam claim all of the Spratlys, while the Philippines, Malaysia and Brunei claim sovereignty over some of the islets (Central Intelligence Agency, 2018; Raine, 2017). All of these countries except Brunei physically occupy islands in the Spratly archipelago. There have been many armed skirmishes, and recent years have seen an increase in intimidation tactics, such as warplane overflights and ramming one another's boats. China's claims over all of the SCS are legally required to be depicted in all maps made in China, including tourist maps and academic cartography.

The SCS claims are typically based upon overlapping assertions of historical control and occupation, as well as each country's own definitions of its territorial economic zones (Lasserre, 2017). At the core of the disputes are the fishing resources of the South China Sea, which are plentiful and productive; the potential of oil and gas reserves underneath the islets and their 200-nautical-mile Exclusive Economic Zones (EEZs); and control of shipping routes between East Asia and the rest of world (Forbes, 2015).

According to international law, rocks or reefs breaching the surface of the ocean that cannot sustain human habitation or support a functional economic system do not possess continental shelves or EEZs (Gjetnes, 2001; Timothy, 2013). To remedy this situation, most claimant states have occupied some of the rocks and islets with military personnel and fishermen during the past 50 years. Many of these islets have also been expanded through land reclamation to the point where they are now physically able to support airport runways, heliports, docks, housing, public services and civilian communities in an effort to demonstrate habitability and thereby expand their EEZs.

To advance their territorial rights claims even further, China, the Philippines, Vietnam, Taiwan and Malaysia have begun to develop tourism on some of their occupied islets or otherwise use tourism as a means of professing sovereignty and asserting political control. Sending tourists to the islands and establishing commercial flights and other tourism services are used by these five states as 'evidence' that their small spots in the ocean are in fact governable portions of their national territory. In the case of the SCS, this is done in two different ways. First, a claimant state establishes a strong tourism presence on an islet. In a couple of cases, small islets have been expanded into functional islands to support tourism through land reclamation to enable airports and hotels to be built. Tourism employees are brought in to staff hotels, resorts, restaurants and airports. Housing is provided for the employees, who typically live among the island's other civilian occupants. The second means of using tourism is belligerents employing their occupied islets as destinations for day trips or cruises, which do not typically require a permanently established tourism superstructure, but do utilize their claims for touristic purposes.

Few of the islets in the SCS have seen tourism capacities of the first type mentioned earlier. The most recognizable example is Layang Layang Island, which is claimed and occupied by Malaysia. The island was originally 6.2 hectares, but with land reclamation for military and tourism purposes, the island has now grown to approximately 35 hectares. It has an airport and a three-star dive resort opened in the early 1990s, as well as a Malaysian naval garrison. Layang Layang is famous for diving, snorkeling and bird watching, and is serviced by seasonal flights from Kota Kinabalu, Malaysia. Predictably, the initial establishment of the resort drew criticism from Vietnam and China, but the situation has settled down considerably as Malaysia has not taken any further steps toward developing tourism on the island or on nearby islands (Huang & Billo, 2015; Rowen, 2018).

Taiwan is considering developing tourism on the 46-hectare Taiping Island, although no actions have yet been taken. Thitu Island, the second largest of the Spratlys, has a population of between 200 and 300 Philippine citizens. There is an airstrip capable of accommodating commercial flights, and the government of the Philippines has recently invested approximately US$32 million to develop a port, repair the airstrip, erect solar panels and improve water supplies as precursors to tourism development (Chubb, 2017). There have also been proposals in the past few years within the government to promote Thitu as an ecotourism and diving destination. Proposals continue to be mulled around regarding the best ways to transform Thitu Island into a tourist destination. There have also been talks underway for several years for Vietnam to renovate its disused airport on Spratly Island (Storm Island) and create a stronger and more permanent tourism presence there (Timothy, 2013). Likewise, the notion of developing a more permanent tourism presence on the Spratlys was introduced formally in Chinese planning documents in 2013, although it had been conceived of much earlier than that (Chubb, 2017; Huang & Billo, 2015).

As for using the islands in other tourism ways, Malaysian tour companies use Dallas Reef for fishing and diving tourism. Vietnam regularly offers cruises to some of its occupied Spratly islets for sun, sea and sand holidays, as well as visits to scientific research stations (Timothy, 2013). China began regular flights to Woody Island in December 2016 and cruises in 2013, and hopes to develop the island in the near future for surfing, diving and wedding tourism (Jennings, 2017).

The touristic uses of the SCS islands are blatantly political and meant to make a statement about a country's undisputable dominion over the region in what Rowen (2014, p. 64) refers to as 'tourism . . . as a technology of state territorialization.' In 2015, Vietnam offered 'sovereignty cruises,' which allowed patriotic citizens on a waiting list to visit beaches and reefs, to fish and dine on local seafood. However, and more importantly, the political dimensions of the trip were of paramount importance and something not lost in advertising. According to marketing materials, the cruise is meant to:

> arouse national pride and citizen consciousness of the sacred sovereignty of the country. . . . Guests will attend the national flag-raising ceremony, commemorate the heroic martyrs, visit a pagoda, get on the lighthouse for a panoramic view of the island, and explore the daily life of citizens and troops on the island.
>
> (quoted in Gady, 2015)

China vehemently opposed Vietnam's sovereignty cruises and insisted that they violated China's sovereignty over the islands (Gady, 2015). It remains unclear whether or not Vietnam will continue to operate sovereignty cruises in the future.

Similarly, China began offering cruises to the Paracel Islands in 2013. Much of China's South China Sea rhetoric aims to foment nationalistic sentiments among its populace, build support for its military activities and buttress its revisionist geographies of the SCS (Roszko, 2015; Swe, Hailong, & Mingjiang, 2017). The cruises aim to reinforce the same doctrines. By 2016, some 23,000 rigorously vetted Chinese tourists had participated on a patriotic cruise, which parallel many elements of its Vietnamese counterpart (Chubb, 2017). They visit a small, uninhabited atoll to participate in a Chinese flag-raising ceremony and proclaim their loyalty to China, dine on fresh seafood on another atoll that is occupied by military forces, and they spend a lot of time on the ship watching presentations that bolster China's official position on Paracel Island sovereignty. Most of the advertising related to the cruise tugs at people's patriotism, describing many times over China's sovereign rights to the islands and nationalistic ideals in promoting the islands. Realizing these implications, Rowen (2018) argues that current Chinese tourism in the area is more about patriotism and politics than it is about sun, sea, sand and sightseeing.

All of these forms of tourism in the SCS have at their core the legitimization of the various states' territorial claims over *terra nullius*. They reflect attempts to 'civilianize' remote ocean outliers that have no indigenous population and which traditionally and naturally could not have supported human habitation, an economic system or government functions. China and Vietnam both disapprove of tourism being developed by other claimant states (Keck, 2014), although they believe their own efforts are warranted. The Philippines has adopted a taunting stance toward China in its tourism efforts in response to China's overbearing presence in the region (Keck, 2014).

Discussion and conclusion

There are hundreds of localities of conflict where tourism is impacted in many ways. This chapter has examined two prominent cases, namely the India-Pakistan border and the South China Sea. Each of these situations is unique in how its nascent tourism sectors interact with territorial conflict (Table 3.1).

While conflict is a significant deterrent to tourism in most parts of the world, it does not appear to be a significant barrier in the SCS, although it clearly is in Kashmir and all along the entire Pakistan-India border. However, both regions exhibit strong indicators that tourism is growing despite the conflict. While border tourism is not permitted at the Pakistan-India frontier, except at Wagah, tourism is thriving in other parts of Kashmir, especially on the Indian side in the areas of scenic Ladakh that are located away from the LoC. Cultural tourism, religious/spiritual tourism and nature-based tourism all appear to be thriving in Ladakh, and are heavily promoted by the state of Jammu and Kashmir, as well as by the national authorities in New Delhi. Although tourism is not growing rapidly in the SCS, this is not a result of the conflict but more likely a consequence of isolation, inaccessibility and limited resources. Nevertheless, tourism continues to grow in the SCS, now occupying a prominent position in claimant countries' national development plans for the maritime region.

There is very little evidence suggesting that the South Asian struggle serves as an attraction, with the exception of the Wagah border ceremony. Access to the Line of Control and the Kashmir Valley is prohibited, and therefore precludes the development of 'dark tourism,' 'solidarity tourism' or other forms of tourism. In

Table 3.1 Conflict and tourism in the India-Pakistan borderlands and the South China Sea

Tourism-conflict relationship	India-Pakistan borderlands	South China Sea
Conflict as deterrent	Strong evidence	Little or no evidence
Tourism growth despite conflict	Strong evidence	Strong evidence
Conflict as attraction	Little or no evidence	Strong evidence
Tourism as catalyst for peace	Little or no evidence	Little or no evidence
Tourism causes hostility	Little or no evidence	Some evidence
Tourism as tool for propaganda	Little or no evidence	Strong evidence
Tourism as justification for territorial claims	Little or no evidence	Strong evidence

the SCS, however, there is strong evidence of the conflict being a major draw. For the Chinese, visiting the Paracel or Spratly islands is a once-in-a-lifetime opportunity with a lengthy waiting list and vetting process for those interested in visiting. Other claimant countries offer tourist experiences that also play on the geopolitical intrigue associated with the well-publicized fracas as a salient element of the region's appeal.

In general, tourism is often touted as a catalyst for peace. However, in areas of direct conflict, it is hard to initiate tourism or even maintain it, let alone manipulate it as a peace-building instrument. While many commentators in South Asia suggest that tourism has the potential to help build cross-border understanding between India and Pakistan, there are few, if any, efforts in either part of the world where tourism actively functions as a means of cultivating more peaceful relations.

Even though tourism is not the root of disharmony in the SCS, it is to blame to some degree for intensifying hostility between discordant states. Each time one of the appellant countries takes action to develop tourism, including building landing strips and lodging facilities, as well as offering cruises, other claimant states lodge complaints with the United Nations or make their own violent threats. This is particularly evident in the relationships between China, Vietnam and the Philippines. In South Asia, tourism does not appear to be a source of conflict.

Tourism is not generally used as a propaganda tool in the India-Pakistan struggle. In the SCS, however, it is a major propaganda focus. The Philippines sometimes uses cruises to rebuff Chinese displays of military might. Chinese cruises to the Paracel Islands abound in nationalistic rhetoric, demonstrations of loyalty and rewards for those who participate. So far, only stalwart supporters of the state's claims to the SCS are permitted to visit. For the most part, these visits reflect a far stronger emphasis on nationalism and solidarity than on sun, sea, sand and sightseeing.

Tourism does not appear to be used as justification for territorial claims in the case of South Asia. In the SCS, the opposite is true. In fact, tourism development on the disputed Paracel and Spratly islands is one of the world's eminent examples of justifying state absorption of *terra nullius*. Massive land reclamation efforts to make the islets liveable; the building of landing strips, ports, airports, and water and energy sources; resettling populations of citizens; planting flags and erecting boundary markers; initiating scheduled flights and cruises; and providing government services are directly related both to military occupation and tourism planning and are proclaimed to satisfy the legal requirements of *terra nullius*.

Many of these relational patterns are because the South Asian example continues to be an active battlefield, while the SCS engagement is more rhetorical with only sporadic and short-lived confrontations. This goes even further when considering that tourism is not allowed at the LoC, and cross-border travel is otherwise extremely difficult in the context of Pakistan and India, while the opposite is true in the SCS.

In disputed Kashmir, there are nascent signs of collaboration and easing of tensions, with tourism playing an increasingly important role in that shift.

Nevertheless, the area continues to be a hotbed of contention, with armed insurgencies attacking Indian military installations as recently as February 2018. In the SCS, hostilities began to escalate in 2011, with some claimant countries beginning to exercise their professed entitlements to fishing and oil exploration. Above all, this has riled China, the most powerful appellant state, which claims sovereign rights to the entire region, even islands and shoals that lie clearly within the territorial waters and EEZs of other states. The SCS hostilities have continued to escalate in the intervening years, with major conflicts continuing in the region in 2017–2018, particularly between China, the Philippines and Vietnam. While Kashmir and the South China Sea have considerable tourism potential, continued active combat plagues both regions and hinders the development of international tourism in two regions that are both attractive and iconic.

References

Aftab, S. (2014). *South Asian regional cooperation: The India-Pakistan imperative*. Robina, Queensland: Bond University, Faculty of Society and Design Publications.

Aggarwal, R. (2004). *Beyond lines of control: Performance and politics on the disputed borders of Ladakh, India*. Durham, NC: Duke University Press.

Ahmad, I. M., & Hussain, N. A. (2011). Impact of turmoil on tourism of Kashmir. *Journal of Economics and Sustainable Development, 2*(7), 1–7.

Allcock, J. B. (1992). *Border and territorial disputes*. London: Longman.

Amer, R. (2014). China, Vietnam, and the South China Sea: Disputes and dispute management. *Ocean Development & International Law, 45*(1), 17–40.

Boucher, D. (2016). The law of nations and the doctrine of terra nullius. In O. Asbach & P. Schröder (Eds.), *War, the state and international law in seventeenth-century Europe* (pp. 77–96). London: Routledge.

Brunet-Jailly, E. (2015). *Border disputes: A global encyclopedia* (Vol. 1). Santa Barbara, CA: ABC-CLIO.

Butler, R., & Suntikul, W. (Eds.). (2013). *Tourism and war*. London: Routledge.

Central Intelligence Agency. (2018). *CIA world factbook*. Washington, DC: Central Intelligence Agency. Retrieved from www.cia.gov/library/publications/the-world-factbook/

Chauhan, V., & Khanna, S. (2009). Tourism: A tool for crafting peace process in Kashmir, J&K, India. *Tourismos, 4*(2), 69–89.

Chaturvedi, S. (2002). Process of othering in the case of India and Pakistan. *Tijdschrift voor Economische en Sociale Geografie, 93*(2), 149–159.

Chhabra, D. (2018). Soft power analysis in alienated borderline tourism. *Journal of Heritage Tourism, 13*(4), 289–304.

Chubb, A. (2017, 6 June). Patriotic tourism in the South China Sea. *East Asia Forum*. Retrieved 3 August 2018, from www.eastasiaforum.org/2017/06/07/patriotic-tourism-in-the-south-china-sea/

Dar, H. (2014). The potential of tourism in border destinations: A study of Jammu and Kashmir. *African Journal of Hospitality, Tourism and Leisure, 4*(2), 1–12.

Equations Team. (2013). Of peoples and places: Tourism and zones of conflict in India. In L. Blanchard & F. Higgins-Desbiolles (Eds.), *Peace through tourism: Promoting human security through international citizenship* (pp. 116–134). London: Routledge.

Evans, A. (2005). Kashmir: A tale of two valleys. *Asian Affairs, 36*(1), 35–47.

Forbes, V. L. (2015). Artificial islands in the South China Sea: Rationale for terrestrial increase, incremental maritime jurisdictional creep and military bases. *The Journal of Defense and Security, 6*(1), 30–55.

Fyall, A., Prideaux, B., & Timothy, D. J. (2006). War and tourism: An introduction. *International Journal of Tourism Research, 8*(3), 153–155.

Gady, F. (2015, 6 June). Vietnam's newest tourist destination: The Spratlys. *The Diplomat.* Retrieved 22 July 2018, from https://thediplomat.com/2015/06/this-is-vietnams-newest-tourist-destination-the-spratlys/

Gjetnes, M. (2001). The Spratlys: Are they rocks or islands? *Ocean Development and International Law, 32*(2), 191–204.

Glassner, M. I., & Fahrer, C. (2004). *Political geography* (3rd ed.). Hoboken, NJ: Wiley.

Hall, C. M. (2006). Buddhism, tourism and the middle way. In D. J. Timothy & D. H. Olsen (Eds.), *Tourism, religion and spiritual journeys* (pp. 172–185). London: Routledge.

Haq, F., & Medhekar, A. (2013). Branding spiritual tourism as an innovation for peace between India and Pakistan. *International Journal of Social Entrepreneurship and Innovation, 2*(5), 404–414.

Higgins-Desbiolles, F. (2008). Justice tourism and alternative globalisation. *Journal of Sustainable Tourism, 16*(3), 345–364.

Huang, J., & Billo, A. (2015). *Territorial disputes in the South China Sea: Navigating rough waters.* Basingstoke: Palgrave McMillan.

Isaac, R. K. (2009). Alternative tourism: Can the segregation wall in Bethlehem be a tourist attraction? *Tourism and Hospitality Planning & Development, 6*(3), 247–254.

Isaac, R. K. (2010). Alternative tourism: New forms of tourism in Bethlehem for the Palestinian tourism industry. *Current Issues in Tourism, 13*(1), 21–36.

Isaac, R. K. (2017). Transformational host communities: Justice tourism and the water regime in Palestine. *Tourism, Culture & Communication, 17*(2), 139–158.

Islam, A. U. (2014). Impact of armed conflict on economy and tourism: A study of the state of Jammu and Kashmir. *IOSR Journal of Economics and Finance, 4*(6), 55–60.

Jennings, R. (2017, 9 April). Travelers visit disputed areas of the South China Sea. *VOA News.* Retrieved 10 August 2018, from https://learningenglish.voanews.com/a/travelers-visit-south-china-sea/3794145.html

Jennings, R. (2018, 22 April). Door opens for new tourism in South China Sea. *VOA News.* Retrieved 1 August 2018, from https://learningenglish.voanews.com/a/door-opens-for-new-tourism-in-south-china-sea/4357944.html

Jeychandran, N. (2016). Specter of war, spectacle of peace: The lowering of flags ceremony at the Wagah and Hussainiwala border outposts. In G. Morris & J. R. Giersdorf (Eds.), *Choreographies of 21st century wars* (pp. 181–202). Oxford: Oxford University Press.

Kalra, V. S., & Purewal, N. K. (1999). The strut of the peacocks: Partition, travel and the Indo-Pak border. In R. Kaur & J. Hutnyk (Eds.), *Travel worlds: Journeys in contemporary cultural politics* (pp. 54–67). London: Zed Books.

Kassis, R., Solomon, R., & Higgins-Desbiolles, F. (2016). Solidarity tourism in Palestine: The alternative tourism group of Palestine as a catalyzing instrument of resistance. In R. Isaac, C. M. Hall, & F. Higgins-Desbiolles (Eds.), *The politics and power of tourism in Palestine* (pp. 37–53). London: Routledge.

Keck, Z. (2014). Philippines military to offer cruise service in South China Sea. *The Diplomat.* Retrieved 3 August 2017, from https://thediplomat.com/2014/08/philippines-military-to-offer-cruise-service-in-south-china-sea/

Kim, S. S., Timothy, D. J., & Han, H. C. (2007). Tourism and political ideologies: A case of tourism in North Korea. *Tourism Management, 28*(4), 1031–1043.

Lasserre, F. (2017). Maritime borders in the South China Sea: Dynamics of claims and legal basis. In B. Courmont, F. Lasserre, & E. Mottet (Eds.), *Assessing maritime disputes in East Asia: Political and legal perspectives* (pp. 136–154). London: Routledge.

Liu, X. (1994). *The Sino-Indian border dispute and Sino-Indian relations*. New York, NY: University Press of America.

Malik, M. I., & Bhat, M. S. (2015). Sustainability of tourism development in Kashmir – is paradise lost? *Tourism Management Perspectives, 16*, 11–21.

Malik, S. A. (2013). Development of difficult region through travel, trade and tourism: A case study of twin border districts Rajouri and Poonch. *International Journal of Marketing, Financial Services and Management Research, 2*(2), 56–65.

Mehra, P. (2007). *Essays in frontier history: India, China, and the disputed border*. Oxford: Oxford University Press.

Michaud, J. (1991). A social anthropology of tourism in Ladakh, India. *Annals of Tourism Research, 18*(4), 605–621.

Moufakkir, O., & Kelly, I. (Eds.). (2010). *Tourism, progress and peace*. Wallingford: CABI.

Murphy, A. B. (1990). Historical justifications for territorial claims. *Annals of the Association of American Geographers, 80*(4), 531–548.

Ngoun, K. (2016). Narrating the national border: Cambodian state rhetoric vs popular discourse on the Preah Vihear conflict. *Journal of Southeast Asian Studies, 47*(2), 210–233.

Nyaupane, G. P. (2009). Heritage complexity and tourism: The case of Lumbini, Nepal. *Journal of Heritage Tourism, 4*(2), 157–172.

Paul, T. V. (Ed.). (2005). *The India-Pakistan conflict: An enduring rivalry*. Cambridge: Cambridge University Press.

Raina, A. K. (2002). *Tourism industry in Kashmir*. New Delhi: Shipra Publications.

Raine, S. (2017). *Regional disorder: The South China Sea disputes*. London: Routledge.

Rasul, G., & Manandhar, P. (2009). Prospects and problems in promoting tourism in South Asia: A regional perspective. *South Asia Economic Journal, 10*(1), 187–207.

Roszko, E. (2015). Maritime territorialisation as performance of sovereignty and nationhood in the South China Sea. *Nations and Nationalism, 21*(2), 230–249.

Rowen, I. (2014). Tourism as a territorial strategy: The case of China and Taiwan. *Annals of Tourism Research, 46*, 62–74.

Rowen, I. (2018). Tourism as a territorial strategy in the South China Sea. In J. Spangler, D. Karalekas, & M. Lopes de Souza (Eds.), *Enterprises, localities, people, and policy in the South China Sea: Beneath the surface* (pp. 61–74). Cham: Springer.

Schofield, V. (2000). *Kashmir in conflict: India, Pakistan and the unending war*. London: IB Tauris.

Sharma, R., Sharma, V. K., & Waris, V. I. S. (2012). Impact of peace and disturbances on tourism and horticulture in Jammu and Kashmir. *International Journal of Scientific and Research Publications, 2*(6), 1–7.

Simmons, B. (2006). Trade and territorial conflict in Latin America: International borders as institutions. In M. Kahler & B. F. Walter (Eds.), *Territoriality and conflict in an era of globalization* (pp. 251–287). Cambridge: Cambridge University Press.

Singh, R. (2014). Evaluating and understanding the tourist experience: An empirical study in Jammu and Kashmir. *Enlightening Tourism: A Pathmaking Journal, 4*(1), 1–29.

Singh, S. (2017). *Tourism in Jammu and Kashmir*. New Delhi: Educreation Publishing.

Soundararajan, R., & Rajan, P. (2006). *Impact of terrorism on Jammu and Kashmir tourism*. New Delhi: Kalpaz Publications.

Swe, L. K., Hailong, J., & Mingjiang, L. (2017). China's revisionist aspirations in Southeast Asia and the curse of the South China Sea disputes. *China: An International Journal, 15*(1), 187–213.

Timothy, D. J. (2001). *Tourism and political boundaries*. London: Routledge.

Timothy, D. J. (2003). Supranationalist alliances and tourism: Insights from ASEAN and SAARC. *Current Issues in Tourism, 6*(3), 250–266.

Timothy, D. J. (2010). Contested place and the legitimization of sovereignty claims through tourism in Polar regions. In C. M. Hall & J. Saarinen (Eds.), *Tourism and change in polar regions: Climate, environment and experience* (pp. 288–300). London: Routledge.

Timothy, D. J. (2013). Tourism, war, and political instability: Territorial and religious perspectives. In R. Butler & W. Suntikul (Eds.), *Tourism and war* (pp. 12–25). London: Routledge.

Van Schendel, W. (2007). The Wagah syndrome: Territorial roots of contemporary violence in South Asia. In A. Basu & S. Roy (Eds.), *Violence and democracy in India* (pp. 36–82). Calcutta: Seagull Books.

Wirsing, R. (1998). *India, Pakistan, and the Kashmir dispute: On regional conflict and its resolution*. New Delhi: Macmillan.

Zhao, S., & Timothy, D. (2017). The dynamics of guiding and interpreting in red tourism. *International Journal of Tourism Cities, 3*(3), 243–259.

4 The attitudes of the Dutch market towards safety and security

Rami K. Isaac

Introduction

Terrorism and conflict represent a big danger for the success of tourism destinations around the world, particularly because most tourists are concerned about terrorism risk. Risky destinations will face difficulties to attract tourists and visitors (Beirman, 2003; George, 2003; Prideaux, 1996; Rittichainuwat & Chakraborty, 2009; Sönmez & Graefe, 1998b), and as a result, there may be a decline in their tourism industries by a reduction of tourist arrivals (Sönmez, Apostolopoulos, & Tarlow, 1999). There is considerable literature that has attempted to examine the connections between risk perceptions, safety fears and tourist behaviour. In particular, studies on the impacts of terrorism in tourism decision-making process include Bonham, Edmond and Mak (2006); Coshall (2003); Floyd, Gibson, Pennington-Gray, and Thapa (2004); Goodrich (2002); Neumayer (2004); Pizam and Fliescher (2002); Ritchie (2004); Sönmez and Graefe (1998)a; and Sönmez et al. (1999); others have studied the impact of risk and safety on travel behaviour (Goodrich, 1991; Hunter-Jones, Jeffs, & Smith, 2008; Irvin & Anderson, 2006; Kozak, Crotts, & Law, 2007; Lepp & Gibson, 2008; Reisinger & Mavando, 2005; Roehl & Fesenmaier, 1992; Seabra, Dolnicar, Abrantes, & Kastenholz, 2013; Sönmez & Graefe, 1998b), and the influence of various other elements on risk and safety perception (Barker, Page, & Meyer, 2003; Lennon, Weber, & Henson, 2001; Lepp & Gibson, 2003; Liu, Schroeder, Pennington-Gray & Farajat, 2016; Reisinger & Crotts, 2010; Reisinger & Mavando, 2006). Nevertheless, only limited research has focused on the specific linkages between terrorism risk perception, and tourism demand. Arana and Leon (2008, p. 300), state that 'despite numerous case studies being conducted on the impact of tourism and terrorism, the impact of terrorism on tourism demand is still under-researched.' To the best of this author's knowledge, no study has so far been published with a focus on the impact of perceived risk of terrorism on attitudes of the Dutch travel behaviour. The aim of this study is to help close this gap in the literature, and therefore, aims to address the issue of how Dutch customers have been reacting to increases in conflict threat levels, both real and perceived, and to explore the role of the tour operators in their destination offerings. In this chapter, terrorism is taken as a surrogate for conflict and conflict-ridden destinations.

Following this introduction, this chapter proceeds to define the relationship between tourism and terrorism, risk perception, and risk perception of international travellers, as derived from the literature. This discussion then moves to a description of the methodology, the presentation of the findings, and discussions and conclusions.

Literature review

Impacts of terrorism

According to Hunter-Jones et al. (2008), terrorism denotes a big danger for the success of tourism destinations, because most tourists are concerned about terrorism risk. Although most terrorist attacks are political or religiously motivated, terrorists frequently choose tourists or tourist destinations to be the target, in order to gain global publicity and attention (Niekerk & Pizam, 2015). Because of worldwide attention, the impact of terrorism on tourism destinations and international tourism industry is crucial (Kılıçlar, Usakli, & Tayfun, 2018). It is proven, however, that the frequency of terrorism in a destination affects the tourism demand for that destination greater than the severity of the terror attack (Pizam & Fliescher, 2002). Early research about terrorism and risk was conducted by Sönmez and Graefe (1998a), who investigated the influence of such risk on foreign tourism decision-making. Many the studies directed at the terrorism arena demonstrate that terrorist activity in a particular place increases the level of perceived risk and uncertainty about that place and thus has negative effects on tourism demand and behaviour, reflected by a drop in visitation (Bar-On, 1996; Blake & Sinclair, 2003; Sönmez, 1998; Sönmez & Graefe, 1998a, 1998b; Wahab, 1996). In addition to the research studies mentioned earlier, other scholars focused on how tourists perceive the risk of terrorism. Still, research on the impacts of terrorism on risk perceptions is not as extensive as could be expected from the previously mentioned studies (Wolff & Larsen, 2017). For example, Reisinger and Mavando (2005) showed risk perceptions to be correlated with travel anxiety, while Sönmez and Graefe (1998b) found that risk perceptions influenced destination choice. Sjöberg (2005) stated that perceived terrorism risk was somewhat low in a Swedish sample. Other research studies (Fuchs, Uriely, Reichel, & Maoz, 2012; Uriely, Moaz, & Reichel, 2007) showed that tourists might disregard governmental travel advisors and still travel to destinations threatened by terrorism. Recent research on Jordan conducted by Liu et al. (2016, p. 296) suggested, 'For most MENA destinations, terrorism and political turmoil have developed into a sustained tourism crisis that has negatively affected the perception held by many source markets.' A recent study of tourism and terrorism conducted by Liu and Pratt (2017) examines tourism's vulnerability and resilience to terrorism. The authors argued that the mindset of international tourists fundamentally changed. The authors claimed that most studies until now focused on the impact of tourism and terrorism. The literature makes it clear that terrorism is no longer the concern of only certain countries or regions, but has global consequences on travel and tourism.

Risk perceptions

Risk perception plays a vital role when it comes to holiday decision-making. Just like risk perception, safety perception is specific to a destination and influences the travelers' choice of a destination (Liu et al., 2016).

Bauer (1967, cited in Seabra et al., 2013) is the first who introduced the term *risk* in research on consumer behaviour in this context; because any individual action of consumption is linked with uncertainty, risk can be seen as implying unanticipated – and possibly unpleasant – consequences (Seabra et al., 2013, p. 503). In the consumer behaviour literature, perceived risk has been defined as 'a consumer's perception of the overall negativity of a course of action based upon an assessment of the possible negative outcomes and the likelihood that those outcomes will occur' (Mowen & Minor, 1998, p. 176). Other authors (Dolincar, 2005; Reisinger & Mavando, 2005; Sönmez & Graefe, 1998b) contend that the relationship between risk perceptions and travel behaviour are travel specific and context dependent, requiring sophisticated scales for their evaluation. Fuchs and Reichel (2006a, p. 84) make a link to the existence of different levels of perceived risk in tourism ranging from 'disappointment in relation to expectations or promised experience, to inappropriate facilities through severe injury and even death.'

Risk perception of international travellers

Corresponding with the findings of Liu et al. (2016) concerning spillover effects, Kozak et al. (2007, p. 240) suggest that 'a single act of terrorism, natural disaster and spread of disease may sometimes lead to forming overall negative image of all the neighborhood countries, resulting in a global devastating impact in the region.' While Liu et al. (2016) considered demographic characteristics to be an unsteady predictor of individual risk perception, Kozak et al. (2007, p. 421) defined age as a stable predictor, stating, 'Elderly people are less likely to change their travel plans if risk threat occurs.' Furthermore, the study of Kozak et al. recommended that travellers' risk perception decreased while their experience increased which is in accordance with the findings of other studies (Sönmez & Graefe, 1998b; Liu et al., 2016; Pearce, 2011), which are related to Pearce's ladder of travel experience, that our behaviour and preferences change as we gain more travel experience.

Destination risk perception

It is argued that personality traits and demographics such as age, gender, education and income are related to perceived risk (Karl & Schmude, 2017). Much research has also identified internal personal factors that determine how strongly an objective risk is perceived by a tourist and these expose a range of relevant factors including personality traits (Reisinger & Mavando, 2005; Roehl & Fesenmaier, 1992); culture and nationality (Kastenholz, 2010); past experiences, where experienced tourists feel less risk (Lepp & Gibson, 2003; Sönmez & Graefe, 1998a, 1998b);

demographics (Lepp & Gibson, 2003); gender (Lepp & Gibson, 2003); and income and education (Floyd & Pennington-Gray, 2004; Mitchell & Vassos, 1997). In addition, several studies have been conducted in tourism segmentation of the tourist market based on risk perceptions (Dolincar, 2005, 2007; Floyd & Pennington-Gray, 2004; Lepp & Gibson, 2003; Roehl & Fesenmaier, 1992). For example, Fuchs and Reichel (2006b) explored the concept of destination risk perception by applying it to a highly risky destination; namely, Israel. The authors' overall assumption is that each destination is characterized by an overall risk perception, as well as by specific categories or items.

Methodology

Survey instrument

This study used several sources to develop the questionnaire (Liu et al., 2016; Sönmez & Sirakaya, 2002). It included demographic variables including age, gender, educational level, profession, income and marital status to provide additional background on the respondents. As Seabra et al. (2013) point out, elements such as culture, nationality, income, education and travel motivations are determinant in one's understanding of what is considered risky or unsafe. The variable of 'children in the household' was expected to be vital and inevitable in the case of the risk perception of the Dutch tourist. The primary questions on safety and security dealt with *the overall importance of safety when booking a holiday at the moment*, with responses ranging from 1 = not important to 5 = very important. Subsequently, the importance of additional aspects when going on holiday, such as price, weather, hospitality and relaxation, were investigated in order to put the safety aspect in the context. Travel behaviour was scrutinized with respect to the extent of travel to destinations. Respondents were asked 'Has your travel behaviour been influenced by the recent terror attacks?' Similarly, the type of information search used by respondents was incorporated in the survey. These features included questions investigating the participants' opinion of the security advice published by the Dutch Ministry of Foreign Affairs, the level of expertise of Dutch tour operators and their perceived most trustworthy information sources. General intention for future travel was evaluated through one question ('In the next 12 months, how likely are you going to travel to Croatia, Egypt, Portugal, Turkey, and Sweden? [1 = very likely to 5 = very unlikely]'). The Dutch tour operators sponsoring the study selected these countries. The survey questions asked respondents to assess their level of risk perception and safety for six popular holiday destinations, some of which have been a target of terror attacks in the past: Spain, Turkey, Egypt, Greece, Italy and France, using a Likert scale, 1 = very unsafe to 5 = very safe.

Questions about preventive measurements and their effectiveness to increase the sense of security were included in the survey and adapted partially from research by Liu et al. (2016). Several measures which could be taken prior to travel, such as registering with the embassy and searching for more information online or in travel guides about how to stay safe were queried, while other questions focused on actions to be taken at the destination itself, such as increased police presence or to adjust respectfully to the local and cultural conditions. Once again, all items were measured using the 5-point Likert-type scale, from 1 = ineffective to 5 = very effective (Ritchie, Chien, & Sharifpour, 2017).

Data collection

The research tool for the present study was a self-administered survey. This tool has been considered useful to reach a wide target sample. The data for this study was collected from January–March 2017. During this period, 504 valid responses were collected. The sample of this study were Dutch citizens over 18 years of age. The survey took place at several central train stations as well as the Tourism Fair in Utrecht, 2017.

Findings

Socio-demographics

Considering the demographics of respondents, the gender proportion was 41.47% males and 58.28% females. Most participants (166) were in the youngest age category, 20–29, followed by age categories 16–19 (113), 30–39 (34), 40–49 (51), 50–59 (67) and 60 and older (49). On 1 January 2017, there were approximately 3.8 million people younger than 20 living in the Netherlands. Those between 40 and 65 formed the largest age group. Together, they numbered approximately six million people. The retired population of the Netherlands consists of approximately three million people. Considering this make-up of Dutch society, it is not surprising there are so many debates around increasing the retirement age (Statistica, 2018).

In terms of education, the greatest number participants had completed secondary school (201), followed by university degree (147), some higher education (139) and primary education (17). In terms of work situation, most (267) were employed, followed by students (184) and retired (24) and house-wives (18). The most common household income (161) was €5,000 per year or less, as the majority of respondents were students, followed by €20,001–30,000 (55), €30,001–40,000 (45), €40,001–50,000 (34), €50,001–60,000 (35) and €60,001 or higher (46). Most participants had no children (338; 67.1%). In terms of marital status, the majority of respondents were not married (211), followed by married (126), legal partners (83), divorced (10) and single (74).

Travelling

Respondents werer asked if they were planning to travel in the coming 12 months to the following destinations: Europe, Asia and the Middle East. The majority of respondents said yes to within Europe (80.1%) and no to the Middle East (94.1%). The majority of respondents also indicated not intending to travel to Asia (81.4%).

Respondents were also asked why not; the majority of respondents stated price (62.3%), followed by distance (21.3%) and language (8.4%). Only 11.6% stated they would not be travelling due to safety and security reasons.

The importance of safety

The respondents were asked 'have the recent safety issues (such as attacks, Turkey, Germany, France, Tunisia, crash of Malaysian airliner) made you reconsider where to travel on holiday?' The majority of respondents stated no (58.45%), followed by yes (31.41%). The rest stated 'do not know' (10.14%). Those respondents who stated yes for reconsidering their travel on holiday were asked how. A majority of respondents (71.95%) stated to avoid affected destinations, to avoid destinations with safety issues (37.20%), family concerns (23.78%), avoiding destinations mentioned on the website of the Dutch Ministry of Foreign Affairs (23.78%), and less likely to travel (9.76%).

In general, it is important to mention that (155) of female respondents valued safety as important and very important, (Figure 4.1) whereas (93) of respondents

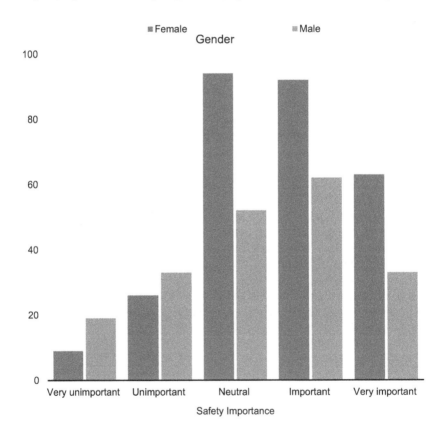

Figure 4.1 Importance of safety and gender

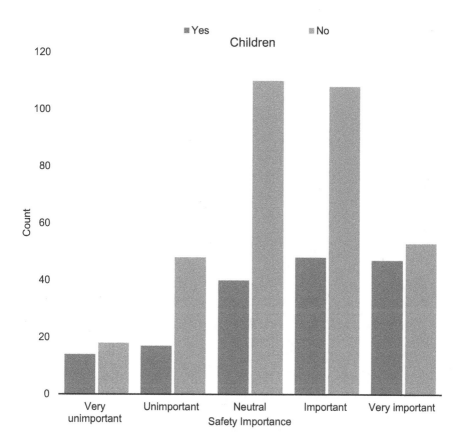

Figure 4.2 Importance of safety and children

stated they were neutral and (32) stated safety was unimportant to very unimportant, while (93) of male respondents considered safety to be important to very important.

Furthermore, in regards to safety, a clear distinction can be made between respondents who have children and the ones who do not (Figure 4.2). Surprisingly, those respondents who have no children (157) value safety as important to very important, while those who have children (92) rank safety with lower importance.

Respondent's risk perception

The respondents were asked 'how safe is it for people from your country to travel to the following countries?' using a Likert scale from 1–5, 1 being unsafe to 5 being very safe. Sweden, Portugal and Croatia were perceived to be the safest destinations (mean 4.54, 4.37 and 4.11, respectively), while Egypt and Turkey (mean 2.50) were perceived to be unsafe travel destinations. Respondents were

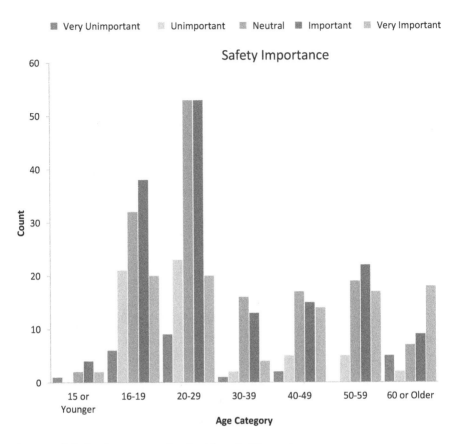

Figure 4.3 Safety importance when booking a holiday and age

also asked 'how likely (is it) that you will travel to the same destinations?'; Portugal scored the highest with a mean of 2.36, whereas Egypt scored the lowest (mean 1.41). Respondents seemed reluctant to travel to the countries mentioned in the questionnaire. In any case, respondents would rather travel to the safest countries than to the unsafe ones. On the question regarding the most important aspect when choosing a holiday destination, the majority of respondents stated weather (64.61%) and price (61.83%), whereas safety scored 37.05%, followed by culture (48.31%), sun and beach (45.42%), attractions (23.86%) and nightlife (16.30%). When asked the question, 'how important do YOU consider safety issues when booking a holiday?', on a Likert scale from 1–5, the majority of respondents stated 'yes,' that safety issues are important, with a mean of 3.55. (Figure 4.3) When cross tabulation is applied between ages and the importance of safety issues, the results revealed that safety is considered very important when booking a holiday. The age categories 16–19 and 20–29 perceived safety to be relatively more important when booking a holiday.

Effectiveness of preventive measures

The respondents were asked 'how effective are the following preventive measures to reduce safety and risk?', with 1 being very ineffective and 5 very effective. Some of these preventive measures occurred prior to travel and others at the destination (Table 4.1). As you can see from the table, most respondents considered these effective preventive measures. Having police in tourist areas, searching for information how to stay safe prior to trip and searching at the website of the Dutch Ministry of Foreign Affairs scored the highest in terms of mean: 3.69, 3.55 and 3.43, respectively.

When cross tabulation between level of education and type of effective measure was conducted, the result showed that highly educated participants are more likely to search the website of the Dutch Ministry of Foreign Affairs and information safety in travel guides regarding safety than other respondents. Participants are likely to undertake organized tours with a tour operator, register at the embassy, keep a low profile and consider safety information from the destinations.

In terms of destination, when the question 'how important do you consider safety information provided by the destination you are visiting?' was asked, 299 of respondents stated this was important, with a mean score of 3.52.

Tour operators

Respondents were asked if they believe that the tour operator channel has sufficient information on safety issues related to tourism destinations. The results show that the expertise of tour operators regarding safety is considered very important; however, the respondents seem divided over the effectiveness of this measure.

Respondents were also asked if travelling with a tour operator is considered safer than any other channel. The relationship between age categories and travelling with a tour operator is important. Moreover, the majority of respondents consider travelling with a tour operator safer, except for the age category between the ages of 20–29.

When cross tabulation is applied between the sample who have children (or not) and the expertise of the tour operators, (Figure 4.6) 69 of those who have children

Table 4.1 Preventive measures and mean

Preventive measure	No. of respondents	Mean
Registering at embassy	178	2.95
Travelling with organized group	184	2.95
Searching for information how to stay safer prior to trip	273	3.55
Searching for information how to stay safe in travel guides prior to trip	230	3.21
Searching at the Ministry of Foreign Affairs	283	3.43
Keeping a low profile at the destination	178	3.01
Having safety brochure in hotel room	190	3.18
Having police in tourist areas	311	3.69

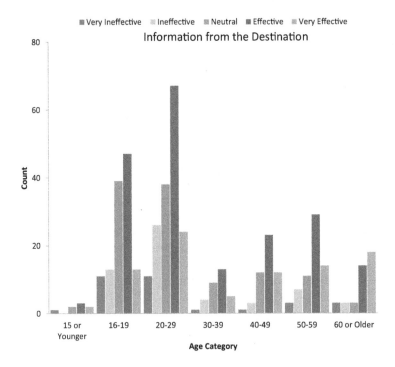

Figure 4.4 Tour operators and information on safety issues

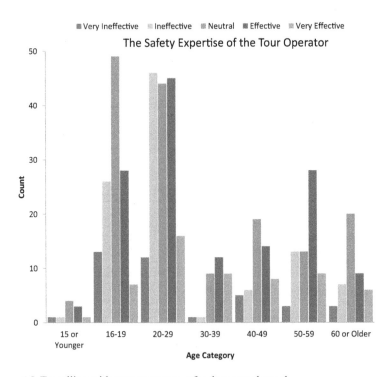

Figure 4.5 Travelling with tour operators safer than any channel

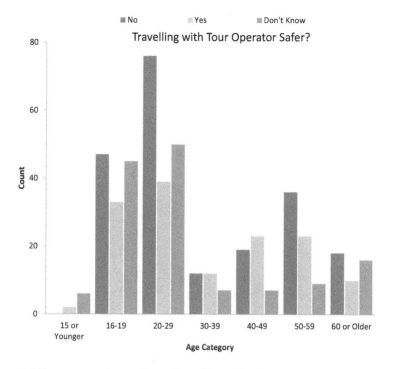

Figure 4.6 Tour operators' expertise and travelling with children

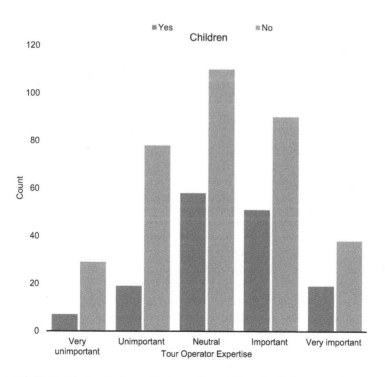

Figure 4.7 Respondents who have children and would travel with tour operators

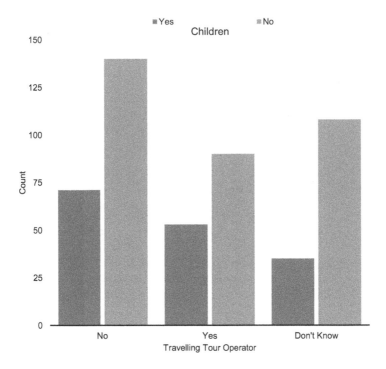

Figure 4.8 Cross tabulation between respondents who have children and would travel with tour operators

said that the expertise of tour operators is effective, while 125 of respondents who have no children state it to be effective.

In addition, when cross tabulation is applied between those who have children and those who would travel with tour operators (53), respondents who have children stated they would travel with tour operators (Figure 4.7).

Discussion

Where respondents discussed engaging in changing travel behaviours, this was mainly expressed through the avoidance of travel to problem countries and countries that had recently experienced safety issues. Explicitly, they choose an alternative destination, which was also found by Sönmez (1998) and Decrop (2010), as well as by Isaac and Velden (2018). In addition, as elucidated by Mansfeld (2006), travel plans do potentially change if the destination is perceived as too dangerous to travel to. In general, the sample voiced a low safety perception of Egypt and Turkey, which is in accordance with the findings of Isaac and Velden (2018) and Liu et al. (2016).

Nevertheless, several survey participants mentioned that even though they were reconsidering their destination choices due to safety issues, in the end, they still decided to travel to the particular destination anyway. This shows that even if a country is perceived as risky to travel to, many tourists might still choose to travel there for various personal reasons. This again is in accordance with the existing literature. A discrepancy between the assessment of the riskiness of a destination and the actual travel behaviour does exist (Karl, 2018). In addition, Liu and Pratt (2017) noted that tourists get used to a heightened level of risk and continue travelling to destinations that are perceived as risky anyway, even despite travel alerts.

Furthermore, as noted, the perceptions of the effectiveness of seven preventive measures on the respondent's sense of security were tested. Four of these measures were to be taken before a holiday, the remaining three at the destination, two by the tourists themselves and one by the DMOs in situ.

All seven preventive measures were thought to be effective to reduce perceived risk in a troubled region. Lo, Cheung, and Law (2011) and Ritchie et al. (2017) also argue that tourists commonly apply risk reduction strategies to reduce the perceived risk. The measures taken prior to the trip, such as searching for information online and in travel guides, seemed to be considered slightly less effective by the sample. Heightened police presence at a destination was especially believed to reduce the risk for tourists, which corresponds with the results of the study by Isaac and Velden (2018). Travelling with an organized tour was also believed to be an effective measure by the majority of the respondents except for the 20–29 age group. Contrarily, the study by Isaac and Velden (2018) found this measure was perceived to be ineffective. However, the finding of this study is in accordance with what Adam (2015) and Karl (2018) stated, that booking a package tour or travelling in groups is indeed helpful to reduce perceived risk. Those risk reduction strategies that minimize terrorism (Paraskevas & Arendell, 2007; Drakos & Kutan, 2003) could have implications for DMOs to help them boost their visitor numbers and revenues from tourism.

Based on this study, there are a few managerial implications that can be considered for some destinations in Europe. Safety is a very important factor that shapes the image of a holiday destination (Fletcher & Morakabati, 2008) and destinations such as France, Belgium and the UK, which have all suffered terrorist attacks, could still experience increasing visitor numbers in the long term and increase their attractiveness if the security issues and resulting risk perceptions of the tourists are resolved. Therefore, the tourism boards in these countries could adapt preventive measures mentioned in this study, focusing on long-term recovery and resilience planning (Ritchie, 2004). Those risk reduction strategies proved to be highly effective, as also found by Lo et al. (2011). Tourism boards and DMOs could thus implement policies that tackle the problems that arise due to the risk of terrorism (Drakos & Kutan, 2003; Paraskevas & Arendell, 2007), specifically to ensure a safe destination, to heighten tourists' confidence in visiting and the appeal of the destination, to hasten the recovery process and to repair a destination's image (Liu et al., 2016). Safety is one of the fundamental conditions for tourism development (Fletcher & Morakabati, 2008), and destinations perceived unsafe will have trouble attracting visitors. A negative image due to a perceived lack of security may be disastrous for the local tourism industry (Goodrich, 2002). Even tourists who consciously seek thrills by aiming for risky regions and destinations prefer minor risk within a 'protected bubble' (Belhassan, Uriely, & Assor, 2014). When destination marketers understand how consumers react to safety and risk perception regarding terrorism, they can construct a more effective marketing campaign to influence consumers' expectations and decision-making.

Tourism boards and destination managers should be aware that safety and risk perceptions nowadays are key attributes that a destination can offer. As a result, risk and conflict avoidance must be considered very seriously and taken into account when choosing a destination. Accordingly, these could be improved by creating security and preventive measures such as increased police presence at touristic sites and resorts.

Conclusion

The aim of this chapter was to address the issue of how Dutch customers have been reacting to increases in threat levels, both real and perceived, and to explore the role of the tour operators in their destination choices. As with every research study, the present research needs to be understood within the context of its limitations. The majority of respondents were between the ages of 20–29, followed by ages 16–19. The outcome might be different for a higher sample with a higher sample with various demographics such as age. Another limitation is the imbalance of gender. The gender proportion was 41.47% males and 58.28% females. All those surveyed considered travel safety and security increasingly important. Those respondents over the age of 40 were especially concerned about security matters and thus more likely to rely on, and put their trust in, tour operators for information. Younger generations were far less likely to alter their destination choice than those over the age of 40. An equal ratio of those in the 40–49 age group were just as likely to continue their holiday as they were to cancel. So in terms of changes in destination choice (as a reaction to security issues), over-40s are much more likely to do so than those under 40. Respondents over the age of 40 expect tour operators to be the 'guardians of their safety' who should offer, where appropriate, practical information concerning destination security in higher risk countries. The perception of trust in the safety expertise of tour operators varies depending on age group, but is below optimal levels. Linking the perception of potential tourists to conflict-ridden destinations and the desire of tourists to avoid conflict areas, it is important to note that the subsequent chapters only apply if tourists' concerns are met, in order to attract tourists and visitors.

References

Adam, I. (2015). Backpacker's risk perceptions and risk reduction strategies in Ghana. *Tourism Management, 49*, 99–108.

Arana, J. E., & Leon, C. J. (2008). The impact of terrorism on tourism demand. *Annals of Tourism Research, 35*(2), 299–315.

Barker, M., Page, S., & Meyer, D. (2003). Urban visitor perceptions of safety during a special event. *Journal of Travel Research, 41*(4), 345–355.

Bar-On, R. (1996). Measuring the effects on tourism violence and of promotion following violent acts. In A. Pizam & Y. Mansfeld (Eds.), *Tourism, crime and international security issues* (pp. 159–174). New York, NY: Wiley.

Beirman, D. (2003). Marketing of tourism destinations during prolonged crisis: Israel and the Middle East. *Journal of Vacation Marketing, 8*(3), 167–176.

Belhassan, Y., Uriely, N., & Assor, O. (2014). The touristification of a tourist zone: The case of Bil'in. *Annals of Tourism Research, 49*, 174–189.

Blake, A., & Sinclair, M. (2003). Tourism crisis management: US response of September 11. *Annals of Tourism Research, 30*(4), 813–832.

Bonham, C., Edmond, C., & Mak, J. (2006). The impact of 9/11 and other terrible events on tourism in the United States and Hawaii. *Journal of Travel Research, 45*(1), 99–110.

Coshall, J. (2003). The threat of terrorism as intervention on international travel flows. *Journal of Travel Research, 42*(1), 4–12.

Decrop, A. (2010). Destination choice sets: An inductive longitudinal approach. *Annals of Tourism Research, 37*(1), 93–115.

Dolincar, S. (2005). Understanding barrier to leisure travel: Tourist fear as a marketing basis. *Journal of Vacation Marketing, 11*(3), 197–208.

Dolnicar, S. (2007), Crisis and scare tourists – investigating tourists travel related concerns. In: B. Prideaux, B. Laws, & K. Chon (Eds.), *Managing tourism crisis* (pp. 98–109). London: CABI.

Drakos, K., & Kutan, A. M. (2003). Regional effects of terrorism on tourism in three Mediterranean countries. *Journal of Conflict Resolution, 47*(5), 621–641.

Fletcher, J., & Morakabati, Y. (2008). Tourism activity, terrorism and political instability within the commonwealth: The case of Fiji and Kenya. *International Journal of Tourism Research, 10*(6), 537–556.

Floyd, M. F., Gibson, H., Pennington-Gray, L., & Thapa, B. (2004). The effects of risk perceptions on intensions to travel in the aftermath of September 11, 2001. *Journal of Travel and Tourism Marketing, 15*(2–3), 19–38.

Floyd, M. F., & Pennington-Gray, L. (2004), "Profiling risk perceptions of tourists." *Annals of Tourism Research, 31*(4), 1051–1054.

Fuchs, G., & Reichel, A. (2006a). *Correlates of destination risk perception and risk reduction strategies progress in tourism marketing* (pp. 161–170). Amsterdam: Elsevier.

Fuchs, G., & Reichel, A. (2006b). Tourist destination risk perception: The case of Israel. *Journal of Hospitality & Leisure Marketing, 14*(2), 83–108.

Fuchs, G., Uriely, N., Reichel, A., & Maoz, D. (2012). Vacationing in a terror-stricken destination: Tourists' risk perceptions and rationalizations. *Journal of Travel Research, 52*, 1–10.

George, R. (2003). Tourists' perceptions of safety and security while visiting Cape Town. *Tourism Management, 24*(3), 575–585.

Goodrich, J. (1991). An American study on tourism marketing: Impact of the Persian Gulf War. *Journal of Travel Research, 30*(2), 37–41.

Goodrich, J. (2002). September 11, 2001 attack on America: A record of the immediate impacts and reactions in the USA travel and tourism industry. *Tourism Management, 23*(6), 573–580.

Hunter-Jones, P., Jeffs, A., & Smith, D. (2008). Backpacking your way into crisis. *Journal of Travel and Tourism Marketing, 23*(2–4), 237–247.

Irvin, W., & Anderson, A. (2006). The effect of disaster on peripheral tourism places and the disaffection of prospective visitors. In Y. Mansfeld & A. Pizam (Eds.), *Tourism, security and safety* (pp. 169–184). Oxford: Butterworth-Heinemann.

Isaac, R. K., & Velden, V. (2018). The German source market perceptions. How risky is Turkey to travel to? *International Journal of Tourism Cities, 4*(4), 429–451.

Karl, M. (2018). Risk and uncertainty in travel decision-making: Tourist and destination perspective. *Journal of Travel Research, 57*(1), 129–146.

Karl, M., & Schmude, J. (2017). Understanding the role of risk perception in destination choice: A literature review and synthesis. *Tourism, 65*(2), 138–155.

Kastenholz, E. (2010). Cultural proximity as determinant of destination image. *Journal of Vacation Marketing, 16*(4), 313–322.

Kılıçlar, A., Uşaklı, A., & Tayfun, A. (2018). Terrorism prevention in tourism destinations: Security forces vs. civil authority perspectives. *Journal of Destination Marketing and Management, 8*, 232–246.

Kozak, M., Crotts, J. C., & Law, R. (2007). The impact of the perception of risk on international travelers. *International Journal of Tourism Research, 9*(4), 233–242.

Lennon, R., Weber, M., & Henson, J. (2001). A test of a theoretical model of consumer travel behavior: German consumer's perception of Northern Ireland as a tourist destination. *Journal of Vacation Marketing, 7*(1), 51–62.

Lepp, A., & Gibson, H. (2003). Tourist roles, perceived risk and international tourism. *Annals of Tourism Research, 30*(3), 606–624.

Lepp, A., & Gibson, H. (2008). Sensation seeking and tourism: Tourist role, perceived of risk and destination choice. *Tourism Management, 29*(4), 740–750.

Liu, A., & Pratt, S. (2017). Tourism's vulnerability and resilience to terrorism. *Tourism Management, 60*, 404–417.

Liu, B., Schroeder, A., Pennington-Gray, L., & Farajat, S. (2016). Source market perceptions: How risky is Jordan to travel to? *Journal of Destination Marketing & Management, 5*(4), 294–304.

Lo, A. S., Cheung, C., & Law, R. (2011). Hong Kong residents' adoption of risk reduction strategies in leisure travel. *Journal of Travel & Tourism Marketing, 28*(3), 240–260.

Mansfeld, Y. (2006). The role of security information in tourism crisis management: The missing link. In Y. Mansfeld & A. Pizam (Eds.), *Tourism, security and safety: From theory to practice* (pp. 271–290). Amsterdam: Elsevier Butterworth-Heinemann.

Mitchell, V., & Vassos, V. (1997). Perceived risk and risk reduction in holiday purchases: A cross-cultural and gender analysis. *Journal of European Marketing, 6*(3), 47–80.

Mowen, J. C., & Minor, M. (1998). *Consumer behavior* (5th ed.). Upper Saddle River, NJ: Prentice Hall.

Neumayer, F. (2004). The impact of political violence on tourism: Dynamic cross-national estimation. *Journal of Conflict Resolution, 38*, 259–281.

Niekerk, M., & Pizam, A. (2015). *How do terrorism and tourism co-exist in turbulent times? An Introduction to conflicting relationship.* Orlando, Fl: University of Central Florida, Rosen College of Hospitality.

Paraskevas, A., & Arendell, B. (2007). A strategic framework for terrorism prevention and mitigation in tourism destinations. *Tourism Management, 28*(6), 1560–1573.

Pearce, P. (2011). *Tourist behaviour: Themes and conceptual schemes.* Clevedon: Channel View Publications.

Pizam, A., & Fliescher, A. (2002). Severity vs. frequency of acts of terrorism: Which has a larger impact on tourism demand? *Journal of Travel Research, 40*(3), 337–339.

Prideaux, B. (1996). The tourism crime cycle: A beach destination case study. In A. Pizam & Y. Mansfeld (Eds.), *Tourism, crime and international security issues* (pp. 77–90). London: John Wiley and Sons.

Reisinger, Y., & Crotts, J. C. (2010). Applying Hofstede national cultural measures in tourism research: Illuminating issues of divergence and convergence. *Journal of Travel Research, 49*(2), 153–164.

Reisinger, Y., & Mavando, F. (2005). Travel anxiety and intensions to travel internationally: Implications of travel risk perceptions. *Journal of Travel Research, 43*(3), 212–225.

Reisinger, Y., & Mavando, F. (2006). Cultural differences in travel risk perception. *Journal of Travel and Tourism Marketing, 20*(1), 13–31.

Ritchie, B. W. (2004). Chaos, crisis and disasters: A strategic approach to crisis management in the tourism industry. *Tourism Management, 25*(6), 669–683.

Ritchie, B. W., Chien, P. M., & Sharifpour, M. (2017). Segmentation by travel related risks: An integrated approach. *Journal of Travel & Tourism Marketing, 34*(2), 274–289.

Rittichainuwat, B. N., & Chakraborty, G. (2009). Perceived travel risks regarding terrorism and disease: The case of Thailand. *Tourism Management, 30*(3), 410–418.

Roehl, W. S., & Fesenmaier, D. R. (1992). Risk perceptions and pleasure travel: An exploratory analysis. *Journal of Travel Research, 30*(4), 17–26.

Seabra, C., Dolnicar, S., Abrantes, L., & Kastenholz, E. (2013). Heterogeneity in risk and safety perceptions of international tourists. *Tourism Management, 36*, 502–510.

Sjöberg, L. (2005). The perceived risk of terrorism. *Risk Management: An International Journal, 7*, 43–61.

Sönmez, S. F. (1998). Tourism, terrorism and political instability. *Annals of Tourism Research, 25*(2), 416–456.

Sönmez, S. F., Apostolopoulos, Y., & Tarlow, P. (1999). Tourism in crisis: Managing the effects of terrorism. *Journal of Travel Research, 38*(1), 13–18.

Sönmez, S. F., & Graefe, A. R. (1998a). Influence of terrorism risk on foreign tourism decisions. *Annals of Tourism Research, 25*(1), 112–144.

Sönmez, S. F., & Graefe, A. R. (1998b). Determining future travel behavior from past travel experience and perceptions of risk and safety. *Journal of Travel Research, 37*(4), 171–177.

Sönmez, S., & Sirakaya, E. (2002). A distorted destination image: The case of Turkey. *Journal of Travel Research, 41*, 185–196.

Statistica. (2018). Ducth population by age 2018. Retrieved January 25, 2019, from https://www.statista.com/statistics/519754/population-of-the-netherlands-by-age/

Uriely, N., Moaz, D., & Reichel, A. (2007). Rationalising terror-related risks: The case of Israeli tourists in Sinai. *International Journal of Tourism Research, 9*, 1–8.

Wahab, S. E. A. (1996). Tourism development in Egypt: Competitive strategies and implications. *Progress in Tourism and Hospitality Research, 2*, 351–364.

Wolff, K., & Larsen, S. (2017). A taxonomy of terror – about the effect of different kinds of terror on risk perceptions. *Scandinavian Journal of Hospitality and Tourism, 17*(2), 111–128.

5 Building destination resilience through community and organizational resilience

Girish Prayag

Introduction

Every destination faces the possibility of experiencing some form of disruptive event. The scale of such events may range from insignificant to catastrophic. In particular, conflict-ridden destinations can suffer multiple disruptive events that last for a substantial period of time (e.g. Syria). In this climate of uncertainty and constant change, the resilience of several stakeholders is required to steer the tourism industry and ensure its survival. Short-term relief following a crisis or disaster is not designed for resilience, but rather it aims at managing the crisis at hand (Blackman, Nakanishi, & Benson, 2017). It is therefore not surprising that much of the tourism literature has focused on crisis management rather than resilience building (Prayag, 2018), although recent publications (Butler, 2017; Cheer & Lew, 2018; Lew & Cheer, 2018; Hall, Prayag, & Amore, 2018) reflect the growing interest in and relevance of the concept to tourism. The purpose of this chapter is to present a conceptual model of destination resilience grounded in the socio-ecological view of resilience. It is argued that destination resilience is very much dependent on linkages with other types of resilience that facilitate the recovery of destinations in the face of disasters and conflicts. Resilience is defined as the capacity of a system to absorb disturbances and reorganize while undergoing change so as to still retain its essential function, structure, identity and feedbacks (Walker, Holling, Carpenter, & Kinzig, 2004). This is one of the most cited definitions of resilience, originating from the field of ecological resilience, but there are other definitions related to the concept of engineering resilience. The tourism field has primarily adopted the ecological resilience approach in its quest to understand the resilience of the tourism system, with the resilience perspective increasingly being used as an approach to understand the dynamics of social-ecological systems (Folke, 2006; Ruiz-Ballesteros, 2017). Vulnerability and resilience are co-constituted, and are constantly in a state of flux, and therefore the two concepts are inextricably linked (Scheyvens & Momsen, 2008). Resilience is therefore a term that finds its meaning in relation to change which can be incremental, extraordinary or cumulative (Hall et al., 2018; Prayag, 2018).

Within tourism, resilience has been researched mainly from an economic perspective, and most resilience research in tourism has focused on case studies rather than advancing theoretical constructs (Lew, 2014). As argued by Hall et al. (2018), community resilience – along with organizational and destination resilience – can be considered as contextual applications of social-ecological resilience. Within these different contexts, it must be acknowledged that 'the resilience approach emphasizes non-linear dynamics, thresholds, uncertainty and surprise, how periods of gradual change interplay with periods of rapid change, and how such dynamics interact across temporal and spatial scales' (Folke, 2006, p. 253). For example, the magnitude of the impacts of disasters on organizations, individuals and communities can vary substantially with post-disaster recovery of the aforementioned happening at different paces. Therefore, a 'one-size-fits-all' approach to building and managing resilience is futile.

There is another aspect of resilience that concerns the capacity for renewal, reorganization and development, and these matters in the aftermath of a disaster or conflict (Becken & Khazai, 2017). In a resilient social-ecological system, disturbance has the potential to create opportunity for doing new things, for innovation and for development (Adger, 2006). For example, in the aftermath of the 2010 and 2011 Canterbury earthquakes in Christchurch, New Zealand, several organizations bounced back by reinventing themselves through new products, business strategies and targeting new markets (Hall et al., 2018). Emergence of new trajectories and renewal of systems due to evolved structures and processes as a result of disturbances happen not only at micro levels (i.e. organizations, stakeholders and communities) but also at macro levels (i.e. regional, destination and even country levels). Hence, this notion of bouncing back with, for example, the emergence of new trajectories is inherent to the concept of resilience (Seville, 2016). It has been argued that individuals, communities and organizations can grow in the face of adversity and do better than pre-disaster (Hall et al., 2018; Reich, 2006). In this way, resilience provides adaptive capacity that allows for continuous development (Smit & Wandel, 2006). Adaptive capacity remains a core concept of resilience, and can be considered as the arrangements and processes that enable adjustment through learning, adaptation and transformation (Parsons et al., 2016).

Systems adaptation is not appropriate for all types of change (Walker et al., 2004), but rather the capacity to manage the impacts and outcomes of change is more important (Bec, McLennan, & Moyle, 2016). As uncertainty can undermine resilience and it is the enemy of successful adaptation (Reich, 2006), the notion of coping capacity is also inherent to the concept of resilience. It refers to the means by which people, organizations and communities use available resources, skills and opportunities to face adverse consequences (Parsons et al., 2016). Hence, this chapter examines the interplay between the two main concepts of resilience (coping and adaptive capacity) and how these contribute to building destination resilience through organizational and community resilience. However, the chapter also acknowledges that long-term resilience building activities, both coping and adaptive capacities, can be undermined by socio-political processes and lack of environmental concerns that heightens the vulnerability of both micro- and macro-level players in the tourism system (Scheyvens & Momsen, 2008). The chapter next discusses the concepts of community, organizational and destination resilience. The last section of the chapter presents a conceptual model that outlines how community and organizational resilience contribute to destination resilience, and also how the model is applicable to both disaster- and conflict-ridden destinations.

Community resilience

Before the chapter moves on to a discussion of community resilience, it is important to clarify what is meant by 'community.' A community can be viewed as 'the totality of social interactions within a defined geographical space such as a neighbourhood, city or county' (Cutter et al., 2008, p. 599). There are often several communities within a tourist destination, with such geographically defined spaces and sub-populations having different levels of coping capacity, vulnerability and resilience that can affect their disaster or conflict recovery trajectories. Communities have the ability to intentionally develop resilience (Magis, 2010), which can increase the community's ability to cope with dynamic environments that are characterized by unpredictability and surprises (Adger, Arnell, & Tompkins, 2005). Resilient communities actively develop community resources (Adger et al., 2005), but this is not the only observable resilient behaviour. Communities can develop resilience strategically via planning, collective action, innovation and learning, and this is facilitated through developing and engaging diverse resources from throughout the community and by encouraging community members to become active agents (e.g. leaders) in the development of community resilience (Magis, 2010). The role of community leaders has been emphasized as critical in shaping the recovery of a community post-disaster. In this respect, community capital is considered critical for resilience building. Community capital refers to resources from the community that are strategically invested in collective endeavours to address shared community objectives (Flora & Flora, 2004). Examples of community capital include financial capital (e.g. financial resources invested in the community for business, civic and social enterprise development, as well as wealth accumulation), built capital (e.g. community infrastructure and physical assets), political capital (community members' ability to access resources and power, and to impact the rules and regulations that affect the community) and social capital (the ability and willingness of community members to participate in actions directed to community objectives) (Flora & Flora, 2004; Magis, 2010).

As argued earlier, community resilience is inherently multilevel. Essentially, in the community resilience literature, it has been argued that the concept is linked to three characteristics of a community: (i) ways in which people relate to each other (e.g. trustworthiness); (ii) interpersonal resources and capacities (e.g. sharing); and (iii) collective resources and capacities (e.g. group identity) (Sheppard, 2017). The more prevalent and strong are these characteristics, the stronger is the ability for the community to respond and recover from adversity (Kimhi, 2016). These characteristics align well with Magis' (2010) idea of community capital. However, it must be pointed out that in destinations ridden by conflicts, community capital may be totally eroded and issues of trustworthiness (e.g. between different communities, or within sub-populations within a community), sharing and group identity may be severely damaged, impeding the ability of such communities to build resilience. The resilience of communities can be built, for example, through: (i) integrating disaster prevention, mitigation, preparedness, and vulnerability reduction perspectives into sustainable development policies; (ii) increasing local capacity for building hazard resilience; and (iii) incorporating risk reduction in the design and implementation of emergency preparedness, response, recovery and reconstruction programmes in affected communities (International Strategy for Disaster Reduction, 2005). These suggestions pertain more to communities dealing with hazards, rather than conflicts. In post-conflict destinations, the built capital (e.g. basic infrastructure and sanitation) may need to be restored first before other forms of capital can be built.

In the context of community resilience, resilience can be considered across economic, ecological, social and institutional dimensions (Berkes & Ross, 2013). Institutions are central to building a community's capacity to adapt (Berkes & Ross, 2013), highlighting the role of government agencies and regional/local institutions to facilitate collective adaptation (Berkes & Ross, 2013). A social system cannot be resilient if the environmental system is vulnerable (Ruiz-Ballesteros, 2011). Therefore, recognizing the cross-scale interactions between economic, ecological, social and institutional factors that impact the resilience of communities can be considered a good starting point for identifying the vulnerabilities of a community. For example, disaster planning activities can be successful only if they cut across these various institutional dimensions, with a major focus on how agencies and governments at the national and local levels should cooperate and coordinate their response, and how they should interact with each other in the face of major crises and disasters (Reich, 2006). In this process, collaboration between stakeholders at community level can increase public confidence; help to share responsibility for planning, prevention, response and recovery; and reduce community reliance on emergency services and government or non-government organizations (Rogers, Burnside-Lawry, Dragisic, & Mills, 2016). In this way, efforts to build community resilience often emphasize capacity building and generative coping mechanisms that involve communities in strategic planning (Prosser & Peters, 2010). Through trust, communication and collaboration, communities can become more resilient to disasters. For example, trust is a vital component of resilience building, given that if community stakeholders trust each other, they are more likely to collaborate beyond the restrictions of hierarchical organizations and daily routines (Rogers et al., 2016).

It has also been noted in the literature that individual capacities matter as much as collective capacities in resilience building post-disaster, hence highlighting the importance of individual or psychological resilience. When seeking to build resilience, community members need to believe that they have the personal resources to achieve their goals following a major disaster. In essence, individual resilience also informs community resilience. Individual resilience can be defined as the ability of an individual to bounce back from adversity (Block & Kremen, 1996).

Individuals within an affected community need to believe they have personal control or the ability to regain personal control following a disaster. The key to bouncing back – and thus, their resilience – is linked to the effort for regaining personal control (Reich, 2006). Disaster planning at the community level should provide constructive rather than destructive pathways for community members to re-establish personal control (Reich, 2006). This interface between individual and community resilience has not been examined within the context of tourism communities (Prayag, 2018). Disaster responding, for example, should protect the drive for coherence through enhancing meaning, direction and understanding during the worst times of the disaster. This is because disasters can destroy the familiar and sense of place, creating behavioural disruption and cognitive disorganization both for the individual and the community (Reich, 2006). Thus, resilience capacities should be the central target of relief efforts to create long-term restoration of the individual and the community (Reich, 2006). A notable characteristic of the behaviour of individuals and communities as a whole is the 'band together' effect, whereby individual and communities seek out each other to help and establish bonds (Reich, 2006). Social support is critical in the recovery phase for individuals and communities. As such, providing instrumental, informational and emotional support to individuals are key components that can enhance the resilience of communities. A resilient community is characterized by interconnectivity between individuals (Allenby & Fink, 2005).

Organizational resilience

The term organizational resilience has been used to describe the inherent characteristics of those organizations that are able to respond more quickly, recover faster or develop more unusual ways of doing business under duress than others (Sutcliffe & Vogus, 2003). It refers to both organizational and employee strength, perseverance and recovery when encountering adversity (Linnenluecke, 2017). Sutcliffe and Vogus (2003) suggest that resilience takes place at multiple levels within an organization (individual and group), and these levels interact to determine the resilience of the organization. The resilience of an organization depends on the quality of three pillars: leadership and culture, networks and relationships it has fostered with others, and how the organization is positioned strategically to be change ready (Seville, 2018). Lack of organizational resilience often stems from organizations working in silos, lack of employee engagement and inability to assess the changing circumstances, among others (Lee, Vargo, & Seville, 2013). To the contrary, organizations that are capable of delivering services under stress (e.g. emergency services as first responders) are agile and flexible in their organizational practices and have networked communication practices that allow them to draw from these strengths to respond to adverse situations (Rogers et al., 2016). Organizational resilience is, therefore, not only about minimizing and managing exposure and risk; it is also about creating organizations that are agile in the way they adapt to unexpected challenges and are capable of seizing the new opportunities presented out of adversity (Seville, 2016).

However, it is widely acknowledged in the literature that there are notable differences between the resilience of different industry sectors and organizations within a sector following major crises and disasters. As shown in the study of Prayag and Orchiston (2016), the tourism sector was less impacted by the 2010 and 2011 Canterbury earthquakes in New Zealand in comparison to the manufacturing and education sectors. However, there were some differences across the sectors in terms of the mitigation strategies that were used by organizations. Several studies in the disaster management literature have established linkages between organization resilience and business recovery (Bruneau et al., 2003; McManus, Seville, Vargo, & Brunsdon, 2008). In addition, it has been highlighted that not all businesses or sectors recover at the same pace and/or in similar ways (Webb, Tierney, & Dahlhamer, 2002). The need to understand organizational resilience across and within sectors is critical for building resilient communities (McManus et al., 2008). The literature recognizes two main aspects to organizational resilience: planned and adaptive resilience. Planned resilience involves the use of existing, predetermined planning and capabilities, as exemplified in business continuity and risk management, which are predominantly pre-disaster mitigation activities (Becken & Khazai, 2017). Adaptive resilience emerges during the post-disaster phase as organizations develop new capabilities through dynamically responding to emergent situations that are outside of their plans (Lee et al., 2013). In the tourism literature, Orchiston, Prayag, and Brown (2016) showed that these dimensions are somewhat relevant to small and micro-enterprises with innovation, collaboration and organizational culture being critical to building organizational resilience. Prayag, Chowdhury, Spector, and Orchiston (2018) go further, demonstrating that organizational resilience of tourism firms has a positive influence on their financial performance. However, this is true only for the adaptive dimension of organizational resilience. Likewise, Biggs, Hall, and Stoeckl (2012) highlighted the importance of human capital in developing organizational resilience. Recovery of organizations following a disaster is closely aligned with restoration of basic infrastructure, which also contributes to community resilience (Chang & Shinozuka, 2004).

Having good employees and getting the best out of them, in times of great stress and unexpected changes, are critical for resilience building (Seville, 2018). Particularly, how employees come together and work together in a way that creates a group that is more resilient that its members on their own can make a difference to organizational survival. However, having resilient employees does not mean that an organization is automatically resilient (Seville, 2018). The notion of employee resilience, which is different from the psychological resilience of individuals, is increasingly becoming an important way to build the resilience of organizations. Employee resilience has been defined as employee capability, facilitated and supported by the organization, to utilize resources to continually adapt and flourish at work, even when faced with challenging situations (Kuntz, Naswall, & Malinen, 2016). Depending on the culture in an organization, management practices can either enhance or erode employee resilience (Seville, 2018). Prayag (2018) argues that the linkages between employee and organizational resilience and their relationships with other levels of resilience such as community and destination resilience have not been examined. The literature offers at times contradictory recommendations on how organizations should build resilience. The need for organizational stability through habits, routines, consistency and control can be at odds with the need for organizational change through experimentation, mindfulness, openness and imagination (Linnenluecke, 2017). As will be argued later in the chapter, there are several reasons why organizational resilience can contribute to building both community and destination resilience.

Destination resilience

Destination resilience is a nebulous concept. There are different aspects to the term in the tourism literature. For example, Hall et al. (2018) identify at least five aspects of destination resilience, namely: socio-ecological, socio-political, urban, community and organizational. According to them, the socio-ecological view of destination resilience stresses the importance of the biophysical and social impacts of, for example, climate change on the vulnerability of destinations (Jopp, DeLacy, & Mair, 2010). From this perspective, resilience of a destination emerges from its capacity to manage vulnerabilities and risks from environmental changes. Following this line of thought, Calgaro, Lloyd, and Dominey-Howes (2014) uses the idea of environmental linkages that form the basis of the vulnerability of an eco-system as the foundation to build the idea of how destinations could become more resilient. Therefore, the socio-ecological view of destination resilience is profoundly linked to changes in the environment and the destination's adaptive capacity with respect to the impact of those changes on the eco-system.

The socio-political dimension of destination resilience has at its core governance structures within a destination. As argued by Hall et al. (2018), a resilient governance structure enhances the adaptive capacity of destinations as well as the institutional changes that are required in times of uncertainty to navigate the destination through both continuous and unexpected changes. Resilient destinations are those that recover quickly by enacting and adapting policies that minimize risks and enhance resilience. There are likely to be diverging outcomes in post-disaster and post-conflict contexts as a result of diverging political will, interests and perspectives (Hall et al., 2018). Often, the diverging political will may impede rather than facilitate recovery and top-down approaches to governance can have negative impacts on tourism planning at national and regional levels (Causevic & Lynch, 2013). As Hall et al. (2018) point out, there can be significant gaps between local community and political interests with respect to recovery and rebuilding strategies, as also noted by Buultjens, Ratnayake, and Gnanapala (2017) in the context of Sri Lanka. Relatedly, the urban view of destination resilience has not received much attention in the tourism literature. However, this view is critical for policy development and for putting in place the governance structure that will deliver the necessary outcomes for the community post-disaster. In this view, the urban system is regarded as a complex and adaptive eco-system that is comprised of socio-ecological and socio-technical networks that extend across multiple scales (Meerow, Newell, & Stults, 2016). There are cross-scale interactions between the socio-political and urban views of destination resilience.

There are different conceptualizations of the relationship between vulnerability, adaptive capacity, coping capacity and resilience (Cutter et al., 2008). In this chapter, within the context of destination resilience, adaptive and coping capacity are considered to be nested within the concept of resilience, which it itself nested within an overall vulnerability structure (Gallopin, 2006), as shown in Figure 5.1. It can be argued that destination resilience is partly a function of community and organizational resilience but will also be affected by the nature of the destination system itself (Hall et al., 2018). The destination sustainability framework (DSF) provides a good starting point to understand the factors that can heightened the vulnerability of tourist destinations (Calgaro et al., 2014) and the role of organizations and communities in reducing vulnerabilities. The DSF is comprised of six factors: shocks/stressors, interconnected dimensions of vulnerability (exposure, sensitivity and system adaptiveness), dynamic feedback loops that express the multiple outcomes or consequences of actions taken in response to the shock/stressor, the contextualized causes and drivers that shape places and their characteristics, scale of change, and multiple timeframes within which social-ecological change occurs. According to this framework, it can be argued that destination resilience can be understood through the lenses of the stability of a socio-ecological system.

Stability is determined by: (i) latitude or understanding the maximum amount a system can be changed before losing its ability to recover; (ii) resistance, which

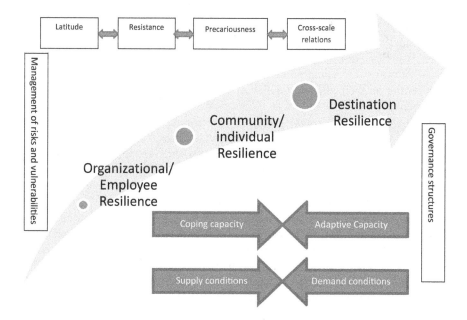

Figure 5.1 Different types of resilience that inform destination resilience

matches the ease or difficulty of changing the system; (iii) precariousness, the current trajectory of the system and proximity to a limit or threshold; and (iv) cross-scale relations, or how the previous three aspects are influenced by the dynamics of the systems at different scales (Folke et al., 2004; Walker et al., 2004). Hence, the resilience of a system (regardless of the context) is determined by the interaction of the four aforementioned factors as shown in Figure 5.1. Embedded within those four factors are also supply and demand conditions for the destination which influence its resilience (see Figure 5.1). The resilience of tourist destinations emerges from an interaction of both supply and demand conditions (Hall et al., 2018). Figure 5.1 also shows that regardless of context (organizational, community or destination), governance structures matter in building resilience (Sheppard, 2017). The lack of an appropriate governance structure including the lack of political leadership within the structure of any tourism destination will undermine its ability to be stable and manage the risks and vulnerabilities affecting the tourism system. Figure 5.1 shows that organizational resilience feeds into community resilience, which in turn feeds into destination resilience. However, the process is linear, as depicted in Figure 5.1. As argued earlier in the chapter, organizational resilience can also feed into building destination resilience and there are feedback loops across all three contexts (organizational, community and destination).

It is also argued, based on Walker et al.'s (2004) notion of the four key characteristics of the socio-ecological resilience of a system (latitude, resistance, precariousness and cross-scale relations) that destination resilience, community and organizational resilience share those characteristics. These four characteristics have inter-relationships among themselves that influence any system, including the tourism system (Figure 5.1). All three contexts of resilience (organizational, community and destination) are subject to the dynamics of both coping and adaptive capacities. For example, tourism organizations within a destination have their own pathways for coping and adapting in the aftermath of a disruptive event. Depending on their planned resilience, these organizations may adapt, survive and recover differently. Likewise, the recovery trajectories of different communities within the same destination may vary, depending on their resilience and the severity of the impacts of the disruptive events. Therefore, the cross-scale relations between community and organizational resilience are complex. There is little knowledge on latitude within the tourism system. While some studies attempt to look at the effects of specific exogenous events (e.g. climate change) on the tourism system but within the context of disasters/conflicts, there are no tourism studies that have explicitly examined latitude with respect to tourism destinations. This remains a significant challenge for understanding destination resilience (Hall et al., 2018). Not knowing the extent to which the resources (financial, human and infrastructural, etc.) of destination can be stretched to cope with the onset of a disaster or conflict can pose significant challenges for multiple stakeholders with respect to charting the recovery trajectories. The lack of knowledge on latitude with respect to financial capital, for example, can undermine the implementation of disaster and recovery plans.

From Figure 5.1, it can also be concluded that a resilient community is likely to reduce the vulnerability of tourism businesses (Biggs, Hicks, Cinner, & Hall, 2015). A resilient destination relies on resilient communities and resilient individuals, which in turn reduces vulnerabilities and increases the coping capacity. However, these linkages may not always work in a linear fashion as suggested by Figure 5.1, where organizational resilience feeds into building destination resilience, for post-disaster and conflict-ridden destinations. For example, in conflict-ridden destinations, the ongoing nature of the disruptive event may imply that the basic infrastructure never recovers to pre-conflict levels. As such, both organizational and community resilience may not be related in any way in building destination resilience. The latter may emerge from activities undertaken by individual members or groups at the community level rather than organizations to facilitate recovery. Figure 5.1 suggests that post-disaster and post-conflict destinations should start their recovery process by examining demand and supply conditions, coping and adaptive capacities, governance structures and how these factors help or hinder the management of risks and vulnerabilities. An examination of these would provide insights that can help shape priorities with respect to building employee, organizational, community and destination resilience.

Conclusion

The purpose of this chapter was to present a conceptual model that outlines the linkages between three resilience-related concepts of organizational, community and destination resilience. The chapter builds on the argument that regardless of the context, the main goal of resilience-building activities is the stability of a socio-ecological system. As such, investments in resilience-building activities should contribute to the stability of the tourism system. A resilient destination relies on the resilience of both organizations and communities, which allow the destination to reduce vulnerabilities by improving both coping and adaptive capacities. Organizational resilience is itself partly determined by the resilience of employees, while community resilience is affected by the resilience of community members (individuals). The chapter also argues that there are multiple views of destination resilience ranging from the socio-ecological view to the urban view. However, no matter what view is adopted by researchers, the four underlying characteristics of stability (latitude, resistance, precariousness and cross-scale relations) must be understood to build the resilience of the tourism system. In a post-disaster context, building destination resilience may require a concerted effort by multiple stakeholders to restore, for example, infrastructure and other basic amenities before organizations can re(build) employee and organizational resilience.

References

Adger, W. N. (2006). Vulnerability. *Global Environmental Change, 16*(3), 268–281.
Adger, W. N., Arnell, N. W., & Tompkins, E. L. (2005). Successful adaptation to climate change across scales. *Global Environmental Change, 15*(2), 77–86.

Allenby, B., & Fink, J. (2005). Toward inherently secure and resilience societies. *Science, 309*(5737), 1034–1036.

Bec, A., McLennan, C. L., & Moyle, B. D. (2016). Community resilience to long-term tourism decline and rejuvenation: A literature review and conceptual model. *Current Issues in Tourism, 19*(5), 431–457.

Becken, S., & Khazai, B. (2017). Resilience, tourism and disasters. In R. W. Butler (Ed.), *Tourism and resilience* (pp. 96–104). Wallingford: CABI.

Berkes, F., & Ross, H. (2013). Community resilience: Toward an integrated approach. *Society & Natural Resources, 26*(1), 5–20.

Biggs, D., Hall, C. M., & Stoeckl, N. (2012). The resilience of formal and informal tourism enterprises to disasters: Reef tourism in Phuket, Thailand. *Journal of Sustainable Tourism, 20*(5), 645–665.

Biggs, D., Hicks, C. C., Cinner, J. E., & Hall, C. M. (2015). Marine tourism in the face of global change: The resilience of enterprises to crises in Thailand and Australia. *Ocean & Coastal Management, 105*, 65–74.

Blackman, D., Nakanishi, H., & Benson, A. M. (2017). Disaster resilience as a complex problem: Why linearity is not applicable for long-term recovery. *Technological Forecasting and Social Change, 121*, 89–98.

Block, J., & Kremen, A. M. (1996). IQ and ego-resiliency: Conceptual and empirical connections and separateness. *Journal of Personality and Social Psychology, 70*(2), 349–361.

Bruneau, M., Chang, S. E., Eguchi, R. T., Lee, G. C., O'Rourke, T. D., Reinhorn, A. M., & von Winterfeldt, D. (2003). A framework to quantitatively assess and enhance the seismic resilience of communities. *Earthquake Spectra, 19*(4), 733–752.

Butler, R. W. (2017). *Tourism and resilience*. Wallingford: CABI.

Buultjens, J., Ratnayake, I., & Gnanapala, A. C. (2017). Sri Lankan tourism development and implications for resilience. In R. W. Butler (Ed.), *Tourism and resilience* (pp. 83–95). Wallingford: CABI.

Calgaro, E., Lloyd, K., & Dominey-Howes, D. (2014). From vulnerability to transformation: A framework for assessing the vulnerability and resilience of tourism destinations. *Journal of Sustainable Tourism, 22*(3), 341–360.

Causevic, S., & Lynch, P. (2013). Political (in) stability and its influence on tourism development. *Tourism Management, 34*, 145–157.

Chang, S. E., & Shinozuka, M. (2004). Measuring improvements in the disaster resilience of communities. *Earthquake Spectra, 20*(3), 739–755.

Cheer, J. M., & Lew, A. A. (2018). *Tourism, resilience and sustainability adapting to social, political and economic change*. London: Routledge.

Cutter, S. L., Barnes, L., Berry, M., Burton, C., Evans, E., Tate, E., & Webb, J. (2008). A place-based model for understanding community resilience to natural disasters. *Global Environmental Change, 18*(4), 598–606.

Flora, C., & Flora, J. (2004). *Rural communities: Legacy and change* (2nd ed.). Boulder, CO: Westview Press.

Folke, C. (2006). Resilience: The emergence of a perspective for social – ecological systems analyses. *Global Environmental Change, 16*(3), 253–267.

Folke, C., Carpenter, S., Walker, B., Scheffer, M., Elmqvist, T., Gunderson, L., & Holling, C. S. (2004). Regime shifts, resilience, and biodiversity in ecosystem management. *Annual Review of Ecology, Evolution & Systematics, 35*, 557–581.

Gallopín, G. C. (2006). Linkages between vulnerability, resilience, and adaptive capacity. *Global Environmental Change, 16*(3), 293–303.

Hall, C. M., Prayag, G., & Amore, A. (2018). *Tourism and resilience: Individual, organisational and destination perspectives*. Clevedon: Channel View.

International Strategy for Disaster Reduction. (2005). *Hyogo framework for Action 2005–2015: Building the resilience of nations and communities to disasters*. Kobe, Japan: United Nations.

Jopp, R., DeLacy, T., & Mair, J. (2010). Developing a framework for regional destination adaptation to climate change. *Current Issues in Tourism, 13*(6), 591–605.

Kimhi, S. (2016). Levels of resilience: Associations among individual, community, and national resilience. *Journal of Health Psychology, 21*(2), 164–170.

Kuntz, J. R., Näswall, K., & Malinen, S. (2016). Resilient employees in resilient organizations: Flourishing beyond adversity. *Industrial and Organizational Psychology, 9*(2), 456–462.

Lee, A. V., Vargo, J., & Seville, E. (2013). Developing a tool to measure and compare organizations' resilience. *Natural Hazards Review, 14*(1), 29–41.

Lew, A. A. (2014). Scale, change and resilience in community tourism planning. *Tourism Geographies, 16*(1), 14–22.

Lew, A. A., & Cheer, J. M. (2018). *Tourism and resilience to environmental change*. London: Routledge.

Linnenluecke, M. K. (2017). Resilience in business and management research: A review of influential publications and a research agenda. *International Journal of Management Reviews, 19*(1), 4–30.

Magis, K. (2010). Community resilience: An indicator of social sustainability. *Society and Natural Resources, 23*(5), 401–416.

McManus, S., Seville, E., Vargo, J., & Brunsdon, D. (2008). Facilitated process for improving organizational resilience. *Natural Hazards Review, 9*(2), 81–90.

Meerow, S., Newell, J. P., & Stults, M. (2016). Defining urban resilience: A review. *Landscape and Urban Planning, 147*, 38–49.

Orchiston, C., Prayag, G., & Brown, C. (2016). Organizational resilience in the tourism sector. *Annals of Tourism Research, 56*, 145–148.

Parsons, M., Glavac, S., Hastings, P., Marshall, G., McGregor, J., McNeill, J., Morley, P., Reeve, I., and Stayner, R. (2016) 'Top-down assessment of disaster resilience: A conceptual framework using coping and adaptive capacities', *International Journal of Disaster Risk Reduction, 19*: 1–11.

Prayag, G. (2018). Symbiotic relationship or not? Understanding resilience and crisis management in tourism. *Tourism Management Perspectives, 25*, 133–135.

Prayag, G., Chowdhury, M., Spector, S., & Orchiston, C. (2018). Organizational resilience and financial performance. *Annals of Tourism Research, 73*, 193–196.

Prayag, G., & Orchiston, C. (2016). Earthquake impacts, mitigation, and organisational resilience of business sectors in Canterbury. In C. M. Hall, S. Malinen, R. Vosslamber, & R. Wordsworth (Eds.), *Business and post-disaster management: Business, organisational and consumer resilience and the Christchurch earthquakes* (pp. 97–120). Routledge: Oxon.

Prosser, B., & Peters, C. (2010). Directions in disaster resilience policy. *Australian Journal of Emergency Management, 25*(3), 8–13.

Reich, J. W. (2006). Three psychological principles of resilience in natural disasters. *Disaster Prevention and Management: An International Journal, 15*(5), 793–798.

Rogers, P., Burnside-Lawry, J., Dragisic, J., & Mills, C. (2016). Collaboration and communication: Building a research agenda and way of working towards community disaster resilience. *Disaster Prevention and Management, 25*(1), 75–90.

Ruiz-Ballesteros, E. (2011). Social-ecological resilience and community-based tourism: An approach from Agua Blanca, Ecuador. *Tourism Management, 32*(3), 655–666.

Ruiz-Ballesteros, E. (2017). Socio-eological balance in community-based tourism experiences: A research proposal. In R. W. Butler (Ed.), *Tourism and resilience* (pp. 41–52). Wallingford: CABI.

Scheyvens, R., & Momsen, J. (2008). Tourism in small island states: From vulnerability to strengths. *Journal of Sustainable Tourism, 16*(5), 491–510.

Seville, E. (2016). *Resilient organizations: How to survive, thrive and create opportunities through crisis and change.* London: Kogan Page.

Seville, E. (2018). Building resilience: How to have a positive impact at the organizational and individual employee level. *Development and Learning in Organizations: An International Journal, 32*(3), 15–18.

Sheppard, V. (2017). Resilience and destination governance. In R. W. Butler (Ed.), *Tourism and resilience* (pp. 53–68). Wallingford: CABI.

Smit, B., & Wandel, J. (2006). Adaptation, adaptive capacity and vulnerability. *Global Environmental Change, 16*(3), 282–292.

Sutcliffe, K. M., & Vogus, T. J. (2003). Organizing for resilience. In K. S. Cameron, J. E. Dutton, & R. E. Quinn (Eds.), *Positive organizational scholarship: Foundations of a new discipline.* San Francisco, CA: Berrett-Koehler.

Walker, B., Holling, C. S., Carpenter, S., & Kinzig, A. (2004). Resilience, adaptability and transformability in social – ecological systems. *Ecology and Society, 9*(2), 5.

Webb, G. R., Tierney, K. J., & Dahlhamer, J. M. (2002). Predicting long-term business recovery from disaster: A comparison of the Loma Prieta earthquake and Hurricane Andrew. *Global Environmental Change Part B: Environmental Hazards, 4*(2), 45–58.

Part II

Tourism and hospitality in conflict situations

6 On killing the 'toured object'

Anti-terrorist fantasy, touristic edgework and morbid consumption in the illegal settlements in West Bank, Palestine

Rodanthi Tzanelli and Maximiliano E. Korstanje

Introduction

Human voraciousness for adventure knows no limits, but the current touristic novelty in Israel might have pushed things too far. In 2017, news circulated that, while on holiday with his family, American comedian Jerry Seinfeld visited a counter-terrorist training academy in an illegal West Bank settlement. 'Caliber 3' helps both tourist visitors and professionals to train like Israeli Defense Forces (IDF) soldiers in simulated situations, including explosions at a Jerusalem marketplace, a stabbing attack, a sniper tournament and a dog attack on humans. Lasting for two hours, the 'training' aims to provide a taste of the Israeli military experience and is proudly advertised by propagandist newspapers such as *Haaretz* (Maltz, 11 July 2017). The news is far from an isolated episode in Israeli tourism. Apparently, such fantasy terror camps have now been established throughout Israel and in the illegal settlements in the West Bank, inviting tourists to shoot terrorists looking suspiciously like Palestinian Arabs in training cut-out pictures. The price for such staged events is very affordable (US$115 per adult and US$85 per child, with discounts available for large groups) and the clientele featured in promotion videos on YouTube is international (Maltz, 11 July 2017).

This shocking phenomenon invites questions: Why would the Israeli state allow such business to blossom in a region already ravaged by conflict? How does a business, which borrows from counter-terrorist plots and tactics, encroach upon a tourist market, which mostly centres on family visitation and pilgrimage? Finally, why would anyone place themselves in such simulated precarious situations while on holiday? A bizarre coexistence of terror with conventional dark/heritage tourist pilgrimage, reinventing the notion of place and culture in a risky world, is suggested. To explore these questions, we place our analysis within a critical mobilities paradigm, focusing on the dark aspects of tourist commodification (Jensen, 2014, pp. 46–47). We argue that designing counter-terrorist packages as a tourist experience in the first place is problematic: such training programmes aim to align tourists' beliefs and behaviours with ethno-nationalist violence, which is advertised as a form of 'edgework' befit for touristic consumption (for an interpretation of tourist marketing, see Moscardo & Ballantyne, 2008).

By 'edgework,' we refer to voluntary engagement in risk-taking practices 'in and through which participants seek to both experience the excitement and "adrenalin rush" of dangerous situations, and to reclaim their sense of agency over a risky lifeworld through the exercise of survival skills and feats of physical and psychological endurance' (Lyng, 1990, pp. 859–860). Considering the managers and training personnel of these fantasy terror camps as Israel's new international tourism experts, who produce techniques and cultural lenses 'that potentially enable tourists to see the physical form and material spaces before their eyes as interesting' (Urry & Larsen, 2011, p. 2), revises histories of victimization in Holocaust contexts (Bauman, 1989). Now placed in the position of the perpetrator of death, allegedly for the engineering of a better, safe society, the Israeli counter-terrorist tourist gaze eliminates what it considers as a socio-cultural abnormality from all domains of human activity, including that of tourism: Palestinian populations and their claims to history and territory. Indeed, our case study suggests a novel marketable revision of memory debated both onsite, through touristic performances, and online, in videos advertising the business, with an aim not to assume responsibility for the past but harmonize false Israeli consciousness with Realpolitik (Huyssen, 2003, pp. 94–95). To explore the intricacies of this issue in connection with the production and management of tourism in the conflict-ridden areas of the illegal settlements in the West Bank, we appraise the Israeli tourism market and consider how this terrorist-tourist novelty fits into it in the second section. In the third section, we consider the price for the staging of such situations online and offline: the withdrawal of compassion from the tourist gaze and experience.

Conflict tourism and heritage: an appraisal of tourist markets, gazes and performances

Israel is situated on the eastern coast of the Mediterranean Sea in the region known as the Middle East, which between 1950 and 2013 ranked among the world's top emerging tourist destinations (Daher, 2007). In 2017, Israel's population was estimated at 8,819,200 (Israel Central Bureau of Statistics, 2018), of which 74.7% were recorded by the civil government as Jews, 20.8% as Arabs, and 4.5% as non-Arab Christians and people who have no religion listed in the civil registry (Jewish Virtual Library, 2018). Despite healthy immigration figures in urban areas, 2013 saw negative migration in Israel's largest cities, including Tel Aviv and Jerusalem, whereas Haifa and the West Bank reported total gains of 2,800 individuals (Jewish Virtual Library, 2018). The West Bank alone only has a population of over 2.5 million, with about 75% declared as Muslims and 17% as Jews (CIA, 2018). The Muslim percentage of population in the region makes Israeli residents a minority but the ruling population. In 2004, the UN Security Council declared the Golan Heights and East Jerusalem (annexed by the Israeli army) as 'occupied territories,' inviting Israel to withdraw from them and other conflict zones in return for normalization of relations with Arab states. Allegations of mass arrests, torture, unlawful killings, systemic abuses and a denial of the right of Palestinians to self-determination (Gelbman, 2008; Tamari & Levine, 2005) should sketch a political landscape incompatible with sustaining tourism. However, regional markets do have a tourist clientele, and the fantasy terror camps provide proof towards this point. IDF Col. Sharon Gat, who in 2003 inspired the establishment of Caliber 3 and several other counter-terrorist camps across the country, disclosed in 2017 that approximately 15,000–25,000 tourists visit the facilities each year, the majority of them American Jews (Carbonated TV, 2017). With over US$10 billion a year in tourism revenues and over three million tourists a year, despite the region's political instability (Israel Ministry of Tourism, 2013, in Collins-Kreiner, 2015), such ideologically ridden additions to Israel's consumption portfolios should not be ignored.

Foreign tourists to the West Bank follow a variety of organized or independent itineraries, and have different motivations for their visit. The whole region of Palestine/Israel is among the most popular dark tourist destinations in the world (Isaac & Ashworth, 2012)

As the sacred or holy land for Christianity, Judaism and Islam, Israel receives both domestic and international tourists. In 2012, 26% of incoming visitors classified their purpose of visit as pilgrimage, out of the 60% of those who recognized themselves as tourists. Among the 26%, 57% were Christian and 24% Jewish. Notably, the largest number of tourists came from the USA (18%), Russia (17%), France (9%), Germany (7%) and the UK (6%), with Jerusalem (77%) and Tel Aviv (56%) the most popular destinations (Israel Ministry of Tourism, 2013 in Collins-Kreiner, 2015). The risk of destruction of heritage sites in conflict zones is great, but we cannot consider visitations to the West Bank and the Holy Lands as 'disaster tourism' or 'conflict tourism.' Likewise, although conflict tourism relates to the idea of societal disruption from widespread human, material and environmental losses exceeding communal ability to cope with the ensued disaster (UNISRD, 2009), it should be considered as a separate phenomenon from 'disaster tourism' and the pilgrimage or Visiting Friends and Relatives (VFR) niches in Israel, especially those connected to Israeli American mobilities (Khalil-ieh, 2016). Comaroff and Comaroff (2009), who warned about the risk of heritage consumption in lands of hostility and conflict, also observed that tourism tends to renew economic and cultural asymmetries with colonialism or other undemocratic legacies or presents. Not only do war disasters form a heritage in their own right to overlay upon heritage sites, they end up contributing to the formation of ideological discourses, which in turn become historically and geographically embedded in social practices (Lacy, 2001; Sather-Wagstaff, 2011). Conventional dark tourism to heritage sites dissects the formation of discourses that feed into national and tourist imaginaries so that sites of mass destruction are sold as products (Johnston, 2013).

We argue that the fantasy camp phenomenon exemplifies the durability and reproduction of systemic mechanisms of what is known as 'military tourism,' a marriage between war and wartime heritage of all sorts with tourism in areas plagued by conflict in the past or present (but see also Isaac & Ashworth, 2012, p. 152). Military tourism, or 'militourism,' is widespread in countries with a history of maintaining military installations from former occupying countries or allied states, which can attract tourists and visitors, enhance the values of militarism in the business of branding the destination, and further consolidate connections between morbid heritage, state-endorsed technological innovations and the creation of public-private sector security alliances (Henderson, 2000). The up-and-coming Israeli militourism of counter-terrorism camps complies with forms of blended state-business governance based on a symbiosis of the gaze of First World tourists to occupied countries (West Bank) with the gaze of military surveillance (Tzanelli, 2017, p. 27; O'Dwyer, 2004). Incidentally, it is also connected to American-inspired audio-visual advertising of counter-terrorist training relevant to our study, which complies with the combined US military involvement overseas during and after the Second World War (Korean War, Vietnam War, wars in Iraq and Afghanistan) and the accelerated growth of tourism infrastructure in the same regions (Feguson & Turnbull, 1999).

But the tourist gaze is only part of the story. At the other end of our morbid spectrum stands the tourist, who enters zones of physical death and emotional attrition. If tourism is a 'mode of being' (Andrews, 2009), how should we define participants in this theatre of violence? The tourists and their gazes or actions have been endowed with different attributes and powers in academic scholarship, covering the entire spectrum of role-playing, from structural dupes with no initiative to strong agents of socio-cultural change (Urry & Larsen, 2011, pp. 7–23). Nevertheless, their representation as culturally illiterate but highly mobile subjects persists (McGabe, 2005), producing value hierarchies in which they occupy lower ranks of worth vis-à-vis, say, professionals or artists. Thurot and Thurot's (1983) research on French tourist advertising introduced a novel genealogical approach to tourist consumption of importance in our consideration of the tourist subject here. Their conception of 'tourism imaginaries' was used to construct an evolutionist schema, impregnated with value (Graburn, 2017, p. 88): to contest aristocratic pretensions, a middle-class return to naturalist egalitarian simplicity emerged as an ideal in tourist advertising, only to be replaced with more adventurous (*gout du risqué*) and well-documented journeys by various classes and especially youth, and, finally, volunteer tourist and educational tourist mobilities. The movement from respect for a sedentary habitus (the early modern aristocratic value of conspicuous consumption at home) to hyper-mobile experiences of moral and pedagogical value is of importance in our argument. For example, allegedly focusing on nurturing the soul and honing moral reason, volunteer and educational forms of tourism are discursively constructed as noble activities by tourists, the media and non-government organizations (NGOs) (Tzanelli, 2016, pp. 38–40). Much like their moralized counterparts, dark and slum tourism, they allow tourist industries to sell an experiential product that surely will contribute to the production of a worthy self-identity for the purchaser.

However, we claim that such neat moral hierarchies also generate their own nemesis: markets which tend to refashion the desire to acquire new aesthetically pleasing experiences all the time, suggesting new alterations to one's lifestyles that reflect wider changing cultural and political trends and circumstances

(Böhme, 2017). There is international evidence that tourism accelerates economic and political recovery in post-disaster contexts (Walters & Mair, 2012; Biran, Liu, Li, & Eichhorn, 2014; Mair, Ritchie, & Walters, 2016) while also adding to societal resilience, but there is not enough analysis on the ways by which markets adapt to protracted conflict situations, building their own resilience mechanisms into affected tourist destinations. Taking this mobility systems approach, we argue that counter-terrorist packages provided in camps such as Caliber 3 are symptomatic of new aesthetic adjustments in tourist mobilities, which, if we follow Thurot and Thurot's schema, announce the making of a new tourist subject to fit the new morbid tourist experience. Borrowing from regressive notions of adventure we find in 'edgework' – emotional, physical and cognitive labour in favour of individual self-betterment – this new subject has to lose its moral compass, which is orientated towards others (what we call an 'ethics of care'). Upon renouncing this moral compass, the tourist subject is equipped by the militourist industry with a new one, which centres on abstract law, facilitated by identifications with national or even imperial state values of securitization *and* market values of pleasure-seeking experiences.

Changing conceptions of moral entrepreneurship: touristified experiences of terror, the racial state and the confused market

Our brief overview of Israeli tourist markets suggests a generous contribution to state revenues by the Jewish Diaspora, with Israeli Americans featuring prominently among those returning 'home' for holidays (Krakover, 2013). The pattern suggests two distinctive but interlocked processes: the first looks to established combinations between diasporic mobilities, dark tourism, pilgrimage and family genealogies or transnational connectivities that may even preserve notions of national identity (Walter, 2009; Mowatt & Chancellor, 2011); the second that, despite the Israelis' minority status in occupied zones, access to rights and conceptions of citizenship favour Israeli populations (Isaac, Hall, & Higgins-Desbiolles, 2016, p. 4). In the case of expatriate returnees and second- or third-generation migrants, citizenship and human rights collaborate with consumer rights in neoliberal Jewish contexts of touristification (Bianchi & Stephenson, 2014), whereas, within the country, Israeli citizens are regarded as colonial classes entertaining all rights. The status of these subjects is further enhanced by the Israeli state's political backing by the USA. It is small wonder then that terror camps, such as that of Caliber 3, are run by Israeli military personnel, whereas their endorsement comes from celebrities of American Jewish ancestry such as Seinfeld. The morbid niche's genealogy is nicely summarized by Hani Sand, founder of Travel Composer, a boutique Israeli agency that specializes in luxury tours: for a long time, military tourism in Israel was popular for Jewish tourists, and especially organized missions, 'to visit Israeli army bases and meet with the soldiers and watch them during their military exercises,' he says. But for those 'who still want to experience the Israeli army, these for-profit facilities provide a great alternative,' and they are an international success (Maltz, 11 July 2017).

One may argue that the problem with the role of business in destination management contexts characterized by political conflict and ethno-national segregation is that it cannot completely excise its agenda from that of the racial state (Goldberg, 2001; White & Frew, 2013). Fantasy terror camps both obey the logic of domination and act as the apotheosis of consumer capitalism (Bianchi, 2006), turning the murder of fellow humans into an anodyne spectacle. As parts of an infotainment industry specializing in blends of morbidity with patriotic values (Barber, 2003), terror camps dictate to tourists that they can have fun with impunity (Korstanje, 2018). One may argue that contemporary terrorism, tourism and the value of hospitality are structurally intertwined with histories of European colonization. Historically, Europeans used tourism and the value of hospitality to legitimate expansion, by fashioning 'civilized' travellers/colonists as 'protectors' and 'educators' of the 'noble savages' in acquired territories (Lester, 2006; Hall & Tucker, 2004; Hollinshead, 2004). However, nowadays, in globalized contexts of terrorist attacks, such structures of hegemony are reinterpreted, placing the law of hospitality in danger. The fear of terrorist disorder dictates to nation-states a withdrawal of hospitality to strangers, especially non-European and non-Western others: civility becomes intertwined with solipsism rather than 'education' of 'ignoble savages' (Tzanelli, 2011; Korstanje, 2018).

Caliber 3's infotainment packaging on YouTube corroborates this argument. The basic package at US$115, including a bombing, a dog attack and a sniper session, can be upgraded to a more advanced programme in combat rappelling, placing the tourist in the adventurous shoes of Israeli commandos on an Entebbe-like hostage rescue mission. Sessions in *krav maga*, the hand-to-hand combat of the Israeli army, are also sold in this upgrade (Maltz, 11 July 2017). However, promotion videos (Caliber 3 – Counter Terror and Security Academy, 25 November 2013) also tell a revealing story about the emotive grounds of preaching to strangers about military ideals and patriotism. As IDF Col. Gat explains to a group of Asian visitors:

> One day, I sat there wondering whether a Jew in the death camp of Auschwitz could have ever dreamed that an academy like this would ever exist in Israel and that it would train members of the German army, he tells them. And then I said to myself that I am going to open this place to the public to show what a long way the Jewish people have come in 75 years.

This 'show,' which for Gat provides even Hollywood celebrities with a taste of reality, grants, according to Israeli authorities, terror experts with the badge of a cultural ambassador (Maltz, 11 July 2017). Funtom, a similar enterprise in Nes Tziona with about 8,000 visitors per year, and Zikit Extreme, based in Jerusalem, offer similar experiences at higher prices for individuals and families. Although the ways training is choreographed in promotion videos do not involve placing visitors in risky situations and do not include a single child, wealth adviser Morgan Stanley reports that he and his wife 'are feeling relieved' that their previously squeamish 10-year-old son became, after his training, 'eager for his next turn shooting an assault rifle' (Fernandez, 18 July 2017).

Let us consider the 'counter-terrorist packages' on offer to think about their significance in tourism development: the distance required for the formation of a relationship of pity does not appeal to physical space, but to the role specific embodied performances are assigned in context (Butler, 2009, pp. 43–44). Watching trained soldiers and experts carrying out fights and murders evidently targeting Palestinian others, and then emulating them as an adventurous tourist, is problematic, when considering that these 'training events' take place in conflict-ridden zones, in a particular spatio-temporal context sustaining mutual hatred. In such contexts, acknowledging the precariousness all humans share in war conditions is simply non-existent – an absence markets exploit in this case to promote dark kitschification for anodyne consumption. Similar to Caliber 3, other facilities sell merchandise, from T-shirts to military equipment, but downplay financial motives in favour of a good moral lesson: 'here the Holocaust is reappraised by its victims, and you can be part of the story' (Fernandez, 18 July 2017). Such staged, symbolic vengeance mirrors Baudrillard's (2003) conception of American 'war-porn,' the televised production of images of terrorism, which allowed for the symbolic humiliation of the (invariably Islamic) other by annihilation. Akin to kitsch souvenirs, terror souvenirs invite their purchasers to ingest 'the experience of [the Jewish] trauma . . . as a fashion statement' (Engle, 2007, p. 76), thus extending fascistic rituals of national unity to a transnational tourist audience. Promoting the visualization and physical engagement of tourists with versions of collective (irredentism) and state-sanctioned violence (counter-terrorism), they cannot be characterized as ethically constructive education. In Sturken's (2011, p. 437) words: 'the mode of re-enactment [of counter-terrorism] is always vulnerable to the charge that it facilitates too easy a connection [to criticism].' There are several critical modes to consider in such a highly charged cultural field, most of them not facilitating leisure and tourism as pathways to wellbeing, individual or collective emotional flourishing and justice (D'Sa, 1999; Fennell, 2009).

If the racial state is the primary arbitrator in the circulation of representations and simulations in media and tourist channels (Boltanski, 1999, pp. 83–85), then we could safely assume that it also has a say in the governance of emotions in the same channels (Butler, 2009, p. 50). Discussing reporting in the 2003 War on Iraq, Butler notes that state authorities wanted to regulate the visual modes of participation in the war so as to craft and validate a particular point of view (Butler, 2009, pp. 64–65). Likewise, the discursive effect of 'soldiering rituals' on consumers in settlements in the West Bank counter-terrorist packages rests in the orchestration of images in their online advertising, in the Anglophone press and on YouTube. Now these messages are addressed to Israelis, but also not to the generic tourist spectator: organizing perception and justifying violence, camera shots are supposed to induce affects that correspond to emotional aspects of the dominant anti-Palestinian ideology. Simulations of violence endorse the touristic desire for edgework under safe conditions, giving the illusion of 'good' action, while encouraging its separation from feelings of critical involvement and compassion – i.e. individualizing the ability to decipher the spectacle of murder, instead of considering it as an issue of collective responsibility (Chouliaraki, 2006, p. 50).

Indeed, the promise of a safe enactment of violence for and by tourists is the most perverted form of dark tourist mobility: complying with an ethos of individualist self-presentation (Herzfeld, 2005, pp. 197–199), these hyper-masculine performances of securitization are examples of resentful edgework. The idea that simulations of murder will educate participants into safety restores the belief in individual agency over a risky lifeworld families and young generations have to master (Lyng, 1990). The advertising videos' instructors speak American English with a Jewish accent and extol the values of military patriotism throughout (Caliber 3 – Counter Terror and Security Academy, 24 January 2017) in line with Seinfeld's family holiday trip to the Caliber 3 camp (Carbonated TV, 2017). Hence, it is not unreasonable to associate such Israeli businesses' attempt to *rebrand the country's conflict zones* with notions of personal security, jingoism and gun violence as these are currently being shaped. Achcar's (2015) conception of the 'clash of barbarisms' already suggests that terrorism and the George W. Bush administration's strategies were two sides of the same coin, in that both sides appealed to radical and extreme policies to legitimate their own perspective. To expand on Achcar's thesis, both sides appealed to stereotypical connections between manliness and civilization to restore a feeling of self-respect (Tzanelli, 2011). By the same token, touristified counter-terrorist edgework in the illegal settlements in the West Bank and elsewhere in the country forms an Israeli-American projection of 'the unique experience of white, middle class, adult males' in dealing with the construction of a trauma (disruption of order in terrorist contexts) narcissistically (Lyng, 2005, p. 11; Lyng & Matthews, 2007).

By 'conflict zones,' we do not refer to the physical places in which atrocities and deaths took place, but to the excision of these traumatic events' symbolic potential from territory and ethnic memory so that their financial capital is amplified and their emotional potential become hyper-mobile – a novel fashioning of what Augé (2008) identified in 'non-places.' Cohen's (2011) coining of the term 'populo' to describe places in which memory is embedded and which promise experiential authenticity of a pedagogical nature to tourists is also modified in our case. The studied simulation camps promise emotional authenticity when it comes to the experience of terror, but they treat the occupied zones' multiple populo sites, where bodies fell and unsung Palestinian or Israeli heroes died, as mobile commodities. At the same time, Israeli state propaganda can strip the self-same places of any Palestinian traces so as to reassign them to the Israeli cause of memory, which then feeds back into tourist markets. In fact, in terms of destination branding, these counter-terrorist camps refashion conventional understandings of pilgrimage as an act of popular religiosity: where pilgrimage sites normally form *axes mundi*, irruptions of the sacred where humans recapture cosmological harmony in a profane social chaos (Eliade, 1959), the camps' simulations of risk look to the restoration of a sense of shared semi-sacred national sentiment, with kitsch as key symbol of national unity in the touristified market (Sturken, 2007, p. 22).

'Masada, the Dead Sea and Jerusalems [sic] Old City are no longer enough,' says Hani Sand, a Tel Aviv-based travel specialist. 'Travelers today are on the lookout for something authentic and different' (Maltz, 11 July 2017).

Concluding reflections

Though fascinationwith death and battlefield tourism is not new, the management of post-conflict destinations seems to be an emerging object of study for social scientists worldwide (Vitic & Ringer, 2008; Black & Gent, 2006; Winter, 2007). Unsurprisingly, this interest, which dates back at least to the Vietnam War, increased after 9/11 and the US-led invasions in Afghanistan and Iraq, and also the scientific exposure of the limitations of the precautionary principle, which originally suggested that risks can be avoided if the experts forecast the future steps of terrorists. The adoption of such theories by policy-makers in the field of tourism was based on the design of a rational programme to protect both tourist destinations and the visitors' ontological security from local crime and international terrorism (Isaac & Ashworth, 2012, pp. 152–154). Overthrowing this precautionary dogma suggested changing the course of action: from then on, specialists would use the 'worst-case scenario' principle in the industrial orchestration of morbid consumption that we associate with military, dark or conflict tourism, as an efficient way to revitalize the affected communities economically and build in them resilience mechanisms. Suffering would be commoditized as a spectacle to cater for visitors in quest of shocking – hence, 'authentic' – experiences. The problem is that new consumption trends can and do wane, so either the clientele demands further innovation, or industries judge that it is time to introduce them. As a result, instead of addressing the trauma of a disaster or conflict, tourist and media industries revitalize or produce new consumption trends featuring fear and suffering as the main attractions (Korstanje, 2016, 2018).

Although the cases we explored in this chapter foster a complicity between tourist consumption, imperialism and racism, they are based on a real global threat meriting dispassionate reappraisal. We argue that the symbolic 'murder' of the Palestinian other – who, in an alternate reality, would have been the legitimate tourist host in the West Bank – in counter-terrorist-tourist simulations happens in the way its framing works together with the powers that be (Butler, 2009, pp. 138–141): language and representation, not only in the region's lifeworlds, but also the global messages controlled by powerful stakeholders in the region, such as the USA. These simulation experiences do not negotiate a healthy relationship between touring spaces of geopolitical conflict and acknowledge which misfortunes deserve addressing with an ethics of care for all sides: there certainly is Palestinian terrorism to account for, but, at the same time, Palestinian claims to independence and autonomy, and brutalization and genocide in the hands of the Jewish Israeli army, cannot be dismissed. On a purely normative level, tourism is supposed to forge peaceful cross-cultural relations, not to sanction geopolitical turmoil (Roberts, 2016, p. 29). But the simulation of combat and murder in these experiential journeys sanctions and disavows violence, withdrawing the duty of care and responsibility, as well as a dispassionate understanding of the situation (Sturken, 2011, p. 424). We therefore conclude that an ability to create and sustain a politics of pity in a region, whereby spectators and sufferers are locked into a relationship of interdependence, is quintessential for the production of a tourist gaze in state-endorsed business contexts, which neither commercializes tragedy nor merely blackmails global visitors into performing an involved volunteer tourist role nor indoctrinates them into a partial narrative of violence.

References

Achcar, G. (2015). *Clash of barbarisms: The making of the new world disorder*. Abingdon: Routledge.

Andrews, H. (2009). Tourism as a moment of being. *Suomen Anthropologi, 34*(2), 5–21.

Augé, M. (2008). *Non-places*. New York, NY: Verso.

Barber, B. (2003). *Jihad versus McWorld*. London: Corgi Books.

Baudrillard, J. (2003). *The spirit of terrorism and other essays*. London: Verso.

Bauman, Z. (1989). *Modernity and the holocaust*. Cambridge: Polity.

Bianchi, R. (2006). Tourism and the globalisation of fear: Analysing the politics of risk and (in) security in global travel. *Tourism and Hospitality Research, 7*(1), 64–74.

Bianchi, R., & Stephenson, M. (2014). *Tourism and citizenship: Rights, freedoms and responsibilities in the global order*. Abingdon: Routledge.

Biran, A., Liu, W., Li, G., & Eichhorn, V. (2014). Consuming post-disaster destinations: The case of Sichuan, China. *Annals of Tourism Research, 47*(1), 1–17.

Black, R., & Gent, S. (2006). Sustainable return in post-conflict contexts. *International Migration, 44*(3), 15–38.

Böhme, G. (2017). *Critique of aesthetic capitalism*. Berlin: Mimesis International and Suhrkamp.

Boltanski, L. (1999). *Distant suffering: Morality, media and politics*. New York, NY: Cambridge University Press.

Butler, J. (2009). *Frames of war: When is life grievable?* London: Verso.

Caliber 3 – Counter Terror and Security Academy. (2013, 25 November). The Israeli pointing method. *YouTube.* [online] Retrieved 22 February 2018, from www.youtube.com/watch?v=UB3El16sw3M

Caliber 3 – Counter Terror and Security Academy. (2017, 24 January). Watch the piece made by ILTV after visiting Caliber 3, broadcasted in 17 countries. *YouTube.* [online] Retrieved 22 February 2018, from www.youtube.com/watch?v=7tf6lKju_34

Carbonated TV. (2017). Seinfeld visits anti-terrorism fantasy camp in illegal settlement. [online] Retrieved 18 February 2018, from www.carbonated.tv/news/anti-terror-fantasy-military-camps-become-tourist-attraction-israel?fb_comment_id=1395154533914224_1557255881037421#f2ae442e62f85b4

Central Intelligence Agency (CIA). (2018). *The world factbook: Israel*. [online] Retrieved 20 February 2018, from www.cia.gov/library/publications/the-world-factbook/geos/is.html

Chouliaraki, L. (2006). *The spectatorship of suffering*. London: Sage.

Cohen, E. H. (2011). Educational dark tourism at an in populo site: The Holocaust museum in Jerusalem. *Annals of Tourism Research, 38*(1), 193–209.

Collins-Kreiner, N. (2015). Israel, tourism. In J. Jafari & H. Xiao (Eds.), *Encyclopaedia of tourism*. Cham, Switzerland: Springer International.

Comaroff, J. L., & Comaroff, J. (2009). *Ethnicity, Inc.* Chicago: University of Chicago Press.

Daher, R. (2007). *Tourism in the Middle East: Community, change and transformation.* Bristol: Channel View.

D'Sa, E. (1999). Wanted: Tourists with a social conscious. *International Journal of Contemporary Hospitality Management, 11*(2/3), 64–68.

Eliade, P. (1959). *The sacred and the profane: The nature of religion.* New York, NY: Harcourt.

Engle, K. (2007). Putting mourning to work: Making sense of 9/11. *Theory, Culture and Society, 24*(1), 61–88.

Feguson, K., & Turnbull, P. (1999). *Oh say, can you see? The semiotics of military tourism in Hawai'i.* Minneapolis, MN: University of Minnesota Press.

Fennell, D. (2009). Ethics and tourism. In J. Tribe (Ed.), *Philosophical issues in tourism* (pp. 211–226). Bristol: Channel View Publications.

Fernandez, B. (2017, 18 July). Holiday in style at Israel's "anti-terror fantasy camps". *Middle East Eye.* [online] Retrieved 22 February 2018, from www.middleeasteye.net/columns/vacation-style-israel-s-anti-terror-fantasy-camps-294950627

Gelbman, A. (2008). Border tourism in Israel: Conflict, peace, fear and hope. *Tourism Geographies, 10*(2), 193–213.

Goldberg, T. (2001). *The racial state.* Oxford: Wiley-Blackwell.

Graburn, N. (2017). Key figure of mobility: The tourist. *Social Anthropology, 25*(1), 83–96.

Hall, C. M., & Tucker, H. (2004). Tourism and postcolonialism: An introduction. In C. M. Hall & H. Tucker (Eds.), *Tourism and postcolonialism: Contested discourses, identities and representations* (pp. 1–24). London: Routledge.

Henderson, I. (2000). War as a tourist attraction: The case of Vietnam. *International Journal of Tourism Research, 2*(4), 269–280.

Herzfeld, M. (2005). *Cultural intimacy: Social poetics in the nation-state.* New York, NY: Routledge.

Hollinshead, K. (2004). Tourism and new sense: Worldmaking and the enunciative value of tourism. In C. M. Hall & H. Tucker (Eds.), *Tourism and postcolonialism: Contested discourses, identities and representations* (pp. 25–42). London: Routledge.

Huyssen, A. (2003). *Present pasts: Urban palimpsest and the politics of memory.* Stanford, CA: Stanford University Press.

Isaac, R. K., & Ashworth, G. J. (2012). Moving from pilgrimage to "dark" tourism: Leveraging tourism in Palestine. *Tourism, Culture & Communication, 11*, 149–164.

Isaac, R. K., Hall, C. M., & Higgins-Desbiolles, F. (2016). Palestine as a tourism destination. In R. K. Isaac, C. M. Hall, & F. Higgins-Desbiolles (Eds.), *The politics and power of tourism in Palestine* (pp. 15–34). Abingdon: Routledge.

Israel Central Bureau of Statistics. (2018). [online] Retrieved 20 February 2018, from www.cbs.gov.il/reader/cw_usr_view_Folder?ID=141

Jensen, O. B. (2014). *Designing mobilities.* London: Routledge.

Jewish Virtual Library. (2018). Latest population statistics for Israel. *American – Israeli Cooperative Enterprise.* [online] Retrieved 20 February 2018, from www.jewishvirtual library.org/latest-population-statistics-for-israel

Johnston, T. (2013). Mark Twain and the innocents abroad: Illuminating the tourist gaze on death. *International Journal of Culture and Hospitality Research, 7*(3), 199–213.

Khalilieh, S. (2016). Diaspora and VFR: An exploratory study. In R. K. Isaac, C. M. Hall, & F. Higgins-Desbiolles (Eds.), *The politics and power of tourism in Palestine* (pp. 113–123). Abingdon: Routledge.

Korstanje, M. E. (2016). *The rise of thana-capitalism and tourism*. Abingdon: Routledge.

Korstanje, M. E. (2018). *Terrorism, tourism and the end of hospitality in the West*. New York, NY: Springer.

Krakover, S. (2013). Developing tourism alongside threats of war and atrocities: The case of Israel. In R. W. Butler & W. Suntikul (Eds.), *Tourism and war* (pp. 132–142). London: Routledge.

Lacy, M. J. (2001). Cinema and ecopolitics: Existence in the Jurassic Park. *Millennium-Journal of International Studies, 30*(3), 635–645.

Lester, A. (2006). Imperial circuits and networks: Geographies of the British Empire. *History Compass, 4*(1), 124–141.

Lyng, S. (1990). Edgework: A social psychological analysis of voluntary risk taking. *American Journal of Sociology, 95*(4), 851–886.

Lyng, S. (2005). *Edgework*. New York, NY: Routledge.

Lyng, S., & Matthews, R. (2007). Risk, edgework and masculinities. In K. Hannah-Moffat & R. Bells (Eds.), *Gendered risks* (pp. 75–98). New York, NY: Routledge-Cavendish.

Mair, J., Ritchie, B. W., & Walters, G. (2016). Towards a research agenda for post-disaster and post-crisis recovery strategies for tourist destinations: A narrative review. *Current Issues in Tourism, 19*(1), 1–26.

Maltz, J. (2017, 11 July). Anti-terror fantasy camps are popping up throughout Israel and the West Bank – and tourists are eating it up. *Haaretz*. [online] Retrieved 22 February 2018, from www.haaretz.com/israel-news/MAGAZINE-anti-terror-fantasy-camps-are-popping-up-throughout-israel-1.5492590

McGabe, S. (2005). Who is a tourist? *Tourist Studies, 5*(1), 85–106.

Moscardo, G., & Ballantyne, R. (2008). Interpretation and attractions: New directions. In A. Fyall, A. Leask, & S. Wanhill (Eds.), *Managing visitor attractions* (pp. 237–252). Oxford: Elsevier.

Mowatt, R., & Chancellor, C. H. (2011). Visiting death and life: Dark tourism and slave castles. *Annals of Tourism Research, 38*(4), 410–434.

O'Dwyer, C. (2004). Tropic knights and Hula belles: War and tourism in the South Pacific. *Journal for Cultural Research, 8*(1), 33–50.

Roberts, L. (2016). The violence of non-places. In H. Andrews (Ed.), *Tourism and violence* (pp. 13–31). Farnham: Ashgate.

Sather-Wagstaff, J. (2011). *Heritage that hurts: Tourists in the memoryscapes of September 11*. Walnut Creek, CA: Left Coast Press.

Sturken, M. (2007). *Tourists of history: Memory, Kitsch and consumerism from Oklahoma city to Ground Zero*. Durham, NC: Duke University Press.

Sturken, M. (2011). Comfort, irony and trivialization: The mediation of torture. *International Journal of Cultural Studies, 14*(4), 423–440.

Tamari, S., & LeVine, M. (2005). *Palestine, Israel, and the politics of popular culture*. Durham, NC: Duke University Press.

Thurot, J.-M., & Thurot, G. (1983). The ideology and class and tourism: Confronting the discourse of advertising. *Annals of Tourism Research, 10*(1), 173–189.

Tzanelli, R. (2011). *Cosmopolitan memory in Europe's "Backwaters": Rethinking civility*. London: Routledge.

Tzanelli, R. (2016). *Thanatourism and cinematic representations of risk: Screening the end of tourism*. Abingdon: Routledge.

Tzanelli, R. (2017). *Mega-events as economies of the imagination: Creating atmospheres for Rio 2016 and Tokyo 2020*. Abingdon: Routledge.

UNISRD. (2009). *Terminology on disaster risk reduction*. Geneva: United Nations International Strategy for Disaster Reductions.

Urry, J., & Larsen, J. (2011). *The tourist gaze 3.0* (3rd ed.). London: Sage.

Vitic, A., & Ringer, G. (2008). Branding post-conflict destinations: Recreating Montenegro after the disintegration of Yugoslavia. *Journal of Travel & Tourism Marketing, 23*(2–4), 127–137.

Walter, T. (2009). Dark tourism: Mediating between the dead and the living. In R. Sharpley & P. R. Stone (Eds.), *The darker side of travel* (pp. 39–55). Bristol: Channel View Publications.

Walters, G., & Mair, J. (2012). The effectiveness of post-disaster recovery marketing messages – The case of the 2009 Australian bushfires. *Journal of Travel & Tourism Marketing, 29*(1), 87–103.

Winter, T. (2007). *Post-conflict heritage, postcolonial tourism: Tourism, politics and development at Angkor*. Abingdon: Routledge.

White, L., & Frew, E. (2013). *Dark tourism, place and identity: Managing and interpreting dark places*. London: Routledge.

7 Tourism as a tool for peace?

Between the lines – Thandaung Gyi in Kayin State, Myanmar

Nicole Haeusler, Zin Mar Than and Frauke Kraas

Introduction

For the past six decades, the area around Taungoo has been strongly affected by a civil war between the Myanmar army and armed ethnic Kayin/Karen groups.

At the end of the first day of a workshop on 'Community Involvement in Tourism and the Peace Process' in 2014, on the way to the restaurant, one of the authors met one of the speakers – a member of the governmental staff. He said:

> Perhaps you are not aware that I lost one of my feet a few miles from here from a land mine. Taking part in such a discussion at such a place with my former enemy helps me a lot to find inner peace. I believe that tourism can be an effective instrument for bringing about peace not only to my inner soul, but to the local people, as well'.

Thandaung Gyi, a former British hill station in Kayin State, is a small town in the steep Thandaung Mountains east of Taungoo, about two hours' drive from the capital city Nay Pyi Taw and six hours from Yangon. The conflict pitted rival armies of the Karen National Union (KNU) against government forces. Based on even pre-colonial tensions (Renard, 1987), fostered by British colonial divide-and-rule-principles, since 1949, Karen groups have fought for independence, self-determination and enhanced autonomy (Core, 2009; Kipgen, 2015). Additionally, economic interests, from border trade to the extraction of resources, play a role not to be underestimated (South, 2011). Ceasefire negotiations resumed in 2011, which led to a preliminary agreement in 2012, but the peace process is still incomplete, because regional stability continues to be fragile.

The KNU has not been the only army fighting for independence. In 1948, Myanmar (or Burma, as it was called at that time) was granted independence as a democratic nation. Following a coup d'état in 1962, it became a military dictatorship under the Burma Socialist Programme Party, which remained in power for 60 years. Armed conflicts between the military regime and as many as 20 different ethnic armed groups have been the order of the day, especially in border areas. In 2011, the military junta was officially dissolved after the 2010 general election, and a civilian government was installed which established a far-reaching political and economic reform process. This, along with the release of Nobel Peace Prize laureate Aung San Suu Kyi and political prisoners, has led to the easing of trade and lifting of economic sanctions. In the election of 2015, Aung San Suu Kyi's party won a majority in both houses. Far-reaching nationwide ceasefire agreements (NCA) were signed on 15 October 2015 by eight ethnic groups, including the KNU (Panyakom & Waters, 2018).

This chapter will describe how informal, facilitated meetings during the initial phase of the case study on tourism and peace have provided a platform for earlier rivalled stakeholders to convene and work towards a common goal: the development of tourism in a post-conflict/ceasefire area in Kayin State. The rationale behind this approach is the perception that economic development and the identification of income-generating opportunities that benefit the local population in particular are prerequisites in supporting and consolidating the peace-building process.

The chapter begins with an overview of tourism development in Myanmar over the past few decades, and of the geography and history of Thandaung Gyi. This is followed by a description of the theoretical concept of stakeholder dialogues and peace-building. Next, it provides an in-depth explanation of the application and evolution of the tourism stakeholder process in Thandaung Gyi and a description of its tourism assets and benefits. The chapter closes with a summary of key lessons that hopefully will be applied in the future in other post-conflict areas of Myanmar, because this case study outlines 'a model for applying community-driven tourism as a tool for peace-building, and highlights its strengths and weaknesses for those who might seek to replicate it' (Carr, 2016, p. 2).

The research project combined a systematic literature review of national and international sources with empirical fieldwork. The mixed-methods approach included field observation, rapid appraisal methods, 24 expert interviews (involving key informants from the government, administration, churches, the private sector and civil society) and 27 conversations and interviews with local households and (inter)national tourists conducted between 2012 and 2018.

Tourism development in Myanmar

Myanmar offers as a destination snowcapped mountains, endless sandy beaches, the pristine Myeik Archipelago, 75 protected areas (Kraas, Spohner, & Myint, 2017, p. 53), outstanding religious sites and secular architecture such as Bagan, a deep-rooted belief in Buddhism, and is considered to have the richest ethnic diversity in Asia, the Bamar (Burmese) being by far the largest group. Other ethnic groups include Shan (9% of the population), Karen/Kayin (7%), Mon, Rakhine, Chin and Kachin (each constituting 5% or less of the population; Ekeh & Smith, 2007).

Although the pre-colonial visits by explorers and missionaries cannot be described as 'tourism' in the narrower sense, the images and impressions that they conveyed attracted growing numbers of investors and merchants, paving the way for the initial phase of early tourism development during the British colonial period (1824–1948). This led to the emergence of international tourism, primarily for the purpose of culture, education, adventure and hunting and mainly was targeted at the elites, towards the end of the 19th century. After the country gained its independence in 1948, however, the length of time that international visitors could feasibly remain in the country and their freedom to travel were initially limited by the impacts of conflict and civil war. Travel was then further constrained by the nationalization of industries and the policy of autarky and isolation from the rest of the world, which were the characteristics of the 'Burmese Way to Socialism' from 1962.

It was not until the introduction of a market-based economy after 1988 that a second phase of tourism development began. This took place in 1996 with the launch of the 'Visit Myanmar Year' marketing campaign, whose systematic objective was to encourage more openness to tourism in general and to facilitate the expansion of a small number of centres, specifically the classic 'quadrangle' comprising Yangon, Bagan, Mandalay and Inle Lake (with a potential extension to also include Ngapali or Ngwe Hsaung beaches) (Kraas & Häusler, 2016). Mercer (2018, p. 169) calls this 'quadrangle' 'the Buddhist heartland,' while peripheral regions of mixed ethnic and religious heritage were announced as problematic and off-limits, (still) providing only poor transport and supply infrastructure. A system of obligatory currency exchange and unrealistically high exchange rates were further impediments to tourism expansion.

A third phase of tourism development began with a rapid increase in visitor numbers triggered by the current transformation process after 2010.

However, these figures (see Table 7.1), published by the Ministry of Hotels and Tourism (MoHT), only stand up to critical scrutiny to a limited extent as they include day trippers from neighbouring countries who crossed the border for the purpose of trade or to visit family (Lawson, 2018). More realistic figures are obtained by looking at Yangon as the main entry point. Out of around one million international arrivals, some 500,000 incoming visitors described themselves as 'foreign individual travellers' (FITs) or as 'package tour' tourists. Most of the rest were travelling on business or visiting family. The Shwedagon Pagoda, Yangon's landmark and main attraction, was visited by half a million tourists, while other key destinations, which mainly attract Westerners and Japanese tourists, report visitor numbers of around 250,000, suggesting that a figure of around 500,000 tourists is realistic; more precise statistics are not available.

However, the Responsible Tourism Policy of 2012 and the Myanmar Tourism Master Plan of 2013 (MoHT, 2012, 2013b), which focus on poverty alleviation, community involvement, environmental protection and good governance, demonstrated the government's commitment to using new ways of working towards a more transparent, open and consultative approach in cooperation with regional governments, the private sector and civil society (Suntikul & Rogers, 2017). Nevertheless, the crisis in Rakhine State at the boarder to Bangladesh has had an impact on the tourism sector. It is expected that the number of Western tourists (i.e. those who stay in the country for up to 14 days and spend over US$150 per night) will decrease by 20–50% in 2018–2019, not only as a result of the country's

Table 7.1 International arrivals into Myanmar by entry point, 2010–2017

Airport	2010	2011	2012	2013	2014	2015	2016	2017
Yangon	297,246	364,743	559,610	817,699	1,022,081	1,180,682	1,080144	1,146,069
Mandalay	13,442	20,912	32,521	89,596	90,011	107,066	128,387	157,860
Nay Pyi Taw	0	5,521	1,250	11,842	19,261	13,835	16,224	17,077
Mawlamyine, Myeik, Muse, Tachileik, Myawaddy, Tamu, Hteekhee	0	0	0	1,250	271	0	47,841	41,942
Land borders	475,877	425,193	465,614	1,144,146	1,949,788	3,379,437	1,634,611	2,080,185
Total	**785,565**	**816,369**	**1,058,995**	**2,044,307**	**3,081,412**	**4,681,020**	**2,907,207**	**3,443,133**

Source: Ministry of Hotels and Tourism (2018)

negative reputation across the world, but also because it is known as an overpriced destination where travelling around is difficult (Lawson, 14 August 2018). This situation is made worse by 'a lack of trained human resources. . ., a weak regulatory environment, corruption, and insufficient public services and infrastructure for tourism' (Hudson, 2016, p. 312).

This unfortunate development does not have any impact on the case study of Thandaung Gyi, however, because most of tourists there are domestic Buddhist and Christian tourists.

Geography and history of Thandaung Gyi

Thandaung Gyi is located at the steep western edge of the wide mountainous area of Kayin State at 914 metres above sea level, with Naw Bu Baw Mountain as highest elevation at 1,454 metres (see Figure 7.1). Due to its location at high altitude, moderate temperatures (annual average: about 20°C) and high, mostly monsoonal precipitation (over 3,800 mm annually) and thus favourable climatic conditions, the British colonial power made the location one of its 'hill stations' in 1852. In the following years, a number of large stone buildings were erected, partly for military, administrative, religious and residential purposes, partly for education, healthcare and public services (Smith, 1902). Missionaries Christianized the resident Kayin/Karen population in the area. With the introduction of tea and coffee plantations from the late 1890s onwards, Nepali and Indian workers were brought in larger numbers in order to work in the newly established

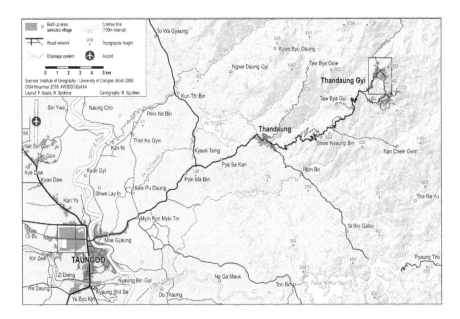

Figure 7.1 Geography of Thandaung Gyi

plantations. In the early 20th century, the previous Methodist English High School building was transformed into the only Kayin tea factory, which still operates today. During the Japanese occupation in 1941, many buildings were destroyed or reutilized with different functions. After independence, Thandaung Gyi fell into oblivion for about five decades, due to civil war and insurgency.

Today's Thandaung Gyi was originally named Thandaung – 'iron mountain.' In 1935, it became administrative centre for the whole area. In 1959, all administrative offices were moved downhill to the newly created Thandaung – while the 'old' place, in order to give it a distinguishable name, was renamed Thandaung Gyi. In 2000, it was upgraded to a town. After the township administrative branch offices moved back in 2002, they were upgraded to main offices in 2006 by the Ministry of Home Affairs. The eastern part of the town was developed as a military training centre. Thandaung Gyi Township (1,413 square meter) belongs to Hpa-an District in Kayin State. Thandaung Gyi Town (315 square meter) comprises five wards, 13 village tracts and 73 villages (GAD, 2018). Today with 4,050 households and almost 21,800 inhabitants in the township and 14,800 urban dwellers (GAD, 2018), it belongs to the group of many small towns in Myanmar with considerable socio-economic development potential. The nearest regional town, Taungoo, about 45 kilometres distant, functions as the major administrative, economic, education and health centre. Beyond cash crops such as coffee, tea and cardamom, the local agriculture produce includes rice, fruits and vegetables, djenkol beans, bamboo shoots and betel nuts.

Until the late 1980s, armed conflicts between the central military government and the Kayin ethnic group's army prevented economic development, including any touristic developments. With the first ceasefire agreements negotiated in the late 1990s, it was possible to start first touristic projects. Thus, in the late 1990s and into the early 2000s, former Prime Minister General Khin Nyunt encouraged local business firms to develop the Thandaung area as a mountain resort. Large Myanmar conglomerates, most of them during those times on the US government's sanctions lists due to their close relationship to the military government – including the Htoo Group of Companies, Asia World and KMA Group of Companies – invested in hotel projects there. International investment was not involved. The projects, however – with the sole exception of the KMA Hotel – stopped when the 2004–2005 ceasefire talks between the same previous conflict parties broke down. Examples of these collapsed projects include the never-completed hotels that still stand in Thandaung Gyi and other projects built at this time, especially for the Visit Myanmar Year in 1996, which have fallen into disuse or disrepair.

These failed infrastructure projects which emerged during a short period of ceasefire talks illustrate how important it is for any projects implemented to actually strengthen the ceasefire and security on different levels – i.e. the military, economic and social development – and jointly between the conflict parties over a long period, rather than simply taking advantage of a temporary lull in fighting to get a project off the ground.

Before we go on to explain how Thandaung Gyi has been established as a tourism destination in recent years based on a stakeholder process among the local community, KNU and the Myanmar military, we will first describe the theoretical framework of this approach.

Stakeholder process in tourism: a tool for democratic development and peace-building

Working towards a more sustainable world makes it necessary to bring together different worldviews and to resolve conflicts of interest in order to promote responsible business activities, people-oriented public services, and a strong civil society (Kuenkel, Gerlach, & Frieg, 2011). A higher level of sustainability in a society requires a change in the mindset of those involved, as well as innovation, inventiveness and, above all, people who are not only inspired by the potential of sustainability, but are also willing to implement change at all levels of the society in which they live. This also applies to the development of responsible tourism. The key stakeholders in tourism planning are governments of all levels, the private sector, national and international NGOs, local communities, development agencies, and international organizations such as the UN World Tourism Organization.

Given this, stakeholder relationships must be based on trust to increase the ability of those involved to communicate and partner with multiple stakeholders: 'The different actors . . . need to communicate respectfully, in a way that shows that they appreciate each other, despite serious differences in opinion' (Kuenkel et al., 2011, p. 13). Such a collaborative approach can become the norm in the daily business of dealing with the challenges of sustainable development, such as peace-building, democratization, sustainable economic development and good governance, all of which are important elements of responsible tourism development in a destination. According to Kuenkel et al. (2011), at the core of stakeholder dialogue is the principle of collective leadership, meaning that a group of leaders contributes to a more sustainable future by assuming joint and flexible leadership for the benefit of all involved. Leaders do not necessarily have to be political or business leaders; what is most important is that they have the strength, the willingness and the ability to contribute to the sustainability of society. In the case of tourism, leaders can be representatives of ministries, tourism associations, local communities, DMOs, local guides and so on. Stakeholder dialogues are structured conversations about certain issues of common interest or concern between:

- People from different sectors or constituencies,
- People with different interests, and
- People with different perspectives and points of view.

These conversations support planning and decision-making, help to resolve problems and contribute to finding innovative solutions or to the design and implementation of joint interventions for change. Ideally, stakeholder dialogues lead to practical outcomes, such as a tourism policy which could otherwise not have been achieved and which is easier to implement because all the stakeholders involved have experienced a higher degree of ownership. In well-facilitated stakeholder dialogues, differences – sometime even conflicts – hold the potential for innovative solutions and can achieve goals that ultimately benefit all. This can lead to:

- Trust building between different stakeholders,
- Forward-looking and constructive cooperation between societal actors,
- Innovative solutions to existing economic or social challenges,
- A higher quality, and broader acceptance, of decisions,
- Ownership of and commitment to implementing agreed-upon results,
- Collective responsibility for change,
- Sustainable outcomes, and
- Long-lasting cooperative structures.

(Kuenkel et al., 2011, p. 18)

This case study of Thandaung Gyi demonstrates that all the factors just mentioned have been important elements towards its development as a tourism destination in a location that was isolated for decades.

Application and evolution of the tourism stakeholder process in Thandaung Gyi: between the lines

According to the Myanmar government, conditions for the implementation of sustainable tourism immediately after the political changes in 2011 were favourable. The rationale behind these efforts was that:

> the Ministry also recognizes that the success of rapid tourism development would not only have a boost on the sector and create a swift economic development, but that it would also have challenges in the long-term success for sustainable tourism development in the country.
>
> (MoHT, 2012, p. 2)

First, initial cautious, informal contacts were facilitated by civil society, mostly religious leaders (pastors and monks) and the local people (who over the years had tried to get on good terms with both the Myanmar military and the KNU) between the conflicting parties. These contacts then led to a consensus over mutual attempts to develop the local economic, especially tourism-oriented development. Thus, a cautious and fragile trust building started to evolve between the lines.

Since early 2012, the MoHT, in collaboration with the Myanmar Tourism Federation (MTF) and Hanns Seidel Foundation (HSF), has initiated coherent stakeholder processes directed at responsible tourism practices and goals which resulted in the outcomes of the publication of two policies: 'Responsible Tourism Policy' (MoHT, 2012) and 'Policy on Community Involvement in Tourism' (MoHT, 2013a). During that period, HSF, MoHT and MTF held workshops on 'Community Involvement in Tourism' for the public and private sector. The concept of 'Tourism and Peace' workshops was developed there, and the policies put forth have provided a framework for ensuring that local communities gain access to opportunities in tourism by setting up small enterprises such as guesthouses, restaurants or souvenir shops. Such policies have promoted the development of community-run tourism activities and enterprises linked to non-financial benefits, including such aspects as: (i) improving livelihoods (in capacity building, managing environmental and socio-cultural impacts, increasing empowerment, improving infrastructure, and dealing with gender and migration issues); (ii) enhancing both partnerships (with the private or public sector); and (iii) participation (by involvement in planning and decision-making processes, strengthening community organizations'[1] capacity in management and negotiation, and making possible the overall improvement of social capital. All these benefits can be achieved only in a peaceful environment.

In 2013, the Myanmar peace process had been gaining speed, with the government signing a total of 13 bilateral ceasefires. The KNU had signed a bilateral ceasefire with the government in January 2012, and 'there was a desire from both sides to bring development to conflict-affected regions of Kayin State' (Carr, 2016, p. 4). Based on an exploratory study for the region, four high potential areas for the development of Kayin State were identified: tourism, agriculture, telecommunication and manufacturing (Carr, 2016). Following this assessment, the PeaceNexus Foundation started to facilitate a large multiple-stakeholder consultation, consistently supported by bilateral (sometimes formal, sometimes informal) consultations with government at both the state and union level, with the KNU and with different communities around Kayin State. The first large-scale consultation event was a workshop on 'Community Involvement in Tourism and the Peace Process' held in the capital city of Kayin State, Hpa-an, in February 2014 and co-hosted by PeaceNexus (PN), the HSF and the MTF. The approximately 70 participants included representatives of government, the KNU, religious leaders, civil society organizations and the private sector (MoHT, MTF, HSF, & PeaceNexus, 24–25 February 2014a).

During the second consultation meeting, entitled 'Responsible Tourism Development in the Kayin State: Stakeholder Dialogues,' which was held in Taungoo in May 2014, the idea of a 'tourism development working group' first arose (MoHT, MTF, HSF, & PeaceNexus, 14–15 May 2014b). At this point, it was decided that the findings should be presented to Kayin State officials, so the next meeting took place in Hpa-an in September 2014 and was entitled 'Responsible Tourism Development in Kayin State: High-Level Stakeholder Meeting.' Discussion at this meeting led to the identification of Thandaung Gyi as a site with high potential for tourism development in respect to its favourable cool climate, the scenic mountainous and forested area, the history as so-called colonial hill station and its rich cultural traditions. As Carr (2016, p. 5) expressed on behalf of PeaceNexus:

> This posted a challenge however, as at the time no foreigners were allowed to visit Thandaung Gyi. It took significant time to secure permission to visit the town, and when the team arrived the municipal officials were noticeably

worried that there would be problems. After spending one night there, however, they relaxed significantly, laying the foundation for future cooperation.

Moreover, the fact that the foreigners – all staff of HSF, PN and MTF – were committed to this project and were willing to be the first pioneers spending the night in Thandaung Gyi demonstrated that sometimes supportive development agencies, in their role as facilitator, must carefully cross a red line to convince the locals that new boundaries can be set up.

The decision was then made to hold the first Thandaung Gyi Tourism Development Working Group (TTDWG) meeting in December 2014 (Figure 7.2). This was attended by more than 25 representatives of the township administration, the KNU and the town church. At this meeting, it was agreed to give the group a three-part structure: an overarching advisory board with KNU, CSOs and government as members; a community-level implementing body; and a supporting body comprising organizations from outside the community such as HSF, PeaceNexus and MTF (later replaced by Myanmar Responsible Tourism Institute – MRTI). According to Carr (2016, p. 5), 'it was made clear that the activities of the group would reflect community priorities, and that the activities would be implemented by community members' – again, an important achievement in a country where the tourism sector has until recently been mainly controlled by a handful of local companies with strong connections to the former military government.

Following the first meeting of TTDWG in December 2014, the group was able to operate throughout 2015 and 2016. At intervals of approximately 2–3 months, meetings were organized to discuss topics such as: (i) structure, objective and vision of TTDWG; (ii) assessment visits to nearby tourist sites; (iii) licence approval process for bed and breakfast (B&B) guesthouses, including overnight stays for foreigners; (iv) hospitality and village guide training; and (v) establishment of a tourism information centre. All these activities were implemented accordingly with the technical and financial support of various International,

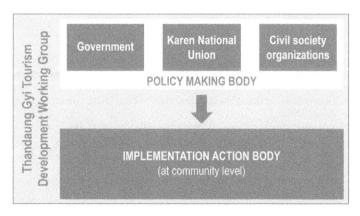

Figure 7.2 Structure of the Thandaung Gyi Tourism Development Working Group (TTDWG)

NGOs ((I)NGOs). The support of skilled foreign volunteers (CUSO, universities) who stayed for several weeks in Thandaung Gyi was very helpful in this regard. However, during a workshop on organizational development of TTDWG in May 2016, it became apparent that the working group need to be more 'institutionalist' in order to improve the capacity to operate sustainably without support from external organizations. As a result, a vision statement and objectives were defined and approved by all members (Schott, 2016, p. 8):

> Vision: 'We aim to establish a community-based organization that promotes responsible tourism development in the Thandaunggyi region, and acts as a role model, supporting locally owned tourism-related businesses, educating the community and helping to conserve natural and cultural resources. The organization aspires to provide a model approach to peace building and help to facilitate free movement in the Thandaunggyi region.'

Additionally, eight objectives were developed, related to the vision and strongly linked to sustainable development topics such as the conservation of natural resources, the maintenance of Kayin culture and environmental management, but as well to become a role model and sharing knowledge on community development in post-conflict areas.

On 26 October 2016, the TTDWG organized a follow-up of the first conference, the 'Thandaung Gyi Community Tourism Development' Conference in Hpa-an, again in strong collaboration with HSF, PNF, MoHT and MRTI. More than 100 participants took part in this event. The audience, again a mixture of representatives of the public and private sectors (including representatives of tourism organizations, such as hotel and tour operator associations), NGOs and 20 members from Thandaung Gyi, discussed the main opportunities and challenges faced so far during the development of community tourism (PeaceNexus, MRTI, TTDWG, MoHT, & HSF, 2016). It was again highlighted by members of

Table 7.2 Objectives of TTDWG

Objective 1	To provide a platform for information exchange for locally owned tourism-related businesses and development actors
Objective 2	To spread economic benefits among the local community
Objective 3	To educate and raise awareness of local communities about conserving natural resources
Objective 4	To provide skills development and capacity building in tourism and hospitality
Objective 5	To promote and provide guidance for sustainable principles (waste management, hygiene, monitoring and evaluation, etc.)
Objective 6	To establish role models for CBT in the region
Objective 7	To maintain Kayin Culture and revive traditional crafts and activities
Objective 8	To share knowledge and lesson-learned on community development in post-conflict areas in Kayin State

Note: CBT, Community-Based Tourism.
Source: PeaceNexus et al. (2016, p. 9)

TTDWG, that the main achievements in tourism and peace-building had been the increasing number of tourist arrivals after the ceasefire agreement in Thandaung Gyi and that the community tourism is part of a trust-building process between the conflicting actors, the Myanmar army and the KNU. However, it was also stressed by the group that the aspect of safety and security is crucial as some areas are still restricted (not only, but also due to landmines) (PeaceNexus et al., 2016). In response, a 'safety and security' poster was created (Figure 7.3).

Figure 7.3 Advice for a safe stay in Thandaung Gyi

Source: Compiled by Myanmar Responsible Tourism Institute with support of Hanns Seidel Foundation

Importantly, in 2015 and 2016, KNU and government representatives also attended the majority of TTDWG meetings, providing a forum for direct exchange between these individuals:

> For example, during opening statements in one early meeting attended by the Township Administrator and the local KNU commander, the KNU commander criticized at length the government army's actions in the region, discussed the limitations of the ceasefire agreement, and noted the Karen's people's rejection of the 2008 Constitution. He then acknowledged the government's efforts in reaching a ceasefire, and affirmed the KNU's commitment to uphold it. In his remarks, the Township Administrator explained clearly that the majority of the villages in the Thandaunggyi areas remained under the control of KNU, and stated that activities outside of the town itself should be cleared with both the government and the KNU.
>
> (Carr, 2016, p. 6)

The early meetings contained several such exchanges. While the management of these relationships could be challenging, in every case, both parties stayed committed to the process. As Carr (2016, p. 6) correctly states, the process was successful due to the careful consultation process undertaken at the beginning of the project:

> This was likely due in large part to the commitments to the project secured in advance from both governmental regional authorities and the KNU Central Committee, which speaks to the need for gradual and multi-level consultation to ensure projects are supported by both side. Ultimately however after the voicing of grievances both parties were willing to work together and were pragmatic in contributing to the discussion of the group.

This statement confirms what was described earlier regarding successful components of the stakeholder process in tourism and peace-building: the willingness to facilitate several meetings of various organizations in different forms and at different levels over a more extended timeframe and to allow people with different perspectives to express and discuss their views.

Tourism assets in Thandaung Gyi

Thandaung Gyi and its surroundings (Figure 7.4) have interesting tourism potential, with beautiful mountains and forests, numerous viewpoints, the Naw Bu Baw (Prayer) Mountain, a waterfall, creek, hot spring and a rock garden. Extensive tea, coffee and cardamom plantations surround the town. Important cultural and religious buildings, among them churches and chapels, a pagoda and a temple, an old British Fort and the Karen New Year Mountain, are interesting as prominent colonial buildings, including a still operating tea factory. At several places, shops sell local products, some especially to tourists, e.g. souvenirs and local coffee, tea

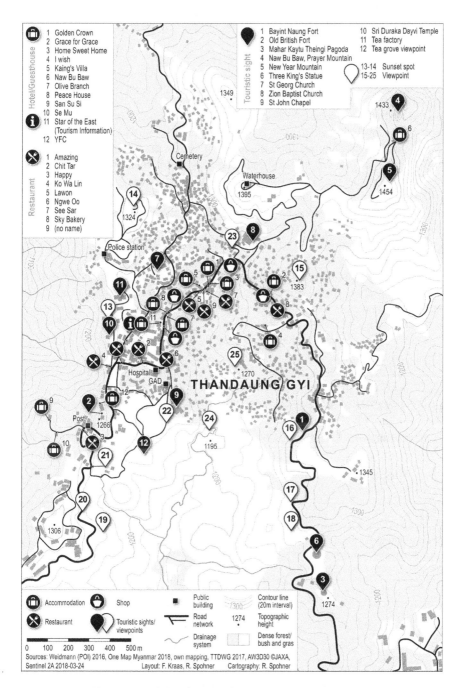

Figure 7.4 Tourism assets of Thandaung Gyi

and cardamom products. The yet unspoilt, hardly developed naturalness of place and people is often emphasized in interviews with tourists.

Benefits of tourism in Thandaung Gyi

The development and expansion of Thaundaung Gyi as a tourism destination has led to a range of benefits for the community, though many are hard to measure. Important first outcomes are raising numbers of domestic tourists and the initial permission for foreigners to visit Thandaung Gyi, followed by permission to stay overnight in 2014. The number of tourists is estimated at between 80,000 and 150,000 day tourists (mostly domestic and religious tourists); overnight tourists account for about 30–40 per week during the peak season between September and April (2016–2017; interview with a local government official), mostly staying at B&B guesthouses and homestays.[2] Ultimately, the process of early tourism development until August 2018, the time of writing, has led to the approval of 12 accommodation and B&B licences for Thandaung Gyi – the first in the country – which has allowed guesthouses also to accommodate foreign visitors.[3]

This licence approval has set a precedent for Myanmar as a whole, and the TTDWG experience has been shared at several conferences in Myanmar – however, three years later, by mid-2018, the national situation had still not changed and Thandaung Gyi was so far the only place with such a special permit.[4] Based on this permit, Thandaung Gyi has now 12 B&Bs and guesthouses (see Figure 7.4), accompanied by nine restaurants.

Beyond these concrete changes, there are less tangible benefits related to the goals mentioned above that will ultimately affect all parties (Table 7.3).

The examples of achievements in Table 7.3 demonstrate that tourism can be used as a tool for internal peace-building by using tourism as a backdoor for collaboration and relationship-building. What is required for improvements in the

Table 7.3 Goals that need to be achieved for successful stakeholder processes and achievements in Thandaung Gyi

Goals	Achievements in Thandaung Gyi
Trust-building between different stakeholders	Positive relationships were built up by religious leaders, supported by external facilitators (PN, HSF) by providing space for informal relationship-building between government and the KNU, where they could work on an issue that was not directly related to peace – in this case, tourism. As Carr (2016, p. 6) pointed out, 'Interviewees reported observing light-hearted exchanges between government and KNU representatives during coffee breaks at meetings.'
Forward-looking and constructive cooperation between societal actors	These first meetings have led to effective collaboration among the government, the KNU and the local community members (including religious leaders).

Goals	Achievements in Thandaung Gyi
Innovative solutions to existing economic or social challenges	Because tourism has been identified as one of the focal economic sectors in this ceasefire area, innovative goals have been set up, such as the licencing of B&Bs, which will allow overnight stays by foreigners and the visit to the tea factory by tourists.
Higher quality, and broader acceptance, of decisions	Owing to meetings arranged at the state and national levels with high-level authorities, the case of Thandaung Gyi is widely accepted as an example of good practice in Myanmar.
Ownership of, and commitment to, implementing agreed-upon results	Because of the history of conflict in the area, community groups historically had little opportunity to mobilize in Thandaung Gyi and had almost no say in the development of the area. The establishment of the TTDWG provided the community with an opportunity to organize, and the partners in the supporting body were able to provide advice on how to manage such a group over time and how to relate to external stakeholders (see Carr, 2016, p. 6).
Collective responsibility for change	These consultative and structured meetings and workshops took place at different levels with stakeholders from different sectors and with differing interests and points of view. Ultimately, they resulted in the successful design of a joint intervention for change. After the first official meetings, all stakeholders agreed to commit to a collective responsibility for change by setting up TTDWG as a joint activity.
Sustainable outcomes	In addition to the institutional strength gained in setting up TTDWG, Thandaung Gyi, as a new domestic tourism attraction, will achieve positive economic incomes.
Long-lasting cooperative structures	The structure, vision and objectives of TTDWG have changed – and will continue to change – as they adapt to the forthcoming political and tourism realms.

Source: Compilation Nicole Haeusler, based on Kuenkel et al. (2011, p. 18)

tourism sector are (as mentioned in several interviews by tourists who have visited the place): improved advertisement and marketing of the colonial and hill-station related history of Thandaung Gyi and of the favourable natural conditions of the mountain area, including the connections with Taungoo; provision of more background information and precise maps with the location of major natural, scenic, cultural and religious tourist attractions within Thandaung Gyi and safe hiking trails around the town of different durations (e.g. to its tea and cardamom plantations, to the waterfalls and the different prayer mountains); and improved overall hygienic and waste situation. Several guests further stressed the importance of development being in local hands as they fear the danger of 'over-development' if external or foreign investors come in, which could destroy the unique, unspoilt natural and authentic character of the destination and the local community.

Lessons learned and outlook

This chapter has illustrated how a town that was once wedged between the forces of two armies for decades – the Myanmar army and the KNU – became an emerging domestic tourism destination within just a few years, with significant impacts not only on economic growth, but also in building a certain trust among different groups of stakeholders. The experience of this case study provides the following lessons within the discussion of tourism and peace:

1   When government and ethnic armed group representatives work together at the local level, it can be an effective means of improving livelihoods in post-conflict communities by using tourism as a tool.
2   Together with stakeholders from the (local) private sector and the civil society, the emerging multiple-stakeholder cooperation can be a solid starting point for a new win-win-situation in tourism.
3   The investment and involvement of the local private sector as motor of community tourism development is important when embedded in an in-depth knowledge of the local, place-based socio-economic setting. Concerns are raised that if external and (inter)national investors appear, their activities would push out and destroy the local enterprises and income-generating chances. This could also lead to mistrust and problems between the stakeholders involved and growing disparities within the community.
4   In the case study, a particular, mediating role was taken by Christian religious leaders who are reinforcing the conflict parties' willingness to cooperate for growing peace by tourism-related activities. They are supported by the actions and attitudes of the local population.
5   When working in conflict-affected environments, it is important for supporting development partners to budget for longer staff time as such projects require time, patience, perseverance and persistence, for as it is necessary to understand the context and parties involved, the development of relationships can take a long time.
6   It also takes time to see whether the working group is inclusive across the whole community, and promote, if possible, broad-based participation with all stakeholders. The establishment of such a working group usually attracts the most interested and engaged community members, but this can raise questions regarding the participatory approach: 'it took a while to work out the connections between the group members' (Carr, 2016, p. 8). In order to understand this context, we recommend applying a rapid community appraisal or a more substantive method called 'Creative Organizational Cultural Assessment (COCA),' which analyzes all but a few aspects of organizational and community cultures on short-term contracts (Häusler, 2017).

7   It yet remains to be seen whether tourism development will become an initial facilitator of wider economic development or will languish as an opportunistic, small, and temporary niche economic feature in times of fragile peace.

8   Furthermore, it is important to define key outcomes and indicators in terms of relationships and community empowerment. According to Carr (2016, pp. 8–9):

> when working in complex conflict-affected contexts, there needs to be a shift in emphasis away from standard development outcomes. While this may not be realistic for many development actors, this project had a full year dedicated solely for assessment and consultations. Once the TTDWG was formed, there were clear limits imposed by the absorption capacity of the local community. . . . As a consequence, this project would fare poorly if measured by standard development metrics: it has been demanding in terms of staff time and staff salaries, with minimal disbursement in the community itself. Yet if conflict-affected communities are to be reached in a way that is sensitive to the challenges of the context, this is necessary.

Of course, the understanding of the context in communities affected by conflict is not only related to the ethnic group of the Karen/Kayin, but to all such communities.

While the last point is of importance for development agencies interested in supporting such a stakeholder process, it reaches further. By seeking to empower communities in conflict-affected areas (or post-conflict/ceasefire areas) using tourism as a tool, it is essential to emphasize and act based on the priority and principle of sustainability. This project is ongoing, and TTDWG still requires continuous coaching, in regard to facilitation of skills and organizational development by allowing a higher level of participation of new community members committed to tourism businesses. In order to avoid growing disparities, community spirit and social cohesion is required. Development needs time, and trust building requires personal encounters and responsibilities.

Notes

1   For example, tourism village committees, youth groups and women's groups.
2   According to non-published research undertaken by the Hanns Seidel Foundation in March 2018, five homestays and eight guesthouses had an average of 100 guests per month between December 2017 and February 2018. Detailed figures are not available.
3   Foreigners are still not allowed to stay in guesthouses or B&Bs in Myanmar, only in hotels (minimum of ten rooms).
4   The owners of the B&Bs in Thandaung Gyi have to apply at an annual basis for the reregistration. All over the country, it is still difficult to get a registration for a B&B with permission for foreigners to stay there overnight.

References

Carr, T. (2016). *Peacebuilding and community-driven tourism development in Kayin state: The Experience of the Thandaunggyi tourism development working group, 2012–2015.* Lausanne and Yangon: PeaceNexus. Retrieved 7 July 2018, from https://peacenexus.org/wp-content/uploads/2016/08/TTDWG-Case-Study-_11-08-2016.pdf

Core, P. (2009). Burma/Myanmar: Challenges of a ceasefire accord in Karen State. *Journal of Current Southeast Asian Affairs, 28*(3), 95–105.

Ekeh, C., & Smith, M. (2007). *Minorities in Burma* (Briefing). Retrieved 8 August 2013, form www.minorityrights.org/?lid=3546

General Administration Department (GAD). (2018). *Thandaunggyi township.* Thandaunggyi. General Administration Department (GAD).

Häusler, N. (2017). *Cultural due diligence in hospitality ventures: A methodological approach for joint ventures of local communities and companies.* Cham: Springer.

Hudson, S. (2016). Let the journey begin (again), the branding of Myanmar. *Journal of Destination Marketing & Management, 5*, 305–313.

Kipgen, N. (2015). Ethnicity in Myanmar and its importance to the success of democracy. *Ethnopolitics, 14*(1), 19–31.

Kraas, F., & Häusler, N. (2016). Tourismusentwicklung in Myanmar. *Geographische Rundschau, 68*(9), 52–57.

Kraas, F., Spohner, R., & Myint, A. A. (2017). *Socio-economic atlas of Myanmar.* Stuttgart: Franz Steiner Publishers.

Kuenkel, P., Gerlach, S., & Frieg, V. (2011). *Working with stakeholder dialogues. Key concepts and competencies for achieving common goals. A practical guide for change agents from public sector, private sector and civil society.* Potsdam: Collective Leadership Institute.

Lawson, B. (2018, 14 August). Letter: To – do list for tourism is only a start. *The Myanmar Times.* Retrieved 9 September 2018, from www.mmtimes.com/news/letter-do-list-tourism-only-start.html

Mercer, D. (2018). Marketing Myanmar: The religion/tourism Nexus in a fragile polity. In R. W. Butler & W. Suntikul (Eds.), *Tourism and religious issues and implications* (pp. 161–181). Bristol: Channelview Publications.

Ministry of Hotels & Tourism (MoHT). (2012). Responsible tourism policy. *Nay Pyi Taw.* Retrieved 19 July 2013, from www.hss.de/fileadmin/suedostasien/myanmar/downloads/120901-Responsible-Tourism-Policy-Myanmar.pdf

Ministry of Hotels & Tourism (MoHT). (2013a). *Policy on community involvement in tourism.* Nay Pyi Taw. Retrieved 19 July 2013, from www.hss.de/fileadmin/suedostasien/myanmar/downloads/130501-Policy-on-Community-Involvement-in-Tourism-Myanmar.pdf

Ministry of Hotels & Tourism (MoHT). (2013b). *Myanmar tourism master plan 2013–2020.* Nay Pyi Taw. Yangon: Ministry of Hotels & Tourism.

Ministry of Hotels & Tourism (MoHT). (2018). *Welcome to Myanmar: Statistics.* Retrieved 9 September 2018, from https://tourism.gov.mm/publications/tourism-statistics/

Ministry of Hotels & Tourism (MoHT), Myanmar Tourism Federation (MTF), Hanns Seidel Foundation (HSF), & PeaceNexus. (2014, 24–25 February). *Project report: Pilot workshop in Kayin state on community involvement in tourism and the peace process.* Hpa-an. Yangon: Ministry of Hotels & Tourism.

Ministry of Hotels & Tourism (MoHT), Myanmar Tourism Federation (MTF), Hanns Seidel Foundation (HSF), & PeaceNexus. (2014, 14–15 May). *Responsible tourism development in Kayin state: Stakeholder dialogues.* Taungoo. Yangon: Ministry of Hotels & Tourism.

Panyakom, S., & Waters, T. (2018). *Myanmar's nationwide ceasefire agreement: Challenges and opportunities on the path to peace-building in Myanmar: A case study of Karen National Union (KNU).* Unpublished Conference Paper.

PeaceNexus, Myanmar Responsible Tourism Institute (MRTI), Thandaunggyi Tourism Development Working Group (TTDWG), Ministry of Hotels and Tourism (MoHT), & Hanns Seidel Foundation (HSF). (2016). *Thandaunggyi community tourism development.* Conference Report, Hpa-an.

Renard, R. D. (1987). Minorities in Burmese history. *Sojourn: Journal of Social Issues in Southeast Asia, 2*(2), 255–271.

Schott, B. (2016). *Report.* Facilitation Workshop "Organisational development of the Thandaunggyi Tourism Development Working Group (TTDWG)", 2–4 May, Yangon.

Smith, J. (1902). *Ten years in Burma.* Cincinnati: Jennings & Pye.

South, A. (2011). *Burma's longest war: Anatomy of the Karen conflict.* Amsterdam: Transnational Institute.

Suntikul, W., & Rogers, P. (2017). Myanmar opening for tourism. In R. W. Butler & W. Suntikul (Eds.), *Tourism and political change* (pp. 123–137). Oxford: Goodfellow Publishers Ltd.

8 Tourism in Chilas, Pakistan

A destination under crisis

Tazayian Sayira and Hazel Andrews

Introduction

This chapter is a discussion of a place that has suffered from a mixture of natural and anthropogenic crises. In terms of the latter, these have taken the form of external and internal conflicts. The first instance refers to the negative media associations of Pakistan with terrorism following the terror attacks of 9/11. In the second instance, terror attacks have also occurred locally. In addition, conflict arises locally when outside agencies brought in to aid development do not consider local sensibilities in the establishment of their development plans.

The discussion is based on tourism in an area of north Pakistan known as Gilgit-Baltistan, but specifically Chilas in the province of Khyber Pakhtunkhwa (KPK, also known as NAP – Northern Areas of Pakistan). The data are based on field research undertaken in Chilas in the period 2010–2012 involving participant observation and the use of interviews. Since then, tourism developments in the region have been followed by examining reporting in the Pakistani media as well as the use of telephone, Skype and WhatsApp correspondence with informants from Chilas, the Pakistan Tourism Development Corporation (PTDC) and the Department of Tourism, Hazara University Pakistan in 2017–2018.

Locating Chilas and tourism

Chilas is situated within the administrative district of Diamer, a place that has long been attractive to outsiders, receiving attention, according to one research informant (2014) from geologists, botanists, archaeologists and historians as well as tourists and hunters. Part of the place's appeal is its location on the famous, ancient Silk Road (now called the Karakoram Highway), linking Europe with China. Chilas is situated on the left bank of the Indus river at a height of about 914 metres above sea level at the foot of the Nanga Parbat mountain, which acts as a wall against the monsoon winds. It is connected to the Chinese cities of Kashghar and Tashkuragan via the Gilgit, Sust and Khunjerab mountain passes. There is an airport, but this is not currently used by passenger airlines. In terms of natural resources, the area is known for its gold; along the banks of the Indus River, gold washers (Maruts) can be seen searching for gold in the water. The

Chilas community owns private montane alpine forests and receives a free grant of timber and firewood from the government of Pakistan. Chilas and the surrounding villages – for example, Thalpan and Shatial – are also known as the meeting point of the world's two greatest civilizations: the Indus valley civilization and the Ghandhara civilization (Dani, 1983). In addition, Chilas is surrounded by the world's highest mountain ranges, i.e. the Himalayas, Pamir, Karakoram and Hindu Kush. Besides the mountains, the area also contains many natural and cultural riches, including ancient rock art, the site of an ancient Buddhist university and a population with unique cultural practices, all of which are attractive to tourists and would satisfy quests for otherness and authenticity (Gandhara Trails, 2012).

Despite the attractive scenery, the area has not thrived in terms of tourism development, due in large part to problems with communication media and the association of the area with terrorism (Sayira & Andrews, 2016). The latter became especially problematic following the attack on the World Trade Center in 2001 and the ensuing military action in Afghanistan. One perception of Pakistan is that it is a terrorist ridden country and generally an unsafe environment in which to travel (Sayira & Andrews, 2016). This is not to say, however, that there is no tourism.

According to a 2018 report by the World Travel and Tourism Council (WTTC 2018), tourism is a growing industry in Pakistan and its direct contribution to GDP is increasing. Predictions are that tourism will continue to grow in the period 2018–2028. As part of this trend, international arrivals for 2017–2018 show an increase compared to the preceding decade. The WWTC figures are based on an analysis of 185 countries in 25 regions of the world. According to the report, the future of travel and tourism in Pakistan is promising. Table 8.1 gives an overview of travel and tourism economics in Pakistan, based on the WWTC report.

Table 8.1 Travel and tourism: economic statistics of Pakistan

Travel and tourism – direct contribution to GDP (2017)	43rd in ranking	US$8.8 billion
Total direct contribution to GDP (2017)	42nd in ranking	US$22.3 billion
Travel and tourism – direct contribution to employment (2017)	12th in ranking	14,928 jobs
Total direct contribution to employment (2017)	13th in ranking	38,940 jobs above world's average
Travel and tourism investment	37th in ranking	US$3.9 billion
Real growth in direct contribution towards GDP in 2018	38th in ranking	5.9% above world's average, i.e. 4.0%
Real growth in direct tourism-related employments in 2018	76th in ranking	2.8% above world's average, i.e. 2.4%
Real growth in travel and tourism investment in 2018	80th in ranking	5.2% above world's average, i.e. 4.8%

(*Continued*)

Table 8.1 (Continued)

Travel and tourism – direct contribution to GDP (2017)	43rd in ranking	US$8.8 billion
Long-term growth (2018) in travel and tourism direct contribution to GDP	23rd in ranking	5.8% p.a. above world's average, i.e. 3.8%
Long-term growth (2018–2018) and direct contribution to employment	71st in ranking	2.7% above world's average, i.e. 2.2%
Long-term growth (2018–2018) visitors' exports	12th in ranking	6.4% above world's average, i.e. 4.1%

Source: Adapted from WTTC (2018)

This trend in tourism growth has also been reported within Pakistan. According to an article in the Pakistani daily English language paper *Dawn*, improvements to security has meant 'tourism in Pakistan has increased by 30 percent over the past few years' (25 April, 2018). *Dawn* also reported on statistics held by the PTDC which gave figures of 1.75 million tourists in Pakistan in 2017, out of which 30% were domestic tourists (*Dawn*, 2018, 25 April); the other 70% were international visitors, returning immigrants and traders. Additionally, Khan (2017) states that the KPK province in which Chilas is situated has seen a huge increase in the number of domestic tourists since 2015. However, Khan (2017) also observes there is still a need to promote tourism at an international level, and to overcome issues relating to 'inadequate infrastructure, negative travel advisory to international tourists, boarding and lodging, poor connectivity through air and road, NoC (non-objection certificate) requirement for foreigners to visit northern areas, trust deficit in private and public sectors, poor tour operators . . . no skilful workers in the industry' and ineffective 'marketing and branding' of tourist destinations in Pakistan, as well as the lack of federal government level coordination of marketing to promote Pakistan as an international tourism destination (Khan, 2017).

In the case of Gilgit-Baltistan (GB) specifically, there are no tourist arrival statistics and the *Dawn* reports of poor conditions to facilitate tourism, for example 'bad roads, lack of accommodation and communication facilities is troubling foreign and domestic tourists in GB' (*Dawn*, 23 June 2018). In terms of tour guides in Chilas, 'there are no skilful tour operators or tour operating agency in Chilas – there are a handful of self-proclaimed local tour operators who would damage the rock carvings . . . sometimes break them into pieces to give them to tourists as souvenirs' (male informant, former staff at PTDC in Chilas, 2018). 'We still see so many tourists coming to the region but there is no proper system of recording them . . . the tourist information centre is always closed and no one bothers' (local male, a returning emigrant, 2018).

There is an increased number of private tour agencies and tour guides since 2014 but due to the worsening conditions of KKH in Kohistan and Diamer districts and lack of standard accommodation facilities, nobody encourages tourists to visit these areas unless tourists are mountaineers or trekkers . . . it isn't cost effective either to ruin your vehicles on KKH passing Kohistan and Diamer . . . but there is a hope of Diamer dam to be completed and then it seems like Chilas is going to flourish.

(male, former staff at PTDC, 2018)

Tourism and anthropogenic crises and conflicts: violent conflicts

Anthropogenic crises, including consecutive reoccurrences of violent conflicts, mainly terrorism and intra-region discomfort, have been hugely influential to the way that Chilas has developed and how its community engages with the 'outside world.' To understand the impacts that these crises and conflicts have had, we will begin by establishing how they are defined and how they impact diverse communities.

In terms of anthropogenic crises, Jha (2010) describes them as those that have occurred due to human negligence, error or the failure of manufactured systems. As such, anthropogenic crises take the form of, for example, conflicts, crimes, civil disorder, terrorism and war. It seems an obvious point, but when a major crisis occurs, the local population may be left without shelter and basic amenities (Patel & Hastak, 2013, p. 95).

In the situations that Patel and Hastak (2013) highlight, a site becomes an under-crisis destination (UCD), and when that place is a tourist destination, or potential tourist destination, the flow of tourists will be disrupted. This will also occur when government agencies external to the site of the disaster develop prohibitive travel strategies towards the destination (see, for example, Bianchi's [2007] paper on the travel ban to Kenya following a terrorist attack). Recovery for a UCD is dependent on various factors: for example, the response of the local community to the incident, and the support available from relevant institutions – including governments and aid agencies – to help the destination recover (Jha, 2010).

The impacts of crises and conflicts are as diverse as the different places in which they occur, but the economic strength of the country will have a significant influence on recovery. For the most developed and wealthiest countries, although they will face different levels of crises, which are, at times, financial crises, they generally have the necessary financial, technological and medical reserves, along with knowledge and skills, to mitigate and overcome disasters more quickly than poorer nations. Also, the impacts of crises are mainly lower than those on developing countries. By contrast, developing and poor regions of countries too often lack the resources, knowledge and skills to prevent or mitigate crises effectively or respond to them in a manner that enables a quick recovery (Jha, 2010).

In terms of conflicts, destinations can suffer as a result of both internal and external disputes.

Pakistan, for example, is reported to be a place where violent conflicts occur in the form of terrorist attacks, with suicide bombers targeting sites of worship, crowded places and foreign embassies (Usmani, 2017). Korstanje and Clayton

(2012) note that where terrorism is driven by an ideological hatred of Western culture and adherence to strict religious beliefs, the promotion of tourism is severely impeded. In relation to Pakistan, Briam noted that Pakistan's tourism has suffered as a result of 'local conflicts' and that 'terrorism' and 'political instability' have a 'direct negative impact on a country's tourism' (2017, p. 32). Additionally, ongoing border disputes with India and Afghanistan as well as 'mutual allegation of supporting terrorism' is another cause of instability in the region (Heidelberg Institute for International Conflict Research, 2017, p. 177). As Richie (2004, 2008) observes, crises have different scales of impact on different communities and tourists. For example, crises and conflicts cause stress, insecurity and anxiety in tourists resulting in them not visiting UCDs (Coombes & Jones, 2010).

Post-crisis development

Peace conferences, peace talks, treaties and third-party involvement, e.g. United Nations organizations, are known tools to ease the level of inter- or intra-national conflicts. To take effective control over crises and conflicts, the National Counter Terrorism Authority (NACTA) of Pakistan was established under the Ministry of Interior in 2008 to plan and develop strategies in order to counter extremism and terrorism in Pakistan (NACTA, 2017) working alongside the existing Anti-Terrorism Act (1997) and Anti-Terrorism Court that was established in 1997. With the formation of anti-terrorism bodies, the rate of terrorism-related activities dropped in Pakistan between 2016–2017 compared to the previous decade (Anwar, 2017; Global Peace Index, 2017).

Crisis management, often involving allocating resources to projects, is quite obviously used to aid recovery in post-crisis and conflict situations (Rosenthal & Pijnenburg, 1990). However, recovery is not immediate. As Arain notes, 'the complex and multifaceted processes of post-disaster recovery and reconstruction extend well beyond the immediate period of restoring basic services and life support infrastructure' (2011, p. 68). That said, Hayashi (2012, p. 193) claims that, 'disasters reveal the deeper layers of society's structure and individual psychology, which are hidden beneath the surface of the social fabric in peaceful times.' This suggests that at times of crisis, the existing structure of a community will be influence the speed of recovery.

Similarly, Arain (2011) argues that the degree of economic development, the type of political leadership, the organizational skills within the community and the existing welfare (in terms of health and education) of the public will also influence the extent of the effects of disasters. Further, De Sausmarez (2007, p. 281) notes, 'the speed of recovery depends not only on the extent of the damage caused by the disaster or crisis but also on how quickly the status quo can be re-established.' He states that there are four 'aspects of post crises recovery: . . . the restoration of confidence, the part played by the media, the role of the stakeholders, and the speed and appropriateness of the response' (De Sausmarez 2007, pp. 281–282). He goes on to suggest that of central importance to post-crisis recovery for tourism is regaining confidence from both international and domestic markets. In this respect 'the importance of the part played by the media during and after a crisis must not be underestimated' (De Sausmarez 2007, p. 282). The reason the role of the media is so important is because as De Sausmarez (2007, p. 282) notes, 'the public's perception of an incident is strongly influenced by how the media reports it.'

As previously noted, NAP has suffered as a result of external conflicts, but there have also been a number of internal struggles; for example, a terrorism-related incident in 2013 known as the Nanga Parbat Massacre and the burning of 12 girls' schools in Diamer, Chilas and Gilgit-Baltistan in July 2018 by militants in a bid to stop women's education. The efforts to promote education for women was a part of the post-crisis development project established with the help of the United Nations following a major earthquake in the region in 2005.

Although negative these violent incidents in some respects had a positive outcome as they attracted attention from numerous different national and international agencies including government, NGOs, researchers, communication and media departments, and crisis management units with short and long-term development plans for the entire region. A number of schemes have been established to encourage entrepreneurial activity. For example, the national government initiated the Prime Minister's Youth Business Loan to encourage young entrepreneurs. This programme enables young people, but mainly women, to start their own businesses subsidized by finances available from the National Bank of Pakistan and the First Women's Bank Limited. Another project is the Economic Transformation Initiative Gilgit-Baltistan (ETI, 2018) which is a seven-year gender- and youth-sensitive community-driven development programme introduced by the Gilgit-Baltistan government. It is co-funded by the International Fund for Agricultural Development and aims to improve income, reduce poverty and decrease malnutrition in the rural areas of Gilgit-Baltistan. This programme is aimed at both women and men in Gilgit-Baltistan, with a view to increasing their skills and giving access to more land to produce local goods and aid regional development. This programme also aims to facilitate positive local community interaction with government officials and by corollary increase trust and confidence issues between local communities and development organizations. To improve levels of education in rural and under-privileged areas of which Diamer is an example the government of Pakistan has introduced a free reimbursement scheme. In this scheme, scholarships are provided to students from under-privileged and remote areas, for example Chilas, to encourage higher educational attainment with a view to enabling youths to better compete in the national job market (Shah, 2017; see also www.sbp.org.pk/smefd/circulars/2013/C10.htm, accessed 7 November 2018).

The area is also starting to benefit from externally funded projects. For example, the China-Pakistan Economic Corridor (CPEC) is a project based in Pakistan but financed by China. It aims to improve the transport infrastructure between both countries to improve trade. An objective of this project is to develop industrial and financial cooperation between both countries in relation to agriculture, tourism, education, human resource development and healthcare, and to increase the safety and security of the region with a view, among other aims, to develop employment opportunities. Research by Shah (2017) indicates that CPEC has had a positive impact, in terms of growth, on the tourism and hospitality sectors in Gilgit-Baltistan.

Arain argues that, 'post-disaster rehabilitation and recovery programs should be seen as the opportunities to work with communities and serve local needs' (2011, p. 68). However, in Chilas, this has not happened because planners and developers did not consult local people before drawing up and implementing their plans. In the words of one local male informant, 'they have not included local community' and specifically 'elders of the community' or 'local policy makers in decision making and planning especially when they decided to appoint female teachers from outside the region . . . build girls' school . . . drown our saqafat[1] to construct the Diamer Basha dam and to complete these projects hiring labour outside Chilas.' Consequently, the local people did not respond well to government initiatives for post-crisis recovery development projects. One way to encourage local involvement is to utilize proper and region-friendly communication and media channels to raise awareness of pre- and post-crises and conflicts projects in an attempt to involve local people in the process. This is perhaps especially pertinent for countries based in Asia, which is known to be a 'disaster-prone region' and appears to suffer from a high number of crises and conflicts compared to other parts of the world (Hayashi, 2012, p. 190).

Community and tourism

The idea that tourism brings benefits to a local community is well-rehearsed in the academic literature (see, for example, Buckley, 2000; Aronsson, 2000). This chapter acknowledges that local communities have a direct connection with tourism, involving a complex set of relationships between various stakeholders, but argues that progress in tourism development procedures can lead to progress in community development, and vice versa. In addition, the more tourism takes place in a destination the more that community is affected, and, as Paul (2004) notes, so is the long-term development of that community.

In the case of Chilas, it was notable that young people felt a sense of loyalty to their place of birth and that by giving them access to training and financial resources, they could potentially increase productivity in relation to tourism. For this to be effective, they need also to take part in decision-making processes. For example, as one male Chilas respondent commented, 'our elders should be consulted before making any plans for Chilas to avoid any confrontation from locals later in the stage.' He was referring in particular to a form of local committee and police called called Zeeto Kalak and Biyaak. Those who sit on these groups act as judges, policy- and decision-makers for the local community in Chilas. Consulting representatives of the local community is needed because it is the local community members who know best about their own traditions, culture and environment. In addition, as Reisinger and Turner argue, 'different cultures have different rules in interaction, [so] the expectations and meanings of rules also differ across cultures. . . . Thus, members of different cultures may misunderstand

and misinterpret the rules of others cultures' (2003, p. 139). Correspondingly, one community's characteristics and attitudes towards tourism and development initiatives differs from that of another as has been shown in Chilas in relation to opening more girls' schools, the construction of the Diamer Basha Dam, labour exchange and the free movement of tourists to the region. Members of the local community have expressed concern about what they identify as a potential loss of local traditions and threats to cultural values and assets. As Briassoulis and Straaten (2000) and Paul (2004) argue, a tourist destination is the home of a community, and changes to the environment that make that home may cause concern for the local people.

During fieldwork in 2011, depopulation was identified as an issue for Chilas. According to one informant, emigration could, in part, be attributed to conflicts of interest and feelings of a lack of 'empowerment within the local community, minimal education and employment opportunities in Chilas' (male, 23, works abroad). A majority of Chilassi community members in the age range 20–40 migrate to other parts of Pakistan or go abroad to seek education and employment opportunities. Very few, if any, return. Of those who do come back, most do so to retire, at which point the returnee's children leave in search of their own employment and educational opportunities. This is the cycle of depopulation in Chilas, as one informant (male, 27, works abroad) advised, 'when my father came back from Saudi Arabia by that time my papers were ready to go there for work. . . . Many people of this area have got the same history as ours because of no availability of standard education and work opportunities here.' To address the issue of depopulation, Fernandes suggests, 'The development of tourism could stem or even reverse this depopulation pattern by serving as a revitalisation process that could contribute to the survival of the communities thereby improving the quality of life of the residents' (2009, p. 19).

Because tourism is labour intensive and is a suitable option for less developed countries (LDCs), where unemployment is a major problem (Cole, 2007a, 2007b), it is also a cause of stress for members of the Chilassi community who are mainly skilled in agriculture-related activities but not skilled in construction and do not possess the necessary abilities to participate in the proposed structural development of the region. It might prove to be more cost effective to hire a trained labour force from outside a region rather than investing financial and physical resources in training the existing potential labour force. This can lead to internal conflict, which has been the case in Chilas. However, if the local population were included, there could be long-term benefits, as one respondent noted, 'investing in local people you have a life time of labour in the region' (informer, male, mountaineer: 2018). Also, employing local people could help to address depopulation. Additionally, Jurowski (2007, 2008), Fleischer and Tchetchik (2005) and Bianchi (2000) note that tourism development in an area may result in people returning to their place of origin, which in turn could support traditional cultural and agricultural practices. The possible help that tourism can bring to a community should not only benefit the most dominant and elite sectors, but also be advantageous to marginalized groups. Cole (2007a) argues that in the provision of low-skilled roles, tourism development in LDCs can potentially be helpful for women and other marginalized groups, who may not possess formal skills or education, but who are nevertheless employable.

Similarly, research by Shah (2017) shows that there is a greater demand for skilled labour in the region, but supply is minimal due to youth emigration. To try to address the issue of unskilled labour, the government of Pakistan has started several training programmes, including the Prime Minister's Youth Skills Development Programme, which is targeted at unemployed young citizens of Pakistan, specifically of rural areas such as the Diamer district, to enable them to become more employable (Prime Minister's Youth Programme, 2018). It is hoped that in the case of Chilas, youth participation in the programme will help reduce outward migration of young Chilassi community members and the region will be able to use its human resources to full potential to aid in the economic development of the area.

Despite all the initiatives, the Chilassi community still resists development policies, especially when the aforementioned Biyaak is not formally consulted. Yoon, Gursoy, and Chen (2000) note that 'Because tourism relies heavily upon the goodwill of the local residents, their support is necessary for the development, successful operation, and sustainability of tourism' (2000, p. 364). In the case of Chilas, the lack of community involvement threatens the sustainability of tourism development. Tourism development is well-known for the benefits it can bring to under-crisis communities, yet they require something more. Such communities also look to tourism to facilitate both national and international recognition of Chilassi cultural practices and traditional activities such as the Biyaak's authority, networking with outsiders, awareness/education, training, anything that can boost their self-esteem and contribute to their empowerment. Economic benefits alone are not enough, as one interviewee from Chilas explained, 'we do not expect earnings from tourists but the recognition,' referring to a perceived lack of acknowledgement of Chilassi cultural practices and traditions with specific reference to the Biyaak and rules associated with the segregation of men and women (male, 34, works abroad).

These findings from Chilas are contrary to those of Jurowski (2007, 2008) and Fleischer and Tchetchik (2005), who argue that tourism works to bring home emigrants and in turn revitalize the local culture and traditions. In Chilas, it seems that the way in which tourism has been initiated has led to dissatisfaction in the area that has contributed to people leaving. The impacts of depopulation in Chilas on local culture and heritage has been exacerbated because it has suffered from crises and conflicts, among them propaganda by unskilled channels of communication media (Sayira & Andrews, 2016), and tourism development that is insensitive to local sensibilities about how to behave, especially in relation to the treatment of women. There is, therefore, a need to pay attention to community attitudes in different socio-cultural and traditional contexts. Tourism development depends upon the basic factors of social exchange theory, which include perceptions of costs and benefits, and trust regarding institutions and power (Nunkoo & Ramkissoon, 2011) that need to be considered when dealing with local communities regarding tourism development matters.

With regards to the study of communities in developing countries, there are several other factors that need to be addressed, especially men's and women's attitudes towards development of communities and destinations. For instance, changes to the existing social conditions makes women more vulnerable in the field of development and the tourism sector in Chilas. Contrary to Bisnath's (2001) arguments, age, class and race are not the first things that establish an understanding of women's position in Chilas. Rather, it is the general socio-cultural setup in the area that has fixed women in a particular position in the development process. For instance, it was noted during the research that a woman of any class and age who would go out to work faces opposition from her male family members, as well as her peers. This is the cultural setup, which states, 'the duty of a woman is to look after children, the husband's family, to do household chores . . . she should not go out for work otherwise the community won't see her as a respectable woman' (male, 42, shopkeeper).

In addition to the cultural and traditional barriers to women's development in UCLDC, it is observed that low male literacy rates in Chilas have a relationship with women's progress in the development process. Those men with lower levels of literacy tend to be more conservative in their attitudes towards women than those who are more literate. In terms of considering women in the study of LDCs, the attitudes and educational levels of the men in the same environment need also to be considered as major obstacles for women's progress and their role in development.

Conclusion

This chapter highlights the fact that destinations struck by crises and conflicts attract attention from various support agencies (both national and international) and research institutes. Chilas has experienced internal conflict with a number of terrorism-related incidents between 2013–2018. In addition, the place has suffered as a result of external conflicts, most notably the 'war on terror' that has seen Pakistan as a whole, but NAP in particular, receiving much negative press that is detrimental to the promotion of tourism. In addition, the area is prone to natural disasters such as earthquakes and avalanches. This chapter highlights that places experiencing or that have experienced crises and conflicts attract attention from organizations and agencies external to the region. In Chilas, this has resulted in a number of proposals, including the plans for the construction of the Diamer Basha Dam; the establishment of an open-air museum to exhibit the unique, ancient rock art under threat from being submerged by waters from the dam; and introducing women's education.

In Chilas, following the various crises and media attention, there have been notable changes. For instance, several national and international NGOs and non-profit organizations have initiated steps to improve the lives of local people by providing them with opportunities for education and training to enhance their employability. They have also opened schools specifically to promote girls' education in the area.

Despite its problems, those tourists who do reach Chilas praise the generous hospitality of the local people. For example, one informant said, 'I have never seen kind and hospitable people like them before' (male tourist, 50s, USA); and another commented, 'Local people are very warm and welcoming' (male tourist, Japan, 47). Therefore, although the Biyaak maintains traditional ways of life that may lead to portrayals of Chilas as a 'very rigid' and 'conservative' community, the experiences of these two male tourists was of a welcoming environment. Indeed, many tourists are repeat visitors to Chilas because of their positive experiences and the development of friendships with local people. However, the lack of women's voices in speaking about community involvement, or their experiences as tourists, suggests that gender segregation remains an issue – and as such, Chilas maintains its reputation as a place in which 'women are nowhere to be seen' (Khan, 2013).

Sayira and Andrews (2016) have highlighted the fact that negative communication media in the region is mainly due to political rivalry between Chilas and surrounding tourist destinations, a situation made worse by the lack of representatives from the Chilassi community in the tourism ministry or the planning and development departments. However, the crises and conflicts suffered in the region have drawn greater awareness to the area, and due to media attention and first-hand information from tourists, the Diamer district in which Chilas is situated attracted a great deal of attention from government development authorities during the period 2008–2018. As discussed in this chapter, the region now receives financial and physical support for the education and skills development of young and female community members. In addition, they are receiving support to start small-scale businesses. All these initiatives would, if they deliver on their objectives, appear to bode well for the continued development of tourism in Chilas, as well as the development of the area as a whole. Some of the projects specifically target women. In so doing, they hold out the hope that women will be provided with a platform for their voices to be heard. At the same time, if successful, women's engagement with the initiatives will allow them to demonstrate that their contributions to the development of tourism and their local communities is something to be recognized and valued. In this, there is hope that these women will cease to be seen as marginal people, but rather will take centre stage in moving their communities forward for their own benefit and that of others.

Note

1 This is an Urdu word to describe local heritage referring to rock art and old houses.

References

Anwar, M. (2017, 19 November). Extremism watch: Report: Noticeable decline in Pakistan's terror fatalities in 2016. *VOA News*. Retrieved 14 October 2018, from www.voanews.com/a/noticeable-decline-in-pakistan-terror-fatalities/4125523.html

Arain, F. M. (2011). An Information Technology (IT) based approach for enhancing prompt and effective post-disaster reconstruction. *Business Review*, *6*(2), 67–79. https://doi.org/10.1016/j.proeng.2015.08.422

Aronsson, L. (2000). *The development of sustainable tourism*. London and New York, NY: Continuum.

Bianchi, R. (2000). Migrant tourist workers: Exploring the contact zones of post-industrial tourism. *Current Issues in Tourism*, *3*(2), 107–137.

Bianchi, R. (2007). Tourism and the globalisation of fear: Analysing the politics of risk and (in) security in global travel. *Tourism and Hospitality Research*, *7*(1), 64–74.

Bisnath, S. (2001). *Poverty in a globalizing world at different stages of women's life cycle – globalization, poverty and women's empowerment*. United Nations Division for the Advancement of Women (DAW) Expert Group Meeting on "Empowerment of women throughout the life cycle as a transformative strategy for poverty eradication," 26–29 November, New Delhi. Retrieved 12 August 2017, from www.un.org/womenwatch/daw/csw/empower/documents/Bisnath-EP3.pdf

Briam, K. M. (2017). *Managing cultural tourism in a post-conflict region – the Kurdistan Federal Region of Iraq* (PhD Thesis). University of Nottingham for the degree of Doctor of Philosophy. Retrieved from www.ethos.bl.uk

Briassoulis, H., & Straaten, J. (2000). *Tourism and the environment: Regional, economic and policy issues*. Tilburg, The Netherlands: Kluwer Academic Publishers.

Buckley, R. (2000). Neat trends: Current Issues in nature, eco and adventure tourism. *International Journal of Tourism Research*, (2), 437–444.

Cole, S. (2007a). Beyond authenticity and commodification. *Annals of Tourism Research*, *34*(4), 943–960.

Cole, S. (2007b). Entrepreneurship and empowerment: Considering the barriers – a case study from Indonesia in tourism. *An International Interdisciplinary Journal*, *55*(4), 461–473.

Coombes, E. G., & Jones, A. P. (2010). Assessing the impact of climate change on visitor behaviour and habitat use at the coast: A UK case study. *Global Environmental Change*, *20*(2010), 303–313.

Dani, A. H. (1983). *Chilas: The city of Nanga Parbat-Dyamar* (p. 120). Islamabad: Chilas Region.

Dawn – The Business and Finance Weekly- Pakistani Newspaper. (2018, 25 April). 1.75m tourists visited Pakistan in 2017, says PTDC. Retrieved 27 October 2018, from www.dawn.com/news/1403800

Dawn – The Business and Finance Weekly- Pakistani Newspaper. (2018, 23 June). Bad roads, lack of accommodation trouble tourists in GB. Retrieved 28 October 2018, from www.dawn.com/news/1415524

De Sausmarez, N. (2007). Crisis management, tourism and sustainability: The role of indicators. *Journal of Sustainable Tourism*, *15*(6), 700–714.

Economic Transformation Initiative (ETI). (2018). *Economic transformation initiative government of Pakistan and international fund for agriculture development Gilgit Baltistan*. Retrieved 12 January 2018, from www.etigb.com.pk/economic-infrastructure/

Fernandes, C. (2009). *Community engagement with local associations and in the development of tourism: A case study of residents of three parishes in the Peneda Geres National Park*. (PhD Thes.), Bournemouth University, Bournemouth.

Fleischer, A., & Tchetchik, A. (2005). Does rural tourism benefit from agriculture? *Tourism Management*, *26*(4), 493–501.

Gandhara Trails. (2012). Chilas. Retrieved August 2018, from www.gandharatrails.com/destinations/details/chilas.html

Global Peace Index. (2017). *Global peace index*. 2018 Report by Institute of Economics and Peace. Retrieved 14 September 2018, from http://visionofhumanity.org/app/uploads/2018/06/Global-Peace-Index-2018-2.pdf

Hayashi, T. (2012). Japan's post-disaster economic reconstruction: From Kobe to Tohoku. *Asian Economic Journal – Journal of the East Asian Economic Association, 26*(3), 189–210. http://onlinelibrary.wiley.com/doi/10.1111/j.1467-8381.2012.02082.x/full

Heidelberg Institute for International Conflict Research (HIIK). (2017). *Conflict barometer*. Retrieved July 28, 2018, from https://hiik.de/2018/02/28/conflict-barometer-2017/?lang=en

Jha, M. K. (2010). Natural and anthropogenic disasters: An overview. In M. K. Jha (Ed.), *Natural and anthropogenic disasters: Vulnerability, preparedness and mitigation* (pp. 1–16). New Delhi: Capital Publishing Company.

Jurowski, C. (2007). Tourism and intercultural exchange. *Annals of Tourism Research, 34*(2), 551–552.

Jurowski, C. (2008). Community development through tourism. *Tourism Management, 29*(2), 394–396.

Khan, M. S. (2017, 11 December). Reviving Pakistan's tourism. *Dawn – The Business and Finance Weekly- Pakistani Newspaper*. Retrieved 26 October 2018, from www.dawn.com/news/1375837

Khan, R. S. (2013). Why I hate Chilas. *Dawn – The Business and Finance Weekly- Pakistani Newspaper*. Retrieved 11 December 2017, from www.dawn.com/news/1022046/why-i-hate-chilas

Korstanje, M. E., & Clayton, A. (2012). Tourism and terrorism: Conflicts and commonalities. *Worldwide Hospitality and Tourism Themes, 4*(1), 8–25.

NACTA. (2017). *National counter terrorism authority annual report 2017*. Retrieved 14 October 2018, from https://nacta.gov.pk/publicationsreports/

Nunkoo, R., & Ramkissoon, H. (2011). Developing a community support model for tourism. *Annals of Tourism Research, 38*(3), 964–988.

Patel, S., & Hastak, M. (2013). A framework to construct post-disaster housing. *International Journal of Disaster Resilience in the Built Environment, 4*(1), 95–114.

Paul, L. K. H. (2004). *Tourism development in less developed countries: The case of Cambodia* (PhD diss.). Bournemouth University, Bournemouth.

Prime Minister's Youth Programme (2018). Retrieved January 2018, from http://youth.pmo.gov.pk/index.php

Richie, W. B. (2004). Chaos, crises and disasters: A strategic approach to crisis management in the tourism industry. *Tourism Management, 25*(6), 669–683.

Richie, W. B. (2008). Tourism disaster planning and management: From response and recovery to reduction and readiness. *Current Issues in Tourism, 11*(4), 315–348.

Reisinger, Y., & Turner, L. W. (2003). *Cross-cultural behaviour in tourism: Concepts and analysis*. Burlington: Elsevier and Butterworth-Heinemann.

Rosenthal, U., & Pijnenburg, B. (1990). Simulation-oriented scenarios: An alternative approach to crisis decision making and emergency management. *Contemporary Crises, 14*, 277–283.

Sayira, T., & Andrews, H. (2016). Impacts of crises and communication media on place image: A case study of Chilas, Pakistan. *Journal of Destination Marketing & Management, 5*(4), 351–360.

Shah, A. S. (2017). *Study on producing skilled workforce for potential economic sectors in Gilgit Baltistan.* Retrieved 14 July 2018, from www.skillingpakistan.org/files/1/Study%20of%20Potential%20Economic%20Sectors%20in%20Gilgit%20Baltistan.pdf

Usmani, Z. (2017). *Pakistan suicide bombing attacks: Most authentic count of suicide bombing attacks in Pakistan (1995–2016).* Retrieved 12 January 2018, from www.kaggle.com/zusmani/pakistansuicideattacks

WTTC. (2018). *World travel and tourism council, report: Travel and tourism economic impact 2018 Pakistan.* London. Retrieved 28 October 2018, from www.wttc.org/-/media/files/reports/economic-impact-research/countries-2018/pakistan2018.pdf

Yoon, Y., Gursoy, D., & Chen, S. J. (2000). Validating a tourism development theory with structural equation modelling. *Tourism Management, 22*(1), 363–372.

9 The moderation effect of branding on destination image in a crisis-ridden destination, Zimbabwe

Joram Ndlovu and Farai Chigora

Introduction

Over the past decade, discourses in destination marketing have analyzed the role of branding in influencing the consumption of tourism destination brands. Hence, the promotion of tourism products has raised various questions among practitioners and academics alike. Currently, there is a dearth of literature on the emerging contradictions in marketing distressed destinations, branding, image and positioning places for market leadership during or after a crisis. Nonetheless, globalization has intensified marketing pressures for tourism destinations to promote their operations at national, regional and international levels (Klimek, 2013, p. 27). As a result, the dynamics of the 21st century have resulted in immense competition, causing organizations in the tourism and hospitality business to adopt new strategic management and operational marketing processes (Gustavo, 2013, p. 13). Globally, the immense returns generated from tourist destinations have caused governments to invest to a greater extent in developing the tourism industry, with the aim of improving its market share (Blanke & Chiesa, 2013). Branding has become one of the important marketing strategies in withstanding the competitive nature of the tourism industry when offering products and services to tourists (Yusof, Ismail, & Omar, 2014, p. 1). Scholars and policy-makers for tourism destinations are not simply focusing on attracting more tourists, but on improving the competitive position of their destinations (Alberti & Giusti, 2012). For this reason, destination marketing has become a fountain for future growth and sustainability of tourism destinations in an increasingly globalized and competitive tourist market (UNWTO, 2013). Thus, destination branding is not a new area, and that is why its relevance is increasing and the tourism industry is largely continuing to grow (Theodhori & Qirici, 2014). Consequently, it has become one of the hottest concepts to both marketers and scholars in destination marketing (Morrison, 2012).

Destination branding is an important concept that has gained popularity in the study of tourism marketing and management (Meža & Šerić, 2014, p. 78). It is responsible for improving visibility of even small destinations, and those popularly known throughout the world. Various areas under destination branding have been explored through research, though there is still a knowledge gap (Qu, Kim, & Im, 2011), especially in relation to the effect of the media on destination branding.

Meža and Šerić (2014, p. 78) note that destination branding is an integrated marketing process, while Da Silva Oliveira (2015) argues that this is a strategic focus in the development of tourism destinations. Morrison (2013) adds that destination branding is a comprehensive concept, since it calls for maximum stakeholder involvement and participation. Thus, branding is all about creating ownership that can extend into the future, which helps in differentiating and improving the identity of a tourism destination (Gartner & Ruzzier, 2011, p. 471). The discussions reveal how destinations use branding as a tool to improve their visibility in a crowd dominated by other similar players. Therefore, the benefits that tourists as consumers attain are mainly in the form of the ability to make tangible and visible their potential travel experience, such that they will not have to search for more information about a destination when they want to visit. So, there is a need to get views and insight in the area of destination branding, with the aim of improving existing strategies dominating the global tourism market.

The main reason for branding in Zimbabwe was to give the destination a name that could improve its identity and global market position. Branding is a continuous process that calls for destination marketers to rebrand over and over again, in order to align a brand concept (Ndlovu & Heath, 2013, p. 947) with the changing tastes, preferences and views of the potential tourists. In order to survive and adhere to the changing market demands, Zimbabwe as a tourism destination has also adopted branding as a marketing strategy, with the aim of holding a high-valued global market position through an extensive brand identity. The problem lies in understanding whether the continuous rebranding exercise is in line with changing needs of the market, or whether it was due to a failure of the brand to attract tourists. The need to maintain a steady growth in tourism gains has increased pressure on marketers and promoters of Zimbabwe as a destination as they strive to attract and convince current and prospective tourists to partake in their tourism offerings. However, their efforts have been affected by a number of factors, mainly the hyper-inflation and unemployment in the country, which have destroyed both the supply and demand for tourism in Zimbabwe. Consequently, the destination has become increasingly expensive, and social unrest has grown. From a political perspective, the country witnessed conflicts and other forms of mayhem, which led to stereotyping and its labelling as being unsafe for tourism. The objective is to demonstrate the extent to which a destination brand could address issues about brand association, perception, image and positioning. Thus, the distinctive nature of the chapter is that it explores the importance of destination branding and its effects on influencing consumer buying behaviour. Based on the importance of branding a destination, the chapter examines the historical development of tourism in Zimbabwe, destination marketing strategies and policies and destination branding challenges in Zimbabwe during a crisis.

The Zimbabwean crisis and its setting

Zimbabwe is endowed with unique tourism products, and the country has been described as Africa's paradise (RETOSA, 2004, p. 8). It is home to the majestic

Victoria Falls and wildlife reserves, and is blessed with an extraordinary land-scape. The country is situated on a high plateau in southern central Africa, between the Zambezi and Limpopo rivers. It is a landlocked country that is bordered by Mozambique to the east and Zambia to the north, South Africa to the south and Botswana to the southwest. Being a unique and fascinating holiday destination, Zimbabwe's tourism industry has the potential to become one of the most important pillars of the country's overall economic sectors if all the available resources are fully utilized (ZTA, 2004). During the 1980s, after Zimbabwe had gained its independence, the new government decided to maintain the status quo as far as tourism was concerned. It continued to target the Western tourism market, which is characterized by high-spending tourists (Child, 1990, p. 4). During the period between 1980 and 1999, the tourism industry grew rapidly. This growth was reflected in the increase in the number of tourist arrivals and receipts from Western markets and in the construction of many hotels, lodges and restaurants. A considerable number of tour operators and travel agents were operating in the country (The National Consultative Forum, 2001, pp. 6–10). It was only in 1999 that, because of its controversial land reform policy, the country began to experience a sharp decline in the number of tourist arrivals. Therefore, it is evident that a tourism destination brand performance can be influenced by both internal and external factors. From a Zimbabwean perspective, the internal socio-economic and political factors have impacted negatively on the attractiveness of the tourism destination brand. As noted, reaction to these internal problems led external media to spread nega-tive publicity, which crippled the tourist arrivals and its brand. The decline was particularly marked in respect of the major Western markets. Consequently, the country suffered a major decrease in its tourism receipts (Sachikonye, 2005). For instance:

> Zimbabwe's tourism fortunes started changing in 2000, the same year politi-cal instability emerged in the country. The sources of political uncertainty in Zimbabwe in 2000 can be attributed to three events, namely: i) the process surrounding the referendum on the draft new constitution which failed to be adopted; ii) the spontaneous 'fast-track' land reform programme which was implemented immediately after the defeat of the draft new constitution, and iii) the heavily polarised parliamentary election in which the opposition won a significant number of seats for the first time in Zimbabwe's history.
>
> (Muchapondwa & Pimhidzai, 2011, p. 2)

In the period after 2002, the utilization of hotel accommodations remained low. Room occupancy rate fell by 4% from an average of 43% in 2004 to 39%, while bed occupancy rates declined by 2% from an average of 30% in 2004 to 28% in 2005 (Koech, 2011). As for clientele composition, the domestic market contrib-uted an average of 87% and the foreign market constituted the remaining 13% of hotel occupancies (ZTA, 2004). Tourism receipts remained low throughout the year, declining by 49% from US$193.7 million in 2004 to US$98.67 million in the year 2005 (Muchapondwa & Pimhidzai, 2011). The publicized causes of tourist decline included the following: fuel, food and water shortages; safety fears of tourists, mainly those from Western countries; high prices that made Zimbabwe an expensive destination, such as multiple connecting flights to Zimbabwe making travelling costs too high for tourists; and inhibiting visa costs and time-consuming logistical travel arrangements (ZTA, 2004).

Zimbabwe's economic crisis and subsequent hyper-inflation were preceded by several years of economic decline and mounting public debt (Zhou, 2016). Output fell 50% between 2000 and 2009, led by a decline in the country's major foreign-exchange cash crop, tobacco, which slid 64% in 2008 from 2000 levels (Koech, 2011). The Zimbabwean currency lost its value at exponential rates amid an imbalance between economic output and the increasing money supply. Thus,

> hyperinflation and economic troubles became so profound such that by 2008, they wiped out the wealth of citizens and set the country back more than a half century. At the height of hyperinflation, prices doubled every few days, and Zimbabweans struggled to save money, and see any real return on their money (ZTA 2011, p.10). For instance, businesses still quoted prices in local currency but revised them several times a day. The government attempted to quell rampant inflation by controlling the prices of basic commodities and services in 2007 and 2008.
>
> (Shumbambiri, 2016, p. 42)

> Authorities forced merchants, sometimes with police brutality, to lower prices that exceeded set ceilings. This quickly produced food shortages because businesses couldn't earn a profit selling at government-mandated prices and producers of goods and services cut output to avoid incurring losses. People waited for hours and days in long queues at fuel stations and stores.
>
> (Koech, 2011, p. 11)

While supermarket shelves were empty, a thriving black market developed whereby goods traded at much higher prices. Underground markets (popularly known as the black market, or 'World Bank' in Zimbabwean circles) for foreign exchange also sprang up in back offices and parking lots, where local notes were converted to hard currencies at much more than the official central bank rate.

Due to the turbulent environment, some businesses closed shop while some tour operators decided to relocate to other countries (Muleya, 2002). It should be noted that, although there was a significant increase in tourist arrivals between 2004 and 2008, this increase was mainly in respect of the Eastern and Asian markets. These tourists are seen as low spenders and their presence could not produce a complete revival of the tourism industry (ZTA, 2008). Researchers and labour and economic organizations have given varying figures of between 70–95% of unemployment, pointing out to the fact that by 2008, Zimbabwe's unemployment rate was the highest in the world.

> The Econometer Global Capital Report (2013) states that unemployment in Zimbabwe rose from 50% and rose to a peak of 95% by 2012. However, the Zimbabwe Statistical Agency gave a conflicting figure of the unemployment rate as 11% which has been rejected by analysts such as Robertson (2013) who have roundly condemned the Zim-Stats data collection instrument as flawed and lacking in both validity and reliability to the extent of grossly understating the unemployment figures.
>
> (Bhebhe, Sulochana, Muranda, Sifile, & Chavunduka, 2015, p. 7)

> The economic meltdown in the new millennium led to incessant closures of formal businesses and thousands of people were retrenched every year forcing them to join the IES. Most manufacturing industries performed below full capacity and the situation kept deteriorating during the years. In 2006 only 27% of the industries operated at full capacity. The situation continued to worsen as capacity dropped to 13% in 2007. By 2008, industries operated at 5% capacity.
>
> (Gumbo, 2013, p. 39)

Bhebhe et al. (2015) found that:

> ZimStat-USAID Central Business Register Inquiry Report (2014) painted a gloomy picture of the capacity of the economy to generate more jobs to absorb the ever increasing numbers of the unemployed educated youths. Findings of the Report showed that 59% of economic activity involved wholesale and retail trade including the sale of second-hand motor vehicles most of which are imported; only 11% of the operators were in the manufacturing industry; 9.2% were in educational services; 5% in other social services; 4.7% in accommodation and food services; Mining and quarrying made up 0.2% of the establishments; 30% of the businesses had an annual turnover of less than US$5,000; only 3% of businesses had an annual turnover of above US$1m; 82% of the business had less than four employees per establishment as at December 2012 and 60% of establishments were sole proprietorships and 19% private limited companies.
>
> (p. 51)

Transportation expenses, in particular, escalated disproportionately as a result of fuel surcharges (Greer, 2003, p. 2). Additional factors that contributed to creating a 'perfect storm" in the Zimbabwean situation included the outbreak of hand, foot and mouth disease in 2003, which caused Europe to ban the imports of Zimbabwean beef; the international market price of tobacco that fell drastically; the International Monetary Fund (IMF) and the World Bank suspended loan facility to the country; and the cyclical drought decreased the national agricultural output

(Greer, 2003, p. 2). These factors and their effects resulted in severe economic problems that have affected the image of Zimbabwe as a tourist destination (ZTA, 2010).

Historical development of tourism in Zimbabwe

In 1980, Zimbabwe gained its political independence from the UK and the name of the country concurrently changed from Rhodesia to Zimbabwe. The transformation of the country's name, from the colonially sanctioned to an indigenously crafted one, concurrently renamed the country's tourism destination. During recent decades, interest in the marketing of countries has grown substantially among academic researchers, formulators of public policies and businessmen (Elliot, Papadopoulos, & Kim, 2011). Thus, applying strategic marketing and branding techniques to countries has been seen as a powerful force for distributing global and cultural wealth, as well as economic development. Strategic marketing of places refers to improving the competitive position of a country in the global market by understanding the forces of the internal and external environments and a country's strengths and weaknesses (Kotler & Gertner, 2002). Hence, country branding activities have become significant not only for export markets, but also for attracting tourists, direct investments and talents to work in the country. The field of study of country branding can be featured as part of two other broader fields: product country image (PCI) and tourism destination image (TDI) (Nadeau, Heslop, O'Reilly, & Luk, 2008). TDI is typically defined as the beliefs that a person has of a particular destination such as certain country, whereas PCI refers to the perceptions about countries from the viewpoint of product evaluation and choice (Lindblom, Lindblom, Lehtonen, & Wechtler, 2017). Studies of country branding have shown that it can help different organizations (such as the ones in the tourism industry) to add value to their offerings.

According to Kotler and Armstrong (2011), a brand can be in the form of a symbol, name or logo that is used for identity by the customer. The statement shows that a name can be used as a branding tool, and changing the country's name to Zimbabwe in 1980 initiated its country's rebranding process. After independence, the tourism industry became one of the targeted pillars for economic prosperity in Zimbabwe (Zhou, 2013; Chibaya, 2013). This resulted in the formation of Zimbabwe Tourism Development Corporation (ZTDC) in 1981, a government body that was meant to be the planner and leader in managing the country's tourism investments (Chibaya, 2013, p. 85). The establishment of ZTDC coincided with the first tourism brand, named 'Discover Zimbabwe' (USAID, 2013). The aim of the brand was mainly to position and form unique identity of the Zimbabwe tourism destination on the global tourism market. However, the 'Discover Zimbabwe' brand failed to gain the expected mileage as a distinctive market-positioning instrument for Zimbabwe. There is limited literature on the issues that resulted in the failure of the 'Discover Zimbabwe' tourism brand, but since the Zimbabwe tourism industry was still at its growth and development stage, the brand did not appeal positively to the target market. Tourists' numbers continued to decline significantly. During the period 1982–1987, there were many reports in the international media regarding the dissident menace where tourists were killed in the Matabeleland region of the country. Other factors that led to the failure of the brand included the inability to consult relevant stakeholders, constructing effective policies and strategies for positioning the destination for market leadership.

In the year 1996, the government transformed the Zimbabwe Tourism Development Corporation into a new marketing oriented establishment known as Zimbabwe Tourism Authority (ZTA) (USAID, 2013, p. 12). The tourism body became a source of marketing vibrancy, justified by an increase in tourists' arrivals from 1,596,696 in 1996 to 2,249,615 in 1999 (ZTA, 2010, p. 1). Branding continued to be a key agenda of ZTA, such that the organization's inaugural rebranding of the tourism destination took the form of 'Africa's Paradise' (Chibaya, 2013). The new brand was meant to sell Zimbabwe as a paradise in Africa. However, the socioeconomic landscape then shifted (Ndlovu & Heath, 2013, p. 948), destroying the coordination of marketing activities. The historical performance of Zimbabwe as a tourism brand can therefore be measured in relation to changes in tourists' arrivals since year 1980, as summarized in Figure 9.1. In 1999, tourists' arrivals were at a peak of 2,249,615; followed by a decline to 1,966,582 in year 2000 (ZTA, 2011, p. 18). Therefore, the worst performance of the Zimbabwe tourism sector can be seen to have started in the year 2000, with the 'Africa's Paradise' tourism brand in place. As a tourist destination, Zimbabwe experienced an evolutionary cycle that is similar to the life cycle of a product in which sales increase as the product evolves through the stages of launching, development, maturity and, finally, decline. According to USAID (2013, p. 15), the years between 2000 and 2008 represented socio-economic stagnation and decline. Zimbabwean tourism could no longer be called a paradise (Chibaya, 2013, p. 87). ZTA (2011, p. 18) noted that 'the major factors that disturbed progress and the desire for a Zimbabwe tourism destination brand were, the political mayhem over the land redistribution programme, the 2008 violent elections and social outcry of the cholera disease'.

The land reform programme resulted in a chaotic state of affairs in the politics of Zimbabwe, wearing down the tourism destination brand immensely. There was an intensive political upheaval in Zimbabwe from the year 2000 onward. The Zimbabwean government – led by its first black president, Robert Mugabe, and the Zimbabwe African National Union Patriotic Front (ZANU PF) – engaged in a chaotic land redistribution led by war veterans and the majority black populace as they sought compensation for their commitment to liberation struggle. Before independence in 1980, large portions of land in the country were owned by a small British white minority, who were labelled Rhodesians, a name borrowed from their colonial leader, Cecil John Rhodes. The subsequent processes and measures that were applied by the post-independence government in redistributing the land antagonized the British property owners in Zimbabwe, together with their acquaintances in other Western countries. Fights and quarrels began in Zimbabwe as the white British settlers snubbed the land reform exercise. Thus, the Zimbabwe tourism brand could not survive the vengeful negative image created for the country by the international media. The media declared Zimbabwe

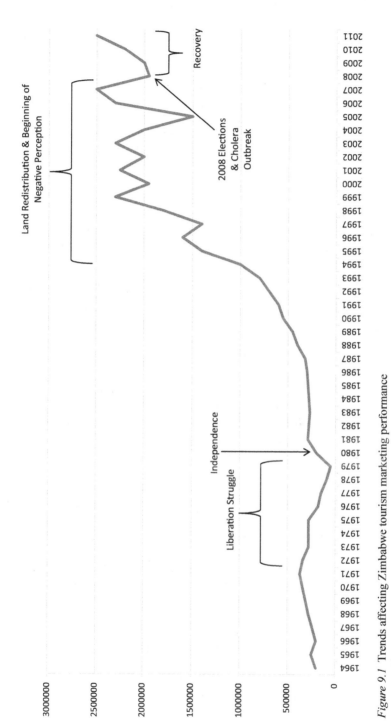

Figure 9.1 Trends affecting Zimbabwe tourism marketing performance

Source: Redrawn data from ZTA (2011, p. 18)

as a hostile and unsafe destination for tourism activities: 'the arrivals of tourists began to drastically fall in years after 2000, that is from 2,249,615 in year 1999 to 1,966,582 in year 2000 and further declined to 1,558,501 in the year 2005' (ZTA, 2011, p. 18).

Political conflict in response to the 2008 and 2013 presidential elections erupted between the two main political parties in Zimbabwe, the ZANU PF and the Movement for Democratic Change (MDC). The MDC, a rival to the ruling ZANU PF, announced to the world that the election results were fraudulent. The majority local populace also endorsed this message as true. The European Union and its Western allies, spearheaded by the UK, shared the same contention that there was no rule of law in Zimbabwe, and that the elections were not free and fair. ZANU PF resisted the efforts by MDC to contest the results, and fought back through the use of state owned media and other manipulative policies. The state of affairs in Zimbabwe worsened, resulting in confusion and unrest, undermining the country as a preferred tourism destination. According to ZTA (2011, p. 18), tourist arrivals fell from 2,505,988 in 2007 to 1,955,594 in 2008.

On 13 February 2009, the two main political parties in Zimbabwe, ZANU PF and MDC, formed a Government of National Unity (GNU), which helped to improve the image and perception signalling peace and stability in Zimbabwe. The GNU redirected the Zimbabwe tourism brand towards excellence. The positive effect was reflected in the yearly improved tourism receipts. The country's receipts from tourism grew from US$5,230,000 in the year 2009 to US$6,340,000 in 2010 and US$6,640,000 in 2011 (ZTA, 2011, p. 8). The period of the GNU was therefore understood as a period of tourism recovery as the country was then portrayed to be peaceful and politically stable (USAID, 2013, p. 15). The international media also responded through reporting this positive development in the country's political ascendancy by spreading favourable news headlines and content reflecting Zimbabwe as a safe tourism destination to visit. Unfortunately, the GNU was short-lived, operating for only five years, and it was dissolved in 2013, after ZANU PF won the presidential elections, reverting the state back to one-party governance. Once again, the elections were purportedly rigged, suppressing the will of the Zimbabwean populace. Perceptions and allegations over political instability resurfaced since the 2013 parliamentary and presidential elections were perceived to be fraudulent by the Western community. Various international media then responded by increasing negative publicity about the new state of affairs prevailing in Zimbabwe's politics. The dire position, image and identity of Zimbabwe as a tourism destination brand resurfaced with its political recovery becoming even more impossible.

Socially, Zimbabwe used a growth equity model after it gained its political independence, and the model was based on transforming the system governing the livelihood of the populace from capitalism to socialism (ANSA, LEDRIZ, & ZCTU, 2012). Thus, the government favoured the indigenous black majority through its management of vital social factors. The populace received free education and healthcare. The free provision of various social amenities meant that the government was running a budget deficit in order to restore society. Agriculture was the main sector sustaining the economy through its export market dominance, and likewise, Zimbabwe was likened to a 'Bread Basket of Africa.' However, since the country was agro-based, it experienced a huge disturbance from the severe droughts that hit the country every ten years, in 1982, 1992 and 2002. Agriculture could no longer sustain the country, and society started to experience alarming poverty. Regardless of their colonial background, the white farmers were far more productive in terms of agricultural output than the new settlers following the land redistribution programme, so Zimbabwe went from a food exporter to an importer and from a bread basket to a begging basket. As a result of the chaotic land reform programme, there was high agriculture-dominated structural unemployment, which resulted in social unrest and donor dependency of the populace. This was exacerbated by an outbreak of cholera between 2000 and 2008. Consequently, the social outcry and health threats created a bad image for the country. As a result, it was labelled as poverty stricken, and unfavourable for tourism. The survival of the brand was therefore threatened again.

Figure 9.2 shows Zimbabwe's historical tourism receipts in US dollars from 2001–2011.

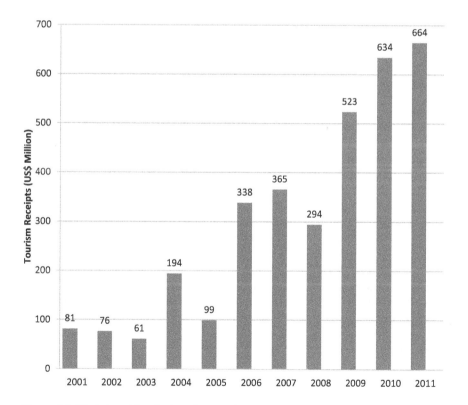

Figure 9.2 Zimbabwe historical tourism receipts

Source: Redrawn data from ZTA (2011, p. 49)

Economically, the tourism industry in Zimbabwe contributed a significant share to the national income in the years just after independence (Zhou, 2013, p. 886). According to the ZTA (2011, p. 49), the tourism receipts grew from US$38 million in 1980 to US$60 million in 1990 and US$232 million in 1996. This is more than 100% growth in revenue between 1980 and 1996. However, as shown in Figure 9.2, the economic vibrancy measured by tourism revenues in Zimbabwe's tourism sector could not continue in the years following the turn of the millennium. In the year 2001, the country received US$81 million from tourism, US$61 million in 2003, US$338 million in 2006 and US$294 million in the year 2008. These booms and slumps in tourism revenues have been mainly attributed to the hyper-inflationary environment that took precedence in the country between 2000 and 2008 (Chibaya, 2013, p. 87).

The loss in value of the country's currency resulted in tourism business establishments closing due to viability problems. The price of tourism products and services were soaring. Tourists plan for their holidays in advance such that they work with budgets for their future spending. Even though tourists from abroad could have found their currency much stronger in Zimbabwe during the hyper-inflation period, the daily changes in prices made planning very difficult. The Zimbabwean government issued the Z$100 trillion bill in early 2009, among the last in a series of ever higher denominations distributed as inflation eroded purchasing power. From 2007 to 2008, the local legal tender lost more than 99.9% of its value (Hanke, 2008). It became difficult for potential visitors to plan for a holiday in Zimbabwe, as their fully committed budgets would not match soaring prices when they came to make a planned visit to the country. By July 2008, when Zimbabwe's Central Statistical Office released its last inflation figures for that year, the rate had reached more than 231 million percent on a year-over-year basis (Hanke, 2008).

> The International Monetary Fund (IMF) put the annual inflation rate in September 2008 at 489 billion percent, with some independent analysts estimating it much higher. With economic decline and hyperinflation eroding the real value of accrued tax liabilities, budget revenue fell from almost US$1 billion (25% of GDP in 2005) to US$133 million (4% of GDP) in 2008.
>
> (IMF, 2009)

Shortly after the Z$100 trillion note began circulating, the Zimbabwean dollar was officially abandoned in favour of foreign currencies (Taylor, 2012). However, in the year 2009, the receipts from tourism started to increase. The improvement in tourism receipts was attributed to the introduction of multicurrency (whereby people were allowed to use different currencies in almost all transactions, such as the US dollar, South African rand and Botswana pula). The multicurrency brought about stability in the purchasing power of tourists, encouraging tourism exchange and revenues of tourism operators. Price stability encouraged savings and consumption of tourism offerings by both local and international tourists. Therefore, there was a restoration of confidence in the Zimbabwean tourism industry, sustaining a positive reflection of Zimbabwe as a tourism brand. The ZTA, as the leading destination marketing organization, responded by introducing another new tourism brand in order to restore identity and attain a new market position for Zimbabwe on the global market. 'Zimbabwe, A World of Wonders' replaced 'Africa's Paradise,' which had become associated with socio-economic and political upheaval (Ndlovu & Heath, 2013). The objective was to showcase the country's tourism destination brand by focusing on its natural wonders.

Destination marketing in Zimbabwe

The marketing of tourism should be taken as a strategic process, done by the leading marketers in a destination. Basically, a marketing strategy is used in order to improve the competitiveness of a tourism destination. 'It is the role of the destination marketing organisations to craft and structure marketing strategies that help in attracting more tourists at any given period in time' (Varghese, 2016, p. 103). It also requires the tourism destination marketers to be able to meet global standards, policies, guides and procedures, which include ability to meet sustainable development practices. The modern customer is highly sensitive to changes in the global tourism market, such that failure to move with the changes will deter success of any tourism marketing strategies. It is important to note that changes in information technology have also affected demand and supply of tourism globally. Technology has made it easier for destination marketers to construct marketing strategies that can reach potential tourists more easily around the world. In addition, customers have relied on the use of technology in order to select a destination to visit, and even view the attractions before making an actual visit. It is then important for tourist destinations to make use of technology as a strategic weapon in selling their tourism offerings.

The gifts of nature, which include animals, forests, landscapes and favourable climatic conditions, constitute the main attractions that have improved the inflow of tourism, resulting in a steady growth of tourism in Zimbabwe. As noted earlier, Zimbabwe was marketed as a tourism destination to countries in the West, including the USA and Europe. The marketing strategy was based on promoting 'Low Volume with High Value' tourism (Zhou, 2013, p. 890). This strategy was premised on serving fewer tourists, who are able to pay higher prices for their tourism activities. The strategy worked for some time, especially in the years between 1980 and 1999, as there was a high inflow of tourists from the targeted source markets (ZTA, 2011, p. 18). Zimbabwe as a tourism destination also engaged in a marketing strategy that was infrastructure-based in the early years after the country's independence. This strategy resulted in the establishment of hotels, travel companies and national parks, which then led to the establishment of three main tourism sectors in the country's tourism industry, namely accommodation, travel and resorts. These sectors became a basis for measuring performance of the Zimbabwe tourism brand in this study. The infrastructure-based strategy resulted in the formation of Rainbow Tourism Group and Africa Sun, which were owned by the government (Chibaya, 2013, p. 85). In addition, since wildlife in the

Zimbabwe tourism destination was another vibrant source of attraction, it resulted in the formation of Zimbabwe Parks and Wildlife Authority through a government act in 1982 (USAID, 2013, p. 16). This new organization was empowered to manage and market all the wildlife in Zimbabwe, including the 'Big Five' of Cape buffalo, elephants, leopards, lions and rhinoceros.

Marketing from a sector perspective can restrict the use of a single brand to sell and promote the tourism destination, since different individuals and organizations will ascribe different views and meaning of the brand they use for market identity and positioning. Therefore, even with this marketing strategy in mind, Zimbabwe as a tourism destination brand is still failing to attract more tourist inflow, despite expectations. Globally, the early years of mass tourism have proved to be a dominant driver for improved inflows and growth of the tourism industry (Harrison, 2015). The problem of engaging this concept as a basis for tourism development in a destination is that it can result in exceeding the carrying capacity, which will in turn destroy the environment and attractiveness of a tourism destination (Maggi & Fredellå, 2010, p. 2). This contradicts the agenda for sustainable management of tourism environments. From a marketing perspective, the strategy can result in the tourism destination losing its appeal to potential modern eco-tourists, who are environmentally conscientious. Some tourism destinations have reacted to this concept by resorting to individualized types of tourism. Individualized tourism marketing strategies are ones that targets specific types of tourists, rather than having a more broadly driven approach. There is still global development of this type of tourism, and Zimbabwe is still lagging behind, which could be a threat to improving growth of its global tourism market share.

Marketing through sustainable tourism is another aspect that has evolved globally, which has a direct effect on the marketing strategy of any tourism destination. A tourism destination can also be marketed from an accessibility perspective. Globally, destinations that are highly accessible have managed to market themselves and attract more tourists. Accessibility of a tourism destination is determined by availability of supporting infrastructure, mainly roads, railways, airports and seaports (Geza & Lorant, 2010). Zimbabwe as a tourism destination has faced challenges in strategically marketing its offerings from an accessibility perspective. This is because there are no links to some of the most promising areas of touristic activities in the country. Even in some areas where there is a link, the transportation networks have deteriorated due to lack of financial capital to refurbish and upgrade the infra- and super-structure that helps to improve accessibility. There is no access via air to various promising areas for tourist activities. This has hindered the Zimbabwe tourism destination marketers' ability to craft packages that encompass all tourism activities in the destination. There is the potential to improve tourism business in the destination if these gaps are addressed in potential touristic areas supported by effective marketing policies and strategies. Usually, tourists prioritize convenience while travelling. Cases where railway lines were vandalized reduced efficiency in travelling by train. The road network is dilapidated, with potholes due to lack of maintenance, making it difficult to travel and access other areas. Even after adopting the multicurrency monetary policy by dollarizing, post-hyper-inflation Zimbabwe still faces challenges on rebuilding public finances, instituting and maintaining credible policies to control government spending, reducing poverty and promoting economic growth.

Considering that Zimbabwe is a land-locked country, making it impossible to access the destination by sea, its marketability as a tourist destination is limited to some degree. Communication instruments play an important role in selling and marketing tourism offerings to potential and existing tourists. The marketing strategy of Zimbabwe as a tourism destination cannot be explained from a specific communication instrument perspective. The ZTA has used various marketing communication strategies in the past, but there is limited literature regarding the most effective type of instrument to use in promoting the destination. The instruments that have been used to promote Zimbabwe as a tourism destination include brochures, websites, newspapers, magazines and presenting in international conferences and exhibitions.

Brand equity in Zimbabwe's tourism sector

Brand equity refers to a brand's worthiness, measured by a combination of variables; namely brand loyalty, name awareness, perceived quality and potency of brand association, together with other key assets such as trademarks, patents, distribution channels and advertising (Kotler & Keller, 2012). The definition shows that the concept of brand equity is an amalgamation of brand awareness creation, image building and loyalty (Gartner & Ruzzier, 2011, p. 473). Destination managers should evaluate their brand equity elements against those of their competitors in order to strengthen their competitiveness on the market (Im, Kim, Elliot & Han 2012). Several reports and studies have been done on Zimbabwe's destination brand, but without directly analyzing the most dominant variable(s) that can lead to high destination brand equity. Pike, Bianchi, Kerr, and Patti (2010, p. 8) have noted that 'even with attempts to measure Consumer- Based Brand Equity (CBBE) of destination brands, there remain a lack of theory to evaluate its applicability in the tourism context thus there is no concrete agreement on the effective measurement of destination brands.'

The power of a brand is measured by the level of its brand equity and ability to be differentiated from other existing brands (Kotler & Armstrong, 2011, p. 243). There is negative Zimbabwe destination brand equity resulting from the tarnished image of the destination by various international media (Chibaya, 2013; Ndlovu & Heath, 2013). In addition, when using brand loyalty as a measurement, there is low brand equity, since the number of tourist arrivals have followed a downward trend over the years. It is therefore difficult to have lasting associates for Zimbabwe's destination and its brand, if corrective measures are not taken. According to Gartner and Ruzzier (2011, p. 472), 'brand equity can be viewed as the process of not only creating ownership for a particular brand but also the value of that ownership of which from a generic product perspective this value is reflected by additional monetary returns that comes from using a brand name.' Pike (2010, p. 125) has meanwhile noted that brand equity is commonly used term that represents brand performance, which is measured in financial value on the corporate balance sheet. This analysis can be related to Zimbabwe as a destination brand, as the revenues from the tourism industry have been staggeringly negative. However, the use of tourism revenues as a measurement of destination brand performance is debatable, since high volumes usually do not reflect high revenues and low volumes also do not mean low revenues. Traditionally, when Zimbabwe as a destination brand was at peak performance, the destination had low volumes of Western tourists with high value. Conversely, the periods associated with poor destination brand performance in Zimbabwe saw a high volume of tourists, with low values, especially after engaging the Look East Policy moving from a 'low volume-high value' to a 'high volume-low value' type of tourism. Therefore, destination brand performance might be measured using tourists' inflows, rather than purely relying on revenues. The reason for this is that brand followership highly reflects the destination's attractiveness in the market.

Destination branding challenges in Zimbabwe

The concept of branding is highly complex, involving many stakeholders for it to be successful. It requires intensive stakeholder consultation, and this is difficult because these stakeholders come from different ideological backgrounds and view the world differently. This makes branding a difficult concept to follow, since it is hard to achieve a common goal when the parties involved are from different backgrounds (Kaplan, Yurt, Guneri, & Kurtulus, 2010). Tourism destinations are an amalgam of many players, who directly and indirectly affect the overall performance of the tourism destination brand. The challenge is for the tourism destination marketers to be able to identify the key stakeholders that they work with closely to achieve a common goal. Even with the consultation of relevant stakeholders, it is difficult to convince them to buy in and share a common vision. The media industry becomes one of the crucial stakeholders in tourism destination branding.

Media publicity requires a huge budget, especially when the focus is on selling the whole tourism destination through a certain tourism destination brand. This is costly, as it requires acquisition of equipment and training of users to use modern communication applications. For the most part, the dynamism associated with the current 21st century requires destination marketers to continuously improve and adhere to modern media technologies. This makes media publicity a necessary subject for continuous research, and developments thus require more investment in terms of both financing and time. A tourism destination brand ought to be communicated to a mass of audiences. The brand message ought likewise to be widely spread. However, for the brand message to reach the targeted potential tourist, it depends on the media coverage. Some media are not able to reach large audiences, which then makes it difficult to improve performance of a tourism destination brand. Zhou (2016) notes that the tourism sector in Zimbabwe went through a rough patch characterized by very low international arrivals, capacity underutilization, economic sanctions, economic instability, bad publicity, withdrawal of airline carriers, catastrophic inflation, shortages of basic commodities and fuel and negative market perception. Poverty and unemployment rose to catastrophic levels, with 70% of the population in need of food assistance and a cholera epidemic claiming more than 4,000 lives (IMF, 2009). The global financial recession of 2008 and the general political conflict exacerbated the conditions. Other notable challenges included violent elections and human rights abuses. Consequently, Zimbabwe's bad image resulted in a massive decline in tourist arrivals, low occupancies recorded in hotels and closure of businesses (Chibaya, 2013).

Based on the described challenges, it should be noted that destination branding is a process that requires coordination of various parties, such that they share a common goal and spread a unified voice among target markets. Coordination of the destination brand exercise requires huge budget commitments. Various countries – especially those in the developing world, such as Zimbabwe – have limited budgets to run all sectors of the economy, which makes it difficult for them to set aside funds to perform a destination branding process. Various forms of communication are needed to spread news about the destination brand before and after it has been launched. The success of a branding exercise requires the destination marketing board to carry out road shows and other travel related promotion across the globe. Thus, destination marketers need to adopt new technologies, which could help in increasing brand publicity, identity and positioning. While destination branding has a moderation effect on destination image, the branding process require enormous financial capital, which is a challenge for many tourism destinations in developing countries in general and Africa in particular. Analysts have regarded Zimbabwe as a country that is financially insolvent and bedeviled by various economic, social and political problems, making it difficult to effectively rebrand and position itself for competitive advantage.

Conclusion

The aim of this chapter was to examine the effect of branding on destination image in a crisis-ridden country. The chapter discussed the importance of branding in moderating the negative effects of a crisis on the image of a destination. The use of the media in the publicity of tourism destination brands has helped in improving brand awareness, brand image, perceived brand quality, brand loyalty and brand association. The media uses various attributes to announce positive issues, improve visibility, identity and positioning of a tourism destination brand. However, the global media can also publicize problems, as has happened with Zimbabwe and is not as easily controlled as the state or local media. These attributes include the use of news headlines, news content and crafting of attractive news. Therefore, the effective use of media can lead to a better performance of the tourism destination brand. Zimbabwe tourism destination marketers should appreciate and engage the media, among others, in order to promote a vibrant tourism destination brand. However, it is also important to appreciate that there are other existing types of media that can also have a positive and a negative influence on the tourism brand. These include social media, broadcast media and direct media, which can also contribute a significant influence to the entire brand variables – mainly the destination image, brand loyalty and brand awareness. Tourists do not readily respond to hype, but want to know what they will get for their money. Repeated exposure to a brand could increase its familiarity and create brand awareness, but the building of an awareness campaign is often enhanced by the development of a slogan, visual symbols, tone of voice, design style and/ or a jingle. Therefore, brand awareness actively pairs the brand and the appropriate purchasing cues, which then create a positive image and effectively promote and communicate the brand in the process. The chapter concludes that branding under uncertain conditions – without changing the social, economic and political landscape – will only moderate the effects of a crisis, thus hindering successful rebranding and marketing of a destination.

References

ANSA, LEDRIZ, & ZCTU. (2012). *Pro-poor and inclusive development in Zimbabwe: Beyond the enclave.* Harare: Weaver Press, Ansa, and Ledriz.

Alberti, F. G., & Giusti, J. D. (2012). Cultural heritage, tourism and regional competitiveness: The Motor Valley cluster. *City and Society, 3*(4), 261–273.

Bhebhe, T. B., Sulochana, N., Muranda, Z., Sifile, O., & Chavunduka, M. D. (2015, September–October). The high unemployment problem among educated youths in Zimbabwe: Lessons that can be drawn from other countries. *IOSR Journal of Economics and Finance (IOSR-JEF), 6*(5), Ver. I, 2321–5925.

Blanke, J., & Chiesa, T. (2013). *The travel and tourism competitiveness report.* Geneva: World Economic Forum.

Chibaya, T. (2013). From 'Zimbabwe Africa's paradise to Zimbabwe a world of wonders: Benefits and challenges of rebranding Zimbabwe as a tourist destination. *Developing Country Studies, 13*(5), 84–91.

Child, B. (1990). *Assessment of wildlife utilisation as a land use option in the semiarid lands in Zimbabwe* (Unpublished report). Harare: National Parks and Wildlife Management.

Eduardo Henrique da Silva Oliveira. (2015). Place branding in strategic spatial planning: A content analysis of development plans, strategic initiatives and policy documents for Portugal 2014–2020. *Journal of Place Management and Development, 8*(1), 23–50.

Elliot, S., Papadopoulos, N., & Kim, S. S. (2011). An integrative model of place image: Exploring relationships between destination, product, and country images. *Journal of Travel Research, 50*(5), 520–534.

Gartner, W. C., & Ruzzier, M. K. (2011). Tourism destination brand equity dimensions: Renewal versus repeat market. *Journal of Travel Research, 50*(5), 471–481.

Geza, T., & Lorant, D. (2010). The connection between accessibility and tourism. *Delhi Business Review, 11*(1), 1–18.

Greer, P. (2003). *Zimbabwe's deteriorating economic situation.* [online] Retrieved from http:/www.hks.havard.edu/cchrp/pdf/greer2003.pdf. Downloaded: July 2, 2007.

Gumbo, T. (2013). *On ideology change and spatial and structural linkages between formal and informal economic sectors in Zimbabwean cities (1981–2010)* (Unpublished Doctor of Philosophy Thesis). Faculty of Science, Stellenbosch University, Stellenbosch.

Gustavo, N. (2013). Marketing management trends in tourism and hospitality industry: Facing the 21st century environment. *International Journal of Marketing Studies, 5*(3), 13–25.

Hanke, S. H. (2008). *Zimbabwe: Hyperinflation to growth.* Harare: New Zanj Publishing House.

Harrison, D. (2015). Development theory and tourism in developing countries: What has theory ever done for us? *International Journal of Asia Pacific Studies, 11*(1), 53–82.

Im, H. H., Kim, S. S., Elliot, S., & Han, H. (2012). Conceptualizing destination brand equity dimensions from a consumer-based brand equity perspective. *Journal of Travel & Tourism Marketing, 29*(4), 385–403.

IMF. (2009). *Public information notice: IMF executive board concludes 2009 article IV consultation with Zimbabwe.* Public Information Notice No. 09/53. Retrieved 7 October 2018, from www.imf.org/en/News/Articles/2015/09/28/04/53/pn0953

Kaplan, M. K., Yurt, O., Guneri, B., & Kurtulus, K. (2010). Branding places: Applying brand personality concept to cities. *European Journal of Marketing, 44*(9/10), 1286–1304. https://doi.org/10.1108/030 9056 1011 06 2844. Retrieved 7 October 2018.

Klimek, K. (2013). Destination management organisations and their shift to sustainable tourism development. *European Journal of Tourism, Hospitality and Recreation, 4*(2), 27–47.

Koech, J. (2011). *Hyperinflation in Zimbabwe.* 2011 Annual report, Gobalization and Monetary Policy Institute. Federal Reserve Bank of Dallas, Globalization and Monetary Policy Institute, Dallas.

Kotler, P., & Armstrong, G. (2011). *Principles of marketing* (14th ed.). New York, NY: Pearson Prentice-Hall.

Kotler, P., & Gertner, D. (2002). Country as brand, product, and beyond: A place marketing and brand management perspective. *The Journal of Brand Management, 9*, 249–261.

Kotler, P., & Keller, K. (2012). *Marketing management.* Upper Saddle River, NJ: Prentice Hall.

Lindblom, A., Lindblom, T., Lehtonen, J. M., & Wechtler, H. (2017). A study on country images, destination beliefs and travel intentions: A structural equation model approach. *International Journal of Tourism Research*, 1–10.

Maggi, E., & Fredellå, F. L. (2010). *The carrying capacity of a tourist destination: The case of a coastal Italian city.* Retrieved 7 October 2018, from https://ideas.repec.org/p/wiw/wiwrsa/ersa10p576.html

Meža, P., & Šerić, N. (2014). Destination branding through the perception of the tourist: Case from Croatia. In *Human capital without borders: Knowledge and learning for quality of life; Proceedings of the management, knowledge and learning international conference 2014* (pp. 77–87). Portorož.

Morrison, A. M. (2012). *Marketing and managing tourism destinations.* London: Routledge.

Morrison, A. M. (2013). *Marketing and managing tourism destinations* (1st ed.). London: Routledge.

Muchapondwa, E., & Pimhidzai, O. (2011). Modeling international tourism demand for Zimbabwe. *International Journal of Business and Social Science, 2*(2), 71–78.

Muleya, D. (2002). *Tourism tumbles in Zimbabwe.* [online] Retrieved 10 October 2007, from http://fr. All ehavi. Com/stories/200211220434.html

Nadeau, J., Heslop, L., O'Reilly, N., & Luk, P. (2008). Destination in a country image context. *Annals of Tourism Research, 35*(1), 84–106.

The National Consultative Forum. (2001). *Zimbabwe economic recovery* (Vol. 2, Issue 1). Harare.

Ndlovu, J., & Heath, E. (2013). Re-branding of Zimbabwe to enhance sustainable tourism development: Panacea or villain. *Journal of Business Management, 1*(12), 947–955.

Pike, S. (2010). Destination branding case study: Tracking brand equity for an emerging destination between 2003 and 2007. *Journal of Hospitality & Tourism Research, 34*(1), 124–139.

Pike, S., Bianchi, C., Kerr, G., & Patti, C. (2010). Consumer-based brand equity for Australia as a long haul tourism destination in an emerging market. *International Marketing Review, 27*(4), 434–449.

Qu, H., Kim, L. H., & Im, H. H. (2011). A model of destination branding: Integrating the concepts of the branding and destination image. *Tourism Management, 32*(1), 465–476.

Regional Tourism of Southern Africa (RETOSA). (2004). *The essence of Africa*. Midrand: RETOSA.

Sachikonye, L. M. (2005). *Keeping on knocking: Zimbabwean labour since independence and its future prospects*. Unpublished National Workshops-Zimbabwe, Harare.

Shumbambiri, G. (2016). *Impact of Quasi fiscal operations on GDP& prices in Zimbabwe: 2003–2008: Impact of Central Bank Quasi fiscal operations on GDP & Prices in an economic crisis: The case of Zimbabwe: 2003–2008*. Saarbrücken: LAP LAMBERT Academic Publishing.

Taylor, T. (2012, 5 March). Hyperinflation and the Zimbabwe example. *Conversable Economist*, Monday.

Theodhori, O., & Qirici, E. (2014). *The impact of destination branding to tourists behavior Albania in focus*. Scientific Papers International Conference, Korca, pp. 1–7.

United Nation World Tourism Organisation (UNWTO). (2013). *Tourism promotion from the perspective of a media channel*. 7th UNWTO Asia pacific executive training program: Tourism branding & communications, UNWTO.

USAID. (2013). *Positioning the Zimbabwe tourism sector for growth: Issues and challenges*. USAID strategic economic research and analysis: Zimbabwe SERA Program, USAID, pp. 1–26.

Varghese, B. (2016). A strategic evaluation on competency of Karnataka destinations through destination management organizations. *American Journal of Industrial and Business Management, 6*, 102–108.

Yusof, M. F., Ismail, H. N., & Omar, R. N. (2014). *A critical analysis on evolution of branding destination in Langkawi Island*. SHS Web of Conferences 12, EDP Sciences, 01002.

Zhou, Z. (2013). A peep into tourism development in zimbabwe: 1980–2010. *Asian Journal of Empirical Research, 3*(7), 884–894.

Zhou, Z. (2016). Post 2010 evaluation of Zimbabwe as a preferred tourist destination. *African Journal of Hospitality, Tourism and Leisure, 5*(1).

Zimbabwe Tourism Authority (ZTA). (2004). *Annual report* (Unpublished annual report). Harare: Harare Research and Development Division.

Zimbabwe Tourism Authority (ZTA). (2008). *Annual report* (Unpublished annual report). Harare: Harare Research and Development Division.

Zimbabwe Tourism Authority (ZTA). (2010). *Tourism trends annual report*. Harare: ZTA.

Zimbabwe Tourism Authority (ZTA). (2011). *Tourism trends annual report*. Harare: ZTA.

10 Dystopian dark tourism, fan subculture and the Ongoing Nakba in Banksy's Walled Off heterotopia

Jamil Khader

Introduction

Recent literature on tourism in Palestine examines the proliferation of different independent forms of alternative and special interest tourism that centres around the occupation (occu-tourism) in the context of conflict-ridden zones, political instability and violence (Isaac, 2013; Isaac, Hall, & Higgins-Desbiolles, 2016). These alternative forms of tourism include justice tourism (Isaac, 2017), solidarity tourism (Higgins-Desbiolles, 2009) and dark tourism (Isaac & Ashworth, 2011; Isaac & Platenkamp, 2018). There are, however, other novel forms of special interest tourism that have been underexplored with regards to recent tourist destinations in the Palestinian tourism industry.

This chapter presents a case study of one of the hottest tourist destinations in Bethlehem, Palestine – namely, Banksy's Walled Off Hotel – in relation to two forms of alternative tourism that have not received much attention in the literature about Palestinian tourism: dystopian dark tourism (Podoshen et al., 2015, p. 316) and pop-culture tourism (Gyimóthy, Lundberg, Lindström, Lexhagen, & Larson, 2015). This chapter argues that Banksy's Walled Off Hotel constitutes a heterotopic counter-site that 'represents, contests, and inverts' (Foucault, 1967) other material and physical sites, temporalities and discursive regimes with which it is linked through unexpected shocking, jarring and disturbing juxtapositions. Through these incompatible juxtapositions, Banksy's Walled Off heterotopia subverts the liberal language and ideology (Foucault, 1966) that informs the media frames, narratives and codes through which the so-called Israeli-Palestinian conflict is filtered and disseminated in the language of moral equivalency and parity. It also stages a rediscovery of accumulative temporality (Foucault, 1967) that sets the Israeli occupation of the Palestinian territories within the historical continuities and genealogies of Western colonialism, the Zionist settler-colonial state and the Israeli apartheid regime.

The chapter shows that dystopian dark tourism in the case of the Walled Off heterotopia is motivated not only by 'an increased insecurity about death' (Podoshen, Venkatesh, Wallin, Andrzejewski, & Jin, 2015, p. 316). Rather, it speculates that unconscious fears and anxieties about the emergence of the global apartheid regime amid the increasing polarization of wealth around the world could be driving this interest in dystopian dark tourism to the Walled Off Hotel and, metonymically, Bethlehem and the occupied Palestinian territories in general. Moreover, the interest in the Walled Off heterotopia can also be attributed to Banksy's international brand name and the vigorous international Banksy fan subculture (Gyimóthy et al., 2015). This chapter also addresses the dialectical relationship between dystopia and utopia that remains under-explored in discussions of dystopian dark tourism (Isaac, 2015). This analysis reveals that the Walled Off heterotopia does not simply register aspects of the dystopian realities in Palestine, but also inscribes a utopian dimension that universalizes the Palestinian struggle for freedom, by linking it to the struggles of other disposable communities around the world.

The Walled Off Hotel in context

The Walled Off Hotel, whose name is a pun and play on the upscale and luxurious Waldorf Astoria in nearby Jerusalem, is a boutique hotel cum art installation, museum and gallery that the elusive, internationally renowned British 'guerrilla' graffiti artist Banksy opened in Bethlehem, Palestine, in partnership with a local entrepreneur, Wisam Salsaa, in March 2017. The ten-room hotel is a three-storey building that used to be a residential building that also hosted a pottery shop on the first floor but which closed in 2000. Dubbed as the hotel 'with the worst view in the world,' the hotel is located at a corner close to the northern entrance of the town of Bethlehem, a few metres away from the Israeli-built separation and annexation apartheid wall that snakes around the Bethlehem governorate in the Palestinian Authority controlled area (Area A). Access to the northern part of town, it is important to note, is controlled by an Israeli military checkpoint, which is commonly known as Checkpoint 300 (Isaac, 2013).

As a boutique hotel, the property on which the Walled Off Hotel was established was remodelled into an art installation. Not only is the building itself a work of art, but it also contains many artworks, artefacts and objects. The building itself is divided into three main parts: a hotel with a Victorian style lobby (a colonial gentlemen's club), a museum and a gallery. The hotel offers three types of rooms: eight scenic rooms, one budget room and a presidential suite, all of which overlook the Israeli-built separation and annexation apartheid wall. The scenic rooms and presidential suite can accommodate up to 25 guests at most, in addition to a budget room that contains six bunk beds. Access to all these rooms gained by guests through a secret door that is painted over as a book case. All these rooms feature original art by Banksy and two other artists, Sami Musa and Dominique Petrin, that offer customers the unique experience of 'sleeping inside a work of art.'

The other parts of the boutique art hotel include the museum and the gallery, as well as a dysfunctional fake elevator on the second floor of the hotel section. The museum is located in the southern part of the first floor past the lobby, featuring a Balfour diorama, a Gaza memorial simulation and an informational wall. The

Figure 10.1 Walled Off Hotel

Source: Author's copyright

Figure 10.2 Walled Off Hotel room type

gallery featuring artwork by Palestinian artists is located on the second floor in an independent wing of the building. The 'out of service' elevator, whose doors are jammed half open only to reveal that the elevator itself is walled off by concrete block, adds a special twist to a boutique art hotel.

Banksy's new project in Bethlehem was believed to bring much-needed attention to the Israeli-built separation and annexation apartheid wall, after it had been overshadowed by other disasters and atrocities in the region. More importantly, it was also believed, according to media reports, to help boost and reinvigorate the captive local Palestinian economy (Graham-Harrison, 2017). It was reported that the hotel employs about 50 Palestinian employees from the area and has become a major attraction for the kind of tourists who do not usually stay in Bethlehem. Unsurprisingly, Banksy's Walled Off Hotel has become a very popular tourist destination in Bethlehem attracting, according to hotel management, over 80,000 visitors since its opening more than a year ago (March 2017), and has been the subject of extensive international media coverage and controversy (Muslemani, 2017).

The Walled Off heterotopia: liberal fantasies, colonial genealogies

In its juxtapositions of different contradictory spatial, temporal and discursive regimes, the Walled Off Hotel is better conceived as a heterotopic site. In his short but controversial essay 'Of Other Spaces, Heterotopias,' Foucault (1967) argues that heterotopias constitute real places that exist 'outside of all places,' in a way that represents, contradicts and inverts all these other material and imagined sites that are linked to these heterotopic space within a particular society. Foucault notes that these other spaces that heterotopias collapse are 'in themselves incompatible' and 'foreign to one another.' While in *The Order of Things*, Foucault reduces incompatibility to disorder, in which 'fragments of a large number of possible orders glitter separately. . . *without law or geometry*' (Foucault, 1966, p. xvii; emphasis added), in his aforementioned essay, he maintains that heterotopias are structured by an underlying logic and a deeper system of 'superimposed meanings.'

As a heterotopic site, Banksy's Walled Off Hotel constitutes a single real place that links together, juxtaposes and collapses different incompatible real and imagined spaces, temporalities and discursive regimes – artistic, cultural, political and ideological, in a dialectic of contestation, critical pedagogy and ideological transformation. Through these juxtapositions, Banksy's Walled Off heterotopia complicates our understanding of the motives and interests of tourists, as well as the dialectical relationship between utopia and dystopia underlying dystopian dark tourism (Podoshen et al., 2015). This heterotopic space will be examined in relation to two features that Foucault associates with heterotopias: language and ideology (Foucault, 1966) and the 'eternity of accumulating time' (Foucault, 1967).

The first feature with which Foucault associates heterotopias relates to language, myth, signifying codes and ideologies. *In The Order of Things*, Foucault writes:

> *Heterotopias* are 'disturbing, probably because they secretly undermine language, because they make it impossible to name this *and* that, because they shatter or tangle common names, because they destroy "syntax" in advance, and not only the syntax with which we construct sentences but also that less apparent syntax which causes words and things (next to and also opposite one another) to "hold together." . . . ; heterotopias (such as those to be found so often in Borges) desiccate speech, stop words in their tracks, contest the very possibility of grammar at its source; they dissolve our myths and sterilize the lyricism of our sentences.'
>
> (1966, p. xix, emphasis in original)

As a heterotopic site, the Walled Off Hotel subverts and undermines not language as such, but a particular type of language and its dominant myths, common names, syntax and grammar; namely, the neoliberal fantasy frame, through which Western journalists, public discourse and travellers (and one might add, quite a few tourism scholars) filter, misconstrue and misrecognize the ugly realities of colonization, genocide and apartheid – what is commonly known as the Ongoing Nakba – in Palestine.

While the liberal mass media, and popular culture in general, mediates and constructs the tourist gaze and experience in general (Urry, 1990), it could be argued that it disseminates certain partisan (pro-Israel) frames and codes in the context of the so-called Israeli-Arab conflict. This neoliberal media coverage is informed by two main frames and codes that posit the Israeli-Arab conflict within Western strategic interests and present the Zionist settler-colonial project, the occupation system and the apartheid regime simply as a 'feud between neighbors' (Gamson, 1992). Needless to mention, these frames privilege the Israeli narrative in all its underlying biblical mythologies, obscure the origins of the Zionist settler-colonial project and the Ongoing Nakba, downplay the extent of the Israeli ethnic cleansing campaign (a term that the Jewish militias and terrorist groups used freely in 1948), encode Palestinians in the racist and Orientalist language of Otherness, and delegitimize the Palestinian right to self-determination and liberation.

As a heterotopic counter-site, then, the Walled Off Hotel exposes and parodies these liberal media frames and codes, exerting 'a sort of counteraction,' 'to use Foucault's words, on the neoliberal position these tourists occupy (Foucault, 1967). In particular, the representational and artistic space of Walled Off heterotopia displays a wide range of objects, images and artefacts that challenges the hegemony of the Israeli narrative, situates the struggle and travel itself within its colonial history and inverts the language of moral equivalency and parity through which the liberal media misrepresents Israel's ethnic cleansing campaign as a symmetrical struggle between two equal and equally legitimate narratives.

Right at the entrance of the hotel's lobby, a large painting on the right side of the lobby depicts the obscenity of the liberal representation of the Israel's ethnic cleansing campaign as a symmetrical power struggle between one of the most powerful countries in the region and the people it has occupied for more than 70 years. Playing on the traditional biblical prophecy that describes the Messiah's millennial kingdom, in which violence will come to an end and predatory animals will live in peace and harmony with domesticated farm animals (Isaiah 11:6), Banksy portrays a leopard lying down with a lamb, exposing the lie of the prophecy in the context of the realities of the Ongoing Nakba outside.

Banksy continues moving tourists and other international travellers out of their comfort zone, by turning a classic idyllic scene in rural Europe into a typical horror scene to which many Palestinians are used. Banksy thus invades the private space of these visitors by reworking a classic Western pastoral painting, in which he inserts a futuristic or cubistic bulldozer into the private space of a European family. Right below it, visitors will be shocked to find a painting of Jesus, his gaze turned up in the direction of a laser red dot that targets his forehead.

In a niche in the wall to the right of the cameras and weaponry display, Banksy reappropriates and inverts the classic Western and biblical underdog master narrative that liberal discourses have invested in to glorify Israel's military power. Banksy mounted one of the most recurrent iconic images of the Palestinian struggle for freedom: Palestinian youth tackling Israel tear gas. In a clear take on Michaelangelo's classic statue *David*, Banksy wrapped the bust of a Hellenized Palestinian youth, whose mouth is loosely covered with a piece of cloth that morbidly looks like a shroud, with the white fumes that are released from a tear gas canister, which he placed at the bottom of the work.

In one of the highlight murals in the heterotopic space of the hotel scenic rooms, moreover, Banksy depicts a pillow fight between an Israeli soldier in full gear and a Palestinian youth, donning civilian clothes with his face completely covered in a kaffiyeh – only his eyes showing. Moreover, the budget room offers visitors bunk beds, which were allegedly recovered from an Israeli military compound. Rather than a post-Holocaust ethical statement about the humanity of the persecutory and colonizing Other, the homosocial and intimate subtext of the pillow fight betrays the dialectic of involuntary participation and forced identification in such power games between persecutors and their victims. The most pertinent historical event, by which this artwork should be gauged is the infamous 'death (soccer) match' at Auschwitz (Sanyal, 2002).

Banksy also pricks the bubble of those Westerners who propose multicultural tolerance, acceptance of the other, and teaching for 'co-existence' as viable solutions to this political struggle. Much has been said in social media and the Palestinian media about the welcoming signs at the entrance and the back of the installation-hotel as well as Banksy's Q&A section on his official website (Muslemani, 2017). The critics contend that Banksy presumably extends an open arm to 'everyone from all sides of the conflict and across the world,' especially young Israelis, to visit Bethlehem and the installation-hotel. For the critics, these must be irreverent calls for normalization. Knowing full well that Israelis are prohibited from travelling into the occupied territories, however, Banksy brings home the illegality of the occupation, an issue that has been long forgotten in Israeli media and public discourse.

The second feature that Foucault associates with heterotopias is their relationship with time. He describes heterotopia as a 'place of all times that is itself outside of time' (Foucault, 1967). For Foucault, heterotopias affect an absolute break with time, but this is not a rupture with time as such (as an abstract category). Rather, heterotopias constitute an absolute cut, or 'slice' as he writes, with 'traditional time' (Foucault, 1967). By reconfiguring traditional time, heterotopic sites set the stage for rediscovering an alternative form of heterochrony, what he refers to as an accumulative temporality that foregrounds historical continuities (Foucault, 1967).

For Foucault, the modern conception of museums and libraries embodies this 'eternity of accumulating time,' since 'time never stops building up and topping its own summit.' As such, heterochronies do not simply offer a respite from the pressures of time, but collapse different temporalities together, by 'accumulating everything, of establishing a sort of general archive, the will to enclose in one place all times, all epochs, all forms, all tastes.' In short, as he states, heterotopias are about organizing 'perpetual and indefinite accumulation of time in an immobile place' (Foucault, 1967).

The Walled Off installation-hotel-cum-gallery and museum constitutes such a heterotopic/heterochronic site that highlights the temporal continuities in the colonial history of Palestine, by linking the legacies of the British colonial mandate – especially the colonial gentlemen's club and the Balfour declaration – to the Zionist settler-colonial project and its history of ethnic cleansing (a term that was used by Jewish terrorists and militias in 1948), occupation and apartheid, or what is usually referred to as the 'Ongoing Nakba' (*Al-Nakba Al-Mostamera*). As Said demonstrates, establishing the genealogy of Zionism and its links and affinities to Western colonialism is important for examining Zionism as an institutional power structure and practice that aims at an accumulation of wealth, land, power and ideological legitimacy as well as the displacement of people, other ideas and prior legitimacy (Said, 1992, pp. 56–57).

Banksy himself issued a statement, in which he situated his installation in the British national debate not only about colonialism, but also about the Balfour declaration – about which the British government has been orchestrating a national revisionist campaign to exonerate Balfour and the British government of any responsibility for the destruction of Palestinian society. He stated:

> It's exactly one hundred years since Britain took control of Palestine and started re-arranging the furniture – with chaotic results. I don't know why but it felt like a good time to reflect on what happens when the United Kingdom makes a huge political decision without fully comprehending the consequences.

> (Sanchez, 2017)

In the heterotopic space of the Walled Off Hotel, Banksy foregrounds this colonial genealogy and history continuity between the UK's imperial legacy and Zionist settler-colonialism in diverse ways. Outside the hotel, a doorman sporting a black top hat and a black overcoat as well as a butler monkey wearing a red waistcoat and a red fez welcome the visitors and guests. Inside, Banksy resituates the Ongoing Nakba in colonial history through the representation of the gentlemen's club and the Balfour diorama that he deposited in the museum in the back of the lobby.

A spectacular fetishized simulation of one of the legacies of colonial history, the gentlemen's club features a mechanical piano, a tea room, a collection of classic Victorian and Royal family plate sets, and three cherubs hanging from the wall wearing yellow oxygen masks. The gentlemen's club replica in its colonial glory offers an anti- or counter-narrative to the exotic nostalgia boom for the British Raj that has swept British public discourses and the media in the last few years (Jeffries, 2015). Moreover, in the specific Palestinian context, the idea of the gentlemen's club itself invokes one of Tel Aviv's boutique hotels, whose décor is supposed to be a throwback to a 1950s gentlemen's club. This other boutique hotel, however, boasts a 'stunning rooftop pool' (Richards, 2015).

The gentlemen's club serves an important function in the inscription of this colonial genealogy – it actually operates as the frame narrative, so to speak, for the hidden narrative of the colonial story-within-a-story of the Balfour Declaration. Past the gentlemen's club and at the entrance to the museum in the heterotopic space of the Walled Off Hotel, Banksy mounted the Balfour diorama. The display features a life-sized diorama of UK Foreign Secretary Arthur Balfour signing the 1917 Balfour Declaration document in repetitive mechanical circles, symbolizing the ongoing cycles of violence and destruction that this document has visited on Palestinians. Banksy thus seems to suggest that the Balfour Declaration is the truth of the colonial spectacle of the gentlemen's club and the Zionist settler-colonial project.

The hidden Balfour diorama is not the only object in the heterotopic space of the installation-hotel that links the UK's colonial legacy to the current Zionist settler-colonial project in Palestine. The western wall of the lobby is adorned with hunting CCTV cameras mounts and a collection of slingshots, as well as two criss-crossed sledgehammers, just above the royalty plate collection. Banksy successfully juxtaposes the technologically sophisticated surveillance system of the Israeli occupation and apartheid regime, as well as the brute force of the sledgehammers with the primitive 'weaponry' that has functioned as an iconic symbol of Palestinian resistance. The threat of the surveillance cameras is heightened by the couple of drones that are hanging to the right of the trophy wall.

In the heterotopic space of the Walled Off Hotel, there is no respite from the ugly realities, and a few artworks bear witness to the Ongoing Nakba under the Zionist settler-colonial project and apartheid regime outside. The entrance of the lobby features a fireplace covered with a pile of rocks that could have been removed, one would presume, from Palestinian homes that were demolished by the Israeli army and its bulldozers. Moreover, the realities of Israel's genocidal policies in the occupied territories and Gaza are registered in a couple of paintings that are self-reproduction acts.

First, Banksy recycles his famous 'Rage, the Flower Thrower' mural in a tripartite frame on the southern wall of the lobby. This painting is a direct condemnation of the Israeli government's genocidal politics in Palestine. As reported in *The New York Times* in the aftermath of the Great March of Return in Gaza, one Israeli colonel responded to a question about Israel's disproportionate lethal attacks on unarmed protestors, by saying that 'It doesn't matter if someone is carrying flowers or if he's tearing down the fence. That's a violent threat' (Abuheweila & Halbfinger, 2018).

Next to 'Rage, the Flower Thrower,' Banksy placed another self-reproduction of his famous mural depicting Gazan children swinging around an Israeli military watchtower in a swing carousel common in amusement parks. In the heterotopic space of the hotel, this painting is linked to a special section of the museum which Banksy dedicates to Israel's genocidal war on Gaza. Not much has been reported in the media about this Gaza memorial, but it is one of the most moving and highly emotional areas of the installation-hotel.

The magnitude of the destruction and death that has resulted from Israel's genocidal wars on Gaza is captured in three different exhibits. A glass case shows children's dusty shoes and a school backpack, probably scavenged from the rubbles in Gaza. There is also an elaborate recreation of the roof-knocking tactic of the Israeli military. A mounted corded white phone continuously rings for visitors to pick up; it re-enacts the call Palestinians receive from an Israeli officer warning them of the coming destruction five minutes before the missiles strike. Earthen statues of a Palestinian mother and children stand close to the mounds of rubble, a testament to the homes that were destroyed. Finally, there is the scale of justice, in which the artist placed heaps of fake teeth to represent the victims of Israel's 'protective edge' war on Gaza.

The museum area also provides a lot of information about different aspects of the Palestinian struggle under occupation. The section is equipped with various interactive technologies, such as an animated 3D map of the history of Palestine, as well as three videos of different aspects of the Palestinian struggle. The section also has an in-house theatre where the Palestinian film *Five Broken Cameras* is screened. In fact, one of these cameras is showcased in a glass case in the theatre room. Many high-quality photographs and posters present the facts about the settlements, the wall and checkpoints. In one interesting glass case, a cross-section from the earth reveals the contrast between the Palestinian and Israeli underground water distribution systems: the narrow rusty iron pipes used in Palestine pale under the thick and wide copper pipes that Israel uses in controlling the water resources and consumption in the area. In an adjacent section, a video loop plays the testimonies of former Israeli soldiers, detailing the daily violations of Palestinian human rights.

The Walled Off heterotopia and dystopian dark tourism

This analysis of the Walled Off Hotel as a heterotopic site in its two dimensions, language and temporal continuity, shows that the Walled Off heterotopia can be related to dystopian dark tourism on many different levels (Isaac & Platenkamp, 2015; Podoshen et al., 2015). At one level, the Walled Off Hotel establishes an overt link to the major themes and motifs in dark tourism such as death and disaster, atrocity and human suffering (Isaac & Ashworth, 2011; Isaac & Platenkamp, 2018). In the larger geopolitical context of the location of the Walled Off Hotel, the fact that it is situated in a conflict zone, it would not be difficult to witness the ravages of war, ethnic cleansing, genocide, occupation and apartheid. The truth of the matter is that as a result of the Zionist settler-colonial project, its ethnic cleansing campaign, occupation and apartheid regime, what is usually referred to as the Ongoing Nakba, no place in historical Palestine was spared from the writing of the disaster. The implications for heritage tourism in this regard are complicated by the lack of access and control of the Palestinian tourism industry over massacre sites (Tantura in the Haifa region, Deir Yasin near Jerusalem) and depopulated areas within Israel proper now.

Within this larger context of dark tourism in Palestine, the Walled Off Hotel can also be identified as a dystopian site, especially in relation to the choice of the hotel's physical location, its architectural structure and its artistic space of representation. In their review of literature on the topic, Podoshen and colleagues mention a few features of dystopian tourism sites, including the presence of ominous topographical features and a hyper-real postmodern space which glorifies artificial and simulated reality and the culture of the spectacle (Podoshen et al., 2015, p. 317), features that are relevant to the understanding of the relationship between the Walled Off Hotel and dystopian dark tourism.

The dystopian dimension of the Walled Off Hotel has to be understood in the context of Banksy's dystopian anti-capitalist aesthetics. In particular, his temporary dystopian anti-theme park project, Dismaland in Weston-super-Mare, England, which the website described as 'a festival of art, amusements and entry-level anarchism,' attracted worldwide attention for its exposure of the dirty and darker side of amusement space, hyper-consumerism, and corporate power until its closure in September 2015.

The hotel's website celebrates tongue in cheek the unique hyper-real and simulated experience of 'sleeping inside a work of art,' the ironic artworks as well as the collection of artefacts and objects that they gathered from manifestations of everyday life under occupation undermine this aestheticized fantasy. This is not an American motel where reality is commodified and presented as an unreal fantasy. Rather, the Walled Off dystopia introduces a gap between the form and the content of this aesthetic experience: the form (the leisurely activity of sleeping inside an artwork or experience reality as unreal) contradicts the content of this art, as will be described following, disclosing the unconscious liberal fantasy that posits Israelis and Palestinians in the same language of moral equivalency and symmetrical power balance.

The Walled Off heterotopia and the new global apartheid regime

Nonetheless, this analysis shows that dystopian dark tourism alone is insufficient to explain the attraction of the hotel tourists and guests. Indeed, as Gyimóthy and colleagues state, 'special interest tourism is driven by more complex processes than those identified in the state-of-the-art literature' (Gyimóthy et al., 2015, p. 15). At one level, literature on dystopian dark tourism suggests that the obsession with special interest tourism reflects a general societal trend addressing 'an increased insecurity about death, society and its relationship to violence and cultural production' (Podoshen et al., 2015, p. 316). However, this analysis does not specify any particular or contextual processes that may accentuate this fascination with dystopian dark tourism.

In the specific context of the Israeli-built separation and annexation apartheid wall, which is one of the main attractions of this hotel with the worst view in the world, it can be speculated that Banksy's Walled Off heterotopia taps into unconscious fears and anxieties about – and perhaps the general complacency with – the emergence of the global apartheid regime in the context of the increasing polarization of wealth around the world. In this new global apartheid regime, as German philosopher Sloterdijk argues, the included, or privileged, elite (the transnational capitalist classes) everywhere live under a protective, self-enclosed cupola that groups and segregates them from the rest of surplus, excluded disposable humanity (Sloterdijk, 2013).

These new forms of apartheid, the philosopher Žižek suggests, remain central to the transformation of the global capitalist system. For him, new forms of capital and profit have privatized the three major commons of humanity, including the ecology, genetics and intellectual property, at the expense of the surplus and disposable part of humanity, the majority of the world's population, in ways that culminate in new forms of apartheid that register the gap between the included and the surplus, disposable and excluded humanity in the global capitalist system (Žižek, 2016, p. 105). Dystopia then is not some imaginary futuristic construct – it is already with us, and Palestine is one of the few places in the world where this emergent global regime can be traced in all its brutality and inhumanity at a more national and collective level.

The Walled Off heterotopia and the Banksy effect: overshadowing Jesus?

At another level, the attraction of the Walled Off Hotel as a dystopian dark tourism site has to do to a large extent with the emergence of a global fan subculture around Banksy and his work. This should be understood in the context of pop-culture tourism and the role that fan subcultures play in motivating fans to travel to conflict zones like Palestine to bask in the shadow of Banksy's artworks and wall art.

Drawing on studies on sport spectators and serious leisure, Gyimóthy and colleagues attribute the travelling and consumption behavior of a fan culture to these fans' ability and willingness to 'invest substantially more time, energy, and money' in their 'object of fascination' than any conventional tourist (Gyimóthy et al., 2015, p 19). Moreover, studies on serious and casual leisure also show that such forms of travel can develop into 'a long-term, systematic engagement with any recreational activity' (Gyimóthy et al., 2015, p. 20). Both of these forms of travel are grounded in fans' identification with their 'object of fascination' and may be 'intertwined with one's self-image, and may mark social status or belonging to a subculture' (Gyimóthy et al., 2015, p. 20).

The appeal and attraction of the Walled Off heterotopia depends to a large extent on a specific 'object of fascination': Bansky's own international brand name, anonymity, status as a British cultural icon artist and reputation as one of the few remaining committed and active political street artists in the world today. The power of Banksy's work lies in his ability to encode his putatively apolitical trademark images, ciphers and signifiers within an overarching semiotic system, complete with its own intertextual references and self-citation that can speak to the universality of the struggle of many disposable communities around the world. As such, Banksy's artwork does not fall into the trap of appropriating and co-opting these particular communities' narratives and symbols or silencing the voices of the colonized and the exploited.

The Walled Off Hotel capitalizes on the popular 'Banksy tourism' in Bethlehem. Banksy first visited Bethlehem in 2005, when he spray-painted several works on Israel's separation and annexation apartheid wall around the town. He also spray-painted a few other works at the Qalandiya checkpoint near Ramallah, Abu Deis and Beit Sahour, where he immortalized his trademark 'Rage, the Flower Thrower' piece on the eastern wall of a local gas station. This project was grounded in an anticolonial vision that sought to vandalize the separation and annexation apartheid wall, which has turned Palestine, as Banksy himself stated, 'into the world's largest open-air prison.'

The power of Banksy's work lies in his ability to encode his putatively apolitical trademark images, ciphers and signifiers within a semiotic system that aims at universalizing the Palestinian struggle for freedom. He thus links it to the struggle of other disposable communities in the region (refugees) and around the world especially, in his native UK (the under-privileged and poor).

The suppressed utopian dimension: universalizing the Palestinian struggle

Banksy's Walled Off heterotopia reworks the dialectical relationship between utopia and dystopia in dystopian dark tourism studies (Isaac, 2015). Dystopian dark tourism scholars have not explained the ways in which every dystopia conceals or screens some utopian dimension. The Walled Off heterotopia does not stop at inscribing the dystopian realities of oppression, genocide and apartheid in Palestine. Rather, the power of Banksy's Walled Off heterotopia lies in its ability to open up the utopian dimension of the fundamental antagonism (class struggle) from within the discursive and architectural contradictions of this heterotopic space. This allows Banksy's hotel to universalize the Palestinian struggle for freedom, by linking it to the international struggles of other disposable communities.

This dialectic between utopia and dystopia is very important for the Walled Off especially, as a heterotopic site, since Foucault's reflections on heterotopia suppress this utopian subtext altogether (Foucault, 1967). In his tentative reflections on heterotopia, Foucault insists on the normative function of specularity and reflection in the way heterotopias are positioned in relation to all other sites and spaces. Foucault thus reinscribes the imaginary in a process of identity production, whereby the subject reflexively reconstitutes itself in the place where it exists in reality. However, he grossly overlooks the act of misrecognition at the core of the imaginary order and the shift from identity to identification in the mirror stage (Lacan, 1949).

The problem with this analysis is that Foucault disavows the Lacanian underpinnings of his theorization of heterotopia, preventing him from articulating his notion of heterotopia in terms of an unconscious ideological fantasy, or the unconscious attachment to a cause, that remains excluded in the formation of such spaces. From a Lacanian perspective, it could be argued that heterotopias are marked by neither the absence of law nor the presence of a deeper logic, as Foucault suggests, but by an ontological gap that heterotopic spaces continue to conceal and disguise; namely, the Lacanian Real. Hence, in Foucault's analysis, heterotopias are reduced to 'a space of illusion that exposes every real space, all the sites inside of which human life is partitioned, as still more illusory' (Foucault, 1967). As Žižek states in his discussion of the film *The Matrix*, however, the Real is not the 'true reality,' whether it's a substantive reality, illusion or a derealized reality, 'but the void which makes reality incomplete/inconsistent' (Žižek, 1999, n.p.). What needs to be recognized is that no reality exists without a constitutive deadlock, a fundamental antagonism, structuring it.

The power of the Walled Off heterotopia is that it succeeds in inscribing this deadlock at the architectural level. It juxtaposes two contradictory structures – namely, the free international circulation of ideas and capital that made this boutique art hotel successful in the borderless world of the global capitalist system, and the restrictions on the mobility of the Palestinians that is represented by the dysfunctional elevator inside the building. This contradiction opens up the 'parallax gap' on which the fundamental antagonism can be encoded and played out in the heterotopic space of the hotel. As such, to paraphrase Jameson's thesis (1981), the Walled Off heterotopia offers imaginary solutions to real contradictions in the global capitalist system, or as Žižek writes, 'architectural projects are answers to a problem which is ultimately socio-political' (Žižek, 2011, p. 246).

By placing the Palestinian struggle in the context of the contradictions of the global capitalist system, the Walled Off heterotopia aims at universalizing the Palestinian struggle, by linking it to the struggles of other disposable communities in the global capitalist system through Banksy's putatively apolitical images, ciphers and signifiers. The intention here is not, as post-colonialists surmise, simply to recover the agency of indigenous communities or reassert 'marginalized or suppressed histories' (Carrigan, 2014, p. 240). Neither it is a 'marriage' between Palestinian art and global art in a way that elevates both Palestinian and universal art. Rather, the idea involves introducing a different universality, not an empty neutral universality that 'enables each culture to assert its identity,' but a 'totally different universality, that of an antagonistic struggle which does not take place between particular communities, but splits from within each community, so that the "trans-cultural" link between communities is that of a shared struggle' (Žižek, 2011, p. 53).

Banksy, thus, first links the Palestinian struggle to the plight of the refugees around the world today. At the entrance of the lobby just above the fireplace on the left, Banksy placed three paintings of a wavy ocean scene, with the orange lifejackets scattered all over the beach, and in some shoes are seen strewn around. The beach is haunted by the absence of the refugees. Under the paintings, the artist placed a small replica of a refugee boat. Insofar as they lack any determinate place in the hegemony of the neoliberal global capitalist regime, these refugees can be said to stand for the system's point of inherent exclusion or exception. Just like the condition of the Palestinians under the hegemony of the Zionist settler-colonial project, ethnic cleansing policies and apartheid regime, refugees expose the lie of the allegedly democratic states and the egalitarian neoliberal global capitalist system.

Banksy also embeds the struggle in Palestine to the struggle of the unemployed and unemployable in the neoliberal global capitalist economy. Behind the bar at the entrance of the lobby of the installation-hotel, there are three clocks marking the time in New York, London and Jerusalem, each of which features the image of the famous Banksy rat in the background. This is the same rat that was previously painted over in Palestine but that Banksy uses as his trademark in most of his street art in Bristol and other places. In their anarchic and libidinal energy, in Banksy's philosophy, rats are the ultimate signifiers of the power of the excluded and disposable communities to represent the ugly truth of the global capitalist system, its constitutive injustice and the inequality from which they are an excluded, even excremental (abject) subject. In one of his memorable statements about the symbolic meaning of rats in his work, Banksy notes: 'If you feel dirty, insignificant or unloved, then rats are a good role model. They exist without permission, they have no respect for the hierarchy of society, and they have sex 50 times a day' (*Erratic Phenomena*, 2008).

These rats hold signs that say 'London doesn't work'; they are not only the unemployed working class, but the increasing number of unemployable workers in the global capitalist system in the UK, as well as in Palestine. As they disclose the inherent contradictions and inconsistencies of the system, by virtue of their exclusion from it, these disposable communities become a symptom of the systemic pathologies of the neoliberal global capitalist system itself.

Conclusion

As a heterotopic site, Banksy's Walled Off Hotel subverts the liberal fantasy narratives and codes, through which the dark political realities in Palestine are framed in the media, public discourse and academia. It also places Bethlehem, and metonymically Palestine, in the context of colonial history, foregrounding the continuity between British imperialism and the Zionist settler-colonial project, its ethnic cleansing campaign, and apartheid regime. Understanding the Walled Off as a heterotopia requires expanding the traditional approaches to alternative forms of tourism in Palestine. Other innovative approaches should be appropriated to account for unique heterotopic sites like the Walled Off Hotel. Moreover, this study concludes that it is time for tourism scholars to reconsider the exclusion of Palestine from the traditional list of genocide-related zones, and to rethink the nationalistic assumptions of Palestinian heritage tourism that ultimately end up fetishizing identity politics, memory and history. This could serve as an antidote to the possible commercial co-optation of all these forms of progressive forms of alternative tourism in the global capitalist system.

Acknowledgement

Research for this chapter was funded by an internal research grant from Bethlehem University, Bethlehem, Palestine.

References

Abuheweila, I., & Halbfinger, D. (2018, 27 April). Plan to storm the fence gets bloody. *The New York Times*. Retrieved from www.nytimes.com/2018/04/27/world/middleeast/gaza-protest-israel.html

Carrigan, A. (2014). Dark tourism and postcolonial studies: Critical intersections. *Postcolonial Studies*, *17*(3), 236–250.

Erratic Phenomena. (2008). Banksy rat appreciation. Retrieved 1 October 2018, from www.erraticphenomena.com/2008/02/banksys-rat-appreciation.html

Foucault, M. (1966). *The order of things*. New York, NY: Vintage.

Foucault, M. (1967). *Of other spaces, heterotopias*. Retrieved from https://foucault.info/documents/heterotopia/foucault.heteroTopia.en/

Gamson, W. A. (1992). *Talking politics*. New York, NY: Cambridge University Press.

Graham-Harrison, E. (2017, 3 March). Worst view in the world: Banksy opens hotel overlooking Bethlehem wall. *The Guardian*. Retrieved from www.theguardian.com/world/2017/mar/03/banksy-opens-bethlehem-barrier-wall-hotel

Gyimóthy, S., Lundberg, C., Lindström, K. N., Lexhagen, M., & Larson, L. (2015). Popculture tourism: A research manifesto. In D. Chambers & T. Rakić (Eds.), *Tourism research frontiers: Beyond the boundaries of knowledge* (Tourism Social Science Series, Vol. 20, pp. 13–26). Bingley, West Yorkshire: Emerald Group Publishing Limited.

Higgins-Desbiolles, F. (2009). International solidarity movement: A case study in volunteer tourism for justice. *Annals of Leisure Research*, *12*(3–4), 333–349. doi:10.1080/11745398.2009.9686828

Isaac, R. K. (2013). Palestine: Tourism under occupation. In R. Butler & W. Suntikul (Eds.), *Tourism and war*. London: Routledge.

Isaac, R. K. (2015). Every utopia turns into dystopia. *Tourism Management*, *51*, 329–330.

Isaac, R. K. (2017). Transformational host communities: Justice tourism and the water regime in Palestine. *Tourism, Culture and Communication*, *17*(2), 139–158.

Isaac, R. K., & Ashworth, G. (2011). Moving from pilgrimage to "Dark" tourism: Leveraging tourism in Palestine. *Tourism Culture & Communication*, *11*(3), 149–164.

Isaac, R. K., Hall, C. M., & Higgins-Desbiolles, F. (Eds.). (2016). *The politics and power of tourism in Palestine*. Abington, Oxon: Routledge.

Isaac, R. K., & Platenkamp, V. (2015). Concrete (dys)utopia in Bethlehem: A city of two tales. *Journal of Tourism and Cultural Change*, *14*(2), 150–166.

Isaac, R. K., & Platenkamp, V. (2018). Dionysus versus Apollo: An uncertain search for identity through dark tourism – Palestine as a case study. In P. R. Stone, R. Hartmann, T. Seaton, R. Sharpley, & L. White (Eds.), *The Palgrave handbook of dark tourism studies*. London: Palgrave Macmillan.

Jameson, F. (1981). *The political unconscious: Narrative as a Socially Symbolic Act*. Ithaca, NY: Cornell University Press.

Jeffries, S. (2015, 19 March). The best exotic nostalgia boom: Why colonial style is back. *The Guardian*. Retrieved from www.theguardian.com/culture/2015/mar/19/the-best-exotic-nostalgia-boom-why-colonial-style-is-back

Lacan, J. (1949). The mirror stage as formative of the function of the I as revealed in psychoanalytic experience. In *Ecrits: A selection*. New York, NY: Taylor and Francis.

Muslemani, M. (2017, 6 March). Banksy's Hotel: Normalizing the wall and its builders. [Funduq Banksy: Altatbee' ma' aljedar wabaneeh]. *Refugeesps*. Retrieved from http://refugeesps.net/post/2838

Podoshen, J. S., Venkatesh, V., Wallin, J., Andrzejewski, S. A., & Jin, Z. (2015). Dystopian dark tourism: An exploratory examination. *Tourism Management, 51*, 316–328.

Richards, N. (2015, 8 September). Where to drink in Tel Aviv. *Suitcase Magazine*. Retrieved from https://suitcasemag.com/travel/explore/best-bars-in-tel-aviv-israel/

Said, E. (1992). *The question of Palestine*. New York, NY: Vintage.

Sanchez, R. (2017, 3 March). Bnaksy opens walled-off dystopian torusin attraction in Bethlehem. *The Telegraph*. Retrieved from www.telegraph.co.uk/news/2017/03/03/walled-hotel-banksy-opens-dystopian-tourist-attraction-bethlehem/

Sanyal, D. (2002). A soccer match in Auschwitz: Passing culpability in holocaust criticism. *Representations, 79*(1), 1–27.

Sloterdijk, P. (2013). *In the world interior of capital*. Cambridge: Polity.

Urry, J. (1990). *The tourist gaze*. Sage Publications.

Žižek, S. (1999). *The matrix, or two sides of perversion*. Retrieved from www.lacan.com/Žižek-matrix.htm

Žižek, S. (2011). *Living in the end times*. London: Verso.

Žižek, S. (2016). *Against the double blackmail: Refugees, terror, and other troubles with the neighbor*. London: Allen Lane.

11 The PEGIDA movement and social conflict in Dresden, Germany

An investigation of the impacts of far-right populism on tourism in Europe

Erdinç Çakmak and Laura Gorlero

Introduction

Recognition of the negative impacts of social conflicts that are often associated with racist and xenophobic attitudes, integration of newcomers, polarization and exclusion has emerged tardily in the academic literature (European Commission, 2011). Since more than 70% of the European population lives in urban areas, the management of social conflict is essential to the wellbeing of the European population (Hamelink, 2008). In addition, a conflict situation has potential for either destructive or constructive development, and policy-makers need to identify creative forms of conflict management (Beall, Goodfellow, & Rodgers, 2010).

In the tourism literature and practice, much attention has given to the impacts of progressive events (e.g. sport and cultural events), and various scholars suggest that hosting events increase the positive image and identity of cities (Richards & Wilson, 2004; Nadeau, O'Reilly, Çakmak, Heslop, & Verwey, 2016). However, little academic attention has been paid to the impacts of negative social events such as those arising from regular demonstrations and protests in cities. Although the radical right populism (RRP) in Western Europe has been widely investigated, there is relatively little scholarly work that investigates this assertion empirically (Muis & Immerzeel, 2017). For instance, rising RRP is dissuading people from visiting eastern Germany (*Financial Times*, 2016). The domestic visitor numbers, based on overnight stays in Dresden, were down 5.1% in 2015 after having five record-breaking years reaching a peak in 2014 (Jahn, 2015). The declining trend continued in 2016 and another 2% decline has been recorded each year since (Jahn, 2015). This is a significant amount when one considers that domestic tourists account for 80% of the total tourism in Germany (German National Tourism Board, 2015).

The aim of this chapter is to explore various stakeholder groups' positions in the tourism system in relation to social conflict. It examines whether and how a radical right populist movement, Patriotic Europeans Against the Islamisation of the West (PEGIDA), affects the tourism industry and the social life of people in a

European urban context. Through focusing on these issues, this chapter seeks to contribute in a number of ways. First, it aims to highlight the complex interplay of social movement and conflict in tourism governance, leading to recommendations on how social conflict can be managed in an effective and constructive way. Considering the contemporary rise of right populist movements and parties across European Union member countries (Heinrich Boll Foundation, 2016), resolving social conflicts is not only academically relevant, but also strategically useful for local governments and decision-makers to add knowledge to this body of research. Second, the study applies the social movement impact theory focusing on economic, social and cultural outcomes of social movements, which is often neglected in many scholarly works (Giugni, Bosi, & Uba, 2013). Moreover the social movement literature has mainly dealt with progressive and egalitarian movements and tended to overlook the negative side of social movement activism (Menocal, 2016).

The context for this study is Dresden, Germany, the destination attractiveness of which has potentially been recently undermined by the rise of the radical right populist movement PEGIDA, which originated at the end of 2014 and grew following the 2015 refugee crisis, along with the rise of anti-European sentiments. Embodying the characteristics of a social movement, PEGIDA mobilized thousands of supporters sharing a common cause, which combines Islamophobic and nationalist sentiments with a mistrust of the media and political institutions. Every Monday in the historical city centre of Dresden, since 20 October 2014, PEGIDA has organized demonstrations characterized by xenophobic sloganeering such as 'Refugees not welcome' or 'Stop the Islamisation of Europe.' The city's official marketing group, Dresden Marketing GmbH, has reported the sharp fall in tourism to Dresden's 'negative image' as a result of PEGIDA's marches that have adversely affected people's business as well as private trips to the city (*The Local*, 2015; *Die Welt*, 2015). The president of the Technical University of Dresden (TUD) was concerned about the city's image and said, 'Before, the image of Dresden was clearly an asset internationally, but now our (foreign) colleagues are concerned for us as far away as (North) Korea. A growing number of international student candidates now hesitate to come to TUD' (*Die Welt*, 2015). Another example comes from the prestigious Max Planck Research Institute in Dresden, which has reported a decrease in new applications from abroad for the first time, as dark-skinned researchers perceive the atmosphere threatening in Dresden (*The Irish Times*, 2015).

Literature review

Social movements and protest

Social movements are a phenomenon of contemporary societies and have become an increasingly visible characteristic of today's social landscape. National daily newspapers in Europe often report social movement activity in relation to strongly contested issues of contemporary times: human rights, environmental protection, gender equality, immigration, nuclear weapons, terrorism, and so on (Snow,

Soule, & Kriesi, 2003). Social movements have received considerable attention from sociologists and political scientists dealing with a wide array of movements, issues and places (Della Porta & Diani, 2006; Van Stekelenburg & Klandermans, 2013).

A social movement is a distinct social process, originating out of voluntary groups that share beliefs and interests, and acts in order to stimulate (or resist) political, economic or cultural changes in society (McGehee, 2002). Although there is no universally accepted definition of social movement, four concepts are considered fundamental to social conflict: namely, a common cause that implies change-oriented goals, conflictual relations with an adversary, collective identity and sustained organization (Della Porta & Diani, 2006; Jasper, 2007). All social movements have a *common cause*, a political perspective and a vision of society that they wish to create. When challenging existing understandings of society, movements propose alternative visions to be achieved by change-oriented goals. In some cases, the aim can be to oppose social change, rather than to encourage it (Horn, 2013).

When social movement actors are promoting or opposing a social change, they engage in political, social or cultural *conflictual actions* with their opponents. In this context, conflict is considered an oppositional relationship between actors who seek control of the same stake and make negative claims about each other. The demands of one group, if realized, may damage the interests of the other group (Della Porta & Diani, 2006).

A social movement process starts only when participants develop a *collective identity*, which brings a feeling of connectedness, a common purpose and shared commitment to a cause (Della Porta & Diani, 2006). New forms of self-knowledge and social knowledge are formed through this collective identity, and social movement participants create in their practice new ways of seeing, being and doing, which they wish to extend to the broader society (Horn, 2013).

Social movements have some degree of continuity and differ from single events such as riots or rallies. Their persistence, *sustained organization*, usually enables them to develop formal organizations, but sometimes they may operate through informal networks. In a social movement, actors are involved in constant exchanges of resources in pursuit of common goals, while keeping their independence. Through constant negotiations between the individuals and the organizations involved in collective action, specific initiatives are coordinated, individual actors' conduct is regulated and strategies are defined. No single actor, no matter how powerful, can claim truthfully to represent a movement as a whole (Della Porta & Diani, 2006).

Protest actions are typically employed by social movements as moments of contestation in which people use symbols, identities, practices and discourses to pursue or prevent changes in institutionalized power relations (Van Dyke, Soule, & Taylor, 2004). Kousis (2000) classifies these actions ranging from non-violent to violent, including formal claims, petitions, meetings, demonstrations, occupations of public buildings, boycotts, strikes, shop closures, threats, road blockades, property damage and collective violence, among others.

One form of protest action commonly used by a social movement is demonstrations. Demonstrations change the urban landscape both visually and functionally. They disrupt traffic, make marginalized people visible in city centres, challenge governments, mobilize police forces and change meanings of places. Most demonstration sites fit in a few main categories: demonstrators may gather outside governmental buildings to communicate with the authorities, at centres of commercial or tourist activity to appeal to a large audience or at places that link them historically, culturally or morally with symbolically significant events (Salmenkari, 2009). Tourism-related protests are frequently part of residents' campaigns against the negative effects and externalities caused by tourism on people and places. In Barcelona, various residents' organizations got together and started quasi-daily 'anti-tourism' demonstrations (Novy & Colomb, 2017). In Hong Kong, the steep rise in mainland Chinese day trippers has been perceived as a contestation of residents' daily lives and led to the emergence of anti-Chinese tourism demonstrations (Rowen, 2016). In 2013 at different cities in Brazil, citizens marched against the social costs of hosting two mega events, the 2014 FIFA World Cup and the 2016 Olympic Games, in a very short period of time. Overtourism, a phenomena of unsustainable tourism (Dodds & Butler, 2019), engenders backlash from residents in many destinations (e.g. Barcelona, Venice, Dubrovnik), which had not happened before at large scale. Since 2017, there have been an increasing number of protests taking place in streets of many overtourism destinations, where residents holding banners saying 'tourists go home' (Francis, 2018).

An important characteristic of protest is the use of indirect channels to influence decision-makers. As Lipsky (1968) stated, protest is a political resource of the powerless, as it is one of the few strategies in which even politically impoverished groups can aspire to engage.

Muis and Immerzeel (2017) argue that social movement protests are generally dominated by 'the left,' while 'the right' prefer to use the electoral channel to voice its discontent, instead of taking to the street. There is no consensus in the literature whether right-wing 'phenomena' could be defined as social movements. Butterwegge (2004) argues that, in terms of content, right-wing populism/extremism can be regarded as an 'anti-social' movement, because it seeks to marginalize certain groups of society and to deny them certain social welfare services or exclude them by coercive measures. Others also share the view that social movements are not always progressive. Religious fundamentalism, neo-Nazism and ethnic nationalism, for example, have all been rooted in and spread by social movements (Horn, 2013; Menocal, 2016).

Examination of the consequences of social movements has been relatively belated in the literature, while scholars focused on their characteristics and dynamics (Snow et al., 2003). Social movement impact theory (McCarthy & Zald, 1977) focuses on assessing the impact that a social movement has on different spheres of society, and which factors might have led to those outcomes. It is one the least studied streams among other major branches of social movement theory, because it poses some conceptual and methodological challenges. For instance, scholars have no consensus on how to define 'success' or 'failure' for social movements, as it may be difficult to assess what a movement's goals are, thus coming to differ-ent conclusions about whether a movement has 'succeeded' (Snow et al., 2003). Often the impacts of social movements are not anticipated before or even do not belong to the movement's goals. Even third parties can act and produce changes in the zone of a movement's interests (Menocal, 2016).

Social movements, conflict and the tourism sector

Rubin, Pruitt, and Kim (1994) defined conflict as a 'perceived divergence of interest, a belief that the parties' current aspiration is incompatible' (p. 78). The connection between social movements and conflict is significantly recognized by scholars, and conflict is seen as a distinctive trait of all social movements (Oberschall, 1973; Touraine, 1973). A social movement develops when a group of dissatisfied individuals seeks a change and, in the process, finds specific adversar-ies. Because the identification of an opponent is a prerequisite for the existence of social movements, social movements could be considered as *products of conflict* (Della Porta & Diani, 2006). When a social movement emerges, it tries to reduce different forms of capital of the opponent group or prevent chances to expand them. For instance, social movements may engage in conflictual relations with the local government, with collective action and protests to forward their demands for social change (Bacallao-Pino, 2016). Thus, social movements are also *produc-ers of conflict*, in the sense that they fuel and expand social tensions in a society. Another example is the sustainable development plain initiated by the local gov-ernment in Calvia, Spain (Dodds, 2007), which did not get enough support from the key stakeholders on the island and the policies were not implemented.

Weissmann (2008) argued that social movements could act as 'resolvers of conflict.' They call attention to injustices, apply pressure to support social changes or reinforce progressive values (Bacallao-Pino, 2016). By restructuring configurations of power and challenging existing ideologies, social movements may affirm the positive, creative role that conflict can play. Yet, in these studies the focus is mainly on 'progressive' social movements throughout history, such as the US women's suffrage and civil rights movements.

Conflict is inherent to every society, but social movements involving conflicts can lead to undesired and harmful economic and social consequences, such as the closure of shops or of schools (Monterubbio, 2017). In any conflict situation, there is a potential for constructive or destructive social change. The danger is not in the conflict itself, but in its escalation to dangerous and violent levels; thus, the challenge is to manage the conflict in constructive ways.

As Isaac (Chapter 4, this volume) has stated in the case of the Netherlands, the tourism sector is fragile in nature, and is greatly affected by broader natural, economic and socio-political events, which can trigger a tourism crisis (Glaesser, 2006). If a tourism crisis occurs, it may generate a downturn in the image of a destination, resulting in a negative impact on the tourism industry and posing a challenge to destination management (Çakmak & Isaac, 2012). However, many studies in the literature are about tourism crises and are preoccupied with crisis management, while less research focuses on the nature and development of factors causing tourism crises (Cohen & Neal, 2010). Social movements resulting in conflicts can lead to tourism crises (Glaesser, 2006). The relationship between social movements and tourism has been mainly studied in one direction – the impact of tourism on generating social movements and collective resistance (Boissevain, 1996) – yet the impact of social movements on tourism is under-researched (McGehee, Kline, & Knollenberg, 2014).

Monterubbio (2017) analyzes the effect of the CNTE movement (a Mexican national teachers' union that firmly opposed education reform in 2016) and its violent protest activities on the tourism industry, using newspaper reports as information sources. While the tourism industry was not the direct target of CNTE protests, the movement was a catalyst for a tourism crisis. Other studies have investigated the tourism-economic ramifications of socio-political unrest involving protests, although such studies do not necessarily refer to social movements. Based on secondary statistical data, daily newspapers and reports, Winckler and Mansfeld (2015) discussed the impact of the Arab Spring's socio-political unrest in bringing about a decline in international tourism arrivals and negative destination images, and how national governments reacted to mitigate the evolving tourism crisis. Nassar (2012) conducted an ethnographical study on the negative impact of socio-political unrest on the tourism industry and the overall economy of Egypt during the nation's revolution in 2011. However, these studies focused only on socio-political unrest and resulting demonstrations and violent conflictual relations between opponent groups. There is a lack of studies considering social movements as *potential disruptive factors* for the tourism industry of a destination. Also, examining tourism crises' causal factors could help tourism managers' design appropriate anticipative crisis control strategies, and tourism managers could become proactive rather than reactive when a tourism crisis occurs (Monterubbio, 2017).

Methods

A qualitative methodology was adopted to understand the perspectives of stakeholders, and to situate their position in Dresden within the wider contexts of their lives. The approach combined ethnographic fieldwork with narrative interviews to gain an understanding of the social conflict and insights into how stakeholders made sense of their status, of others and of the situations they encountered through *storied experiences* (Mishler, 1995, p. 1999). Ethnographic research has certain characteristics: (i) the study consists of one or a small number of cases usually over a lengthy period of time; (ii) the study adopts a wide initial focus at the start of the study and avoids testing narrow and defined hypotheses; and (iii) it uses several types of data (e.g. observational and/or interview data, documents, statistics, questionnaire data) and has minimal pre-structuring of the data (e.g. detailed field notes, audio and video data) (Konu, 2015). In this study, an emic approach was used to collect the data and to make sense of it following a local's view and also researchers' perspectives (Fetterman, 2010).

The ethnographic fieldwork was conducted in Dresden, Germany, over eight weeks from July to October 2017, including the following: observing protesters in their demonstrations; acting as a tourist in interactions with residents; participating in conferences, workshops and podium discussions; working as an internship at the DMO; conducting semi-structured interviews with experts, tourism professionals and policy-makers; and finally, analyzing media sources about PEGIDA (see Table 11.1).

Narrative approaches have been used widely in tourism studies to explore people's experiences and their identities (McCabe & Foster, 2006; Çakmak, Lie, & McCabe, 2018). Informants express their status, interpretations of object and others, and their emotions through narrative telling of their experiences.

A judgmental sampling method was used to capture a variety of perspectives towards PEGIDA and its impacts on the lives of stakeholders at the destination. All the interviews were conducted in German and translated later into English in the analysis process. The dataset consists of jottings and field notes, policy documents from city hall and other public organizations, promotion materials from tourism professionals, maps, photos, media stories and 29 interviews and conversations collected from key informants working in the public and private sector, tourists, residents, volunteers at civil society organizations and refugees.

An interpretive approach was taken to analyze the data. To interpret meanings, the authors analyzed the context of each story and narrator, and the stated discourse, with a focus on symbol and insights. Later, the narratives were compared in order to detect similarities, contradictions in content and interpretation across informants' positions in the field. Finally, the stories are categorized as big, intermediate and small stories illustrating insights, understandings and interpretations of stakeholder's perspectives in the field.

Such narratives were grouped into three categories: the big stories (Bamberg, 2006), the intermediate stories (Verloo, 2015) and the small stories (Bamberg & Georgakopoulou, 2008). The categories enable a clear division of the most relevant stakeholders and facilitate the explanation of the findings about stakeholders' reactions and positions with regards to the social conflict.

Table 11.1 Fieldwork overview and primary data collection

Ethnographic fieldwork	*Quantity*	*Period*
Interviews with experts	9	20–31 July 2017
Informal interviews and conversations	20	24 July–16 October 2017
(Non)participant observation at demonstrations, café meetings, seminars, podium discussions	8 different locations	20 July–16 October 2017
Conferences and events attended	8	24 August–29 September 2017
Internship at Dresden Marketing Board		7 August–7 November 2017

Findings and discussion

Big stories

The big stories are generated from people, who usually occupy important positions in society and are highly visible in public discourse. They are actively involved in the decision-making processes regarding the social conflict, and have a legitimate mandate to be involved in making those decisions. They also hold the responsibility to come to terms with the conflict, and cannot ignore it. They have the most power and influence to cause changes, as they have authority, a team of people and a sufficient amount of funds at their disposal. Therefore, they have the resources to eventually lead to the conflict's resolution or transformation. However, as a result of their high profile, they are often locked into positions where they feel that they must be cautious as they may represent an entire city and its people, and as such they should act in the best interest of the residents and seek their support. The local government has always guaranteed the *freedom of assembly* and not banned PEGIDA protests, as long as the police could assure that public safety and security were under control during a demonstration. One officer from the city hall said:

> the fact that the city recognises that there is a part of the population that has this kind of opinion [referred to PEGIDA] is an assurance that democracy works in Germany.

However, the City Council sent a clear message through advertising campaigns, public relations, and hosting events (e.g. 'Multicultural Dresden' and 'Citizens Festival') that it does not tolerate racism and does stand for integration and multiculturalism, thus condemning PEGIDA's ideas. These events were largely attended by the residents and generated some positive media coverage.

The local government's strategy was to portray Dresden in a positive light, spreading colourful messages and showing that the city is worth living in and it is cosmopolitan.

A representative of the Tourism Division at the City Hall admitted:

> When PEGIDA first started to march on the streets of Dresden, it was not perceived or recognized as a problem to be dealt with. After the first months of demonstrations and the consequent wide media coverage, it became clear that the issue could not be avoided. This is when the Dresden Marketing Board put into motion a number of strategies to win back visitors to the city and to repair the damaged destination image.

The DMO's strategies mainly aimed to improve the city's image, while at the same time to identify PEGIDA is an important issue to be discussed and dealt with. On the one hand, they attempted to limit the negative press coverage, for instance by intensifying press trips of journalists and bloggers who would spread a more positive view of the destination. On the other hand, they created space in which PEGIDA and related issues were directly addressed and discussed, such as in the *Dresden Magazin* (e.g. 'Interview with the mayor of Dresden and the alderman of culture'; 'Dresden we love you: four famous Dresdners tell their love to their city').

Intermediate stories

Intermediate stories are told by the stakeholders, whose business and operations have been damaged by the PEGIDA activities or as a consequence of the created negative image. These people are mostly the tourism professionals working at hotels, tour operators, transport companies, entertainment providers, in the gastronomy and retail sector, or at cultural and educational institutions like museums and universities. Unlike the key players of the big stories, these stakeholders do not feel an obligation to engage in the social conflict, as their survival does not depend on the worsening, nor resolving, of such conflict. Their position out of the immediate attention provides them with space and the possibility to manoeuvre more freely.

Surprisingly, not every tourism professional did not want to comment on the problematic situation originated by PEGIDA, though many such as hotels and shops in the city centre have been affected by the PEGIDA demonstrations. The famous Taschenbergpalais Kempinski Hotel in the city centre is one of the businesses which comments on the image of Dresden. The manager of the hotel told the national newspaper *Die Welt:*

> The public image of Dresden is catastrophic now. PEGIDA has absolute impact on the volume of Christmas shopping and bookings. Although the occupancy rate in the month December has to be one of the highest, many reservations at the hotel decreased by 50 percent this year compared to previous years.
>
> (*Die Welt*, 4 December 2015)

However, some hotels, in front of which protests happened and whose employees are questioned by confused tourists, are hesitant to comment. They preferred to remain silent and neutral about the situation, refraining from getting engaged in the discussion on public media, and responded their 'business as usual.' An officer working at the Dresden Marketing Board stated:

> International hotel chains chose this approach because they did not want to take a political position, considering their guests or staff could have supported PEGIDA's ideas. I am very disappointed by this passive approach. Despite these entrepreneurs want to present themselves to the international tourism market, they do not take a position against xenophobic attitudes and actions.

However, not all tourism professionals remain silent and some industry associations stated their opinion through their website or the press. For example, one of the hotels in the city centre has posted on its website a few comments from guests who chose not to visit Dresden again because of PEGIDA:

> We had been looking forward to staying in your hotel! But what has been happening on the streets of Dresden for some time now, ruins the visit to this beautiful city. . . . This makes us really angry!

This hotel's director further stated:

> Our hotel employees distance themselves from PEGIDA's ideas and they are disappointed how the movement is negatively impacting the tourism sector. I hope Dresden will soon present itself again as the cosmopolitan city with full of international culture that actually is.

In contrast, non-profit-driven stakeholders, such as cultural and educational institutions, have opted for an active approach of condemning PEGIDA's actions and words, and showed their support for multiculturalism and foreign integration. They preferred to hold a strategy of delivering counter-messages aiming to battle the negative perceptions of the destination. For example, a poster over the entrance of Dresden State Art Collection's recites a slogan that reminds readers of the international influence that shaped the city:

> 14 museums with works from all continents. A large house full of foreigners. We are one nation.

Similarly, the Opera House, the front door of which has been repeatedly used as the location of PEGIDA protests, has displayed colourful banners and flags with slogans advocating for an open and tolerant society.

Small stories

Small stories are presented by the Dresden population at large and reflect the realities of everyday people. These stories are closest to the realities of people who are involved in the social conflict, but have little formal access to the elite. They include people who have contributed to the creation of the conflict and/or added to it, or those who struggle daily with the consequences of it, as well as people who are only sometimes reminded of the conflict; for example, through acts they see, words they hear and images they see. As the social conflict in Dresden revolves around PEGIDA, the 'small stories' include: (i) locals, who are PEGIDA sympathizers – though this is a minority of the population (Police Department Sachsen, 2017); (ii) people who publicly show that they are against PEGIDA; (iii) people who condemn PEGIDA's ideologies but do not openly show they are against PEGIDA; and (iv) people who are undecided or do not have an opinion.

While some of these people have contributed to the creation of the conflict or added to it, others struggle with the consequences of conflict in their daily lives. Yet, all the people, who are involved in the social conflict, have little formal access to the decision-making process in policy formation.

A large number of the interviewed residents distanced themselves from PEGIDA and its ideology; but only a few of them stated that they have participated in anti-PEGIDA demonstrations. As one student stated:

> At the beginning, many creative forms of counter protests were organised by groups of students or by associations such as 'Dresden Nazifrei' or 'Herz statt Hetze'. But then we had no energy anymore, and we also realised that many people didn't take part, we were only around 1,500 people.

Some volunteers working at civil organizations showed actively their detachment from PEGIDA and engaged with social projects advocating pro-multiculturalism. One volunteer said:

> Working in the social projects is more productive than spending time to participate in the counter protests.

The documentary *New City – das bunte Dresden*, directed by a Spanish director, shows the 'positive side' of Dresden, taking the alternative quarter of the Neustadt as an example of multiculturalism in Dresden and narrating projects helping integration between Germans and refugees, such as the Football Club Borea.

However, these event organizers receive some critiques from residents. One stated:

> The city spent taxpayers' money to talk about how allegedly open and multicultural Dresden is, without doing anything to solve real problems. They think Dresden is multicultural but it is not the reality. I like the initiative of the Opera House installing a screen showing some short statements those support integration and diversity, which are written by their employees. This initiative is more 'authentic.'

Besides this project, there are also other counter-social movements against PEGIDA initiated by the community members advocating for a peaceful and inclusive society. For example, 'Cooking Action, the Banda Internationale' have been driven by the residents, who support multicultural values and integration throughout the city and find creative ways to show their socio-cultural engagement. An employee from the Dresden Integration and Foreigners' Commissioner confirms this:

> Since PEGIDA grew bigger, we have seen an enormous increase in events and projects and cooperation partners, we are proud of this, it shows that the society is now more engaged.

Conclusion

The findings of this study confirm the relation between social movements and conflict, supporting Oberschall's (1973) idea that a social movement is a carrier of societal conflicts, and Della Porta and Diani's (2006) conceptualization that social movements are inherently connected to conflict. In addition, our study demonstrates that a social conflict might undermine the attractiveness of a destination and negatively impact social relations within community members.

First, our findings show that PEGIDA is the product of conflict, as it has been formed on the basis of *unspoken grievances* and became a channel to vent feelings and opinions that were already present in the society. Therefore, the movement can be considered as a part of larger social conflict that grew its roots before the movement started. Second, the study suggests that PEGIDA is also a producer of conflict, because it has contributed to enlarge the social tensions among the Dresden community members. PEGIDA has fuelled fights and tensions at community level, as part of the community formed an *anti-PEGIDA* front, while the City Council was faced with the challenge on how to best deal with the thousands of *concerned citizens*, weekly demonstrations causing disruptions, rising acts of discrimination against foreigners and the negative presence of Dresden in the media that damaged the city's reputation.

Furthermore, the present study proposes a new statement, namely that the social conflict is formed by two components: a visible part, and a hidden part. The visible component comprises observable and empirically measurable aspects of the conflict. The most obvious examples are the PEGIDA demonstrations, which are visible to anyone who is in Dresden at a certain time and place. But more importantly, demonstrations become visible to people elsewhere through the media, since both online and offline media promulgate visuals and texts. The visible part of the conflict is therefore easy to perceive by outsiders, who are not involved with the social conflict. Under the visible component of social conflict, three categories can be distinguished: actions, communications and physical signs. Actions include PEGIDA protests and counter-protests, as well as the public events that are a visible source of tension and sometimes violence. Communications occur when someone talks about or refers to the conflict (i.e. during public speeches), particularly when conflicting parties communicate with each other through online and offline media reports related to the conflict. There are also physical signs in the city that represent a visible manifestation of the conflict; for example, the banners of cultural institutions put on their building façades, where they refer to their anti-PEGIDA positioning and in favour of multiculturalism. It can be said that a considerable part of the visible component of the conflict revolves around PEGIDA, as the movement triggered a larger social conflict on the basis of previous social tensions.

At the level of practice, cultural and educational institutions may create new social spaces where people from diverse cultures can interact with each other, city council may promote narratives wherein migrants are presented as integral members of the society and show how they contribute to the wellbeing and economy through increasing available diverse skills and innovation potential at the destination. Finally, the DMO may coordinate events and campaigns wherein residents, business people and volunteers from non-profit-driven organizations work together with a purpose to improve the place brand by highlighting international aspects of the city.

This study and its findings have a number of limitations. Since it involves only one country and one destination context, replication of the study is in order. In addition, this study does not include interviews with PEGIDA sympathizers.

Future research is needed at other destinations afflicted by a social conflict showing similar characteristics to the one in Dresden, where a catalyst such as a social movement intensifies conflictual tensions. The economic, social and cultural impacts of non-progressive or reactionary social movements on tourism destinations need to be determined. Further insights can be gained by applying these methods, which distinguish a visible and a hidden component of conflict. This would allow a confrontation between the outcomes, and improve the consistency and the applicability of recommendations for other destinations. In particular, further research on the impact of radical right populism in Europe is strongly recommended, given its emergence in both Western and Eastern European contexts and a lack of studies on the topic (Muis & Immerzeel, 2017). Finally, as cultural outcomes appear in the long term, it would be interesting to investigate the cultural impact of PEGIDA in Dresden.

References

Bacallao-Pino, L. M. (2016). Agents for change or conflict? Social movements, democratic dynamics, and development in Latin America. *Voluntas*: *International Journal of Voluntary and Nonprofit Organizations*, *27*(1), 105–124.

Bamberg, M. (2006). Stories: Big or small: Why do we care? *Narrative Inquiry*, *16*(1), 139–147.

Bamberg, M., & Georgakopoulou, A. (2008). Small stories as a new perspective in narrative and identity analysis. *Text & Talk*, *28*, 377–396.

Beall, J., Goodfellow, T., & Rodgers, D. (2010). *Cities and conflict*. London: Crisis States Research Centre.

Boissevain, J. (1996). *Coping with tourists: European reactions to mass tourism*. Oxford: Berghahn Books.

Butterwegge, C. (2004). *Rechtsextremismus und Jugendgewalt: Erklärungsmodelle in der Diskussion*. Retrieved 11 June 2018, www.christophbutterwegge.de/texte/Rechte%20 Jugendgewalt.pdf

Çakmak, E., & Isaac, R. K. (2012). Image analysis of Bethlehem: What can destination marketers learn from their visitors' blogs? *Journal of Marketing & Destination Management*, *1*(1–2), 124–133.

Çakmak, E., Lie, R., & McCabe, S. (2018). Reframing informal tourism entrepreneurial practices: Capital and field relations structuring the informal tourism economy of Chiang Mai. *Annals of Tourism Research*, *72*, 37–47.

Cohen, E., & Neal, M. (2010). Coinciding crises and tourism in contemporary Thailand. *Current Issues in Tourism*, *13*(5), 455–475.

Della Porta, D., & Diani, M. (2006). *Social movements. An introduction*. Oxford: Blackwell Publishing.

Die Welt. (2015, 4 December). Retrieved 12 November 2018, from www.welt.de/wirtschaft/article149602145/Pegida-ruiniert-Dresden-das-Tourismusgeschaeft.html

Dodds, R. (2007). Sustainable tourism and policy implementation: Lessons from the case of Calvia, Spain. *Current Issues in Tourism, 10*(4), 296–322.

Dodds, R., & Butler, R. (2019). *Overtourism: Issues, realities and solutions.* Berlin: De Gruyter Oldenbourg.

European Commission. (2011). *Cities of tomorrow: Challenges, visions, ways forward.* Brussels: European Union.

Fetterman, D. M. (2010). *Ethnography: Step by step.* Los Angeles, CA: Sage Publications.

Financial Times. (2016, 21 September). Retrieved 12 November 2018, from www.ft.com/content/66733e8a-8004-11e6-8e50-8ec15fb462f4

Francis, J. (2018). Overtourism: What is it, and how can we avoid it? *Responsible Travel* website. Retrieved 1 November 2018, from www.responsibletravel.com/copy/what-is-overtourism

German National Tourism Board. (2015). Summaries of key facts and figures. *GNTB* website. Retrieved 18 November 2018, from www.germany.travel/en/international-press/facts-figures-information/facts-and-figures.html

Giugni, M., Bosi, L., & Uba, K. (2013). Outcomes of social movements and protest activities. In *Oxford bibliographies in "political science".* Oxford: Oxford University Press.

Glaesser, D. (2006). *Crisis management in the tourism industry.* London: Routledge.

Hamelink, C. J. (2008). Urban conflict and communication. *The International Communication Gazette, 70*(3–4), 291–301.

Heinrich Boll Foundation. (2016). How to counter right wing populism and extremism in Europe. *Heinrich Boll Stiftung-European Union.* Retrieved 5 January 2018, from https://eu.boell.org/en/right-wing-populism-and-extremism-europe

Horn, J. (2013). *Social movements: Evolution, definitions, debates and resources.* Brighton: BRIDGE Gender and Social Movements, Institute of Development Studies. Retrieved 11 June 2018, from http://socialmovements.bridge.ids.ac.uk/sites/socialmovements.bridge.ids.ac.uk/files/07.%202.%20Social%20Movements.pdf

The Irish Times. (2016, 28 September). Retrieved 12 November 2018, from www.irishtimes.com/news/world/europe/foreigners-avoid-dresden-as-pegida-creates-poisonous-mood-1.2807747

Jahn, E. (2015, 10 September). Image problem leads to visitor decline in Dresden. *Deutsche Welle.*

Jasper, J. M. (2007). Social movements. In G. Ritzer (Ed.), *Blackwell encyclopedia of sociology* (pp. 4451–4458). Oxford: Blackwell Publishing.

Konu, H. (2015). Case study: Developing a forest-based wellbeing tourism product together with customers – an ethnographic approach. *Tourism Management, 49,* 1–16.

Kousis, M. (2000). Tourism and the environment: A social movements perspective. *Annals of Tourism Research, 27*(2), 468–489.

Lipsky, M. (1968). Protest as political resource. *The American Political Science Review, 62*(4), 1144–1158.

The Local. (2015, 6 December). Retrieved 12 November 2018, from www.thelocal.de/20151206/romantic-dresden-fears-anti-foreigner-demos-hurting-tourism

McCabe, S., & Foster, C. (2006). The role and function of narrative in tourist interaction. *Journal of Tourism and Cultural Change, 4*(3), 194–215.

McCarthy, J. D., & Zald, M. N. (1977). Resource mobilization and social movements: A partial theory. *American Journal of Sociology, 82*(6), 1212–1241.

McGehee, N. G. (2002). Alternative tourism and social movements. *Annals of Tourism Research, 29*(1), 124–143.

McGehee, N. G., Kline, C., & Knollenberg, W. (2014). Social movements and tourism-related local action. *Annals of Tourism Research, 48*, 140–155.

Menocal, R. A. (2016). *Social movements.* GSDRC Professional Development Reading Pack no. 50. Birmingham: University of Birmingham.

Mishler, E. G. (1995). Models of narrative analysis: A typology. *Journal of Narrative and Life History, 5*(2), 87–123.

Monterubbio, C. (2017). Protests and tourism crises: A social movement approach to causality. *Tourism Management Perspectives, 22*, 88–89.

Muis, J., & Immerzeel, T. (2017). Causes and consequences of the rise of populist radical right parties and movements in Europe. *Current Sociology Review, 65*(6), 909–930.

Nadeau, J., O'Reilly, N., Çakmak, E., Heslop, L., & Verwey, S. (2016). The cameo effect of host country and the transitory mega-event: Patterns of effect on sponsorship evaluation for sport tourists and residents. *Journal of Sport Management, 30*(6), 656–671.

Nassar, M. A. (2012). Political unrest costs Egyptian tourism dearly: An etnographical study. *International Business Research, 5*(10), 166–174.

Novy, J., & Colomb, C. (Eds.). (2017). *Protest and resistance in the tourist city.* London: Routledge.

Oberschall, A. (1973). *Social conflict and social movements.* Englewood Cliffs, NJ: Prentice-Hall.

Police Department Sachsen. (2017). *Annual criminal facts report by police in 2015.* (in German) Retrieved from www.polizei.sachsen.de/de/9549.htm

Richards, G., & Wilson, J. (2004). The impact of cultural events on city image: Rotterdam, cultural capital of Europe 2001. *Urban Studies, 41*(10), 1931–1951.

Rubin, J. Z., Pruitt, D. G., & Kim, S. H. (1994). *Social conflict: Escalation, stalemate, and settlement.* New York: McGraw-Hill Book Company.

Rowen, I. (2016). The geopolitics of tourism: Mobilities, territory, and protest in China, Taiwan, and Hong Kong. *Annals of the American Association of Geographers, 106*(2), 385–393.

Salmenkari, T. (2009). Geography of protest: Places of demonstration in Buenos Aires and Seoul. *Urban Geography, 30*(3), 239–260.

Snow, D. A., Soule, S. A., & Kriesi, H. (2003). *The Blackwell companion to social movements.* Oxford: Blackwell Publishing.

Touraine, A. (1973). An introduction to the study of social movements. *Social Research, 52*(4), 749–787.

Van Dyke, N., Soule, S. A., & Taylor, V. A. (2004). The targets of social movements: Beyond a focus on the state. *Authority in Contention, 15*, 27–51.

Van Stekelenburg, J., & Klandermans, B. (2013). The social psychology of protest. *Current Sociology, 61*(5–6), 886–905.

Verloo, N. (2015). Develop stories, develop communities: Narrative practice to analyze and engage in Urban conflict. In E. Gualini (Ed.), *Planning/conflict: Critical perspectives on contentious urban developments.* New York: Routledge Publishing.

Weissmann, M. (2008, October). *The missing link – bridging between social movement theory and conflict resolution.* Gothenburg: University of Gothenburg. Retrieved 11 June 2018, from the website: https://warwick.ac.uk/fac/soc/pais/research/researchcentres/csgr/garnet/workingpapers/6008.pdf

Winckler, Y., & Mansfeld, O. (2015). Can this be spring? Assessing the impact of the "Arab Spring" on the Arab tourism industry. *Tourism Review, 63*(2), 205–223.

Part III

Tourism and hospitality in post-conflict destinations

12 Memorial entrepreneurs and dissonances in post-conflict tourism

Naef J. Patrick

Introduction

This chapter, which examines cases in Colombia and the former Yugoslavia, seeks to analyze the role of tourism, and in particular related discourses and representations, in the construction of peace. By analyzing the practices and narratives of various stakeholders and citizens directly or indirectly involved in the tourism sector in post-conflict countries, it challenges the idea that the development of tourism naturally contributes to reconciliation and peace-building. Although public bodies and international organizations often present tourism as a tool that helps enhance peace, research has demonstrated that the reality in the field is often much more complex (Naef, 2016a; Viejo-Rose, 2011; Baillie, 2011). In 2004, the French Ministry of Tourism stated in a convention signed with the Secretariat of State for Veterans that 'in times troubled by large international events, tourism of memory [*tourisme de mémoire* in French in the text] appears like a vector of peace, of exchange and of mutual respect between people' (Convention, 2004 cited in Hertzog, 2013, p. 54). Similarly, UNESCO discourses frequently highlight the way cultural tourism contributes to the production of a shared memory. After the war in Bosnia-Herzegovina, the reconstruction of the Old Bridge in the Bosnian city of Mostar – one of the main historical and touristic landmarks of the country – has been repeatedly pointed out as a symbol of reconciliation. The World Heritage list describes it as follows: 'The reconstructed Old Bridge and Old City of Mostar is a symbol of reconciliation, international co-operation and of the coexistence of diverse cultural, ethnic and religious communities' (UNESCO, 2005). However, more than 20 years after the war, while the architectural and technical success of this reconstruction is undeniable, the tense and polarized context still prevailing in this historical town casts doubt on this statement. Some would even argue that the reconstruction of the bridge benefits exclusively the tourism trade, a sector that is becoming the only reliable economic generator in the town. Calame and Pašić (2009, p. 15) note that for certain residents of Mostar, 'if they had been forced to choose, a factory on the outskirts of town would have been preferable to the restored Old Bridge at its center.' Indeed, for them, factories would have provided jobs, 'while the reconstructed Old Bridge merely reminds them of a past that seems irretrievable' (Calame and Pašić, 2009, p. 15). More generally, Young (2012) shares this view of polarized benefits for residents and tourists, pointing out that projects aimed primarily at attracting tourists rarely seek to improve the quality of life of permanent residents.

There is thus a crucial need for academics and practitioners to reach beyond easy metaphors, like the ones featuring bridges and reconciliation, and to take a thorough look at the role of tourism and cultural heritage in divided societies. As will be shown here, stakeholders involved in tourism and peace-building should be cautious when promoting tourism as a tool to enhance peace. This sector can no doubt contribute to a reconciliation process. It can, however, also be a source of tensions. While tourism can contribute in some cases to fostering an 'alternative form of diplomacy' (Kim & Crompton, 1990) and a 'rhetoric linked to peace and international cooperation' (Hertzog, 2013, p. 54), it would be over-simplistic to consider this as a given. In post-conflict settings, tourism activities can reappear quickly after the end of a war, in a highly unregulated setting. Private entrepreneurs, often former war actors, seize this opportunity, offering their services as tour guides or transforming war sites into tourist attractions, as it has been the case for instance in Bosnia-Herzegovina, Croatia and Colombia (see Chapter 13, this volume). By analyzing the practices and discourses of what are conceived here as 'memorial entrepreneurs' (Dwyer & Alderman, 2008; Jordan, 2006; Naef, 2018a), this chapter will show how different and sometimes competing actors contribute to building new touristscapes in these countries, using conflicting narratives and representations. The data presented here are the result of ten years of research focusing on these memorial entrepreneurs in different settings: Bosnia-Herzegovina, eastern Croatia and Colombia. Centred mainly on urban contexts (e.g. Medellín in Colombia, Vukovar in Croatia, Sarajevo in Bosnia-Herzegovina), this research sought to identify these actors and to look at the different ways they exploited war memory and heritage in various cultural practices, including tourism. The methodology is grounded on the anthropological corpus: observation of sites and participation in tours linked to war heritage, semi-structured interviews and focus groups with so-called 'memorial entrepreneurs' and stakeholders from the tourism sector, and a thorough content analysis of print, video and Internet elements.

Memorial entrepreneurs in the realm of tourism

First, the concept of 'memorial entrepreneur' needs to be defined. Building on the work of the sociologist Fine on 'reputational entrepreneurs' (1996), leading experts in the field of memory studies such as Dwyer and Alderman refer to memorial entrepreneurs as people who seek to shape our understanding of the past: 'individuals, alone or in league with others, who endeavour to influence the meaning of social issues and debates about the past' (Dwyer & Alderman, 2008, p. 7). Adopting a broader view than the one proposed by Fine – who limits his conception to the role of social actors in shaping the reputation of historical figures – the two geographers explore the place of commemoration and activism in modelling not only the reputation of historical figures, but also that of the places associated with remembrance. Sharing this view, Jordan (2006) highlights the vital role Berlin's memorial entrepreneurs play in anchoring an official collective memory in one place. Focusing on 'official' memory, she adds that in non-democratic settings, when memory culture is the domain of a single party or a single leader, the role of memorial entrepreneurs is far less important.

In the French context, Michel (2010) develops the concept of 'entrepreneurs of history' (*entrepreneurs d'histoire* in French), also relating it to 'official' memory, when he examines what he refers to as 'memorial governance.' Demonstrating that states have lost their quasi-monopoly in terms of public memory production, Michel limits his conceptualization to public or semi-public actors such as teachers, historians and scholars. Representatives of civil society are excluded from this definition, even if Michel acknowledges that increasing pressure from grassroots movements tends to question the vertical power relation that imposes an official public memory. Building on Dwyer and Alderman's conception of 'memorial entrepreneurs,' the objective here is to expand this definition to include actors from civil society (e.g. artists, novelists, tour guides, journalists, community leaders, NGO volunteers, war veterans, former criminals) in addition to public agents (e.g. public museum curators, government employees, UNESCO collaborators, elected officials). Using an anthropological approach and drawing on an interest in the tourism sector, the author will take a close look at these 'non-official memorial entrepreneurs,' to explore their strategies and the limits they face when expressing and representing a dissonant memory associated with war heritage. A 'memorial entrepreneur' is defined here as an individual contributing to the production of discourses and representations, for commercial or non-commercial purposes, and associated with specific contexts and events, through artistic, documentary, scientific, touristic or heritage practices (Naef, 2018a). In what follows, the study will examine the role of some of these memorial entrepreneurs in the tourism sector, in various settings around the world, specifically highlighting practices associated with so-called 'memorial tourism,' 'heritage tourism' and 'historical tourism.' The author is particularly interested in the way these practices can contribute to diffuse dissonant – and sometimes hegemonic – narratives and representations on the wars in question.

Heritage, tourism and dissonances

In post-conflict contexts, when one leaves the court of law and enters the tourism sphere, or more broadly the domain of heritage management, interpretation takes on a more prominent role. In a sector related to leisure and guided by commercial imperatives, the notion of 'truth' becomes increasingly blurred, raising the question of whether it is the role of tourism to present 'true facts.' Moreover, reconciliation is generally not a priority in the management of museums or other tourism and heritage sites; on the contrary, as the author's personal research has demonstrated, they can participate in spreading significant antagonistic discourses (Naef, 2016a). The concept of 'dissonant heritage' developed by Turnbridge and Ashworth (1996) leads us to explore how a single heritage site or object can be associated with different – and sometimes competing – values and meanings. War and slavery sites around the world show the conflicting viewpoints these places may represent. When war is the issue, definitions such as 'perpetrators,' 'victims,' and 'bystanders' are far from being homogenous and are highly dependent on the interpretation of history. The 'reconciliation vs. division' dichotomy is shaped by many power relations: dominant groups can promote some objects, sites, values, or interpretations and exclude others (Naef, 2016a). As stated by Logan and Reeves (2008, p. 11), one always faces the risk 'that only those places that reflect the official interpretation of historical events are likely to be commemorated and that those places that do not reflect the ideology of the regime in power or the dominant social, ethnic or racial group are neglected.'

It is thus of prime importance to discuss the various practices, discourses and representations promoted by so-called 'memorial entrepreneurs' in the field of tourism, in order to understand how tourism development in post-conflict contexts can serve as a tool for peace and reconciliation. The following focus on cases in Colombia and the former Yugoslavia, and presents various strategies that different actors – tourism stakeholders or simple citizens – use in order to achieve specific objectives, which lie somewhere between division and reconciliation.

Tourism stakeholders and narcos as memorial entrepreneurs in Colombia

Colombia certainly represents an instructive example when it comes to memory work and peace-building. On 17 June 2018, a right-winger, Ivan Duque, was elected president, succeeding the 2016 Nobel Peace Laureate Juan Manuel Santos. One of the first moves of the new president was to announce that he would modify the peace treaty achieved by his predecessor. Although he guaranteed that he would not call into question the peace deal that represents a beacon of hope for many Colombians in a country rent by more than 60 years of armed conflict involving the army, guerrillas, paramilitaries and narcos, the new president – following the hard line of his mentor, former president Alvaro Uribe – clearly stated that he did not want to see guerrilla leaders and narco-traffic patrons walking freely in the streets of the country.

Colombia also experienced a 'memory boom' (Huyssen, 2003; Winter, 2007; Naef, 2018a) after the 2011 'Victims and Land Restitution Law' was signed, a decree that acknowledged the existence of an armed conflict and thus opened the way for stronger protection for the victims. Numerous commemorations and museums focusing on the war sprang up all over the country, as victims exercised their 'right to remember' (Hoskins, 2014). Furthermore, Colombia is now seeing an increasing number of foreign tourists in certain regions where security has progressively improved over the last decade, principally in the Caribbean North. According to the United Nation World Tourism Organization (2016), tourist arrivals in the country rose from 933,000 in 2005 to 2,978,180 in 2015. While many tourism stakeholders, eager to attract foreign visitors and investors, generally aim to do away with the country's violent image – promoting instead touristic resources such as natural beauties, coffee production or Fernando Botero[1] – the heritage and memory associated with the war and drug trafficking are neverthe-less exploited by other entrepreneurs, some of them closely associated with this context of violence. Thus, different and sometimes competing actors contribute to building the Colombian touristscape, using conflicting narratives and representa-tions (see also Chapter 13, this volume).

Representing (or not) Colombia's violent past

> Former gang members (*pandilleros* in Spanish) from the *Egipto* neighbour-hood will take us to what was once a territory where war was waged between gangs and criminal groups. Today it is just a place that aims to help the youngest recover through tourism, art and sport. . . . One former gang mem-ber known as *Calabazo*, will allow us into his house, to tell us what he has lost in his life.

Together with some recommendations on what to bring (money, because 'tips to the locals are part of the community support' and an umbrella 'because there is always a possibility of rain in Bogota'), this is how Zomos, a global travel plat-form, presents its '*Barrio Egipto* Tour' (Zomos, n.d.). The *Egipto* neighbourhood, now part of the *Candelaria* area that hosts many restaurants, guesthouses and museums of the Colombian capital, is known for its invisible borders and its gang wars (in which more than 1,400 people died between 1990 and 2004, according to the *Externado* University, Kowol, 2017). But in addition to being situated just next to one of the most touristy areas of Bogota, it is also near the *Externado* University, one of leading academic institutions in the country. In 2016, the uni-versity, well-known for its tourism administration programme, offered tour guide training to 20 youngsters who had left the *Egipto* gangs. This lead to the creation of the 'Breaking Borders' initiative, where tourism is described as a 'powerful weapon for positive transformation and generation of opportunities': 'See how tourism trumps violence in this amazing tour in Bogotá. These ex-gang members have turned their life around and chosen peace. . . . Be enchanted by the stories of former gang members that now have new dreams, goals and hopes.' (Impulse Immersive Travel Experience, 2018). For a little more than US$50, these tour guides propose a four-hour tailored visit of the area, described as 'unexplored and one of the most antique neighbourhoods of Bogota,' and including sites such as a soccer field, the main cobble-stoned street and even a tasting of the local craft alcoholic beverage: the '*Chicha*.'

As this comment posted by a foreign tourist on the Facebook page of 'Breaking Borders' (n.d.) shows, some of the public authorities, like police officers, may still have doubts about this new tourism venture:

> Jaime is a legend, if you can stomach his history. . . . Halfway through, cops did arrive on motos, and told us these guys were gangsters and would rob us, that we had to come with them to the station to report them. But the two of us believed in Jaime and Alejandro, and we finished the amazing tour.

In other words, while this tour may now feature as a 'top cultural choice' in the *Lonely Planet* travel bible (n.d.), its local recognition is still limited. Similarly, the author's personal research in Medellín (Naef, 2016b, 2018b) has shown that tours focusing on the violent past of the second city of Colombia are chiefly taken by foreigners, mostly North Americans and Europeans. Moreover, although the situation is changing, public bodies related to the tourism sector usually distance themselves from any representations of the violent years that plagued the country (Naef, 2018b; Giraldo, Van Broeck, & Posada, 2014). Andrés, one of the tour guides involved in the '*Barrio Egipto* Tour,' commented to *VICE* (Kowol, 2017) on the complete absence of the state in efforts to enhance peace in his neighbourhood. Besides the support of the private University *Externado*, the creation of this tour in 2016 was inspired by the existence of a similar undertaking in another neighbourhood and another town, also well-known for a context of violence, Commune 13 in the outskirts of Medellín.

Colombia's second largest city, once considered as one of the most dangerous in the world thanks to the Medellín drug cartel and its boss, Pablo Escobar, is now attracting increasing numbers of visitors from all over the world. While local authorities are more than reluctant to feature the city's darkest years – most of the tours promoted by public tourism bodies focus on tango, the flower fest and what is referred to as 'social innovation' – many private entrepreneurs are capitalizing on this violent past through so-called 'narco tours' (or 'Pablo tours') and '*comuna* tours.' When he was released from jail, Roberto Escobar, brother of Pablo Escobar and former treasurer of the Medellín Cartel, converted a house formerly belonging to his brother into a museum dedicated to the drug lord and himself (Naef, 2018b). Dozens of Western backpackers, channelled by local tour guides working with Roberto Escobar, visit this informal museum daily, eager to get a selfie with the former narco-trafficker, especially since the success of the Netflix series *Narcos*. Similarly, after 23 years in jail, Jhon Jairo Velásquez (alias Popeye), Pablo Escobar's main hitman, attempted to move into the tourism scene. According to the regional newspaper *El Pais*, the former narco offers four-hour tours for up to US$1,000 (Palomino, 2017). In another initiative, in 2016 a Puerto Rican tourist operator proposed a four-day trip in Colombia for US$1,449 dollars, labelled '*Medellín en Halloween.*' Aside from the main attractions usually offered during 'narco tours' (the grave of Pablo Escobar, his hacienda in the countryside and other sites related to the drug lord), the key moment of this tourism package was a dinner with Popeye (Restrepo, 2016).

In Medellín's touristscape, Popeye and Roberto Escobar are not the only ones cashing in on the city's violent past. Many 'narco tours' are now available for tourists, most of them foreigners, since locals generally look on this practice with something between curiosity and disgust. Not all tourist and memorial entrepreneurs are former criminals: most of them are citizens who have studied abroad, mainly in the USA, where they learned foreign languages, enabling them to interact with international tourists (Naef, 2018b). Some are also indirectly related to the tourism sector. Pablo Escobar's ex-butler, for example, is now managing a restaurant next to the farm *La Manuela*, near the resort town of Guatapé, where one can participate in the 'Escobar Paintball Tour.'[2] Whatever their background, in one way or another, all these actors are moving into the growing touristscape of Medellín and its region, spreading various and often competing narratives and representations of the drug war and its main symbol, Pablo Escobar; these discourses include condemnation, of course, but some also promote the legitimization, glorification, glamorization and trivialization of Colombia's narco past (Naef, 2018b).

Tourism, memory and transformation

Over several decades, informal neighbourhoods sprang up in the hills surrounding Medellín as widespread violence in the countryside led to the displacement of many inhabitants of rural areas. Guerrillas took advantage of the poverty-stricken social tissue in these settlements to recruit the local youth and develop the illicit trade of drugs and weapons (National Centre for Historical Memory, 2011). At the end of the 1990s, a social cleansing process began, largely supported by paramilitary groups backed by the state: the main objective was to banish guerrillas from Medellín. However, this so-called '*limpieza social*' (social cleaning) also targeted other individuals, such as prostitutes, union leaders and petty criminals. Commune 13, on the western side of the city, was specifically targeted and became an infamous symbol of this process after several military and paramilitary operations took place there. On the other hand, Medellín has won praise globally for its transformation, often referred to as 'the miracle of Medellín' (Navarro, 2014; Moss, 2015). An ambitious 'social investment' programme, launched at the beginning of the 2000s, prioritizes public space recuperation and social projects. Commune 13 plays a key role in the branding of the 'new Medellín.' It has seen the development of large-scale projects, such as the construction of its celebrated outdoor electric stairways. The transformation of Medellín is being used as a tourism resource, especially by the public authorities, who exploit it to sell the image of a city which has recovered from many dark years of violence. In this context, tour guides now offer so-called '*comuna* tours' (Naef, 2016b; Chapter 12, this volume), taking tourists to the informal settlements of Medellín, with Commune 13 being the most visited.

'*Comuna* tourism,' sometimes called 'transformation tourism,' thus gives memorial entrepreneurs directly or indirectly involved in tourism opportunities to disseminate particular representations of the violence associated with Medellín's peripheral neighbourhoods, as well as of the transformation of the city. The author's research (Naef, 2016b) demonstrated that the narrative that is conceived as 'the miracle of Medellín' is a hegemonic and selective discourse, favouring heroic and romantic representations of this process, and covering some of the darker aspects of a city still facing many problems of violence and equity. Here again, memorial entrepreneurs – whether public authorities implicated in the branding of the new Medellín or community leaders trying to make their voices heard – spread different and sometimes dissonant levels of discourse on the city's violent past and its transformation. To limit stereotypes and oversimplifications of the past and the transformation of Medellín, various readings of the city must be encouraged. Tourism can play a significant role in this dynamic by allowing public as well as private entrepreneurs to integrate Medellín's touristcape, hence contributing to showing the numerous aspects of this multifaceted city.

War veterans as memorial entrepreneurs in the former Yugoslavia

Former war actors are also active in tourism practices related to a situation in Europe: they are operating in the post-war cities of Sarajevo (see also Chapter 14, this volume), the capital of Bosnia-Herzegovina, and the town of Vukovar in eastern Croatia. During the wars that rent Bosnia and Croatia, both cities were besieged by the JNA[3] (the Yugoslav People's Army) – which became the Serbian army in the course of the conflicts – and paramilitary groups. The siege of Sarajevo lasted almost four years; the siege of Vukovar went on for three months. Both events caused heavy casualties and left the inhabitants with traumatizing memories. They are now memorialized in contrasting ways; in memorials, commemorations and museums, but also in the touristscapes of these two cities. Divisions caused by the wars, and also by the ways these are memorialized, have been the topics of many debates within academia and international agencies (see, for instance, Baillie, 2011; Baker, 2009; Calame & Pašić, 2009; Capuzzo-Derkovic, 2010; Glasson Deschaumes, 2005; Duijzings, 2007; Kardov, 2007; Naef, 2016a; Petritsch & Dzihic, 2010). Drawing on notions such as 'divided memories' (Baillie, 2011) or 'ethnized heritage' (Kaiser, 2000), scholars have shown how history and memory have been used as instruments of political manipulation, promoting nationalistic discourses, and often causing harsh confrontations between the communities in the region. In 2010, Petritsch and Dzihic (2010, p. 20) stated that 'diverging memories and selective narratives of the recent past are still dominant in the former states of Yugoslavia. There are still no traces of dialogic remembering at all.' Colin Kaiser (2000), former director of the UNESCO office in Sarajevo, has said that technical problems related to reconstruction in the former Yugoslavia are far less serious than the ethnic divisions caused by heritage management.

However, while scholars have had intensive discussions on issues of war memory and division in the former Yugoslavia, the role of tourism has been underexplored until recently (Naef, 2016a; Dragićević Šešić & Rogač Mijatović, 2013; Aussems, 2016; Kamber, Karafotias, & Tsitoura, 2016; Arnauld, 2016; Čorak, Mikačić, & Ateljević, 2013). The wars in Bosnia-Herzegovina and Croatia had catastrophic impact on their tourism sectors. Croatia recovered rapidly, but Bosnia-Herzegovina took more than ten years to regain its pre-war tourism market, a market far smaller than that of its neighbour. Nevertheless, the wars related to the breakup of Yugoslavia gave rise to cultural heritage production and the touristification of war sites, memorials and museums. In the post-conflict settings of Vukovar and Sarajevo, private memorial entrepreneurs started to offer visitors 'war tours' (Naef, 2016a). These tailored tours are conducted by former war actors, such as ex-soldiers or fixers, or individuals less implicated in the conflict, such as students who were exiled during the sieges, but who – as in the case of Medellín's 'narco tours' – speak foreign languages and can thus interact with international visitors. These guides propose visits to war sites such as front lines and destroyed buildings. In addition, both cities have significant numbers of war museums and memorials that are heavily promoted by the tourism sector, especially in Vukovar, which is considered in Croatia to be a symbol of the martyrdom, bravery and independence of the country. Indeed, at the end of the 1990s, the town experienced a form of memorial tourism in which Croats from all over the country came to pay their respects to this martyred town and region (Kardov, 2007).

The memory of the war and its unilateral interpretation

Vukovar, close to the Serbian border, is a divided city. Croats have a hostile relationship with the local Serbian community, which stayed in their hometown after the period in which the region came under Serbian control and was named the 'Serb Republic of Krajina' (Kardov, 2007; Baillie, 2011). This division is noticeable in many ways: in political declarations, in discrimination in the employment market and even in public inscriptions (in Cyrillic for Serbians and in Latin for Croats). Moreover, due to the symbolic role of Vukovar in the Croatian imagination, the tourism sector is intrinsically associated with the memory of the conflict: most of the landmarks promoted are memorials underlining the martyrdom of Croatia, and hence the guilt of Serbia. The city map distributed by the Vukovar Office of Tourism in 2010 is illustrative of this phenomenon: 13 of the 20 sites singled out for visitors are directly related to the war: memorials, cemeteries or ruined buildings. In addition, the back cover of the map features the emblematic illustration of 'The Croatian Association for Prisoners in Serbian Concentration Camps' (Naef, 2016a). Many jobs in museums and memorial centres at that time were held by Croatian war veterans, some of them named '*Braniteljis,*' a reference to soldiers and inhabitants who decided to stay in the town to fight the assailants. These memorial entrepreneurs were thus influential in diffusing hegemonic and unilateral narratives on the past war, presenting Croats as solely 'victims' and inevitably, Serbs as solely 'perpetrators.' Serbian memorial entrepreneurs and material symbols are therefore almost absent in Vukovar's memorialscape; but in surrounding villages dominated by Serbian majorities, the opposite is true.

In Sarajevo, a somewhat similar, but certainly more nuanced, phenomenon can be seen. Like the country[4] of which it is the capital, the city is officially divided. 'East Sarajevo,' mostly composed of suburbs, is predominantly inhabited by a Serbian population. The rest of the city, encompassing the old city and most of the touristic highlights and museums, is more diverse, but is predominantly populated by Bosniaks (or Bosnian Muslims). This political division has produced a touristscape entirely administered by the Canton of Sarajevo in which museums and other historical sites are managed by Bosniak actors, leaving only the administration of surrounding natural parks to local Serbian tourism stakeholders. As a collaborator of the Ministry of Tourism and Trade of the *Republika Srpska* (the Serb Republic of Bosnia-Herzegovina) commented in 2011:

> Most part of Sarajevo is within the Federation. In the Republika Srpska we have mostly the suburbs, but the core is in the Federation. . . . There are less tourism attractions in the Republika Srpska, so we don't do much. And all the international institutions and foreign companies are in the Federation.
>
> (Personal communication, 11 July 2011, cited in Naef, 2016a)

At the state level, tourism management is almost non-existent and financial resources are scarce. Cantons (in the Federation) and municipalities (in the Republika Srpska) are thus the chief actors in this context, a dynamic often leading to the diffusion of one-sided and nationalistic narratives. As a result, discourses and representations of the history of the siege in museums and other cultural sites in Sarajevo are presented solely by Bosniak memorial entrepreneurs. Of course, these narratives are far from being homogenous, and it would be over-simplistic to describe them all as unilateral representations of the last war. Nevertheless, Serbian memorial entrepreneurs are left without any way of participating in the construction of Sarajevo's memorialscape. This dynamic can also be observed in the practices of Bosniak 'war tour' guides, who often encourage tourists participating in their tours to 'learn from the other side' (Naef, 2016a). Unfortunately, in the Republik Srpska, 'war tours' are not available.

Memorial entrepreneurs in a contested touristscape

In the former Yugoslavia, in the post-war cities of Vukovar and Sarajevo, tourism is an active participant in memory conflicts. Different memorial entrepreneurs – tourism stakeholders, war veterans and simple citizens – take part in the construction of contested memorialscapes through the touristification of war memorials and the intense promotion of 'war tours' and war museums. While some tour guides and museum projects clearly try to diffuse a message of peace and reconciliation detached from the overwhelming nationalistic narratives characterizing the former Yugoslavia (see, for instance, the History Museum of Bosnia-Herzegovina's permanent exhibition 'Sarajevo Under Siege' which focuses on the inhabitants without mentioning their nationalities), a significant majority of tourism representations and discourses related to the memory of the war tend to present a unilateral version of history, involving clear-cut categories of victims and perpetrators. In parallel with the wide corpus of work on domains like politics, media and cultural heritage management, analyzing tourism practices is thus crucial to understanding memorial issues in the region. In the former Yugoslavia, tourism has been sometimes hastily presented as a tool for peace and reconciliation by international bodies (e.g. UNESCO, UNWTO, the European Commission). However, as the author's research has demonstrated, it can also contribute to increasing tensions.

Although rooted in very distinct contexts, cases like Vukovar and Sarajevo can provide interesting insights into the development of tourism in post-conflict Colombia. In Medellín's rapidly evolving touristscape, memory of violence is expressed in ambivalent ways. Private memorial entrepreneurs cash in on the fascination that the narco-world can exert on an international audience (see, for instance, the Netflix series *Narcos*), but also on the local population (for instance, the success of so-called *narconovelas* in the country). These new actors in the field of tourism propose 'narco tours' – an offer that is now one of the most popular with the city's foreign visitors – and play a role in spreading contested narratives and representations on the narco-related past. Moreover, the touristification of the memory of violence that plagued the country also inspires rejection within public bodies trying to promote the image of a transformed city, as well as among locals (many of whom are direct or indirect victims of the narcos).

The objective of this chapter has been to focus on the individuals involved in memory practices and their role in the development of tourism in post-conflict contexts. While all of them are to some extent involved in the tourism sector of the cases explored, the scope of the subject goes beyond the study of tourism stakeholders. For an in-depth understanding of the role of tourism in post-conflict contexts, it is of foremost importance to enlarge the focus to other actors in the tourism sphere. Artists, former criminals, community leaders, war veterans and NGO collaborators, to mention only a few, can play important roles in the dissemination of tourism narratives and representations associated with the memory of war. Studies often tend to overlook these 'alternative tourism stakeholders' and focus on only one side of the problematic. Therefore, the concept of 'memorial entrepreneurs' advocated here is a broad one that includes official as well as non-official actors involved in tourism and memorial practices. It is particularly interesting in how grassroots initiatives evolve in the burgeoning – and sometimes unregulated and free-ranging – touristscapes of post-conflict cities. By giving close attention to what is excluded or included in these memorial entrepreneurs' narratives, we will gain a better understanding of the role of tourism and memory in sites recovering from wars.

Conclusion

This chapter has stressed the importance of carefully analyzing problematics identified in tourism and dissonant memory in post-conflict contexts. While the complex relationships between tourism and memory of war have been widely explored in tourism studies, this topic is still surprisingly under-explored in the case of the former Yugoslavia and Colombia. The work briefly presented here aims to partly fill this gap and lay the foundations for future research. Through a close look at the role of official and non-official memorial entrepreneurs in tourism practices, this chapter has sought to explore some of the power relations associated with dissonant interpretations of post-war memory, in order to demonstrate that, although tourism is often presented as an instrument for peace and reconciliation, it can also serve as an ideological tool to adapt, obliterate or reinvent dissonant memories.

Notes

1 A famous Colombian painter and sculptor.
2 Havis (2018). www.escobarpaintball.com/
3 Jugoslovenska narodna armija.
4 Following the Dayton Agreement that ended the Bosnian war, Bosnia-Herzegovina was divided in two entities: the Federation of Bosnia and Herzegovina (FBiH), with mostly Bosniaks and Croats, and the Republika Srpska (RS), with mostly Serbs.

References

Arnauld, F. (2016). Memorial policies and restoration of Croatian tourism two decades after the war in former Yugoslavia. *Journal of Tourism and Cultural Change, 14*(3), 270–290.

Aussems, E. (2016). Cross-community tourism in Bosnia and Herzegovina: A path to reconciliation?. *Journal of Tourism and Cultural Change, 14*(3), 240–254.

Baillie, B. (2011). *The wounded church: War, destruction and reconstruction of Vukovar's religious heritage* (PhD). University of Cambridge, Cambridge.

Baker, C. (2009). War memory and musical tradition: Commemorating Croatia's Homeland War through popular music and rap in Eastern Slavonia. *Journal of Contemporary European Studies, 17*(1), 35–45.

Breaking Borders Facebook page (n.d.). Retrieved 9 July 2018, from www.facebook.com/pg/breakingBordersCol/reviews/

Calame, J., & Pašić, A. (2009). *Post-conflict reconstruction in Mostar: Cart before the horse*. Divided Cities/Contested States Working Paper Series 7. Cambridge: University of Cambridge.

Capuzzo-Derkovic, N. (2010). Dealing with the past: The role of cultural heritage preservation and monuments in a post-conflict society. In W. D. Offenhässer, C. Zimmerli, & M.-T. Albert (Eds.), *World heritage and cultural diversity*. Bonn: German Commission for UNESCO.

Čorak, S., Mikačić, V., & Ateljević, I. (2013). An ironic paradox: The longitudinal view on impacts of the 1990s homeland war on tourism in Croatia. In R. Butler & W. Suntikul (Eds.), *Tourism and war* (pp. 161–175). London: Routledge.

Dragićević Šešić, M., & Rogač Mijatović, L. (2013). Balkan dissonant heritage narratives (and their attractiveness) for tourism. *American Journal of Tourism Management, 3*(1B), 10–19.

Duijzings, G. (2007). Commemorating Srebrenica: Histories of violence and the politics of memory in Eastern Bosnia. In X. Bougarel (Ed.), *The new Bosnian mosaic: Identities, memories and moral claims in a post-war society* (pp. 141–166). Farnham: Ashgate.

Dwyer, O. J., & Alderman, D. (2008). *Civil rights memorials and the geography of memory*. Athens: University of Georgia Press.

Fine, G. A. (1996). Reputational entrepreneurs and the memory of incompetence: Melting supporters, partisan warriors, and images of president harding. *American Journal of Sociology, 101*(5), 1159–1193.

Giraldo, C., Van Broeck, A. M., & Posada, l. (2014). El pasado polémico de los años ochenta como atractivo turístico en Medellín, Colombia. *Anuario Turismo y Sociedad, 15*, 101–114.

Glasson Deschaumes, G. (2005). Mémoires en excès, mémoires en creux dans les pays de l'ex-Yougoslavie. In M. Aligisakis (Ed.), *Europe et mémoire: une liaison dangereuse?* (pp. 115–141). Geneva: Institut européen de l'Université de Genève.

Havis, M. (2018) Pablo Escobar's ruined mansion is now a paintball venue. *Daily Mail*, 2 July. Retrieved January 28, from 2019, https://www.dailymail.co.uk/news/article-5908489/Mansion-Pablo-Escobar-stashed-cocaine-cash-secret-compartments-paintball-venue.html

Hertzog, A. (2013). Quand le tourisme de mémoire bouleverse le travail de mémoire. *Espaces, 313*, 52–61.

Hoskins, A. (2014). Media and the closure of the memory boom. In K. Niemeyer (Ed.), *Contemporary nostalgia and media: Yearning for the past, the present, and the future* (pp. 118–125). Basingstoke: Palgrave Macmillan.

Huyssen, A. (2003). Diaspora and nation: Migration into other pasts. *Contemporary German Literature, 88*, 147–164.

Impulse Immersive Travel Experience. (2018). Retreived July 9, 2018, from https://impulsetravel.co/tour-operator/en/bogota-tours/day-trips/sightseeing-tours/bogbreak/breaking-borders

Jordan, J. A. (2006). *Structures of memory: Understanding urban change in Berlin and beyond*. Palo Alto, CA: Stanford University Press.

Kaiser, C. (2000). En ex-Yougoslavie, la destruction du patrimoine culturel a brisé l'identité commune des citadins, et satisfait un rêve archaïque dans les campagnes. *Le Courrier de l'UNESCO, 8*, 41–42.

Kamber, M., Karafotias, T., & Tsitoura, T. (2016). Dark heritage tourism and the Sarajevo siege. *Journal of Tourism and Cultural Change, 14*(3), 255–269.

Kardov, K. (2007). Remember Vukovar: Memory, sens of place, and the national tradition in Croatia. In S. P. Ramet & D. Matić (Eds.), *Democratic trandision in Croatia: Value transformation, education and media* (pp. 63–88). Austin, TX: Texas University Press.

Kim, Y.-K., & Crompton, J. L. (1990). Role of tourism in unifying the two Koreas. *Annals or Tourism Research, 17*, 353–366.

Kowol, M. (2017, 5 September). Egipto: de barrio bravo a "destino turístico" en Colombia. *Vice*. [online] Retrieved 9 July 2018, from www.vice.com/es_mx/article/paa93n/egipto-de-barrio-bravo-a-destino-turistico-en-colombia

Logan, W., & Reeves, K. (2008). Introduction: Remembering places of pain and shame. In W. Logan & K. Reeves (Eds.), *Places of pain and shame: Dealing with "difficult heritage"*. Oxon: Routledge.

Lonely Planet. Colombia. (2018) Retrieved 9 July 2018, from www.lonelyplanet.com/colombia/bogota/activities/breaking-borders/a/poi-act/1581858/363308

Michel, J. (2010). *Gouverner les mémoires: Les politiques mémorielles en France*. Paris: Presses Universitaires de France.

Moss, C. (2015, 19 September). Medellín, Colombia: A miracle of reinvention. *The Guardian*. [online] Retrieved 15 August 2018, from www.theguardian.com/travel/2015/sep/19/Medellín-colombia-city-not-dangerous-but-lively

Naef, P. (2016a). *La ville-martyre*. Geneva: Slatkine.

Naef, P. (2016b). Touring the "comuna": Memory and transformation in Medellín, Colombia. *Journal of Tourism and Cultural Change, 16*(2), 173–190.

Naef, P. (2018a). L'escombrera' de Meellin: une fosse commune entre reconnaissance et oubli. *Géographie et culture, 105*, 27–47.

Naef, P. (2018b). "Narcoheritage" and the touristification of the drug lord Pablo Escobar in Medellín, Colombia. *Journal of Anthropological Research, 74*(4).

National Centre for Historical Memory. (2011). *La Huella invisible de la guerra: Desplazamiento forzado en la comuna 13.* Bogota: Taurus.

Navarro, A. (2014, 26 January). La ejemplar metamorfosis de Medellín. *El Faro.* [online] Retrieved 15 August 2018, from https://elfaro.net/es/201401/internacionales/14559/

Palomino, S. (2017, 23 June). La cara b del 'narcotour' de Pablo Escobar desmitifica al capo de Medellín. *El País.* [online] Retrieved 9 July 2018, from https://elpais.com/internacional/2017/06/23/colombia/1498172784_237146.html

Petritsch, W., & Dzihic, V. (2010). Confronting conflictual memories in (South East) Europe: An introduction. In W. Petritsch & V. Dzihic (Eds.), *Conflict and memory: Bridging past and future in (South East) Europe* (pp. 15–27). Baden-Baden: Nomos.

Restrepo, V. (2016, 29 September). Agencia que vendió paquetes turísticos para ver a alias "Popeye" será investigada. *el Colombiano.* [online] Retrieved 9 July 2018, from www.elcolombiano.com/antioquia/agencia-turisticos-de-puerto-rico-vende-paquetes-para-visitar-a-alias-popeye-en-Medellín-CA5075602

Turnbridge, J. E., & Ashworth, G. J. (1996). *Dissonant heritage: The management of the past as a resource in conflict.* Hoboken, NJ: John Wiley & Sons.

United Nations Educational, Scientific and Cultural Organization (UNESCO). (2005). *World heritage list: Old bridge area of the old city of Mostar.* [online] Retrieved 7 July 2018, from https://whc.unesco.org/en/list/946

Viejo-Rose, D. (2011). Memorial functions: Intent, impact and the right to remember. *Memory Studies, 4*(4), 465–480.

Winter, J. (2007). The generation of memory: Reflections on the memory boom. *Contemporary Historical Studies, Archives & Social Studies: A Journal of Interdisciplinary Research, 1,* 363–397.

World Tourism Organization. (2016). *Compendium of tourism statistics dataset.* Madrid: UNWTO. [online] Retrieved 7 August 2018, from http://statistics.unwto.org/news/2016-02-22/methodological-notes-tourism-statistics-database-2016-edition

Young, Y. E. (2012). *City branding and urban tourism: A case study of Seoul and Taipei.* 6th Conference of the International Forum on Urbanism. [online] Barcelona: TourBanism, pp. 1–10. Retrieved 15 August 2018, from http://hdl.handle.net/2099/12607

Zomos. (2012) Retrieved 9 July 2018, from https://zomoz.travel/co/activities/4134/tour-barrio-egipto-el-barrio-que-utiliza-el-turismo-para-la-paz

13 Taking tourism matters into their own hands

Phoenix tourism in Moravia, Medellín, Colombia

Anne Marie Van Broeck

Introduction

Since a peace treaty was signed in 2016 between the Colombian government and the guerrilla FARC (Revolutionary Armed Forces of Colombia), Colombia is entering a 'post-conflict era' (although some prefer calling it a 'post-agreement' phase) and the country is shedding little by little its image as a dangerous place in the world; it is no longer considered a no-go zone for tourism. In Medellín, long considered among the most dangerous cities in the world because of violent conflicts between several different non-state groups and between these groups and state actors, violence has dropped drastically over the years (Doyle, 2016, 2018). Together with urban transformations, this has contributed to a better image of the city, making Medellín attractive for tourists, some of whom want to learn something about the (violent) past. Many know, for instance, before arriving about the drug lord who left a strong mark on the city, due to the popular Netflix series *Narcos*. For others, upon arrival in town, the 'curiosity factor' makes them wonder about the conflicts and violence they have heard about.

The *Museo Casa de la Memoria* gives visibility to these conflicts and their victims. Also in – generally contested (Van Broeck, 2018) – tours about Pablo Escobar, tourists get some information about the crime-related past. Yet in general, the violence and conflict is (deliberately) not a central theme in the city's tourism image. The theme does pop up (generally only briefly and indirectly addressed), mainly in several tours in 'transformed' neighbourhoods, which have been (and still are) strongly associated with poverty and violence.

This chapter presents the results from an investigation conducted in 2017 and 2018 in Moravia, one of these 'transformed' neighbourhoods, and explores the local residents' perspective – in particular, their response to tourism development in their community.

After presenting some relevant literature, the research is contextualized, describing Medellín. Moravia and tourism development are then introduced, followed by the findings. These are presented in the context of 'Phoenix tourism' (Causevic, 2008; Causevic & Lynch, n.d., 2008, 2011), which refers to tourism development in a post-conflict setting through the visiting of conflict-related sites, and the way members of the local community which was involved in the conflict become included, integrated in and empowered for tourism, resulting in social reconciliation, community revitalization and urban regeneration.

Dark tourism, local residents and Phoenix tourism

Research on tourism and war is not new; within different disciplines and from different approaches, the relationships between them have been under scrutiny (Butler & Suntikel, 2013; Van Broeck, 2017). As such, various authors have placed the visiting of battlefields, war cemeteries and other war- or conflict-related sites under the label of cultural or heritage tourism; others have looked at this from the angle of dark tourism, broadly defined as tourism to places where tragic events have taken place in the past or to sites associated with tragedies, disasters and death. This research will borrow from this latter field, and reflections are made with some dark tourism literature as a backdrop.

Light, after reviewing two decades of academic research into dark tourism and thanatourism, concluded that 'the perspectives of local communities as a stakeholder group have been largely neglected to date,' suggesting that 'future research might focus on the ways in which local communities are impacted by, negotiate, and respond to becoming the focus of tourist interest based on a particular instance of death or tragedy' (Light, 2017, p. 296). Authors who have taken a look at the communities' perception of and/or response to tourism – such as Coats and Ferguson (2013) and Wright and Sharpley (2016) on disaster tourism after earthquakes in New Zealand and Italy, respectively; Kim and Butler (2015) on crime-related tourism in South Australia – address the need for inclusion of local residents' perspective and voices. Also in slum tourism literature, frequently considered a niche of dark tourism, the perspective of residents remain largely unknown (Slikker & Koens, 2015; Kieti & Magio, 2013). For the involvement of local communities in tourism to sites of recent conflict, the publications of Causevic and Lynch shed some light (Causevic, 2008; Causevic & Lynch, 2008).

> It is not possible to force people to start developing tourism as if nothing has happened. It is not that easy to forget. A society needs some time to rise from the ashes. That time is phoenix tourism.
>
> (Causevic, 2008, p. 353)

Phoenix tourism cannot be considered a type of tourism, but is rather a transitionary phase. It is a kind of tourism 'in between' (Causevic, 2008; Causevic & Lynch, 2008, 2011).

Several recurrent themes appear in research on the perception and/or the response of the local residents. The chronological distance to the event is an important determinant. Generally, the closer to the event, the more emotional the connections, and people might not have had the time to 'heal.' As such, it is considered easier to talk about the conflict when 'sufficient' (or a long) time has passed. Then, it concerns an interpretation of an already 'historical' site, and the occurred has become part of the historical memory (Causevic, 2008). As such, when tourism arrives (too) early, often some resentment could be observed, while more acceptance is noticed over time.

Factors contributing to leniency are the business opportunities and/or economic benefits tourism might generate for local residents, even indirectly; for instance, by way of a donation to contribute to the (recovery of the) community. When, to the contrary, external private businesses or public instances get the benefits, they might be considered 'unethical and insensitive to seek profit from the disasters and misery' (Coats & Ferguson, 2013, p. 37). Also,

> profit-generating business activity related to viewing the site of the disaster was acceptable if there was a financial contribution towards the recovery; without such a donation, residents felt as though they were 'being taken advantage of.'
>
> (Coats & Ferguson, 2013, p. 56)

Similar reactions were observed in Belfast (Boyd, 2013; Causevic, 2008), where locals considered the commodification of their struggles by outsiders as an exploitation of the legacy of the conflict.

As dark tourism is frequently related to a 'difficult past' (Knudsen, 2011) and 'dissonant heritage' (Tunbridge & Ashworth, 1996), there is among the residents a concern about the story told, and possible inauthenticities and biases: Who is telling the story? Whose story is told? And how is it been told? (Coats & Ferguson, 2013; Kim & Butler, 2015; Van Broeck, 2018; Causevic & Lynch, 2008). Communities often feel proprietorial; since it is their story, they should tell to the world (Causevic, 2008). Also, the selection of the narratives is very complicating: stories might present partial truths, be an official story, collide with efforts to (re) define collective memory, to forget or remember, etc.

Wright and Sharpley (2016, p. 9) comment also that, especially when the elapsed time is rather short, 'focal points . . . that could symbolize the human tragedy' and/or 'places where the human story . . . could be told, contemplated or understood' are still missing. Memorials or sites to commemorate the victims, for instance, are of primary importance for the community but can also evolve to become of interest by tourists.

Urban conflicts, social transformation and tourism in Medellín

Medellín has long been known as one of the most violent and lethal cities in the world. Between 1975 and 2012, the city counted 90,000 homicides (Martin, 2014). Between 1980 and 2014, about six of every 100 persons had been a direct victim of armed conflict and associated violence, including forced displacement and disappearance, recruitment of minors, kidnapping, sexual violence, massacre, torture, social cleansing and extortion, caused by paramilitary groups (25%), guerrillas (15%), groups after demobilization (15%) and the state (1%). In the majority of these cases, nevertheless, the victimizer remained unrecognized (Centro Nacional de Memoria Histórica, 2017).

Violence was originally mainly related to crime, in particular the drug trade. Since the 1980s, several generations of drug traffickers have used Medellín as a centre of their activities and developed criminal actions within the framework of their expansion as drug cartels. Well-known is Pablo Escobar and the Cartel of Medellín, but also other drug-related groups operated in the city during his life and mainly after his death, such as 'La Oficina de Envigado.'

While at first the political conflict took mainly place in rural areas, by the end of the 1980s the guerrillas also arrived in the city, forming the so-called militias, extending their influence into several peripheral barrios. Paramilitary organizations responded immediately to this, often with the support of important sectors of the political and economic elites of the region, eliminating the militias. These paramilitary groups (and occasionally earlier, the guerrillas) 'grafted' themselves onto existing structures of various city gangs in these areas, thereby imbedding themselves in the local communities. Since these local criminal groups were often important in the control of the drug trade, drug-related crimes and armed political conflict became entwined.

After 1991, the most violent year in the city's history, violence in the city reduced due to several causes (see Doyle, 2016). At the beginning of the 21st century, the urban conflict could mainly be characterized by the violence of criminal groups (locally called BaCrim), who were in control in several neighbourhoods and associated with micro-trafficking, charging protection money from local businesses and public transportation, the intimidation of locals, invisible frontiers and curfews. Especially heavy turf wars with rival groups caused a majority of the homicides in Medellín (Avendaño, 2015). By the end of August 2017, a non-aggression agreement between major criminal actors brought some tranquillity ('Se ajusta el pacto,' 2017).

It was Mayor Sergio Fajardo (2004–2007) who included the concept of 'social urbanism,' which is considered the driving force of the transformation of several *comunas* (a conglomerate of neighbourhoods) in the city politics. Through investment of public resources in architecture, urbanism and community projects (infrastructure, education, mobility, cultural promotion), driven by his and subsequent administrations, in these formerly marginalized and neglected, poorer areas of the city, Medellín passed 'from fear to hope' (Alcaldía de Medellín, 2007) and – little by little – was transformed. This led to international recognition in 2013 as 'the most innovative city' (Camargo, 2013), for 'the infrastructural developments perceived to have contributed to the rapid decline in violence' (Doyle, 2016, p. 8). Although some authors (Gil Ramirez, 2013; Doyle, 2016, 2018) dispute how much credit should be given to social urbanism policies for this decline, the official discourse tends to point out to the successes of the transformation, supported by research results; for example:

> The decline in the homicide rate was 66% greater in intervention neighborhoods than in control neighborhoods . . . and resident reports of violence

decreased 75% more in intervention neighborhoods. . . . These results show that interventions in neighborhood physical infrastructure can reduce violence.

(Cerdá et al., 2012, p. 1045)

In contrast to other cities in the world (see e.g. Buckley & Witt, 1985, 1989), tourism was not used in Medellín as a strategy to bring about urban regeneration. Even more, it was not considered in the urban intervention policies (López Zapata, Sepúlveda, & Gómez Gómez, 2015, 2017). Rather, tourism came to these renewed areas in the city in the wake of the urbanistic interventions. While hosting the 7th World Urban Forum (2014), some tours were organized by the municipality to proudly show the international visitors the transformation of the city. During approximately the same time period, tourism actors were also invited to discover these neighbourhoods to be promoted as new tourism products (Naef, 2018; tour operator, interview 2017).

By the end of 2017, the municipality promoted the '*Rutas de Turismo Comunitario*' in eight selected areas in the city, among which were some of the transformed neighbourhoods formerly little or not considered in the city's tourism marketing. It mainly promotes existing the local initiatives in neighbourhoods, associated with strong community dynamics (Sub Secretary of Tourism, interview 2018), instead of directly creating opportunities to bring about urban regeneration. As such, the *comunas* of Medellín are changing from trenches of war into tourist destinations (*Las2orillas*, 2018).

Research methods

The findings presented are partial results of ongoing explorative and qualitative research about tourism in Moravia. The first phase took place during 2017, in collaboration between researchers from the Instituto Universitario Colegio Mayor de Antioquia and the Corporación Universitaria de Sabanata (Unisabaneta), both from Medellín, and the Catholic University of Leuven (KU Leuven), Belgium. The second phase was started with a visit in June 2018 by the author.

The research is based on fieldwork, including visits in the neighbourhood and participant observation during two half-day tours (Real City Tours, in 2017; Colombia Immersion, in 2018), and several interviews with community leaders (individually and in groups), tour providers in Moravia and public tourism stakeholders. A debate organized in Moravia in May 2017, in the context of this research, shed light on how the community was looking at the tours passing through their barrio. All interviews were digitally recorded and transcribed. The interviewees are identified by anonymous names to protect privacy when cited in this chapter. Some complementary desk research and web analysis (review of the tour websites) was done, also.

Local youngsters from Moravia, studying tourism, were asked to develop scripts for touristic routes related to memory and peace, transformation and hope in their neighbourhood, thus illustrating what they considered to be important places to show to visitors.

Between December 2017 and June 2018, significant changes could be observed in the local residents' response towards tourism. While writing/publishing this chapter, things are changing continuously; therefore, this chapter should be considered a snapshot.

A history of Moravia: conflicts in a 'transformed' barrio

The origin of Moravia is related to the migrations from rural areas to the Medellín during the 20th century, at first driven by the industrialization, but later by the war. People arrived in Moravia from the 1960s onwards. Between 1977 and 1984, the administration located the main dumpsite of the city in this neighbourhood – yet the place continued attracting victims of the violence in the countryside who settled on the hill of tons of waste, on 'El Morro.' On several occasions fires destroyed many precarious dwellings and Moravia became associated with bad living conditions, poverty and violence.

The city's urbanization policy led – once again – to the (forced) relocation of several families (Osorio Gaviria, 2014; *Kienyke*, 2014). Many people were opposed to this displacement, and police intervention was used (Naef, 2018; Chaparro, 2017). Even today, some families still refuse to leave their home on the hill, continuing to offer resistance (*Medellín Travel*, n.d.). Several persons feel discontent about what took place and mention it as a conflict with the municipality.

The neighbourhood had its share of urban violence, drug traffic- and crime-related, as well as violence due to the presence of guerrillas and paramilitaries. There are links between Moravia, Pablo Escobar and the *sicarios* of the cartel of Medellín (*Kienyke*, 2014); turf wars were fought between local gangs; the neighbourhood was also known for being one of the traditional dumps of corpses of the city ('La Curva del Diablo': Medina, 2006); and the Milicias Populares del Valle de Aburrá (MPVA, a guerrilla-related militia) also centred its actions in this neighbourhood from 1989 onwards until they demobilized in 1994 (*El Tiempo*, 1994), as did also other non-state groups in 1998 and 2003 (Dardanya, 2011).

It would be too optimistic to consider the reduced and less visible violence and the (armed) conflicts completely over, as some conflicts still exist. The interviewees pointed out that several actors (such as former perpetrators) are still around and have changed 'hats' several times. Demobilizations and reintegration are often just like a 'turnstile,' by which one leaves one violent actor group, reintegrates, but next (re-)enters the conflict by association with another actor group (community leader, interview 2017).

These situations have led to silence(s), and there are still many 'innombrables,' unnamable/unmentionable topics (community leader, debate 2017), which hinder the collective construction of the memory of the violent past; yet, some steps have been taken. Some community leaders succeeded in creating a commonly agreed-upon timeline with pictures representing the neighbourhood's history/story, as a collective memory. These photos are shown in the Center of Cultural Development of Moravia. Dardanya (2011) worked also with the community to visualize elements of their history. In both, obviously, the violent past was present.

Tourism in Moravia: *recorridos* and tours

Traditionally, the Center of Cultural Development of Moravia (CDCM), and in particular the Center of the History of the Neighborhood, has been the gateway to Moravia for many visitors, such as volunteers or visitors of local NGOs. Employees of this Center and community leaders frequently were asked to guide visitors around in a *recorrido* to provide a general view of the barrio, or on the specific topic of their interest – such as environmental issues, the urban development of the barrio, the transformation or the urban violence – especially in those days when the neighbourhood was perceived as dangerous and people feared to enter the territory.

Four years after the participants of the World Urban Forum could take a tour to get to know the transformed Moravia (World Urban Forum, 2014), nine tour operators are offering a visit to this neighbourhood, either as a specific tour (such as those the author participated in) or including the neighbourhood in a broader tour. Real City Tours, which started in September 2016, and has brought between then and July 2018 around 1,500 tourists to Moravia (Álvarez, personal conversation, 2018), is perceived as the one most frequently visiting the neighbourhood. Recently, the visits of Medellín, City of Contrast also are on the rise (community leader, conversation 2018). While the former focuses completely on Moravia, the latter tour operator spends less time in the neighbourhood, with it being only a part of a broader tour in the city.

All commercial tours (in contrast to the non-commercial *recorridos*) were managed and run by people from outside the neighbourhood, but in June 2018, two local start-ups appeared on the horizon: Moravia Tours and Memoria Tours (community leader, conversation 2018).

The community of Moravia has been absent or marginal in participating in the delivery of these commercial tours, except for giving some explanation at a particular site, such as in the greenhouse on top of 'El Morro." 'By 2018, some change could be observed: two community leaders were contracted to accompany once weekly a group of Real City Tours and also Medellín Soul Tourism had a youngster from the neighbourhood participate in their tours (community leader, interview 2018).

Community leaders formulated their discontent with the fact that outsiders were bringing in tourists. This relates in the first place to the question about who has the right to tell about Moravia. Residents pointed out that often tour guides, who themselves only recently came to know the neighbourhood, are following a memorized script. Some considered that only those who had experienced life in Moravia – and the conflicts – have the right to talk about it, a position obviously challenged by external tour providers, who see also a place for an external view and narrative.

> I think that this tourist activity does serve us, to visualize this memory, but that it is important, that we, the inhabitants of the territory do this activity, because there may be people who have a very good investigation, . . . but it

is not the same, because one can tell the story but one will always have questions. . ., so these stories only have them who lived them.

(community leader, debate 2017)

Just as one cannot hide themes, one cannot hide voices, . . . so everyone has the right to talk about everything, it is absolutely fundamental that people can talk; the issue that people who have lived closer to the conflict feel more authority is absolutely natural . . . but also. . ., I think you cannot despise the one who did not live it, who studies it from afar, the one who looks from the outside.

(tour operator, interview 2017)

During the fieldwork in June 2018, a related reason for this resentment became clear: several community leaders perceived they were not valued (even that they were looked down upon) as competent storytellers by some external providers, since they do not know English nor have the 'adequate' experience.

Finally, community leaders complained about the fact that external tour operators make profits with these commercial tours while relating their story, while on the contrary, tourism leaves few or no economic benefits to the residents or the community. A strong resentment is felt towards those tour operators who make promises to take the community into account, such as in sharing some benefits, and then do not deliver. Some other tour operators have a strong commitment with the community, such as Real City Tours, which returns some of its profits in social processes in Moravia, and also Medellín Soul Tourism, which considers itself to have a social responsibility.

The story (to be) told: transformation and conflict

Based on analysis of the relevant websites, tour operators seem to present mostly a more general story of the barrio and emphasize its transformation. Most of the tour names refer to this urban process or its results: 'From Garbage to Gardens: Discovering El Morro de Moravia' (Bauman, 2016); 'Moravia: Gardens and Flowers' (Siclas, n.d.); the 'Barrio Transformation Tour' (Real City Tours, 2017); 'Medellín Renace: Moravia' (Medellín Soul Tours, 2018); 'Memory and Social and Urban Transformation' (Medellín, City of Contrast, 2018a, 2018b); 'Medellín Social Urbanism' tour (Juan Camillo/Tours by Locals, 2017).

Several tours refer mainly to positive aspects, as such following the official discourse, although some do seem to put raise questions. Tour operator Haus refers in its text to the 'struggles to avoid being displaced from their homes' (Casa Encuentro Guatape, 2015). Real City Tours puts the transformation under scrutiny by asking on its website: 'are you wondering whether there is an untold truth behind this iconic story?' During the tour, the guide aimed to give a balanced view on what had happened, trying to let all voices be heard and therefore did not avoid describing the conflicts with the municipality, pointing out how the transformation also left victims. The guides of Colombia Immersion also touched on these different facets.

On the other hand, there is little reference to other conflicts in the website descriptions of the commercial tours. Colombia Immersion refers to the past violence in the city in general terms, and to the conflict which led to the displacement of people towards and within the city (Bauman, 2016).

Medellín Soul Tours refers very explicitly to the violent past while promoting the tour in English (something which is not done in the Spanish version):

> The first thing you may think about when having our invitation to visit a humble neighborhood of our city, is it safe to go there? We say: of course! All our neighborhood share the same history; state abandonment, violent wars and booms of big drug traffickers coming out of their streets. Also, they share a present that is drawn differently and that is something that fills us today with pride: the transformation, the hope and the push of its people to see their neighborhood reborn. Each neighborhood in our city has its own way of telling the consequences of those years of war, its struggle and its new bet.
>
> (Medellín Soul Tours, 2018)

The topic of the violent past of Moravia was also rather limited developed during the tours. Pablo Escobar was mentioned as a supporter at the soccer field, and Colombia Immersion also referred to the neighbourhood the narco built and the houses he donated to several poor families of Moravia. Real City Tours only mentioned this when asked about it. Both tour guides did also mention at the soccer field the turf war between two local gangs, which was resolved in 2009 by a symbolic soccer game ('*El partido de las locas*': Kienyke, 2014). Real City Tours also took the time to explore the photos in the CDCM.

In contrast, the script for the *recorridos* developed by some community leaders in an attempt to standardize the information presented ('Guía Visita Guiada,' n.d.), does refer to several social problems (prostitution, use of drugs and common crime). It elaborates also on the origins and presence of self-defence groups and local gangs, and the practice of collection of protection money. In addition, the negotiation and the following demobilization of the MPVA and their reintegration as a civilian organization in 1994 is described and illustrated by one of the pictures of the timeline in the Center. Another picture, representing the communal labour by which the barrio (sewerage, aqueduct, etc.) was constructed, evokes the story of a conflict with the municipality about property rights, being one of several perceived social injustices. The written script is further rather neutral and limited in information about the transformation and the conflictive relocation of the inhabitants of 'El Morro' ('Guía Visita Guiada,' n.d.), and therefore seems to avoid elaborating on the conflicts with the municipality's administrations. Nevertheless, when the interviewees talk about their neighbourhood, this topic surfaces frequently and easily.

Although a little bit more elaborate, the script of the *recorridos* is also rather brief on the conflicts of the neighbourhood ('Guía Visita Guiada,' n.d.). Nevertheless, there seem some stories ready to be told about the conflict, the resilience and resistance. An independent reflection by one of the leaders (Hernández, 2017), the scripts developed by several youngsters studying tourism and the interviews for this research revealed an incipient cartography of several places representative of the conflicts, which could become 'focal points' (Wright & Sharpley, 2016, p. 9) where the story could be told. Moravia counts with little physical memorials, remembering the past conflicts or their victims (interviews with community leaders 2017, 'Programa de Atención a Víctimas,' 2010); however, mid 2018, a mural appeared referring to Father Vicente Mejia, who played an important role in the formation of popular urban organizations. Tourism could take advantage to tell here his role in the social conflicts.

Various cultural expressions, such as graffiti and hip-hop, illustrate the resilience of the population (Bejarano, Arroyave, Saldarriaga, Urrego, & González, 2017). Therefore, another initiative to follow up on is the 'Flames walking tour Moravia,' sharing the story of Moravia through encounters between tourists and local youngsters, who found a way to resist and survive the conflict through dance and music. As such, the local culture might lure the tourists to get to know life in Moravia (similar to what happened in another area in the city, *Comuna 13*, with graffiti and hip-hop).

As one of the community leader suggested:

> We have to know first the living heritage within the territory, then sit at a desk, where we can visualize all the actors in the territory, all the ways of telling our story, it would be excellent if all Moravia could count all his stories, because Moravia cannot yet tell all his stories, because its actors are still being part of this difficult subject, being the war in our country; so Moravia cannot openly tell his stories. But there are ways in which art can do it, and we have a good reception of the histories of the territory, in performance, in other forms of culture that can tell these stories, these experiences, and make a tourism that does not make the situation of the territory dangerous. So, for me, it is possible that a responsible tourism is done within the territory.
>
> (community leader, debate, 2017)

Local participation in tourism

Local participation in tourism is mainly limited to a few brief encounters (mutual greeting, small talk) between tourists and locals, or related to an occasional small purchase, such as green mango juice in a local business or *patas de gallina* or water from a street vendor (stops included in the tour). Since there is no local tourism infrastructure, like coffee shops, restaurants or hostels catering specifically to tourists, tourism is leaving few direct (economic) benefits.

At first hesitatingly, some community leaders looked for greater involvement. By October 2017, the desire to get involved was clear, as was a need for capacity building. After having taken a course on touristic and cultural entrepreneurship (offered by I.U. Colegio Mayor de Antioquia, as a consequence of this research), some participants felt empowered and addressed the Municipality about not being included in the 'Community Tourism Routes' (see earlier). This led in April 2018 to the inauguration of 'la Mesa del Turismo of Moravia' whereby different local stakeholders started combining forces. Several leaders are at present following a course on Community Tourism (SENA). Ideas are sprouting; new opportunities for local informal and formal entrepreneurship, and alternatives to benefit more economically from the tourists while visiting the area, are looked for. Since more and/or appropriate tourist infrastructure near the greenhouse on top of the hill (bathrooms, shady places, etc.) is required, some are helping and looking for alliances with international NGOs. They hope that tourists might even contribute to Moravia's further development.

Social reconciliation, community revitalization and urban regeneration

Some particularities of the urban conflict should be taken into account when considering social reconciliation through tourism development in Moravia. In contrast to Belfast, where a peace agreement was signed between opposing parties where the different actor groups can be easily defined (delimited) and are considered 'equals,' the situation is not as clear-cut in Moravia's conflicts. In some tours in Belfast (Causevic, 2008), as well as in Israel/Palestine (Isaac, 2010; Mejdi Tours, 2017), people from (formerly) opposing groups are telling together both sides of the story to tourists, as such offering multiple narratives. This is not yet the case in Moravia, and presently no such partnership has been found. The society has not yet really incorporated the reintegrated *guerrilleros* or paramilitaries, and also for them, silence offers often more security, especially in view of possible reprisals as vengeance. It is not yet time to have such multiple narratives in Moravia. Notwithstanding, in our conversations with the community leaders in 2017, some expressed prudently that they could imagine this dual vision in the future.

So, while such partnerships do not seem present or easily within reach, others are being developed, aligned with the residents' growing involvement in tourism development. Although there are still very different opinions within the association of community leaders, and personal or leadership rivalries, by 2018 several leaders seemed to have become more conscious about the advantages of working together ('If we don't unite, we drown' was heard during a meeting in 2018), participating in and creating as community tourism projects. Several have chosen to take part in the courses offered to them, and steps forward are taken.

Another partnership is that between the different local stakeholders who are part of the 'Mesa de Turismo.' Even alliances with entrepreneurs/residents from *La Comuna 13*, another transformed area which went through a similar tourism development, have been established, when several community leaders went for the first time in their life to this neighbourhood, in the context of capacity building. Although some leaders still show some reluctance, others have made alliances with tour operators as a step in getting involved in tourism development.

Post-conflict tourism can contribute to urban regeneration and community revitalization (Causevic & Lynch, 2008). Although it was not used as a strategy by the Municipality, the new tourism developments in Moravia might obviously further contribute to these dynamics, which were set in motion before. New tourist infrastructure such as the one planned on top of the hill is an example. Also, the expected boost to small businesses will contribute to community revitalization. Finally, residents seem happy with the fact that now foreigners are visiting their neighbourhood, they feel recognition and are proud to show them around. This resembles the following observation:

> Although tourists come to the area to see the sites of the previous conflict, they tend to show interest in the community and their way of life and in that sense bringing pride and self-esteem back to the community.
>
> (Causevic & Lynch, 2008, p. 12)

Some final thoughts

This chapter has focused on the local residents' perspective (primarily of several community leaders) on tourism in the post-conflict setting of Moravia, in particular their response to the so far externally steered tourism development in their community.

Interesting to note was their discontent, not as such with the tourists, but rather with the external tour operators and tour guides. This could be partly explained by the fact that locals were missing out economic benefits while others were obtaining profits telling their story. The residents felt that they should tell their story, since they were the ones who had lived it; even more so as they feared that the story told might not be the whole truth. Since the official discourse (of the municipality) sees the transformation only as a success, there clearly is some dissonance with the story the local residents want to communicate.

Although the short time since the violent conflicts in the neighbourhood brings without doubt an emotional connection, there is also another issue at stake when one considers it too soon to talk about some histories. This has more to do with some prudency, since some actors of the conflicts are still around. For the moment, some things are still *innombrables*, but one day, hopefully in the near future, the stories of the conflict might be part of the collective memory and of the preserved heritage. It is not yet clear how and what the residents will tell when they tell their own stories, yet their lives have been continuously intertwined with survival, resilience and resistance, and therefore probably the (past) conflict will be part of their stories. It would also be interesting to research the tourists' perspective. What do they know – and want to know – about the (violent) past of this neighbourhood, or for that matter, of the city? Do they just want to get off the beaten track and visit a 'different' (marginalized, poor, etc.) neighbourhood? Is this just a 'slum tour'?

Although incipient, the elements mentioned in the definition of 'Phoenix tourism' are present: a (relatively) post-conflict setting, visiting conflict-related sites, and a growing participation of the local community in tourism. The local community is getting empowered by capacity building and the installation of the 'Mesa del Turismo'; some residents are starting small businesses or preparing to tell the story of Moravia themselves. It might be interesting to look in the future at the evolution of this development within the framework of community-based tourism, its threats and opportunities, without discarding the post-conflict context. If not yet through partnerships with actors of the violence, tourism has contributed to new social dynamics, and can strengthen community revitalization and urban regeneration. Residents see a role for tourism in the further development of the neighbourhood.

For now, the Phoenix (and Phoenix tourism) is starting to arise from the ashes of Moravia: the residents are taking tourism matters into their own hands.

References

Alcaldía de Medellín. (2007). *Del miedo a la Esperanza.* [pdf] Medellín: Alcaldía de Medellín. Retrieved 18 March 2018, from www.scribd.com/document/357637 539/66114877-Sergio-Fajardo-Del-Miedo-a-la-Esperanza-pdf

Análisis Urbano. (2017, 28 August). Se ajusta el pacto del fusil. Retrieved 19 March 2018, from http://analisisurbano.org/se-ajusta-el-pacto-del-fusil/

Avendaño, M. (2015, 12 March). Medellín: menos homocidios, pero. . .'. *El Espectador.* [online] Retrieved 17 March 2018, from www.elespectador.com/noticias/nacional/Medellín-menos-homicidios-articulo-549125

Bauman, A. (2016). From garbage to gardens: Discovering El Morro de Moravia. *Colombia Immersion.* Retrieved 18 March 2018, from www.colombiaimmersion.com/2016/06/17/urban-project-Medellín-moravia/

Bejarano, H., Arroyave, M., Saldarriaga, M., Urrego, C., & González, D. (2017). El turismo urbano como oferta turística alternativa en Medellín: Comportamientos espaciales de la ciudad como destino turístico. *Revista Humanismo y Sociedad, 5,* 8–16. doi:10.22209/rhs.v5n1a02

Boyd, S. (2013). Tourism in Northern Ireland: Before violence, during and past violence. In R. Butler & W. Suntikel (Eds.), *Tourism and war* (pp. 176–192). London and New York, NY: Routledge.

Buckley, P., & Witt, S. (1985). Tourism in difficult areas: Case studies of Bradford, Bristol, Glasgow and Hamm. *Tourism Management, 6*(6), 205–213.

Buckley, P., & Witt, S. (1989). Tourism in difficult areas II: Case studies of Calderdale, Leeds, Manchester and Scunthorpe. *Tourism Management, 10*(2), 138–152.

Butler, R., & Suntikel, W. (Eds.). (2013). *Tourism and war.* London and New York, NY: Routledge.

Camargo, M. (2013, 1 January). Medellín, la ciudad más innovadora del mundo. *Semana.* [online] Retrieved 17 March 2018, from www.semana.com/nacion/articulo/Medellín-ciudad-mas-innovadora-del-mundo/334982-3

Casa Encuentro Guatapé. (2015). Haus, Moravia: Fall in love with Medellín. Retrieved from http://casaencuentro.co/tour-moravia-2/

Causevic, S. (2008). *Post-conflict tourism development in Bosnia and Herzegovina the concept of Phoenix tourism* (PhD). University of Strathclyde, Strathclyde.

Causevic, S., & Lynch, P. A. (2008, 21 October). Tourism development and contested communities. *EspacesTemps.net, Works.* Retrieved 17 March 2018, from www.espacestemps.net/en/articles/tourism-development-and-contested-communities-en/

Causevic, S., & Lynch, P. A. (2011). Phoenix tourism: Post-conflict role. *Annals of Tourism Research, 38*(3), 780–800. doi:10.1016/j.annals.2010.12.004

Causevic, S., & Lynch, P. A. (n.d.). *The significance of dark tourism in the process of tourism development after a long-term political conflict: An issue of Northern Ireland.* Conference paper. Retrieved 17 March 2018, from www.mecon.nomadit.co.uk/pub/conference_epaper_download.php5?PaperID=1355&MIMEType=application/pdf

Centro Nacional de Memoria Histórica. (2017). *Lanzamiento de Medellín: memorias de una guerra urbana.* Retrieved from www.centrodememoriahistorica.gov.co/noticias/noticias-cmh/Medellín-memorias-de-una-guerra-urbana

Cerdá, M., Morenoff, J., Hansen, B., Tessari Hicks, K., Duque, L., Restrepo, A., & Diez-Roux, A. (2012). Reducing violence by transforming neighborhoods: A natural experiment in Medellín, Colombia. *American Journal of Epidemiology, 175*(10), 1045–1053. doi:10.1093/aje/kwr428

Chaparro, I. (2017). The Oasis: A story of displacement and resistance. *Esempi di architettura.* Retrieved from www.esempidiarchitettura.it/ebcms2_uploads/oggetti_articolo_267_ITA_EMEaNRmmaUgPPUpeXtJx3TtyUfcTrH5VmAVYg8ah.pdf

Coats, A., & Ferguson, S. (2013). Rubbernecking or rejuvenation: Post earthquake perceptions and the implications for business practice in a dark tourism context. *Journal of Research for Consumers, 23,* 32–65.

Dardanya, P. (2011). *La memoria reciclada.* Project realized for the Encuentro Internacional de Medellín, MDE11. Retrieved from www.pepdardanya.com/?p=372&lang=en#_ftn5

Doyle, C. (2016). Explaining patterns of urban violence in Medellín, Colombia. *Laws, 5*(1), 3, 1–17. doi:10.3390/laws5010003

Doyle, C. (2018). "Orthodox" and "alternative" explanations for the reduction of urban violence in Medellín, Colombia. *Urban Research & Practice.* doi:10.1080/17535069.2018.1434822

El Tiempo. (1994, 8 April). En firme, proceso de paz con milicias de Medellín. Retrieved from www.eltiempo.com/archivo/documento/MAM-96223

Gil Ramírez, M. (2013, 26 May) Medellín: entre la esperanza y el miedo. *Razón Pública.* Retrieved from www.razonpublica.com/index.php/regiones-temas-31/6851-Medellín-entre-la-esperanza-y-el-miedo.html

'Guía Visita Guiada. Sector Moravia.' (n.d.). Not published script for recorridos by the local community leaders.

Hernández, L. M. (2017). *Moravia Chuliao.* Not published document to develop touristic route in Moravia, Medellín.

Isaac, R. K. (2010). Alternative tourism: New forms of tourism in Bethlehem for the Palestinian tourism industry. *Current Issues in Tourism, 13*(1), 21–36. doi:10.1080/13683500802495677

Juan Camillo, J./Tours by Locals. (2017). *Medellín social urbanism II.* Retrieved form www.toursbylocals.com/SocialUrbanism-II

Kieti, D., & Magio, K. (2013). The ethical and local resident perspectives of slum tourism in Kenya. *Advances in Hospitality and Tourism Research (AHTR), 1*(1), 37–57.

Kim, S., & Butler, G. (2015). Local community perspectives towards dark tourism development: The case of Snowtown, South Australia. *Journal of Tourism and Cultural Change, 13*(1), 78–89.

Knudsen, B. (2011). Thanatourism: Witnessing difficult pasts. *Tourist Studies, 11*(1), 55–72.

Las2orillas. (2018, 5 April). Las comunas de Medellín: de trincheras de guerra a destinos turísticos. Retrieved from www.las2orillas.co/las-comunas-de-Medellín-de-trincheras-de-guerra-destinos-turisticos/

Light, D. (2017). Progress in dark tourism and thanatourism research: An uneasy relationship with heritage tourism. *Tourism Management, 61,* 275–301.

López Zapata, L., Sepúlveda, W., & Gómez Gómez, J. (2015). El Rol del turismo en los planes de ordenamiento territorial de Medellín. *ABET (Anais Brasileiros de Estudios Turisticos), 5*(2), 26–34.

López Zapata, L., Sepúlveda, W., & Gómez Gómez, J. (2017). El turismo en sectores informales a partir de la experiencia en el mejoramiento integral de barrios en Medellín. *Revista de Turismo, Patrimonio y Desarrollo, 3*(5), 48–70.

Martin, G. (2014). *Tragedia y Resurrección: Mafias, Ciudad y Estado. 1975–2013.* Bogotá: La Carreta Editores.

Medellín, City of Contrast. (2018a). *Free tour.* Retrieved from www.freetour.com/ Medellín/medell%C3%ADn-city-of-contrasts-free-tour

Medellín, City of Contrast. (2018b). *Historic center and its contrasts.* Retrieved from https://ogusakira.wixsite.com/Medellíncitycontrast

Medellín *Kienyke.* (2014, 7 December). Moravia: el barrio que floreció sobre una montaña de basura. Retrieved from www.kienyke.com/historias/moravia-Medellín-el-barrio-que-florecio-sobre-una-montana-de-basura

Medellín Soul Tours. (2018). Medellín Renace: Moravia. Retrieved from http://Medellín-soultours.com/tour/Medellín-renace-moravia/

Medellín Travel. (n.d.). Jardín de Moravia: de cómo una ciudad transforma la basura en vida. Retrieved from https://Medellín.travel/MedellínTravelWeb/trends/237/jardinmoravia Medellín

Medina Franco, G. (2006). *Una historia de las milicias de Medellín* (1st ed.) [pdf]. Medellín: Instituto Popular de Capacitacion. Retrieved 17 March 2018, from http://209.177.156.169/libreria_cm/archivos/pdf_762.pdf

Mejdi Tours. (2017). Multiple narratives. Retrieved from www.mejditours.com/why-mejdi/ multiple-narratives/

Naef, P. (2018). Touring the "comuna": Memory and transformation in Medellín, Colombia. *Journal of Tourism and Cultural Change,* 16(2), 173–190. doi:10.1080/14766825. 2016.1246555

Osorio Gaviria, D. (2014). *Moravia: The story of a slum on a hill of garbage.* Unpublished Paper, Master of Human Settlements, KU Leuven. Retrieved from www.academia. edu/10623171/Moravia_The_story_of_a_slum_on_a_hill_of_garbage

Programa de Atención a Víctimas del Conflicto Armado de la Secretaría de Gobierno de la Alcaldía de Medellín. (2010). *Imágenes que tienen memoria.* Medellín: Alcaldía de Medellín.Real City Tours. (2017). Barrio transformation tour. Retrieved from www.real citytours.com/barrio-transformation-tour/

Siclas. (n.d.). *Moravia: Gardens and flowers.* Retrieved from www.siclas.org/en/tours/

Slikker, N., & Koens, K. (2015). "Breaking the silence": Local perceptions of slum tourism in Dharavi. *Tourism Review International, 19,* 75–86. doi:19.10.3727/1544272 15X14327569678876

Tunbridge, J. E., & Ashworth, G. J. (1996). *Dissonant heritage: The management of te past as a resource in conflict.* Chichester: J. Wiley.

Van Broeck, A. M. (2017). *Conflicto y turismo: una revisión bibliográfica.* Memorias Conferencias Centrales CONPEHT Medellín. Turismo Sostenible para la Paz (ISSN 2590-6208), Medellín, 21–25 de octubre, pp. 1–7. Retrieved 20 July 2018, from conpeht. com/revistas/r1/1.%20Art%C3%ADculos%20cortos/1.1%20CONFlICTO%20Y%20 TURISMO.%20UNA%20REVISI%C3%93N%20BIBLIOGR%C3%81FICA.pdf

Van Broeck, A. M. (2018). Pablo Escobar tourism – unwanted tourism: Attitudes of stake-holders in Medellín, Colombia. In P. R. Stone, R. Hartmann, T. Seaton, R. Sharpley, & L. White (Eds.), *The Palgrave handbook of dark tourism studies* (pp. 291–318). London: Palgrave Macmillan.

World Urban Forum. (2014). Medellín lab tours. *The New North*. Retrieved from http://wuf7.unhabitat.org/Medellín-lab-tours

Wright, D., & Sharpley, R. (2016). Local community perceptions of disaster tourism: The case of L'Aquila, Italy. *Current Issues in Tourism*, *21*(14), 1569–1585. doi:10.1080/13683500.2016.1157141

14 Narrating the scars of Sarajevo

Reminiscent memories of war and tragedy in the landscape

Nicholas Wise

Introduction

The creation of a war-tourism destination in the period following a conflict is often temporary, but memories of war in the landscape and media narratives suggests war is embraced as part of the attraction (Jansen-Verbeke & George, 2013). Sarajevo (in Bosnia-Herzegovina) was negatively impacted by a siege that lasted more than 1,000 days between 1992 and 1995. After the war, the city attempted to recover as journalists and early tourists who visited Sarajevo experienced what was considered an open-air museum of tragedy and destruction. Over time, tourism increased, but the city's landscape remained scarred. Tourism opportunities and visitor attractions aimed to educate visitors about war and conflict in Sarajevo and (across the Balkans) in the early 1990s. This chapter will focus on narrations of Sarajevo's landscape and memories of war as presented in newspapers accessed from LexisNexis Academic, now called Nexis Uni, to link narratives with critical observational reflection and interpretation. The analysis is framed around three sections: (i) landscapes frozen in the 1990s; (ii) touring the tunnel of survival; and (iii) roses of remembrance. Interpretations and discussion of the content and observations will be guided by theories of landscape, memory and representations of destinations post-conflict. War impacts a destination in numerous ways, especially the visitor economy, which was difficult to calculate during the Balkan conflict until a tourism office was established in 1997 (Izvor, 2014). Tourism statistics before the siege in Sarajevo, for all of Bosnia-Herzegovina, as part of the Republic of Yugoslavia, note that in 1986, tourism peaked with over two million visitors, with the majority of visitors spending time in Sarajevo (Osmanković, 2017). Average annual growth of over 10% in the decade since the war ended has since been recorded (Osmanković, 2017); 2006 was the first year the city attracted over 100,000 tourists (*Nanaimo Daily News* [British Columbia], 16 August 2008), and the city surpassed 300,000 by 2014 (Izvor, 2014).

This chapter offers a discussion of reminiscent memories of war and tragedy in Sarajevo's landscape. The author of the chapter has conducted research across the Balkans region and has spent time in Sarajevo assessing and analyzing the scars that provoke remembrance of conflict. War did not destroy Sarajevo's elegance. In 2007, the World Travel and Tourism Council estimated only 12% of

Bosnia-Herzegovina's economy was directly linked to tourism and that war sites were among the more popular attractions (*Nanaimo Daily News*, 16 August 2008). There are several key attractions that, lest we forget, memorialize what happened in Sarajevo, and from the point of arrival into the city visitors simply need to see the bullet holes and bombed structures throughout the city that persist as landscape remembrance (see Wise, 2011). This is where the everyday urban landscape tells a story of Sarajevo's past, with building façades bearing scars. For a more formal tour of Sarajevo's struggles during the war, visitors make their way to the city's airport to visit what remains of the Tunnel Museum which acted as a lifeline for those who risked their lives to protect the city. While a small part of the tunnel remains, it gives those who visit a chance to try to understand the difficulties of bringing in supplies and getting people to safe territory. Finally, the Roses of Sarajevo are also distinct points of landscape remembrance as dedicated memorials created shortly after the war to remind people where someone lost their life, with mortar impressions filled in with red paint (now faded pink in hue). People remember and create formal and informal memorials in different ways; in Sarajevo, these roses bear meaning for those who lost loved ones. By filling the cracks in the pavement with concrete and paint, a rose gives way to memory and meaning where tragedy struck.

This chapter will now turn to a review of the literature on landscape, image, memory and post-war tourism. Much work builds on discussions from the work of human social and cultural geographers, and considers how tourism scholars have borrowed and conceptualized their understandings in tourism studies. The following section is comprised of the three subsections outlined earlier using content from newspaper articles as well as reflections and interpretations from the author's experience of tourism research in Sarajevo. The chapter will conclude with some research directions going forward concerning the need to look at how memories of war fade with time.

Landscape, image, memory and post-war tourism

This chapter relates to several areas of academic literature, linking notions from human geography and tourism studies. Acknowledging work on landscape provides insight on how images and memories in post-war tourism destinations are consumed (Lennon & Foley, 2000). From a social and cultural geographical understanding, a cultural landscape results from collective human transformations often updated or altered by different style and activities (Cresswell, 2014; Morin, 2003; Wylie, 2007), and when places are impacted, this can significantly scar (or erase) landscapes (Ashworth & Hartmann, 2005; Wise, 2011). Rowntree (1996) argues that landscapes are impacted by historic narratives, but as noted in this chapter, descriptions of tourist and journalistic accounts suggest perceptions of landscapes are 'not just the world we see, it is a construction, a composition of that world. Landscape is a way of seeing the world' (Cosgrove, 1984, p. 13) and the accounts that directly alter and affect places – such as war and conflict. Because landscapes are scenes, they reflect a unique sense of place identity in a locale; therefore, an image is portrayed, and when something tragic happens, we seek ways to memorialize places and spaces.

While war impacts the landscape, it greatly impacts perceptions of places; thus, the image of a destination (Vanneste & Foote, 2013). Image research is important to acknowledge in this chapter, given the wide discussion in the tourism literature (see, for example, Beerli & Martín, 2004; Cartier & Lew, 2005; Hall, 2003). Linked to the wider discussions in this chapter, image and memory are complementary conceptualizations, because it is the past that makes people aware of a place's image and reputation (Wise & Mulec, 2012). Images are presented to prospective visitors through the media as textual or visual discourses, offering subjective imaginations of places and destinations (Lehtonen, 2000). Thus, landscape scenes are often presented, and such visuals are crucial because they leave lasting impressions in people's memories given more permanent scars in places impacted by war. Conceptually, this is made evident by Clouser (2009, p. 7), who suggests: 'the power of a landscape can be seen in its ability to mold thoughts, evoke memories and emotions, reinforce and create ideologies, and to relay to the world the values and priorities of a place.' The media covered the Balkan conflict in the early 1990s, and created lasting memories of violent conflict so that war became synonymous with Bosnia. Today, destination images are increasingly becoming associated as brands, despite these being different conceptualizations, but the image of war tourism is treated as a destination brand because of the development of niche tourism (see Morgan, Pritchard, & Pride, 2010; Wise, 2017). This relates to Milman and Pizam's (1995) point that a destination's image is promoted vis-à-vis what awareness people have of a place.

In many cases, awareness is dependent upon a place's image and associated memories, or the imagination of how people perceive a place (Winter, 2009; Wise, 2011). In this regard, an image represents a vision (or an imagination) that may have been constructed during some point in the past (see Govers, Go, & Kumar, 2007). Places are also dependent upon positive perceptions, while negative visions can potentially burden a places reputation (Winter, 2009), but not in all cases. Impressions refer to attractions, uniqueness, the physical environment, accommodations, safety, public management and user facilities, each intended to develop 'imagescapes' (see Cartier & Lew, 2005). Aligned with this point, Hernández-Lobato, Solis-Radilla, Moliner-Tena, and Sánchez-García (2006, p. 343) suggest that a 'tourism destination image is a mental schema developed by a tourist on the basis of impressions.' Thus, destination images are mental schema producing touristic knowledge alongside branding a place's image to generate a distinctive imagination (Beerli & Martín, 2004).

Wars cast a negative image on destinations and often create images of fear, deterring people from visiting a destination, as detailed by Müller (2002). Moreover, Wise and Mulec (2012, p. 58) argued that it is difficult for destinations after a conflict initially to overcome negative images because images of war make people feel insecure about visiting a place. A topic discussed in the literature recently on post-war tourism is how destinations may attempt to (re)create an image to change perceptions of a destination and move beyond the memory of war (see Cooper, 2006; Wise, 2011, 2017; Wise & Mulec, 2012, 2015). The other option is for destinations to include the impacts of war into tourism agendas, which is something that Sarajevo has done well, and has also been seen in Vietnam (Henderson, 2000), Cambodia (Winter, 2008), Montenegro (Vitic & Ringer, 2007), Guatemala (Clouser, 2009), Japan (Figal, 2008), Lebanon (Kanso, 2005) and Germany (Guy, 2004). Each of these studies articulates on the notion of war tourism, relating to the literature on dark tourism (e.g. Lennon & Foley, 2000). Many of these studies address the significance of constructed monuments, storied places or manifested memorials as part of the narrative. Moreover, landscape features represent the remembrance of tragic events first-hand (Foote, 2003). Concerning destination image and post-war tourism, Wise (2011) presents a conceptual three-fold typology for interpreting the directions destinations take after a conflict: landscape remembrance, fading memory and replacing memory. Important in this chapter is landscape remembrance, or what Foote (2003) would refer to as 'designation.' Wise's (2011) conceptualization of landscape remembrance is relevant here because features and façades across Sarajevo designate reflections of war, visions of the past. These are especially evident as a tourist observes the scenes and impact of the war right across the city from the bullet holes in the 'Welcome to Sarajevo' sign outside the train station to bullet holes in buildings or the 'Roses of Sarajevo.' Based on this understanding, scenes in the landscape convey images of war, allowing visitors to reminisce about past imaginations of a (particular) place. War tourism continues or extends the narrative of the conflict and becomes an essential part of a place niche tourism agenda, destination image and/or branding techniques (Butler & Suntikul, 2013).

Narrating the scars of Sarajevo

Sarajevo was perceived as an ideal place to live where different ethnic and religious groups cohabited. However, after the atrocities of war that devastated the image of Sarajevo between 1992 and 1995, 'war tourism' became a phrase commonly used to describe the city. There was also the Olympics, however: 'most people forget that Sarajevo hosted the Winter Olympics in 1984' (*Sunday Telegraph*, 10 June 2007). The 1984 Winter Olympics held in Sarajevo were an attempt to bring the international sporting community to what was then the Republic of Yugoslavia as a way of easing rising tensions across the region following Josep Broz Tito's death in 1980. While the Olympics were an attempt to encourage peace in the region, it would be less than a decade until the city of Sarajevo and all the Balkans succumbed to war and tragedy. Research has assessed media narratives and representations of the Balkan conflict's impact on tourism across the region (see Arnaud, 2016; Bevan, 2006; Hall, 2003; Morrison, 2016; Müller, 2002; Naef & Ploner, 2016; Pašić, 2016; Pilav, 2012; Wise, 2011, 2017; Wise & Mulec, 2012). The conflict left Sarajevo with new visitor attractions in the years after the conflict, enabling tourists to see and understand first-hand the devastation which was broadcast on television. One of Sarajevo's earlier museums showcased the incident that sparked a global conflict: 'Sarajevo was famous in another war. On June 28, 1914, Archduke Franz Ferdinand of Austria was assassinated in the city, lighting the fuse for the First World War' (*The Halifax Daily News*, 7 April 2007). Sarajevo is a city linked to war, and while conflict burdens a destination during and in the period after the conflict, war-torn destinations become in some ways *terra incognita*, or an unknown destination that viewers came to know so much about, but would not consider visiting, at least initially.

The chapter now moves on to address three key narratives of Sarajevo as a post-conflict destination, based on the following three points of discussion: (i) landscapes frozen in the 1990s; (ii) touring the tunnel of survival; and (iii) roses of remembrance. Each section considers how the Balkans war is memorialized in Sarajevo, and for some, the city is considered an open-air museum of the Balkans conflict that burdened this region throughout the 1990s. The following sections are supported by newspaper content gathered by searching articles on tourism, war and memory and Sarajevo accessed from LexisNexis Academic (Nexis Uni). The quotes presented from newspapers help frame and position the wider narrative, whereas conceptual interpretations from the academic literature help make sense of the meanings portrayed.

Landscapes frozen in the 1990s

Walking around Sarajevo is like walking around a museum, but instead of seeing images of destruction, visitors can see remnants of war first-hand. Stories and narratives are captured and framed in newspapers to position not only a city negatively impacted by war, but a city that has much to gain and showcase. Impacts of war in Sarajevo are blended with the beauty of the city; according to *The Independent* (28 July 2015), we are presented with:

> a striking testimony to the resilience of a people targeted for extermination just 20 years ago. Sarajevo's tragic history, which dates back far longer than Bosnia's civil war, is laid bare upon the bones of its exquisite natural beauty and fine architecture that neither bombs nor snipers could manage to eradicate in four years of bloody conflict.

The discussion is picked up in other stories distinguishing between then (being the time of war) and now (referring to the current time of writing) in several papers, perhaps as a way of reassuring people that Sarajevo is safe to visit:

> An elegant city eclipses its scare; TRAVEL SARAJEVO
> (*Australian Financial Review*, 10 June 2005)

> with the bullet holes of Berlin's Brandenburg Gate being only recently repaired, perhaps it's no bad thing that Sarajevo's scars remain to remind us of what lies beneath the surface.
> (*Australian Financial Review*, 10 June 2005)

A similar approach was considered in Dubrovnik, Croatia, where just inside one of the main entrances to the city, visitors are presented with a map showing what parts of the city were impacted by the siege on the city (noted in Wise & Mulec, 2012). Wider narratives are important to consider as well, from the *Australian Financial Review* (10 June 2005), a reporter describes the urban landscape of Sarajevo:

> Apart from the bullet holes and Sarajevo roses, there are other mementos of the deadly siege. I was staying in the frumpy Holiday Inn (not one of the chain's finest properties) on what used to be the infamous Snipers' Alley, where civilians had to run the gauntlet of bullets from the hills opposite. Every morning when I awoke I was greeted by the view of a charred building opposite. And just up the road, away from the city centre, office buildings and colleges have memorials to those killed in the siege.

Similar stories are presented widely to create a distinct awareness of Sarajevo as a destination with a myriad of landscapes:

> the National Library, which is still eerily beautiful despite being riddled with bomb scars and being boarded up since the siege that lasted more than three years and took more than 10,000 Bosnian lives. . . . I looked up and around at the architecture: a hybrid of pastel secessionist townhouses with ornate facades of floral molding, and Oriental domes and minarets woven together with the occasional scars of a mortar explosion along a pedestrian promenade.
>
> (*Australian Financial Review*, 10 June 2005)

> The pavement and cobble stone of Sarajevo's downtown core is gouged, cracked and pock-marked like most European cities. The difference here is in the patchwork. Rather than being tarred over in black, Sarajevo's pot holes and sidewalk rents are filled with a bright-scarlet rubber-like substance. The effect – that of a city scattered with petrified blood puddles – is both intentional and appropriate. These are not pot holes but bomb pits. They mark scars of an almost four-year siege (May 2, 1992 to Feb. 26, 1996) during which over 10,000 people died and more than 50,000 were wounded, a great number of whom remain invalids.
>
> (*The Globe and Mail*, 10 January 2001)

Even today 'it is impossible to visit cities such as Sarajevo and not be confronted by the legacy of war' (*The Daily Telegraph*, 2 October 2010). The *Sun Herald* (26 March 2006) made apparent:

> Ten years after the Dayton Peace Agreement of 1995 ended the war, this famously picturesque city of 388,000 people, now the capital of Bosnia and

Herzegovina, has slowly begun to lure tourists again. In 2004 Paddy Ash-down, a former British MP and the country's then-top civilian peace adminis-trator, even toured Europe touting Bosnia and Herzegovina as the continent's last great undiscovered tourism destination.

There has been much communicated about Sarajevo that positions how war remains a central component of the discourse; for instance: 'Rising from the ashes . . . where history is never buried' (*The Sun Herald*, 26 March 2006); 'While many of its buildings were destroyed, its sense of soul remains intact' (*Sunday Herald Sun*, 17 July 2006); 'A day in Sarajevo can be the most interactive, inad-vertent history lesson you'll ever have' (*The Guardian*, 11 November 2006); 'Things do change: war leaves and a battered city rebuilds' (*The Halifax Daily News*, 7 April 2007); and 'Bosnia's capital is shrugging off its tragic past' (*Sunday Telegraph*, 10 June 2007). As observed in the preceding quotes, war was central to Sarajevo's tourism narrative.

While the war did detract visitors to Sarajevo while it was taking place, much of the narrative conveyed by journalists in their newspaper articles focused on three emerged themes: how welcoming the Bosnian people were, notions of the war's memory in the landscape and the commodification of war paraphernalia (discussed ahead). *The Daily Telegraph* (31 March 2007) ran a travel section spe-cial on Sarajevo that attempted to highlight undiscovered European cities:

> Sarajevo is one of them. For all sorts of reasons, mainly war related, trav-ellers have been reluctant to go there. . . . Now the dangers are in the past. . . . Former war zones are great places to visit. The prices are mod-erate, people are really pleased to see you, and so much new history has accumulated along with the old . . . and the war has given them new mate-rials to work with.

Additionally, the *Sunday Herald Sun* (17 July 2005) notes:

> Despite everything that has happened, the people of Sarajevo somehow still reserve a smile of welcome for visitors, forgiving the world's neglect, deter-mined to show that its troubled years were an aberration for what remains an otherwise urbane and cultured city.

These quotes put emphasis on how post-war destinations offer a combination of old and new history and are referred to as undiscovered destinations. In mak-ing sense of the quotes presented this far, notions of memory, if only informally intended, created and (re)created imaginations of Sarajevo during the time of war and as a destination. During the war, the media made people around the world aware of the atrocities, but the new directions offered in the articles ten years after the conflict brought forward the imaginations of war, showing us how the media can present the same story to showcase the same narrative in a different light – thus (re)creating imaginations. We see how some articles can position how memories of the war have become a part of the visitor attraction:

> In the city's buildings a few [are] still bullet-ridden and pockmarked with shell holes – one sees the reflection of the city's battered self-esteem, the vivid cartography of its recent tragic history.
>
> (*Sunday Herald Sun*, 17 July 2005)

> War still shades everything – and not just the buildings scarred by machine gun fire or the half-finished repairs on others that can make it seem some-times that the predominant colour of Sarajevo is plaster filler. The damage lingers in unexpected places, as in the people on New Year's Eve who say they cringe at the bottle rockets that crack over the Ferhadija district.
>
> (*The Sun Herald*, 26 March 2006)

> Entering Sarajevo today, it looks as though the siege ended only weeks ago. The bus station is on the outskirts of town, and the walk into the centre along the Miljacka River takes you past the ruins of bombed- out buildings and caved-in homes spilling down the banks. Bullet holes dent the sidewalk, and now and then you come across a 'Sarajevo Rose' left by exploding mortar shells. Those filled with a red resin indicate a fatal hit.
>
> (*The Halifax Daily News*, 7 April 2007)

> The infamous Snipers Alley, where hundreds of residents were gruesomely picked off by hilltop gunmen on their way to and from work. It is a sobering feeling strolling down the now peaceful promenade that follows the Miljacka River, seeing the bullet holes replaced with red cement (The Sarajevo Roses).
>
> (*Sunday Telegraph*, 10 June 2007)

However, it is not only the physical scars that construct the narrative of Sarajevo as a war-tourism destination. Locals have found employment opportunities post-war by telling their story and by creating experiences for visitors that convey what life was like during the period of war between 1992 and 1995, such as how the Tunnel Museum discussed in the next section was an initiative by a local family.

Touring the tunnel of survival

Sarajevo's Tunnel Museum is a formal landmark dedicated to the conflict in the early 1990s, as explained in this reporter's encounter:

> Hunching over with a 50-kilogram backpack while trudging through part of the tunnel gives you an idea of what Sarajevans went through to get supplies during the Serbian siege. We visited the tunnel with 'Sarajevo Sonny,' who was a teenager during the war and is now a tour guide. He'll tell you how he had to carry water and firewood to his home while dodging sniper bullets.

Sonny's two-hour tour will also take you to the hilltops from which snipers terrorized a stretch of city streets.

(*The Globe and Mail*, 8 September 2007)

Building on the previous section, many newspapers discuss the scars of war, and although these remain as memories of the siege, the Tunnel Museum was often discussed as a specific war-tourism attraction. Although controversial, the designation of the museum did create some tension, but it was argued it would create another experience for tourists, as described in the *Nanaimo Daily News* (16 August 2008):

> 'It should be reconstructed to remember those times and show Bosnians and the world how we lived, how we survived,' said Ismet Hadzic, a general during the war who ran one half of the tunnel. 'If the city rebuilds it, it would become the premier tourist destination in the city.'

Moreover, by designating the tunnel a tourism attraction, the same article made comparisons to similar attractions around the world:

> Like Vietnam's Cu Chi tunnels or the Anne Frank House Museum in Amsterdam, the tunnel that helped ordinary people survive in Sarajevo through more than 1,000 days under siege embodies the local spirit of resistance.
>
> (*Nanaimo Daily News*, 16 August 2008)

Following the war and once Sarajevo's international airport was rebuilt, most of the tunnel was lost. However, 25 metres did remain intact – and one year after the war where this intact stretch remains, the family whose home the tunnel enters opened the 'Tunnel Museum' (*Nanaimo Daily News*, 16 August 2008). The local story was initially part of the visitor offering, noted in the *Financial Times* (29 November 2003):

> The only way in and out for ordinary people was an 800-metre tunnel under the runway, linking the city centre to a sliver of safe territory beyond Serb and UN lines. To this day, beyond the runway, the tunnel leads toward town from the shrapnel-battered house of the Kolar family, who built and guarded it.

The Tunnel Museum relates to two of Foote's (2003) conceptualizations: sanctification and designation. It is an attraction that brings visitors into the experiences of war and survival during the siege of the city. But to some, visiting the Tunnel Museum is a slightly sanitized experience, but meeting siege survivors in their homes and hearing their personal war stories over dinner is truly haunting (*The Independent*, 28 July 2015). It is clearly a designated site where goods and supplies (i.e. food and ammunition) were brought from the free Bosnian territory into the city that was surrounded. In another regard, this site can be interpreted as sanctification, because it is a site of remembrance that has a lasting meaning to locals and to visitors who seek such attractions.

There were debates for some time as to how to dedicate the site, given that it had been a lifeline for many, and was now a tunnel of hope in the form of a popular visitor attraction today:

> The narrow tunnel that ran beneath Sarajevo airport was people's only escape route during the longest siege in modern history, a symbol of a brutal war that split families and pitted neighbours against each other. After marking the 15th anniversary of the now largely destroyed tunnel's opening, some in the capital of Bosnia hope to reconstruct the passage which meant escape or at least brief relief from desperate times. Yet the sensitive project lacks funds and they say it may be an opportunity for foreign investors.
>
> *(Nanaimo Daily News*, 16 August 2008)

> Evidence of war remains in the bombed-out buildings and memorials scattered throughout the countryside. In Sarajevo, where more than 10,000 Bosnians died during a siege that lasted almost five years, mortar-pocked walls sit next to new skyscrapers. A museum at the Tunnel of Hope, dug to smuggle in supplies from the West, serves as a monument to the indomitable human spirit.
>
> *(The Gazette*, 30 August 2014)

The story of dedicating a site with a unique history surrounding struggles to survive and secure Sarajevo is an attraction that promoted hope and survival, but the next section considers memorialized scars, dedicated to those less fortunate.

Roses of remembrance

The Roses of Sarajevo are what many articles refer to as makeshift memorials or manifested memorials:

> The red splotches now serve as miniature, makeshift war monuments. For the foreign visitor in Sarajevo today strolling through the city's lively downtown core, every red splotch underfoot serves as an eerie reminder of the horrors this place has seen. . . . The Roses are, in effect, Sarajevo's memory of violence made manifest.
>
> *(The Globe and Mail*, 10 January 2001)

> Following the siege of Sarajevo – which lasted four years and during which as many as 14,000 people were killed, many of them civilians – the city filled mortar blast marks on sidewalks and roads with red resin to mark the places where people had been killed by shells. Less than 20 years later, only four of these 'Sarajevo Roses' remain.
>
> *(Ottawa Citizen*, 27 December 2013)

The *Australian Financial Review* (10 June 2005) adds to the wider narrative concerning the roses:

> A decade after the end of a bitter siege, Sarajevo is humming with new life. . . . In most cities it would be unusual to gaze out of a cafe window and see walls pockmarked with bullet holes. But not in Sarajevo. And although the fighting finished 10 years ago many other reminders of the war remain, none more poignant than the Sarajevo roses which dot the pavements. They are not flowers, but rather a tribute set in the concrete to those killed by mortar fire: a gruesomely appropriate red plastic compound fills in the craters that were made by exploding shells.

We get a sense of how the discourse is changing. The preceding article discussed how Sarajevo was undesirable following the war, and now a decade later, Sarajevo is being referred to as an undiscovered destination worth the visit. Despite the discussion of war negatively impacting a place's image, the discourse of war, tourism and Sarajevo has taken a different approach to show how the city is integrating the conflict into the city's tourism management plan.

The focus from the quoted articles generates imaginations of the landscape, vivid in memories of war and tragedy – but with much hope in that the roses have become part of the visitor journey in understanding what happened in the early 1990s. Such context of awareness relates to Wise's (2011) notion of landscape remembrance, and how memories of war remain through discussions of war's scaring, such as: bullet holes noticeable in façade, the red 'Roses of Sarajevo' symbolizing where mortar shells had been and tragic and burnt out buildings/edifices. While complementary to the discussions of memory, journalists also focused on the remnants of the war for sale in bazaars and how merchants acquired war paraphernalia to sell as mementos of the conflict. Here we see two different ways of consuming: the roses are memories, while some have found opportunities to commercialize elements of the war so visitors can purchase war remnants and remove them from the city. For instance, in discussing war paraphernalia in the local bazaars:

> Inside the shops . . . coppersmiths hammer flower-print designs into vases made from discharged artillery shells found on the hilltops that surround the city. Others remove gun powder from unused sniper bullets and replace it with springs and ink cartridges, turning once-lethal ammunition into souvenir pens.
> (*The Globe and Mail*, 8 September 2007)

It was shells that caused the harm, leading to the roses, that one now sold to visitors. But artefacts, such as war paraphernalia, have become a part of the new tourism narrative and attraction. In some ways, this refers to the commodification of the war materials, but as discussed earlier, such souvenirs became an inherent part of the visitor experience as tourists made their way through Sarajevo's Baščaršija (the Bazaar), passing roses along the way.

Conclusion: memories of war fading with time

Remnants of conflict are still displayed and consumed in Sarajevo, as remnants of the war remain in a city devastated more than 20 years ago. Looking at findings from neighbouring countries in the region, there were much earlier attempts to fade memories of war from the landscape and media narrative (see Wise, 2011; Wise, Flinn, & Mulec, 2015; Wise & Mulec, 2015). Online representations and attempts to rebrand the destination see a replacing of memory to remove narratives of war (see Wise, 2012). Destinations need to maintain a level of competitiveness and provide a niche product to distinguish themselves from similarly sized, or regional, destinations. Sarajevo has a unique tourism product in that landscapes and attractions across the city still display a city burdened by conflict in recent memory. But as time passes, and with pressures to redevelop urban spaces due to real estate demands, people invest and upgrade structures, which removes the scars of war from buildings (bullet holes) and pathways (mortar shell impressions). This fading removes the presence of war, but it also symbolizes moving on. While memories fade in the landscape, media and online narratives have oftentimes moved on. Consumers and travellers then look to media narratives to gain an awareness of understanding of a destination. From the quotes and reflections presented in this chapter, we get a sense of how reporters describe a destination, but they channel the reader's attention to address that while tragedy struck, they reassure the reader that the destination is open for tourism and there is no threat to the tourist. This was a point Wise and Mulec (2012) emphasized regarding the notion of fading memory – that communications of conflict are starting to disassociate a destination and its place image. Although their study focused on Dubrovnik, Croatia, findings display numerous similarities with the case of Sarajevo, with shifts in meaning across the different media narratives to alter place images after times of trouble/conflict.

What is observed in this research, and needs to be further explored, is how travel narratives in the media can also restore place images by transitioning contexts to (re)create associations with places. While much of the work conducted by the author of this chapter has looked at newspaper content, there is need to consider user-generated narratives produced by travellers to conflict-ridden destinations, because this positions the traveller/tourist as the storyteller who consumes and recreates the discourse. This is seen in research looking at narratives presented through different online communication/social media outlets including TripAdvisor (e.g. Easton & Wise, 2015) and Facebook (e.g. Wise & Farzin, 2018). As a society, we are also moving towards consumer accounts presented on social media and virtual discussions areas more so than newspapers. While newspapers can be a reliable and reputable source for consuming information, we have succumbed to a time of over-communication resulting in fake news – but communication between tourists and sharing experiences is gaining momentum as we attempt to understand new place narratives through social media (see Wise & Farzin, 2018). The challenge here is that consumers are emphasizing their experiences opposed to the wider narrative. This is where newspaper content becomes important to evaluate because this can present several narratives across different moments in time to position past and present. From such content, we can better understand how memories are reinforced or fade over time, and it is the longitudinal narrative that is important for destinations to show what has occurred and how a destination overcame a negative image in a competitive tourism marketplace. The niche of post-conflict tourism that Sarajevo has to offer is slowly fading as landscapes are altered, consumer demands change and new stories arise.

References

Arnaud, F. (2016). Memorial policies and restoration of Croatian tourism two decades after the war in former Yugoslavia. *Tourism and Cultural Change, 14*(3), 270–290.

Ashworth, G., & Hartmann, R. (Eds.). (2005). *Horror and human tragedy revisited: The Management of sites of atrocities for tourism.* New York, NY: Cognizant Communication Corporation.

Beerli, A., & Martín, J. D. (2004). Factors influencing destination image. *Annals of Tourism Research, 31*(3), 657–681.

Bevan, R. (2006). *The destruction of memory: Architecture at war.* London: Reaktion Books.

Butler, R. W., & Suntikul, W. (2013). *Tourism and war.* London: Routledge.

Cartier, C., & Lew, A. A. (Eds.). (2005). *Seductions of place: Geographical perspectives on globalization and touristed landscapes.* London: Routledge.

Clouser, R. (2009). Remnants of terror: Landscapes of fear in post-conflict Guatemala. *Journal of Latin American Geography, 8*(2), 7–22.

Cooper, M. (2006). The Pacific War battlefields: Tourist attractions or war memorials? *International Journal of Tourism Research, 8*(3), 213–222.

Cosgrove, D. (1984). *Symbolic formation and symbolic landscape.* Madison, WI: The University of Wisconsin Press.

Cresswell, T. (2014). *Place: A short introduction.* Oxford: Blackwell.

Easton, S., & Wise, N. (2015). Online portrayals of volunteer tourism in Nepal: Exploring the communicated disparities between promotional and user-generated content. *Worldwide Hospitality and Tourism Themes, 7*(2), 141–158.

Figal, G. (2008). Between War and tropics: Heritage tourism in postwar Okinawa. *The Public Historian, 30*(2), 83–107.

Foote, K. E. (2003). *Shadowed ground: America's landscapes of violence and tragedy.* Austin, TX: University of Texas Press.

Govers, R., Go, F. M., & Kumar, K. (2007). Promoting tourism destination image. *Journal of Travel Research, 46*(1), 15–23.

Guy, S. (2004). Shadow architectures: War, memories, and Berlin's futures. In S. Graham (Ed.), *Cities, war, and terrorism: Towards an urban geopolitics* (pp. 75–92). Oxford: Blackwell.

Hall, D. (2003). Rejuvenation, diversification and imagery: Sustainability conflicts for tourism policy in the eastern Adriatic. *Journal of Sustainable Tourism, 11*, 280–294.

Henderson, J. C. (2000). War as a tourist attraction: The case of Vietnam. *International Journal of Tourism Research, 2*(4), 269–280.

Hernández-Lobato, L., Solis-Radilla, M. M., Moliner-Tena, M. A., & Sánchez-García, J. (2006). Tourism destination image, satisfaction and loyalty: A study in Ixtapa-Zihuatanejo, Mexico. *Tourism Geographies, 8*(4), 343–358.

Izvor, F. (2014). *U KS-u 2013. je najuspješnija turistička godina od kad se vodi statistika.* Retrieved 7 July 2018, from www.akta.ba/bs/Vijest/kapital/u-ks-u-2013-je-najuspjesnija-turisticka-godina-od-kad-se-vodi-statistika/34489

Jansen-Verbeke, M., & George, W. (2013). Reflections on the Great War centenary: From warscaapes to memoryscapes in 100 years. In R. W. Butler & W. Suntikul (Eds.), *Tourism and war* (pp. 273–287). London: Routledge.

Kanso, A. (2005). Reinvigorating the "Switzerland of the Middle East": How the Lebanese government can use public relations to reposition the country as a premier tourism destination. *Journal of Hospitality and Leisure Marketing, 12*(1/2), 135–156.

Lehtonen, M. (2000). *The cultural analysis of texts.* London: Sage.

Lennon, J., & Foley, M. (2000). *Dark tourism.* London: Thomson.

Milman, A., & Pizam, A. (1995). The role of awareness and familiarity with a destination: The central Florida case. *Journal of Travel Research, 33*(3), 21–27.

Morgan, N., Pritchard, A., & Pride, R. (2010). *Destination branding: Creating the unique destination proposition.* Oxford: Elsevier Butterworth-Heinemann.

Morin, K. M. (2003). Landscape and environment: Representing and interpreting the world. In S. L. Holloway, S. P. Rice, & G. Valentine (Eds.), *Key concepts in geography* (pp. 319–334). London: Sage.

Morrison, K. (2016). *Sarajevo's holiday inn on the frontline of politics and war.* Berlin: Springer.

Müller, J.-W. (Ed.). (2002). *Memory and power in post-war Europe: Studies in the presence of the past.* Cambridge: Cambridge University Press.

Naef, P., & Ploner, J. (2016). Tourism, conflict and contested heritage in former Yugoslavia. *Journal of Tourism and Cultural Change, 14*(3), 181–188.

Osmanković, J. (2017). Bosnia and Herzegovina. In L. L. Lowrey (Ed.), *The SAGE international encyclopedia of travel and tourism* (pp. 159–161). London: Sage.

Pašić, L. (2016). *20 years after Dayton: Where is Bosnia and Herzegovina today?* Belgrade: BalkanAnalysis.

Pilav, A. (2012). Before the war, war, after the war: Urban imageries for urban resilience. *International Journal of Disaster Risk Science, 3*(1), 23–37.

Rowntree, L. B. (1996). The cultural landscape concept in American human geography. In C. Earle, K. Mathewson, & M. S. Kenzer (Eds.), *Concepts in human geography* (pp. 127–159). Lanham, MD: Rowman and Littlefield Publishers, Inc.

Vannestes, D., & Foote, K. (2013). War, heritage, tourism and the centenary of the Great War in Flanders and Belgium. In R. W. Butler & W. Suntikul (Eds.), *Tourism and war* (pp. 254–272). London: Routledge.

Vitic, A., & Ringer, G. (2007). Branding postconflict destinations: Recreating Montenegro after the disintegration of Yugoslavia. *Journal of Travel & Tourism Marketing, 23*(2–4), 127–137.

Winter, C. (2009). Tourism, social memory and the Great War. *Annals of Tourism Research, 36*(4), 607–626.

Winter, T. (2008). Post-conflict heritage and tourism in Cambodia: The burden of Angkor. *International Journal of Heritage Studies, 14*(6), 524–539.

Wise, N. A. (2011). Post-war tourism and the imaginative geographies of Bosnia and Herzegovina and Croatia. *European Journal of Tourism Research, 4*(1), 5–24.

Wise, N. A. (2012). Landscape remembrance, fading memory, and replacing memory: Conceptualizing destination image and place imaginations, post-War. *e-Review of Tourism Research, 10*(4), 86–91.

Wise, N. A. (2017). Interpreting media content post-conflict: Communications of "travel" and "Bosnia and Herzegovina" in US newspapers, 20 years post-Dayton. *Drustvena Istrazivanja, 26*(3), 363–383.

Wise, N. A., & Farzin, F. (2018). "See you in Iran" on Facebook: Assessing "user-generated authenticity". In J. Rickly & E. Vidon (Eds.), *Authenticity & tourism: Productive debates, creative discourses* (pp. 33–52). Bingley: Emerald.

Wise, N. A., Flinn, J., & Mulec, I. (2015). Exit Festival: Contesting political pasts, impacts on youth culture and regenerating the image of Serbia and Novi Sad. In O. Moufakkir & T. Pernecky (Eds.), *Ideological, social and cultural aspects of events* (pp. 60–73). Boston, MA: CABI.

Wise, N. A., & Mulec, I. (2012). Headlining Dubrovnik's tourism image: Transitioning representations/narratives of war and heritage preservation, 1991–2010. *Tourism Recreation Research, 37*(1), 57–69.

Wise, N. A., & Mulec, I. (2015). Aesthetic awareness and spectacle: Communicated images of Novi Sad (Serbia), the Exit Festival, and the Petrovaradin Fortress. *Tourism Review International, 19*(4), 193–205.

Wylie, J. (2007). *Landscape*. London: Routledge.

15 Bangkok street food

Conflicting visions of modernity

Raymond Boland

Introduction

This chapter analyzes the campaign (occurring at the time of writing in 2018) approach to Bangkok street food by the authorities there as an aid to understanding the wider, deeper conflict about modernization. Social and economic change in all societies produces conflict, and winners and losers. The drive to industrialize in the UK in the late 18th and early 19th centuries, for example, saw a massive expansion in productive capacity and wealth creation, but also resistance from groups such as the Luddites, whose traditional patterns of life and income were made obsolete by the new factories. These fundamental conflicts can be difficult to comprehend, but in the same way that quantum physics turned to the study of the smallest units of matter to help understand the universe, so an analysis of small conflicts – such as over street food – can help us understand bigger deeper processes.

An optimistic take on history sees modernization as a relatively benign process in which the forces of progress and reason overcome those of backwardness and superstition. However, modernization in the West involved a substantial amount of repression by elites in their colonies and against various poor and disenfranchised sections of their own societies (Mishra, 2017). Modernization in Bangkok is also characterized by marginalization of the poor, as in the process of gentrification and in the campaign against street food vendors, whereby cheap housing and opportunities to earn a living are disappearing.

History does not repeat itself directly, but current politics in Thailand can be seen as a replay to some extent of these modernizing processes in the West. In many ways, the suspicion of Bangkok's conservative elite and middle class of the rural and urban poor reproduces the 19th-century European ruling class fear of 'the mob' and the uneducated, who are not yet ready for democracy (Connors, 2012).

Bangkok street food constitutes a microcosm whereby we can clearly observe these contemporary contradictory forces: a neoliberal drive to empower markets and finance combined with increased control of the poor, in which the benefits of modernization accrue primarily to the already successful; and a more inclusive form of modernization which recognizes human values, seeks to curb the excesses of free markets and promotes self-organization, equality, creativity and flexibility. The campaign against street food vendors in Bangkok is both a reflection of global neoliberal development and of domestic political forces. This chapter also considers the question of who should decide what happens in the streets – the people who live, work and socialize there, or the planners and authorities who are more remote.

Food (and street food) features strongly in the image of Thai tourism. However, studies of tourism which just focus on management, marketing and cultural questions marginalize political issues embedded in the wider processes of change. The tourist demand for the different and the authentic, and the tendency to exoticize (de Botton, 2003) distant destinations, means that there is a resistance from this sector to change. Western tourists visit cities such as Bangkok partly because they promise something different to what can be experienced at home. So, in many ways, tourism can function as a reactionary force in its drive to conserve and protect physical and intangible heritage (Ganesh, 2018). If tourism does have a role in the future of Bangkok street food, it may well be to defend street food.

Nevertheless, tourists and the tourism industry are not the most important players in this process in Bangkok. Essentially, the conflict arises from the different social classes and their views on the prospective costs and benefits of change. For the aspirational urban middle class in Bangkok, a city such as Singapore – where street life is highly regulated and society is organized and efficiently administered – is undoubtedly an attractive prospect. So, the campaign against street food vendors may well receive tacit support as it is seen as a step towards a more modern metropolis. For the street food vendors and their working-class customers, the threat of loss of income or affordable food and the lack of available suitable alternatives (either in terms of employment prospects or in source of nourishment) is an existential threat to their way of life.

The conflict is also one between two basic human drives that Nietzsche (1993) characterized as Apollonian and Dionysian. The Apollonian drive is to order and structure, while the Dionysian is towards creativity and chaos. The drive by the Bangkok Metropolitan Authority to regulate and control street food is obviously Apollonian, while the street food vendors' preference for flexibility, lack of regulation and spontaneity is Dionysian. If we as human repress the Dionysian too much, we deny ourselves the pleasure of living.

This chapter argues that a turn away from some aspects of neoliberalism and a more flexible attitude to regulation and inclusion could help push through modernization of street food in Bangkok in a successful manner, avoiding unnecessary social conflict and hardship. To some extent, this will rely on the self-organization of, and cooperation between, different sectors of society.

Thailand, like most countries in southeast Asia, currently faces contradictions arising from the processes of modernization, development and globalization. Bangkok itself currently faces the same 'dual compression' as many Asian cities, whereby not only the pressure from the sheer size and density of the growing population, but also the forces of neoliberal global capitalism, constrict urban space (Huang, 2004), especially for the poor. The population of Bangkok increased from 1.4 million in 1950 to 9.1 million in 2004 (UN-HABITAT Urban Indicators Database, cited in Davis, 2017, p. 4) placing increasing demands on space and resources. Furthermore, low interest rates in the West help stimulate property speculation in cities such as Bangkok (as Western capital seeks locations where higher returns on investment are available), leading to increased rents and property prices and to a reduction in available space for the poor.

Street food plays a very important social and economic role in cities such as Bangkok, where public space is gradually being privatized by shopping malls, new hotels and condominium developments. Space traditionally occupied by street food vendors, such as in Sukhumvit Soi 38 (a once popular street food location for residents, workers and tourists just off one of the city's busiest main roads in the heart of one of the key business districts) in Bangkok, is often sold for property development, leading to the removal of street food stalls (Yongcharoenchai, 2015).

This compression has been intensified by the campaign by the Bangkok Metropolitan Authority and the central government to clean up the streets. In the year up to August 2016, for example, it is estimated that more than 15,000 street vendors (not just street food vendors, it should be noted) were removed from On-Nut, Siam, Sathorn, Sukhumvit and Silom (Sauers, 2016). Estimates of the actual number of street food vendors in Bangkok vary from between 100,000 and 300,000 (CitiScope, 2018), but whatever the true figure, this is a considerable reduction.

The authorities in general and planners in particular see street food as disruptive, old-fashioned and impossible to regulate. They would like to see a more regulated, organized city, maybe along the lines of Singapore – a vision attractive, as already mentioned, to some extent to Bangkok's rising middle class. The street food vendors and customers see street food as an essential economic and cultural element of the city. For the vendors, it is also a way to make money and improve their lives.

Thailand's food is central to the country's tourism promotion – see for example, the Thailand 'Kitchen of the World' adverts (Thai Select [Canada], 2013) or the 2018 Amazing Thailand 'Open to New Shades' posters, where gastronomy features as one of the six visual panels. Bangkok itself is widely believed to have some of the greatest street food in the world. Therefore, on the surface, the continued pressure from central government and the Bangkok Metropolitan Authority to clear street food vendors from many traditional areas in the city may seem paradoxical. However, change is never linear and mono-directional: it involves choices, conflicts and detours. All developmental and modernization processes unleash social and economic forces, and ideological responses which conflict and which are eventually resolved in one way or another, before new forces and conflicts arise.

As Gramsci (1971) notes, no one group in society can gain sufficient power and legitimacy (hegemony) to achieve their goals, and so they need to persuade other groups to join them and to believe that their interests will be best served by such an alliance. The process of modernization in general, and street food in Bangkok specifically, will be shaped to a large extent by the way in which different social formations coalesce and cooperate. These historic blocks (political alliances between various social groups) in Gramsci's (1971) terms are always contingent and shifting, but can be sufficiently stable to drive through change.

The street food contradictions

Economic development in Thailand since the 1970s has raised the living standards of all Thais – however, not all at the same rate (Glassman, 2011). On the one hand, the export-oriented growth policies pursued by all governments since then combined with some minor attempts at wealth redistribution have reduced levels of poverty in Thailand. Ninety-five percent of Thai households have electricity, and the country has the second highest pickup truck market in the world, trailing only the USA (Crispin, 2012). In 2015, 7.2% of the population was estimated to live below the poverty line (Central Intelligence Agency, n.d.), which compares favourably with many of the country's neighbours. On the other hand, Thailand's Gini coefficient has worsened 'from about 0.4 in the 1960s to 0.5 and above in the period since the 1980s' (Hewison, 2012, p. 149).

The forces unleashed by this economic development in Thailand are irreversible. The traditional conservative elite dream of a stable, placid and subservient rural peasantry living from subsistence farming is no longer tenable. Members working in Bangkok or abroad support practically all rural families, and all have access to the good life via their televisions and the Internet. They have 'already tasted the capitalist consumer modernity' (Glassman, 2011, p. 42), and they want more of it.

Many street food vendors see the efforts to clean up the street food scene as an attempt to concentrate street food in the hands of large corporations and landlords (Dunlop, 2017), and redistribute the profits from the poor to the rich – a process not unusual in neoliberal capitalism. Unsurprisingly, they would like the economic benefits of street food to be primarily theirs. On the other hand, the authorities see the process as one of promoting hygiene and food quality, dealing with criminal elements and removing inconvenience for pedestrians and motorists, as food stalls block pavements and encroach into the roads.

The Tourism Authority of Thailand and the government are well aware of the importance of food and street food in Thailand's national image, so they almost certainly do not want to damage that aspect of the brand. Nevertheless, if we look at the promotion of street food festivals in corporate areas such as hotels and malls and the Thailand 'Kitchen of the World' advert (Thai Select [Canada], 2013), it appears that they would prefer that street food can be made to appeal to better-off tourists. 'The idea behind the ban [on street food] is to create a place where tourists feel comfortable about spending money, perhaps in covered malls' (Nualkhair, 2017, as cited in Dunlop, 2017).

Food in Thailand, as elsewhere, is in a continuous process of diversification, renewal and reinvention (Mak, Lumbers, & Eves, 2012). Influences from Portugal, India, China and Laos, for example, are all reflected in Thai cuisine. Thailand's export-oriented growth policies of the last 30 years or so have produced a growing urban middle class with a taste for consumption (Koanantakool, 2002). Migrants and expatriate communities have created new markets and brought new dishes with them, so that along Sukhumvit one can find Japanese food around Soi 33, while Middle Eastern food is located around Soi 3, and Yaowarat offers numerous types of Chinese and Thai food. Som tam, a spicy green papaya salad originally from Isaan in the northeast of Thailand, has become popular in Bangkok after being brought there by internal migration. This process of innovation and creativity will be suppressed if street food is more strictly regulated (Dunlop, 2017).

Prepared food is ubiquitous in Thailand. Snacks and meals are readily available from mobile push-carts that usually specialize in one or two dishes. Some of these can transform into street restaurants if part of the pavement is taken over by small plastic tables and chairs. These are almost always temporary, occupying a particular stretch of pavement for only a few hours a day, and offer a specific meal such as breakfast or lunch, for example. A less transitory version of these street restaurants is offered by the shop-house restaurants, which again tend to specialize in a small number of dishes and/or meal times. Large numbers of locals, expatriates and tourists use these options for many of their everyday meals, as prices are low (between 40 and 80 Baht – a little over €1–2 for a meal) and the selection is wide (Sriangura, 2018).

A more recent addition is the food court in shopping malls, where a variety of meals served from separate small stands are offered. Branded chain restaurants in shopping malls and retail centres cater to the middle classes, if they want a more special meal out, and often offer international cuisine such as sushi or Sichuan hot-pot. Of course, Bangkok also has many high-end restaurants such as David Thompsons Nahm, which in 2014 was voted the best restaurant in Asia in the San Pellegrino Asia's Best Restaurant Awards (*The Bangkok Post*, 2014) and which was awarded a Michelin star in 2017.

The Bangkok Metropolitan Authority (BMA), like many other urban authorities, sees street vendors as 'symbols of underdevelopment' (Maneepong & Walsh, 2013, p. 39), and so promotes actions to remove them. It appears unaware or uncaring of the disastrous impact this can have on street vendors' businesses and their families. Street vending provides opportunities for women, helps single women look after their families and creates urban spaces where women can operate safely (Maneepong & Walsh, 2013). Research by Nirathon (2016, cited in CitiScope, 2018) shows that 70% of street food vendors in Bangkok are women, 70% are older than 40 and more than 40% have only obtained primary-level education. The economic impacts caused by this campaign on those traders affected will undoubtedly be severe.

The authorities argue that displaced street food vendors will be relocated to more suitable locations, such as shopping malls. However, for many vendors, the cost of renting a place in a private building such as a mall would be unaffordable (Dunlop, 2017). Furthermore, the presence of women and activity in the streets, especially at night, is also one of the reasons why much of Bangkok is relatively safe to walk around. De-populating the streets and removing activity will certainly make them less safe and welcoming.

As in many places, people move to Bangkok not because they are attracted by jobs, but because they cannot make enough in the countryside. A process of 'overurbanisation' (Davis, 2017, p. 16) means that people have to go there. The absence of stable jobs in the city once they arrive means they have no recourse but to earn a living informally. These informally employed are seen as a political threat by many, and so city governments attempt to move them on (Davis, 2017). As in many cities, street vending is one way of earning a living in Bangkok for these internal migrants.

Thailand has the world's seventh-highest ratio of income derived from the informal sector (Maneepong & Walsh, 2013). So the lack of regulation, 'ease of entry and reliance on indigenous resources, family ownership and small scale operation' (Mateo-Babiano, 2012, p. 456) and available demand all make street vendor start-ups easy and potentially profitable. In 2007, for example, street vendors were found to 'earn twice the daily income of general workers in Bangkok' (Maneepong & Walsh, 2013, p. 39).

However, the opportunity for these small businesses to grow much beyond a low level of profit is limited, as they tend to become crowded out as more entrepreneurs enter the market, driving down prices and profits. With their limited access to capital and lack of organizational skills, the potential to branch out or grow into more profitable production or services is low (Chang, 2011).

Street food is also important for its consumers, both local and tourist, as it is a source of excellent, readily available cheap food. Osborne (2006, p. 137) claims that 'Bangkok has the best street food on earth,' and it is hard to disagree with him. It also provides Bangkok with part of its memorable character (Sukphisit, 2010). 'Biting into a stewed pig leg or grilled squid long after midnight on the sidewalk tables of Sukhumvit's little *soi*, you cannot help but reflect that this elemental pleasure would be illegal virtually anywhere in the West' (Osborne, 2006, p. 137). Unfortunately, this 'elemental pleasure' (Osborne, 2006, p. 137) may soon not be so easy to find in Bangkok, either.

Street food politics

For many, Thai streets are smooth, striated spaces (in Deleuzian terms) and are not just for walking on. The same space can be used for a multiplicity of functions at the same or different times. In fact, the street food stalls are an aspect of the assemblage that construct the place (Dovey, 2010). Everyone is felt to have equal right to use the streets, whether it be for watching TV, cooking or serving street food (Mateo-Babiano, 2012). To some extent, Bangkok street food can be seen as 'a survival of nomadic food-on-the-go' (Osborne, 2006, p. 137).

These street food stalls become sites of spontaneous public interaction. They are one of the few places where social classes interact in the city (Sauers, 2016). Although they do not conform to the official ideal image of a public space, these lively public spaces are much more dynamic than the 'dead empty spaces' created by well-meaning urban planners (Nathiwutthikun, 2012). Street food plays a role in making the city streets liveable, attractive and places where people want to be.

In many ways, street food represents many of the elements that are necessary to make cities liveable and pleasant places. It offers flexibility – it is responsive to immediate needs as changes can occur quickly without the need for regulatory control. It makes the streets safe as entrepreneurs and customers are part of a collective mutually supportive group. It allows bottom-up development reflecting the needs of suppliers and consumers. It allows for diversity and creativity. It is human-scaled and allows for free and open exchange away from a corporate environment (The Why Factory, 2012).

Conclusions: the future

The rather sterile Apollonian (Nietzsche, 1993) presentation of the Thai dining experience in tourism promotion and in the planners' visions contrasts with the more Dionysian experience of many. Sitting on plastic chairs at a low table perched precariously on the pavement on a hot and humid Bangkok evening, drinking cold beer and eating hot and spicy food is an experience that no restaurant can hope to replicate.

Thai food – and especially street food – is one of the world's great cuisines. Although it is always changing and adapting, it would be a tragedy for the businesses themselves, for the consumers and for the quality of street life if speculative neoliberal development of condominiums, hotels and shopping malls and attempts at modernization drove this culture to extinction in Bangkok. Similarly, well-meaning attempts to regulate the business may well stamp out the creativity that can be currently observed there.

The BMA has a case that street food stands create traffic (pedestrian and motorized) congestion and contribute to litter and waste disposal problems. However, the urban density partly created by street food makes spaces lively and vibrant. Prioritizing social interaction in the streets rather than vehicular mobility may be a much more sustainable long-term solution – especially if combined with investment in public transport such as the BTS and MRT systems (see Gehl & Svarre, 2013, for a more detailed defence of this position). Making it easier to move around Bangkok by car will not solve the traffic problems in the city. In fact, Singapore's policy of suppressing demand for cars may be a much more attractive policy option.

Shopping malls are an essential part of the city in Bangkok, and are utilized by many sections of society. Nevertheless, they provide a very corporate environment and a limited experience. If the forces of neoliberalism are allowed too much free reign, they will crowd out other environments and experiences. The authorities in Singapore wisely ensured that in their process of modernization, space was maintained for local food traders in the hawker centres. Bangkok could well follow his model, but keep the traders in the street rather than in designated controlled spaces.

Thailand and Bangkok have a well-deserved reputation for 'pluralism and tolerance' (Montesano, 2012, p. 2), and so a more bottom-up, less planned response to the issues surrounding street food would both reflect this and provide a basis for resilient and inclusive modernization in this sector. Seoul's Haebangchon Hill Village and the Tsukishima are of Tokyo demonstrate that a more flexible and bottom-up approach to planning and regulation do not have to be in conflict with progress and modernization (The Why Factory, 2012).

Although the potential for street food vendors to develop and expand their businesses is low, at least these businesses currently provide a liveable income. In the absence of alternative better employment, street food vending is an attractive option for work for Bangkok's urban poor, and one worth defending. One way for the street traders to protect their livelihoods is to build political alliances with the middle classes. If they ally with journalists, the urban middle class, lawyers and town planners, they can show how street food is an essential part of the social and economic ecology of the city. In this way, greater pressure can be put on the authorities to recognize their interests. For example, an informal riverside *kampung* in Jakarta recently took this approach, approaching journalists and lawyers, and used discourses about sustainability to protect their home from bulldozers threatened by the city government (Sofian, 2018) – demolition which was to be undertaken in the name of progress, and initially with the support of the urban middle class.

Tourism can also play a role here. For example, the street food vendors around the Khao San and Yaowarat Road areas have been partially exempted from the clean-up because of their importance for tourism in the area. The danger in pandering to tourism for developing nations is that if the tourism industry is economically significant, it can lead to an 'ossification' (Ganesh, 2018, p. 20) of particular locales: tourists don't want change, so the place doesn't change. The result of this can often be the loss of any dynamism and economic development in the destination. What was once a living local phenomenon used by residents and tourists (and therefore valued by tourists) becomes something just for tourists (and therefore of little value to tourists). See Ganesh (2018) for a fuller discussion of this argument.

Singapore has great food in its food courts, and they operate very effectively in the context. So, it is easy to see its attractiveness as a model for other cities in the region. However, the food courts tend to have limited opening hours (most closing around 21:30) and require an effort to find them, go in, look around and choose a meal. Bangkok street food is just there 24/7 and enables much more spontaneous choices. If something looks good, why not just sit down and eat it?

A more relaxed bottom-up approach to street food would help preserve the economic, social and culinary benefits of street food, while coping with the problems more fluidly. Bangkok is a great city with a resilient, entrepreneurial and creative population. If these good qualities are acknowledged, street food and its attendant positive contributions to the life of the city can still flourish there.

If the poor are given more stake in the future and greater prospects for economic and social advancement, they may well pleasantly surprise some. This, prospect, however, does require a turning away from some of the aspects of neo-liberalism (property speculation, and downward pressures on wages and job security, spring to mind) which penalize the poor disproportionately. It also requires an acceptance that cities can be sometimes messy and chaotic, but that this is what makes them such dynamic and innovative places. Perhaps occasionally the desire for order (Apollo) has to be replaced by the celebration of creativity and life (Dionysus). Liveable cities, and cities attractive to tourists, require space for all (rich and poor) – and sometimes, less planning from above.

References

The Bangkok Post. (2014, 25 February). Nahm named best restaurant in Asia. Retrieved from www.bangkokpost.com/breakingnews/396892/nahm-named-best-restaurant-in-asia

Central Intelligence Agency (CIA). (n.d.). *The world factbook East and Southeast Asia: Thailand*. [Data set] Retrieved 20 July 2018, from www.cia.gov/library/publications/the-world-factbook/geos/print/country/countrypdf_th

Chang, H.-J. (2011). *23 Things they don't tell you about capitalism*. London: Penguin Books.

CitiScope. (2018, 19 January). What Bangkok's crackdown tells us about the multiple roles of street vendors everywhere. *Asian Correspondent*. Retrieved from https://asiancorrespondent.com/2018/01/bangkoks-crackdown-tells-us-multiple-roles-street-vendors-everywhere

Connors, M. K. (2012). Notes towards an understanding of Thai liberalism. In M. J. Montesano, P. Cachavalpongpun, & A. Chongvilaivan (Eds.), *Bangkok May 2010: Perspectives on a divided Thailand* (pp. 97–107). Singapore: Institute of Southeast Asian Studies.

Crispin, S. W. (2012). Thailand's classless conflict. In M. J. Montesano, P. Cachavalpongpun, & A. Chongvilaivan (Eds.), *Bangkok May 2010: Perspectives on a divided Thailand* (pp. 108–119). Singapore: Institute of Southeast Asian Studies.

Davis, M. (2017). *Planet of slums*. London: Verso.

De Botton, A. (2003). *The art of travel*. London: Penguin.

Dovey, K. (2010). *Becoming places: Urbanism/architecture/identity/power*. Abingdon: Routledge.

Dunlop, N. (2017, 27 August). Will Bangkok's street food ban hold? *The Guardian*. Retrieved from www.theguardian.com/global/2017/aug/27/will-bangkok-street-food-ban-hold

Ganesh, J. (2018, 1–2 September). Arrested development: The ossification of cities. *The Financial Times International Weekend Edition Life and Arts*, p. 20.

Gehl, J., & Svarre, B. (2013). *How to study public life* (K. A. Steenhard, Trans.). Washington, DC: Island Press.

Glassman, J. (2011). Cracking hegemony in Thailand: Gramsci, Bourdieu and the dialectics of rebellion. *Journal of Contemporary Asia*, *41*(1), 25–46. doi:10.1080/00472336.2011.530035

Gramsci, A. (1971). *Selections from the prison notebooks* (Q. Hoare & G. Nowell Smith, Trans., & Eds.). London: Lawrence and Wishart.

Hewison, K. (2012). Class, inequality and politics. In M. J. Montesano, P. Cachavalpongpun, & A. Chongvilaivan (Eds.), *Bangkok May 2010: Perspectives on a divided Thailand* (pp. 143–160). Singapore: Institute of Southeast Asian Studies.

Huang, T. (2004). *Walking between slums and skyscrapers: Illusions of open space in Hong Kong, Tokyo and Shanghai.* Hong Kong: Hong Kong University Press.

Koanantakool, P. C. (2002). The middle-class practice of consumption and traditional dance: "Thai-ness" and high art. In C. J. W.-L. Wee (Ed.), *Local cultures and the "New Asia": The state, culture and capitalism in Southeast Asia* (pp. 217–241). Singapore: Institute of Southeast Asian Studies.

Mak, A. H. N., Lumbers, M., & Eves, A. (2012). Globalisation and food consumption in tourism. *Annals of Tourism Research, 39*(1), 171–196. doi:10.1016/j.annals2011.05.010

Maneepong, C., & Walsh, J. C. (2013). A new generation of Bangkok street vendors: Economic crisis as opportunity and threat. *Cities, 34,* 37–43. doi:10.1016/j.cities.2012.11.02

Mateo-Babiano, I. B. (2012). Public life in Bangkok's urban spaces. *Habitat International, 36*(4), 452–461. doi:10.1016/j.habitatint.2012.04.001

Mishra, P. (2017). *Age of anger: A history of the present.* London: Allen Lane.

Montesano, M. (2012). Introduction: Seeking perspectives on a slow burn civil war. In M. Montesano, P. Cachavalpongpun, & A. Chongvilaivan (Eds.), *Bangkok May 2010: Perspectives on a divided Thailand* (pp. 1–9). Singapore: Institute of Southeast Asian Studies.

Nathiwutthikun, K. (2012). Jane Jacobs and the diversity of use of public open space in Thailand. In S. Hirt & D. Zahm (Eds.), *The urban wisdom of Jane Jacobs* (pp. 181–195). Abingdon: Routledge.

Nietzsche, F. (1993). *The birth of tragedy* (S. Whiteside, Trans.). London: Penguin Classics.

Osborne, L. (2006). *The naked tourist.* New York, NY: North Point Press.

Sauers, C. (2016, 23 August). Bangkok's disappearing street food. *BBC.* Retrieved from www.bbc.com/travel/story/20160817-bangkoks-disappearing-street-food

Sofian, E. V. (2018, 4 April). Jakarta's urban poor have found a new way to fight City Hall – and win. *The Guardian.* Retrieved from www.theguardian.com/cities/2018/apr/04/jakartas-urban-poor-have-found-a-new-way-to-fight-city-hall-and-win

Sriangura, V. (2018, Auguat 10). Street food is life. *Bangkok Post.* Retrieved from www.bangkokpost.com/news/special-reports/1519134/street-food-is-life

Sukphisit, S. (2010, 14 February). Dining on the streets Thailand's truly distinctive phenomenon. *Bangkok Post, Brunch,* p. 20.

Thai Select (Canada). (2013). *Thailand: Kitchen of the world.* [Video clip] Retrieved from www.youtube.com/watch?v=m9UmLPcMsm4

The Why Factory. (2012). *The vertical village: Individual, informal, intense.* Rotterdam: NAi Publishers.

Yongcharoenchai, C. (2015, 24 May). Popular Soi 38 food stalls face developer's axe. *Bangkok Post.* Retrieved from www.bangkokpost.com/news/general/570883/popular-soi-38-food-stalls-face-developer-axe

16 Post-conflict tourism development in Northern Ireland

Moving beyond murals and dark sites associated with its past

Stephen W. Boyd

Introduction

A simplistic view of tourism is about getting people from 'over there to over here, and while over here getting the greatest spend from their stay.' One major determinant in achieving that objective is offering them a conflict-free destination to visit. Not all places can claim to be successful at tourism, but those that are fortunate enough to offer a setting free of political insecurity and conflict have a greater chance than those that have had to develop tourism in a post-conflict climate. Where conflict has existed, those affected regions have to develop their tourism profile against that negative backdrop.

The focus of this chapter is therefore to understand how tourism develops in a post-conflict context, what is the nature of the tourism offer, what type of market it looks to attract, and to what extent destinations that have endured a long period of conflict can move beyond an early stage of post-conflict, often referred to as Phoenix tourism, to evolve into mature and normal tourism destinations. Using Northern Ireland as a case study, this author illustrates the sequence of changes that a destination post-conflict may encounter. Attention is also given to the role of dark tourism, how this is presented within the destination region as a whole and also how this is manifested at the scale of individual communities in how the era of conflict helps define their tourism product development, especially around murals. The case study also helps to outline the extent to which destinations coming out of conflict can develop their tourism, which moves beyond the Phoenix stage to resemble that which is viewed as 'normalization' within conflict-free destinations. Prior to discussing the case study, attention turns to a wider discussion of what is meant by post-conflict tourism development.

Post-conflict tourism development

Post-conflict tourism is the opposite of tourism that has developed in a conflict-free context, where tourism has been able to develop as part of a wider issues agenda for regions, facilitated by a policy arena and environment supportive of tourism as a development tool. When destinations are not conflict-free, tourism in this context has had to struggle, adapt and evolve within what have been termed 'difficult environments' often shaped by negative images and perceptions, experiencing shocks and stressors, chaos and unpredictability, where tourism exudes a high degree of vulnerability (Mansfeld, 1999; McKercher, 1999; Faulkner, 2001; Wall, 2007). Destinations rocked by shocks (rapid-onset events, such as the outbreak of civil unrest and political instability) and stressors (slow-onset events, such as a long timeline to achieve a ceasefire in the conflict) have had the added challenge of living with conflict and dealing with crises. As such, they have had to develop resilience strategies, both at the scale of destinations as a whole and within individual communities that have been directly affected by the violence and conflict (Wall, 2007; Boyd, 2013). It is, therefore, not surprising that regions that have endured a long period of political insecurity and conflict often take longer in their recovery (Boyd, 2017; Butler & Suntikul, 2013, 2017). The extent to which they recover is often determined by the presence of crisis management thinking and strategy, something that few destinations responding to crisis could turn to for assistance (Sharpley, 2005).

There are a number of distinct attributes about post-conflict tourism development. First, there is a strong aspect of peace-building involved. Tourism, peace and the relationship that can exist between both have long been recognized, particularly in shaping tourism policy at a global and international level (Moufakkir & Kelly, 2010). At the scale of individual destinations, that association often manifests itself in specific product development (e.g. dark tourism, political tourism, reconciliation tourism) or the creation of new tourism spaces (tourism borders, peace parks). At the scale of individual communities, dissonance within the cultural heritage of affected communities is illustrated directly within the landscape (e.g. murals) or told through the stories and memorabilia of warfare showcased within community museums, or the conversations that occur between guide and visitor at dark conflict sites along a defined trail or route (Chapter 13, this volume).

Second, post-conflict tourism development often aligns itself with dark and/ or political tourism: sites and events that connect the visitor to elements of the past conflict. Dark tourism scholars make a distinction between sites 'of' and sites 'associated with' events linked to death, dying, disaster and the macabre (Sharpley & Stone, 2009). It is the former that relate to destinations that have either experienced conflict – either as war, genocide or long-term terrorism – or currently face development of tourism alongside the threat of war, occupation and atrocities; in both cases, much of those region's tourism product development is conflict-related (Boyd, 2013; Isaac, 2013; Butler & Suntikul, 2017).

Third, post-conflict tourism development takes place within affected communities and it is their stories that the visitor wants to hear; it is the memorabilia that communities showcase that visitors want to see; it is the actual sites or death, atrocity that visitors want to physically touch (Causevic & Lynch, 2011; Boyd, 2016). These community spaces represent a distinct cultural heritage, a heritage which is closely tied to their past, customs and traditions. It is dissonance heritage as it belongs only to them; it is heritage of 'us' and not 'them' (Tunbridge &

Ashworth, 1996) and it is showcased within small community museums that tell their side of the conflict and it is the murals on display that showcase their cultural heritage (McDowell, 2008; Simone-Charteris & Boyd, 2010). It also presents an opportunity to improve the economic welfare of community citizens by actively engaging with tourism product development around the region's dark history (Chapter 14, this volume), but development that is driven by and has the support of the community.

Fourth, post-conflict development is short term; it is tourism development that takes place immediately after the violence, unrest or conflict is over. It is the early form of tourism development that takes place in a post-conflict era, and to some it has been labelled as 'Phoenix tourism' (Causevic & Lynch, 2011; Miller, Gonzalez, & Hutter, 2017). It is often favoured by the private sector side of the industry where unique products and attractions develop around the region's dark and difficult past and often involve key people, sites and events. This is in contrast to the public sector that avoids developing specific dark tourism opportunities and focuses on wider product development that capitalizes on a region's unique natural and cultural capital; namely, its natural and cultural heritage (Boyd, 2016, 2017). Differences also exist over the value assigned to Phoenix tourism. Causevic and Lynch (2011) view the Phoenix stage not as economic development but development of the affected communities; their storytelling of the conflict to visitors becomes a catharsis, a form of healing and of reconciliation. Peace-building and community healing take on greater prominence than the economic benefit of development of tourism products and services. Others see Phoenix tourism as a niche form of tourism that facilitates a region and or community to recover from disasters and conflict – to regenerate, rehabilitate, reimage and revitalize (Miller et al., 2017).

Finally, if viewed at a wider destination scale, post-conflict tourism development must be seen as part of a wider timeline that extends backwards through the conflict era to possibly a time before conflict started, but also forward to where a region is developing into a mature normal tourism destination (Chapter 2, this volume). This timeline is set out in Table 16.1, against which eight key attributes are evaluated: namely, safety and security, the perception that is held concerning the destination, the attraction mix (extent of supply present), entrepreneurial climate, access to the region, market reach, levels of investment and industry size (Boyd, 2019). The table illustrates the development pathway and the nature of that development in a series of development eras, pre-conflict, during conflict, post-conflict (Phoenix) and post-conflict (normalization). The pre-conflict era represents characteristics of a normal tourism destination, but at a lower scale of development found in mature tourism destinations; in short, characteristics of early tourism development. In contrast, the conflict era illustrates how such early tourism development is not only curtailed, but in many cases ceases to exist, and that for tourism to survive, it is reliant on the resilience of the industry and the strength of the domestic market. The table subdivides post-conflict era into a Phoenix stage and a normalcy stage. In terms of the Phoenix era, recovery of tourism and building on what survived during the conflict era is dependent on how safe people see the destination to be, both in reality and perception. As argued

Table 16.1 Destination change over time: pre-conflict to post-conflict

Aspect	Pre-conflict	Conflict	Post-conflict (Phoenix)	Post-conflict (normalcy)
Concern over safety and security	Limited	Extensive	Reduced	Limited
Perception of destination	Safe	Dangerous	Changing	Greater feeling of being safe
Attraction mix	Established (small)	Natural and cultural heritage dominant	Emergent dark tourism with existing heritage	Diversifying; event tourism, signature attractions (includes dark tourism)
Entrepreneurial climate	Established (accommodation focused)	Resilience (few attractions and accommodation sector)	Opportunity around dark and political tourism (private sector driven)	Public-private arrangements; signature build (public over private sector)
Access	Driven by domestic and Great Britain market	Limited routes facilitating VFR and regional market	New routes open (regional and international)	Changing pattern of route development (overall one of growth of route network)
Market	Local and national	Local (national – VFR)	Local, national (holiday), growing international	Local, national and international
Investment	Limited	Little to non-existent	Narrow focus (private sector – dark products, public sector – natural and cultural heritage)	New accommodation stock (private sector), event bidding and showcasing (public sector)
Industry size	Small (stable)	Declining, some resilience, slow growth toward peace	Growing (around selective products and services)	Extensive growth (diversified portfolio of products and services)

in Table 16.1, if these are viewed as 'reduced' (where people have less of a concern of visiting in terms of their safety and security) and 'changing' (where the image of the destination is much more positive), respectively, then the remaining aspects in Table 16.1 will also see change, which suggests overall recovery of the region but one that is clearly built around an interesting the region's past. Market reach is extended, visitor numbers rise and more come to see the destination as a holiday region and not one just associated with visiting friends/visiting relatives (VF/VR), new access opens up to capitalize on new experiences and products, but also because a peaceful environment is in place. The Phoenix stage is one that demonstrates recovery of tourism, but the size of the industry remains small and limited. The second stage of post-conflict may be termed as a period of 'normalcy.' The characteristics of this stage, as shown in Table 16.1, resembles the characteristics of a destination that has developed free of conflict and instability: it is one of growth and development beyond a limited base around dark tourism and tourism associated with the conflict era; the destination is highly accessible, the product mix is appealing to both domestic and international visitors, extensive investment in tourism takes place by the private sector (new visitor attractions open, new serviced accommodation stock is built), and public sector bodies seize the opportunity to showcase the destination through bidding for and hosting of major tourism events.

It is important to understand that the changes a destination may go through or experience across a 'pre-conflict' to 'post-conflict normal' timescale have also been shaped by the wider macro environment that takes into account political, economic, social and technological change, as well as the arena in which tourism policy has been made; the geographic context, setting and the stakeholders involved (Boyd, 2019). Figure 16.1 models destination change across a timescale before, during and after conflict. The model implies that the post-conflict eras offer the opportunity to plan and consider policies to develop tourism, but often in the early post-conflict stage, unrealistic targets are set by a government's renewed interest in the sector. Policy and planning become more realistic the longer the post-conflict era lasts; often building on an extant heritage base, developing attractions that have international market appeal, and tapping new markets such as niche tourism, especially events tourism. However, the private sector may continue to promote an element of the Phoenix era as illustrated by the dotted arrow; product range remains closely tied to dark tourism. Equally, communities that have not benefited from years of peace remain reliant on tourism products that are closely tied to the past conflict; they tap into an international marketplace still fascinated by the small community museums that provide a narrative and storytelling of the conflict era. The model suggests that the post-conflict Phoenix stage is where the destination from a tourism point of view starts to recover, building on the resilience of the sector that endured the conflict era. It is recovery in addition to what early development (pre-conflict) survived the conflict era. This stage of post-conflict tourism development sets the stage against which post-conflict normalcy era is possible. This 'normalcy era,' however, is dependent on a long-term peace arrangement, where the conflict has ended many decades ago, and the

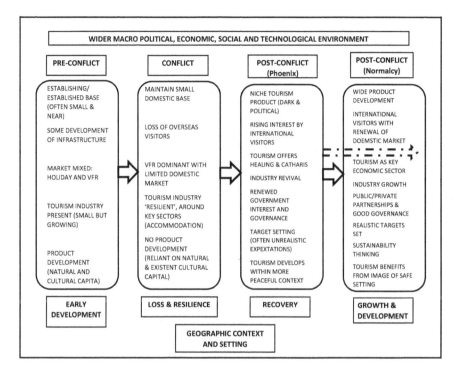

Figure 16.1 Wider macro-political, economic, social and technological environment

opportunity to develop tourism in a climate of long-term peace, safety and security facilitates ongoing growth and development of the tourism sector.

Attention now turns to illustrate how many of the aspects of post-conflict tourism development, as shown in both Table 16.1 and Figure 16.1, can be applied to a real-life case study. The chosen case that reflects this development pathway is Northern Ireland. Discussion is offered at both the scale of the country as a whole, and also at the level of individual communities when issues associated with dissonance heritage and community narrative (small community museums, murals, memorials, interface regions) are involved. It is also important to set the scene of tourism in Northern Ireland, both before and during the years of conflict, as tourism that evolved from conflict had close ties to the regions' past.

Post-conflict tourism development: the case of Northern Ireland

Pre-conflict era

It is often forgotten in the negative viewpoint that has been taken on Northern Ireland in the past by commentators that the country enjoyed many decades of a normal environment where tourism was able to develop and flourish. For a country which is to yet celebrate its centenary (having been established in 1922), Northern Ireland, prior to the outbreak of civil unrest in 1969, had moved quickly to develop a tourism profile. In almost 50 years of peace, an early tourism association was set up (the Ulster Tourist Development Association came into being in 1923) to promote the beaches and coastal communities along Northern Ireland's seashore to the UK marketplace; many of these resorts resembled the Victorian and Edwardian coastal resorts found along the English and Welsh coastline. The Ulster Tourist Development Association was the forerunner of the Northern Ireland Tourist Board, and then later, the country's National Tourism Organisation (NTO) was set up in 1948, and was also the first region of the UK to formally establish a tourist board. The Giants Causeway, claimed as one of the historical seven wonders of the world (announced to the world as early as 1693 in the form of lithographs, artists' painting and early travelogues), would quickly become the most visited attraction in Northern Ireland, promoted heavily by the NTO to the UK and international markets (Boyd, 2016, 2017), and now under National Turst ownership. In 1964, an open-air museum called Cultra opened to showcase a past Irish rurality focused on the built vernacular of the region's past and Irish rural life. By the end of the 1960s, a tourism product mix fashioned on both natural and cultural heritage capital was in place, alongside what would be viewed as quintessential cold-water bucket and spade seaside resorts. Records of early visitor numbers are sparse; they only started to be officially collected in 1959, when 633,000 tourist trips were recorded. A decade later and on the year that conflict started (1968), tourist trips had reached over one million (Boyd, 2013). Six years (1963) before the conflict started, the Royal Air Force airbase at Aldergrove was opened to civilian flights, and this played a pivotal role in this early pattern of growth. NITB records reveal that the tourism flow to Northern Ireland by 1967 was mainly driven by the VF/VR market and the holiday market, 38% and 26%, respectively. The country had a tourism accommodation sector of 210 hotels that offered a maximum capacity of 4,368 beds; a sizeable sector demonstrating the strength of the tourism industry (Boyd, 2013). Tourism in Northern Ireland over the pre-conflict era resembled the characteristics outlined in Table 16.1 and Figure 16.1.

This early development of tourism in Northern Ireland was quickly curtailed with the outbreak of violence by the Irish Republican Army (IRA) and its campaign against British presence and rule in Northern Ireland in 1969. The English media termed this 'The Troubles,' ushering in 25 years of violence and terrorism before a lasting peaceful resolution to the violence could be found. Northern Ireland would experience a quarter of a century when a loss of tourism investment and development resulted in tourism declining, although small sectors of the industry did demonstrate some degree of resilience.

Conflict era

The decline in tourism numbers was dramatic in the early years of conflict; 435,000 trips were recorded in 1973, a decline of 53% on figures for 1968.

Accommodation loss was also equally dramatic, down in the same period from 210 to 137 hotels as the Great Britain (GB) market collapsed (NITB, 1980). By the end of the 1980s, tourist trip numbers remained below those enjoyed in pre-conflict times, and accommodation stock had slumped further to 120 hotels (NITB, 1990). The tourism industry relied almost exclusively on its domestic and VFR markets. While at no time were tourists viewed as legitimate targets by the IRA, the perception of a region heavily policed by the British army was a major detractor to out-of-state visitors.

Commentators have been critical about the lack of investment and initiative taken by the Northern Ireland tourist authorities (Leslie, 1999), but much accommodation stock had been damaged or was closed down due to lack of market demand. What remained intact was a strong heritage base of attractions geographically located away from incidents of violence and terrorism. By the start of the 1990s, the numbers of visitors, while increasing, were still lower than those in the late 1960s, and room capacity in the hotel sector had been reduced by a third (Boyd, 2013). Despite this, the tourism industry demonstrated considerable resilience, driven by the hotel sector, and total visitor spending between 1974 and 1989 defied expectations and rose tenfold from £13 million to £136 million (NITB, 1990). Toward the end of the conflict era, a return to stronger governance was emerging, with clear targets and actions being set out by the national tourism organization (Northern Ireland Tourist Board), which predicted tourism numbers by 1994 of 1.6 million. In reality, 1.3 million would be achieved (Boyd, 2013), and that year is significant as it marked a major ceasefire, and 1995 would be the first year that was conflict-free. This year saw a 20% rise in visitors to 1.55 million, with double digit growth in all market regions, illustrating how quickly tourism benefits when the perception of safety and security changes for the better (Boyd, 2000).

An audit of tourism attractions between 1994 and 1997 revealed a natural and cultural heritage (including historical, industrial and educational) base (Boyd, 2000), with the development of a new attraction cluster across the capital city of Belfast emerging, along with the existing attraction cluster that had been established in pre-conflict times on the north coast. During the conflict era, Belfast was a closed city that lacked visitor appeal, whereas the heritage attractions across the North Coast cluster were little affected and were viewed as being far removed from the violence that was taking place elsewhere. Despite a more peaceful environment being established, the border region with the Republic of Ireland (RoI) was not viewed as having much tourism appeal (Boyd, 1999). It was not until 1998 that the official end of the conflict was announced with the signing of the Good Friday Agreement and the initial steps were taken to restore local government in Northern Ireland. The tourism industry was ill-prepared to capitalize on a changing political climate and the opportunity it created for tourism, as there were underlying problems of a lack of capacity of accommodation stock, poor service standards and a small workforce with many lacking professional qualifications (Boyd, 2013, 2017).

The era of conflict had seen violence concentrated in specific regions of the country, across both the two largest cities (Belfast and Londonderry) and in the border area with the RoI. Those regions affected during the conflict projected a sense of community which saw expression in displaying dissonance in their cultural heritage, often illustrated in murals that showcase either a British and Unionist or Catholic and Nationalist/Republican identity. These murals would form an important part of the Phoenix tourism era when tourism would start to see a recovery as a wider GB/international market sought out these open-air galleries. What visitors did not realize was that the murals, while they told a certain narrative, also illustrated dissonance in heritage (namely 'it's my heritage, not yours') as well as territoriality, in that these became very clearly demarcated spaces, albeit also tourism space. The murals would become a very important element in the post-conflict recovery of tourism, particularly in Belfast and Londonderry, and help shape what is viewed as Phoenix tourism in the Northern Ireland context.

Post-conflict 'Phoenix' era

As already stated, the murals formed an integral element of a dark tourism product that the out-of-state visitor came to see after the permanent ceasefire in 1997. That year the travel writer Simon Calder encouraged visitors to see what he termed the 'magnificent open-air galleries,' despite the fact that many of the murals were politically charged canvases that took in a mix of conflicting narratives (Boyd, 2000; Carden, 2017). Murals on Divis Street (West Belfast) became known as the 'International Wall' that depicted images of other conflicts and regional struggles (e.g. the Basque region, Israeli/Palestine, Syria) and lauded past freedom fighters and peacemakers (e.g. Che Guevara, Nelson Mandela). The canvases for these murals were the 'peace walls' that were erected during the Troubles in the interface regions to separate Catholic and Protestant communities (like those in Bethlehem, Palestine, separating Palestinians from Israelis; see chapter 10 in this volume). Walls of division quickly became walls of narrative and spaces where visitors could add their own personal messages of support for peace; a place where that expression for some became a form of catharsis against the struggles they were facing in their own homeland. It is not surprising that Belfast quickly emerged as a destination that people could visit as a place of learning about conflict resolution.

Catholic West Belfast, in the early 2000s, was marketed as the Gaeltacht Quarter – in all things, such as food, music, and traditions, and support of the Irish language to be widely spoken. In particular, the Catholic Falls Road in West Belfast became a 'city within a city,' a ghetto of Irish identity that quickly became 'gazed upon' by out-of-state visitors. Historical decisions had concentrated the Catholic community into this space, and cultural expression connected to Irishness, which was well entrenched in the fabric of this community, soon became visible to the visitor. In contrast, visitors could view the strength of Britishness and support for the Union when they travelled down the Protestant Shankill Road in West Belfast. These two community spaces in close proximity to each other became the 'political tourism section' of tours where visitors were given the tour guides' narrative of Northern Ireland's past. In early years this narrative varied; some guides were very historically factual in recounting a multiplicity of facts and incidents, while others talked about the wider role of conflict resolution and peace reconciliation by the communities themselves. The latter perhaps was a deliberate, if not official, company policy of railing against the emergence of the so-called 'Troubles tourism'; walking tours by ex-prisoners and black taxi tours of the 'black spots' of the conflict.

Calder also noted that these open galleries might not be there for long, as he feared that government and city officials would be keen to sanitize some of the most provocative ones. Beyond the galleries depicted on certain peace walls, there existed a myriad of murals of a distinct cultural and community heritage, often on the gable ends of houses, that conveyed strong messages of territoriality. The early visitors in peacetime would encounter phrases within murals such as 'You are entering Protestant. . .' or where flags of the Republic of Ireland and militant scenes depicting guns would be central within Republican community murals. Here on display was a clear example of dissonance heritage, where communities were proud of that heritage and where they used murals not just as an art form but where it became the means of expression of their heritage, politics and identity. According to Skinner and Jolliffe (2017), murals can take on a heritage, politics and identity theme. Belfast had the competitive advantage of being able to promote itself as a destination where visitors were able to view all three themes as the murals across the communities of both West and East Belfast were heritage-, politics- and identity-centric.

There are no official figures to say how many tourists visited the peace walls and their murals; they certainly added to the rise in visitor numbers after the Good Friday Agreement of 1998, a significant milestone that conveyed a message of openness and of a region that was safe to visit. In the early post-conflict years, there was no new tourism infrastructure development, and any growth built on the extant heritage attraction base (both natural and cultural) that had survived the Troubles. The appeal of the murals was a new dimension to that extant heritage base (Boyd, 2019).

The Phoenix stage of recovery did not morph into what may be termed the 'corporate stage,' whereby deliberate policy and planning was undertaken to facilitate tourism development that resembled normalcy for mature destinations. Instead, it saw government bodies (Art Council), city councils (Belfast) and to some extent community (Community Cohesion Units) intervention to reimage the murals; take the politics out, sanitize some and reposition the narrative around sporting heroes (e.g. footballer George Best), maritime past (e.g. East Belfast and its close association with the RMS *Titanic*) and literary figures (East Belfast and C.S. Lewis) (Boyd, 2016; Simone-Charteris, 2017). To some extent, the Phoenix focus has become less dark and more cultural heritage-centric, with some communities looking to promote their cultural identity through festivals and small community museums, and to share some of the dividend possible with a lasting peace.

Post-conflict 'normalcy' era

The official bodies (NITB and Tourism Ireland; the latter a cross-body organization created as part of the Good Friday Agreement) could market Northern Ireland
as a safe destination to visit. Corporate plans became more realistic as opposed to
idealistic, but growth remained slow; it took a decade after the 1998 Agreement
before out-of-state visitor figures reached two million and revenue from the market segment approximated £500 million (Boyd, 2019). Like any other region coming out of conflict, there were major obstacles to overcome: a highly fragmented
industry structure (Devine & Devine, 2011), lack of quality serviced accommodation stock and a lack of new tourism infrastructure and funds to develop new
attractions (Boyd, 2019).

Despite the financial downturn of 2008–2011, the Devolved Government of
Northern Ireland's NI *Programme for Government* (PfG) of 2008–2011 invested
heavily in developing new tourism product that would have international appeal.
The programme was formally labelled as the 'Signature Projects' and developed
out of the earlier 2004 NITB 'Strategic Framework for Action.' These have been
discussed elsewhere (see Boyd, 2013), and resulted in significant investments
in new tourism development that created not only a 'wow' factor but allowed
Northern Ireland to promote itself in a global marketplace. Of the five attractions,
two were particularly instrumental in achieving international recognition. 'Titanic
Belfast' (a new visitor attraction built around the RMS *Titanic* and Belfast, where
it had been conceived, designed, built and launched) opened in 2012 for the centenary of the sinking of RMS *Titanic*. Second, a new visitor centre opened at
the Giants Causeway. Alongside the other projects, the combined investment in
tourism-related infrastructure was £300 million. The NITB saw 2012 as a tipping
point year. The NI2012 campaign 'our time, our place' saw over one million visitors coming to a 2012 event which generated an economic impact of £18 million
and a tourism impact of £42 million (Northern Ireland Tourism Board, 2012).
The NI2012 included the opening of the MAC arts facility in Belfast, the 50th
anniversary of the Belfast Festival at Queen's, the Peace One Day concert in
Derry~Londonderry, the Cultural Olympiad and the Clipper Round the World
Yacht Race and Maritime Festival, to name but a few. This corporate response was
to deliberately plan and development around a boosterism and economic/industry
approach. Community-driven tourism was not a priority, and as such, the focus
on 'big build' received considerable criticism outside corporate and commercial
tourism circles. Many communities looking to capitalize on the peace dividend
did not figure in corporate thinking. Despite criticism, this decision paid off; in
2017, the Giants Causeway received over one million visitors for the first time
and *Titanic* Belfast has received major global tourism industry awards, with five
million visitors since it opened in 2012.

A second deliberate strategy by NITB (rebranded as Tourism Northern Ireland
in 2015) was to focus on events. The first major event to be hosted was the EMA
MTV Music Awards in Belfast in 2011, and it demonstrated that Northern Ireland
could host such events. What followed is a success story: Northern Ireland hosted

the Irish Open (Golf) in 2012, 2015 and 2017 and the G7 Summit in 2013 and the starting stages of Giro d'Italia cycling race; Derry/Londonderry showcased events across 2013, as the first city to be named a UK City of Culture; and 2016 had a whole year of events to celebrate Northern Ireland's food and drink. Recently, Belfast was awarded a City Deal by the UK government with one of its strategic thrusts being to grow cities' tourism economies.

The country has also benefited from the filming of the HBO series *Game of Thrones*, which has generated economic benefits (£30 million generated in the local economy, Tourism Ireland, 2016) and has opened Northern Ireland to new international markets, in particular the outbound Chinese market.

The corporate strategy has been a focused one with a draft Tourism Strategy 2030 of doubling the value of Northern Ireland tourism to £2 billion and creating 20,000 new jobs (in addition to the 61,000 recorded by Northern Ireland Statistics and Research Agency in 2016; Northern Ireland Statistics and Research Agency, 2017a, 2017b). Northern Ireland has reached the condition of 'normalcy'; it is seen as a visitor destination as opposed to a VF/VR destination and over the course of the next decade the strategy is one of developing and marketing what Tourism Northern Ireland calls 'an internationally compelling experience brand built upon landscape, heritage and culture.'

Conclusion

Destinations that have endured any conflict, particularly one that has been long and protracted, will struggle to reach a state of normalcy as they exude a degree of fragility, are beset with a negative perception in the marketplace and have a legacy of a lack of trust to overcome. It is therefore not surprising that recovery or the emergence of tourism in a post-conflict state takes on characteristics of that conflict – and as such, dark tourism can take on greater precedence than is officially preferred. Northern Ireland's tourism recovery story fits that mould to a certain extent. There has been the development of a dark tourism product and brand, but this has been mostly driven by the private sector and has not been official public policy. Tourism Northern Ireland recognizes that there is market potential there, but it looks to market it more broadly as 'People, Place and Politics.' Communities that have been affected by the conflict and have not had a great tourism-peace dividend are keen to use the dark tourism hook to develop community-driven tourism around the past but also to provide visitors with a wider cultural heritage-centric narrative. The ongoing growth and development of tourism in Northern Ireland will depend on how attractive the signature attractions remain, as there is emerging concern that some of the most popular attractions and spaces are becoming congested, with issues of sustainability and overtourism arising, as at the time of writing, Northern Ireland does not have a functioning Devolved Government, and the Brexit agreement (the UK exiting the European Union) remains to be finalized. Both factors are important in the context of post-conflict tourism development. First, despite the absence of a Devolved Government, Tourism Northern Ireland has been able to provide strategic direction for the sector. The sector as a whole has been able to develop momentum, perhaps because it has the assurance that the destination is now firmly seen in the eyes of the consumer to be a safe one to visit. To that end, the private sector has taken a greater initiative, and the Northern Ireland tourism industry is less reliant on the public sector as it reaches a mature state. As for Brexit and the post-Brexit relationship, the RoI is an important market, and the return to a hard border would certainly have a negative impact. Northern Ireland tourism predominantly takes place away from the border region, and the presence of a hard border would have a more dramatic impact at a regional as opposed to a national scale, but when factored into national statistics, it would inevitably impact both visitor numbers and spending.

This chapter has attempted to achieve two outcomes: to suggest a possible schema of recovery for destinations moving out of conflict and to apply that thinking within a specific case study. Each destination recovering from conflict will inevitably chart its own tourism path, but it is not unreasonable to expect this will initially take on a conflict narrative before it broadens to a development scenario akin to conflict-free destinations. If, however, it fails to make that shift, it is unlikely to develop as a destination that has anything to offer beyond a narrative of the past conflict – which, ironically, prevented it from becoming a mature destination. That would be a dangerous risk to take if becoming a mature destination is the end goal.

References

Boyd, S. W. (1999). North-South divide: The role of the border in tourism to Northern Ireland. *Visions in Leisure and Business, 17*(4), 50–71.

Boyd, S. W. (2000). Heritage tourism in Northern Ireland: Opportunities under peace. *Current Issues in Tourism, 3*(2), 150–174.

Boyd, S. W. (2013). Tourism in Northern Ireland: Before violence, during and post violence. In R. W. Butler & W. Suntikul (Eds.), *Tourism and war* (pp. 176–192). London: Routledge.

Boyd, S. W. (2016). Heritage as the USP for tourism in Northern Ireland: Attraction mix, effective storytelling and selling of a dark past. In G. Hooper (Ed.), *Tourism and heritage in Britain and Ireland* (pp. 245–362). London: Palgrave Macmillan.

Boyd, S. W. (2017). Tourism and political change in Ireland, North and South: Identity, modernity, contrast and moving toward convergence. In R. W. Butler & W. Suntikul (Eds.), *Tourism and political change* (2nd ed., pp. 153–168). Oxford: Goodfellow.

Boyd, S. W. (2019). Tourism policy and planning in post-conflict destinations: Comparative cases of Northern Ireland and Sri Lanka. In K. Andriotis, D. Stylidis, & A. Weidenfeld (Eds.), *Tourism policy and planning implementation: Issues and challenges* (pp. 53–77). Oxford: Routledge.

Butler, R. W., & Suntikul, W. (Eds.). (2013). *Tourism and war*. Oxford: Routledge.

Butler, R. W., & Suntikul, W. (Eds.). (2017). *Tourism and political change* (2nd ed.). Oxford: Goodfellow.

Carden, S. (2017). The Gaeltacht quarter of mural city: Irish in Falls Road murals. In J. Skinner & L. Jolliffe (Eds.), *Murals and tourism: Heritage, politics and identity* (pp. 236–253). Oxford: Routledge.

Causevic, S., & Lynch, P. (2011). Phoenix tourism: Post-conflict tourism role. *Annals of Tourism Research, 38*(3), 780–800.

Devine, A., & Devine, F. (2011). Planning and developing tourism within a public sector quagmire: Lessons from and for small countries. *Tourism Management, 32*, 1253–1261.

Faulkner, B. (2001). Towards a framework for tourism disaster management. *Tourism Management, 22*(1), 135–147.

Isaac, R. (2013). Palestine: Tourism under occupation. In R. W. Butler & W. Suntikul (Eds.), *Tourism and war* (pp. 143–158). London: Routledge.

Leslie, D. (1999). Terrorism and tourism: The Northern Ireland situation – a look behind the veil of certainty. *Journal of Travel Research, 38*, 37–40.

Mansfeld, Y. (1999). Cycles of war, terror and peace: Determinants and management of crises and recovery of the Israeli tourism industry. *Journal of Travel Research, 38*(1), 30–36.

McDowell, S. (2008). Selling conflict heritage through tourism in peacetime Northern Ireland: Transforming conflict or exacerbating difference. *International Journal of Heritage Studies, 14*(5), 405–421.

McKercher, B. (1999). A chaos approach to tourism. *Tourism Management, 20*(4), 425–434.

Miller, D. S., Gonzalez, C., & Hutter, M. (2017). Phoenix tourism within dark tourism: Rebirth, rebuilding and rebranding of tourist destinations following disasters. *Worldwide Hospitality and Tourism Themes, 9*(2), 196–215.

Moufakkir, O., & Kelly, I. (Eds.). (2010). *Tourism, peace and progress*. London: CABI Publishing.

Northern Ireland Statistics and Research Agency (NISRA). (2017a). *Northern Ireland annual tourism statistics 2016*. Belfast: Tourism Statistics Branch.

Northern Ireland Statistics and Research Agency (NISRA). (2017b). *Trips taken in Northern Ireland and revenue generated 1959–2016*. Belfast: Netherleigh.

Northern Ireland Tourist Board (NITB). (1980). *Tourism facts 1979*. Belfast: NITB.

Northern Ireland Tourist Board (NITB). (1990). *Tourism facts 1989*. Belfast: NITB.

Northern Ireland Tourism Board (NITB). (2012). *NI2012: Our time, our place: Our story*. Retrieved January 24, 2018, from https://tourismni.com/globalassets/facts-and-figures/research-reports/impact-of-events/impact-of-events-ni2012-review.pdf

Sharpley, R. (2005). International tourism: The management of crises. In L. Pender & R. Sharpley (Eds.), *The management of tourism* (pp. 275–287). London: Sage.

Sharpley, R., & Stone, P. R. (Eds.). (2009). *The darker side of travel: The theory and practice of dark tourism*. Clevedon: Channel View Publications.

Simone-Charteris, M. (2017). State intervention in re-imaging Northern Ireland's political murals: Implications for tourism and the communities. In J. Skinner & L. Jolliffe (Eds.), *Murals and tourism: Heritage, politics and identity* (pp. 217–235). Oxford: Routledge.

Simone-Charteris, M., & Boyd, S. W. (2010). Northern Ireland re-emerges for the Ashes: The contribution of political tourism towards a more visited and peaceful environment. In O. Moufakkir & I. Kelly (Eds.), *Tourism, progress and peace* (pp. 179–198). Wallingford: CABI.

Skinner, J., & Jolliffe, L. (Eds.). (2017). *Murals and tourism: Heritage, politics and identity*. Oxford: Routledge.

Tourism Ireland. (2016). *Tourism Ireland annual report*. Retrieved January 24, 2018, from https://www.tourismireland.com/TourismIreland/media/Tourism-Ireland/About%20Us/Corporate%20Publications/Tourism-Ireland-Annual-Report-2016.pdf?ext=.pdf

Tunbridge, J. E., & Ashworth, G. J. (1996). *Dissonant heritage: The management of the past as resource in conflict*. London: John Wiley and Sons.

Wall, G. (2007). *The tourism industry and its adaptability and vulnerability to climate change*. Warsaw: Institute of Geography and Spatial Organization, Polish Academy of Sciences.

17 Visitor-host encounters in post-conflict destinations

The case of Cyprus

Anna Farmaki

Introduction

Tourism, as a social phenomenon, has long been considered as holding unrealized power in improving the perceptions, attitudes and relations among people. Unsurprisingly, the tenet that tourism may contribute to global peace, through the cultivation of understanding among people, is widespread. Emanating from the inspiring work of D' Amore (1988), who invited researchers to consider the role of tourism in establishing peace, a significant body of research on the tourism and peace nexus emerged. Research on the interface between tourism and peace was performed from a variety of angles, and was placed within different settings. For instance, pertinent studies look mostly into socio-cultural and political perspectives of the tourism and peace nexus, through the lens of corporate social responsibility, globalization and alternative tourism (e.g. Higgins-Desbiolles, 2003; Isaac, 2010a, 2010b). Likewise, there is a plethora of case studies, including the former Yugoslavia, Palestine, Vietnam, Ireland, Afghanistan, the USA, Mainland China and Taiwan, which provide insights on the contribution of tourism in reconciliation and peace (Alluri, 2009; Causevic & Lynch, 2011; Durko & Petrick, 2015; Guo, Kim, Timothy, & Wang, 2006; Kim & Prideaux, 2003; Zhang, 2013).

Extant literature posited that tourism may contribute to peace through contact brought about by travel. With the phenomenon of tourism being deeply rooted in social structures, networks and behavioural aspects, it is not surprising that tourism is widely regarded as a force for peace (Farmaki, 2017), with the traveller seen as an 'ambassador' of peace (Salazar, 2006), given the potential of travel to bring people closer together. Indeed, Nyaupane, Teye, and Paris (2008) argued that travel-induced contact may positively influence international politics and foster global peace by reducing cultural and psychological gaps among people. The proposition that, through contact, visitors' negative stereotypes of an opposing group are eliminated, gave potency to the contact hypothesis within the tourism-peace literature. The majority of pertinent studies adopted the contact hypothesis in their investigation of the role of tourism as a contributor to peace, with supporters of the hypothesis claiming that contact brought by travel may increase understanding between people of different races and cultural and national origin. Nonetheless, the contact hypothesis within the tourism context has been greatly criticized. In relation to peace-building, the positive effects of travel-induced contact remain equally contested. In fact, scholars have questioned the validity of the causal relationship between tourism and peace (Anastasopoulos, 1992; Pizam, Jafari, & Milman, 1991), with Litvin (1998) suggesting that tourism is a beneficiary of peace rather than a cause of peace. Indeed, it is widely acknowledged that tourism cannot flourish in the midst of conflict, with sceptics arguing that people have always travelled, yet such travelling tendencies have neither minimized the propensity of nations to enter into conflict nor eliminated gaps among diverse communities.

So far, the rhetoric on the contributory role of tourism to peace remains fragile, as inconsistency characterizes the findings of relevant studies. Farmaki (2017) argues that tourism's economic orientation and political relevance makes the potential contribution of tourism to world stability and peace more complex. Additionally, the assumption that travel-induced contact may improve human relations is somewhat optimistic, ignoring the nature of the contact and/or the context in which contact occurs. In this regard, Tomljenovic (2010) questioned the strength of previous studies using contact theory, as most focused on student groups visiting for a short period of time as part of an educational trip. In occasions of an organized trip, tourists are sheltered in an environmental bubble and depict little willingness to learn about the host community, leading to minimal quality contact with the host community. Therefore, there is a need to investigate the nature of encounter between visitors and the hostile visited community, if understanding is to be gained on the conditions under which travel-induced contact may contribute to peace.

This chapter attempts to examine the nature of encounter between visitors and hosts in conflict-affected countries. Drawing from the Cyprus setting, which is well-known for the conflict between its Greek Cypriot and Turkish Cypriot communities, the chapter aims to shed light on the contextual conditions shaping the nature of contact among people in post-conflict destinations, where political uncertainty and fragility exists. Indeed, countries such as Cyprus that have experienced prolonged conflict offer an interesting background for the examination of travel-induced contact and its effect on the relationship of hostile groups. While the host-guest relationship has been extensively researched within tourism, there is less knowledge on the nature of the encounter between people from potentially hostile societies. Indeed, as Sharpley (2014) postulated, much research on the visitor-host relationship is tourism-centric, largely ignoring the socio-cultural and historic framework in which the encounter between people occurs and which influences people's perceptions and attitudes. Consequently, this chapter may contribute to knowledge on the visitor-host relationship beyond a predetermined tourism space. The chapter begins with a review of the literature on the role of travel-induced contact in fostering world stability and peace before proceeding to discussing visitor-host encounters. Following, the study context and methodology adopted are explained, whereas the discussion centres on the key themes emerging from the examination of the visitor-host encounter in the Cyprus context. Last, implications are discussed which may be relevant to other destinations whose societies have been affected by conflict.

Tourism and peace

The effect of peace on tourism development is well-established. Contrarily, the rhetoric on the contributory role of tourism to peace remains questionable, with previous research yielding inconclusive results of the nature of the relationship. It has been suggested that contact through travel elevates tourism's role as an agent of change, bringing down barriers among people and encouraging cooperation among nations (Askjellerud, 2003; Causevic, 2010). Based on the contact hypothesis, scholars have positioned tourism as an agent for establishing rapport between divided communities (Causevic, 2010) and recognized tourism as a confidence-building measure encouraging cooperation (Sönmez & Apostolopoulos, 2000). Similarly, it has been argued that tourism may exert political influence and facilitate peace through increased interaction and mutual appreciation (Kim & Crompton, 1990). In fact, to denote the potential impact of tourism on peace-building, Causevic and Lynch (2011) coined the term 'Phoenix tourism' (see Chapter 13, this volume), indicating its role in destination renewal, through the normalization of social relationships. While there are some studies showing positive effects on visitors' perceptions and attitudes following visitation to the hostile outgroup (e.g. Chen, 2010; Kim, Prideaux, & Prideaux, 2007), the majority of studies are discouraging about the potential effect of tourism on peace. For example, early studies found no, or only marginal, improvement in attitudes, highlighting the rigidity of negative views towards hostile communities (Milman, Reichel, & Pizam, 1990; Pizam et al., 1991). Anastasopoulos (1992) concluded that travel does not necessarily improve perceptions between 'traditional enemies.' More recent studies concur that tourism is a beneficiary of peace rather than a cause for peace (Chen, Lai, Petrick, & Lin, 2016; Cho, 2007; Guo et al., 2006; Kim & Prideaux, 2006).

Critics of the contact theory have proposed that the optimistic view on the contributory role of tourism to peace ignores the economic and political orientation of tourism (Farmaki, 2017). Indeed, several factors were recognized in extant literature as inhibiting tourism cooperation and the improvement of political and social relations between hostile nations, including nationalistic sentiment (Altinay & Bowen, 2006), distrust and miscommunication (Selwyn & Karkut, 2007), political tensions (Cho, 2007; Kim & Prideaux, 2006) and trade issues (Guo et al., 2006). In this respect, the nature of encounter was identified as influential on its positive effects on perceptions and attitudes of people. Within this context, it has been suggested that mistrust between visitors and hosts may be alleviated if their interactions are positive, based on mutual respect and if there is little social distance between interested groups (Askjellerud, 2003). Building on Allport's (1954) argument, Pettigrew and Tropp (2006) suggested that relationship improvements may arise if participants are of equal status and have common goals and intimate and voluntary contact among participants. Indeed, investigations into Israeli ecotourist attitudes towards Jordanians reported improvement following visitation to Jordan (Pizam, Fleischer, & Mansfeld, 2002), with researchers concluding that the positive attitude change resulted due to the presence of equal status between host and visitors, intimate contact and governmental support for interaction. Likewise, the positive effect of intergroup contact was noted in studies examining student groups working on collaborative projects (e.g. Durko & Petrick, 2015).

Although the results of these studies are promising, they primarily investigated student groups travelling to a hostile outgroup as part of an educational trip and for a short period of time (Tomljenovic, 2010). Less attention has been paid to the encounters between members of the society of conflict-ridden destinations. Indeed, Yu (1997) highlighted the importance of low politics activity in positively influencing the political relations between hostile countries. Examining the visitor-host encounter within the politically uncertain setting of countries that have undergone prolonged conflict may illuminate existing knowledge on the conditions under which tourism may contribute to peace.

Visitor-host encounters

There is a proliferation of research on the 'visitor-host' relationship. The burgeoning body of work dedicated to visitor-host relations is unsurprising, considering that the interaction between the host community and visitors is part and parcel of travel. Smith (1977) argued that visitor-host relations are fundamental to tourism, as they largely determine the tourist experience. Similarly, the nature of visitor-host relations may yield significant impacts on the residents of a destination (Wall & Mathieson, 2006), thereby influencing residents' perceptions of tourism development and visitors. Early studies on the visitor-host relationship have focused primarily on the structure and setting in which the interaction took place (e.g. Krippendorf, 1987). Within this context, Sutton (1967) argued that contact between the host community and visitors is transitory and characterized by imbalance. Although both parties seek satisfaction from the encounter, it is 'business as usual' for the host community. Indeed, a UNESCO paper published in 1976 characterized the encounter between visitors and the host community as being restricted by time and space, with the relationship being largely unequal and predetermined. Evidently, as contact between the two parties takes place within an organized tourist space, the visitor-host encounter is conditioned by the commercially based nature of tourism (Reisinger, Kozak, & Visser, 2013). Nonetheless, there are different forms of visitor-host encounters, ranging from regular contact to no contact (Krippendorf, 1987), as well as from structured, commercial-based exchanges to spontaneous informal engagements. According to De Kadt (1979) there are situations when visitors and the host community may find themselves side by side as 'the two parties come face to face with the object of exchanging information or ideas' (p. 50).

Central to the visitor-host relationship are the perceptions and attitudes of local residents towards visitors. Over the years, researchers diverted their attention to residents' perceptions of the potential impacts of tourism, which from the 1960s onwards came to be seen as being in conflict with the environment in which tourism developed (Dowling, 1992). Evidently, the vast majority of pertinent studies on the visitor-host relationship investigate primarily host communities' perceptions and attitudes towards tourists and/or tourism development. There has been minimal consideration of visitors' perceptions of the host community. Additionally, recognizing the multifaceted and complex phenomenon of visitor-host interactions, as well as the heterogeneity of visitor-host relations, Sharpley (2014) called for greater academic attention to the socio-cultural and historic framework in which the visitor-host encounter occurs and which shapes people's perceptions and attitudes. In this respect, post-conflict settings offer an interesting context for the examination of visitor-host encounters. First, characterized by fragile socio-political environments, post-conflict destinations represent a promoting background on which understanding of the visitor-host encounter may be advanced. Considering the current context of instability in which global tourism operates and the intensification of negative prejudice influencing the tourism activity, knowledge from post-conflict countries may illuminate extant literature on the conditions shaping the visitor-host encounter in situations of vulnerability and instability. Second, in light of the assumption that travel-induced contact may improve the relations between people from conflictual destinations by positively influencing perceptions and attitudes of one another, an examination of the visitor-host encounter in post-conflict destinations may provide interesting insights into the role of tourism as a peacemaker. This chapter draws from the Cyprus post-conflict context in evaluating visitor-host encounters between people of conflict-affected destinations, affected by conflict.

Study context

Cyprus represents an interesting case of political instability, as it is known for its frozen conflict where there is no active violence, yet the political dispute is ongoing. The island of Cyprus has been divided since 1974, when Turkish forces occupied approximately 37% of the island's northern part (Fisher, 2001). The Turkish invasion of Cyprus was the aftermath of ongoing tensions between the island's two main communities, the Greek Cypriots and the Turkish Cypriots, and led to the geographical partition of the two communities, with around 185,000 Greek Cypriots being internally displaced to the south of the island and 45,000 Turkish Cypriots respectively relocating in the north (Webster & Timothy, 2006). As a result, the two communities developed separate institutional and governance structures: the Republic of Cyprus (an internationally recognized state and member of the European Union) in the south and the Turkish Cypriot administration in the north, which remains a non-recognized de facto state economically and politically dependent on Turkey. Crossing into the 'other' side was made possible only in 2003. Within a year and a half, more than four million crossings had been registered by Greek and Turkish Cypriots; whereas by 2014, more than 13 million crossing were registered for Turkish Cypriots compared to almost eight million crossings by Greek Cypriots (European Commission, 2017). Interestingly, while the Turkish Cypriot community is numerically smaller – representing approximately a quarter of the Greek Cypriot community – the number of crossings registered for Turkish Cypriots is noticeably higher. A selective number of investigations (e.g. Dikomitis, 2004; Webster & Timothy, 2006) looking into Greek

Cypriots' visit motives to the northern part of Cyprus sheds some light on this discrepancy.

As reported by Dikomitis (2004), Greek Cypriots forced out of their homes in 1974 wished to take their children back to their ancestral places, while others crossed simply out of curiosity about the 'other' side. Nonetheless, the initial euphoria of the first crossings subsided when the experience of returning as a kind of domestic tourist led to many Greek Cypriots deciding against a future visit (Bryant, 2010). Interestingly, a large proportion of the Greek Cypriot community has never visited the northern part of Cyprus (Webster & Timothy, 2006). As Scott (2012) postulated, the requirement to show identification to Turkish Cypriot guards upon crossing is a deterring factor for many Greek Cypriots as it is a reminder of the power politics at play. Indeed, resistance to cross emanates from a concern that doing so will grant political legitimacy to the 'other' side. In highlighting the complex reality on the island, Webster and Timothy's study (2006) identified looking for ancestral land, gambling, visiting sacred places and curiosity as key travel motives for Greek Cypriots. In contrast, Turkish Cypriots cross to the 'other' side for shopping and employment, in addition to looking for ancestral land. Greek Cypriots' perceived ethical barriers were identified as an inhibiting factor on visitation, with many Greek Cypriots being bound by an ethical imperative not to spend money in the north, even in the case of a visit (Webster & Timothy, 2006). For example, staying in a hotel, buying goods and gambling are regarded as acts of immoral behaviour (Webster & Timothy, 2006). Although these studies are informative of the complexity surrounding visitation to the 'other' side, they are less helpful in advancing understanding on the nature of the encounter between visitors and the visited community. To this end, this chapter aims to contribute to existing knowledge by examining the visitor-host encounter from the Greek Cypriot perspective. In other words, the opinions of Greek Cypriots visiting northern Cyprus were sought in relation to (i) visitation patterns and (ii) contact with their counterparts on the 'other' side.

Methodology

A qualitative research framework was deemed as appropriate in collecting and analyzing the empirical data. Specifically, we interviewed Greek Cypriots residing in the southern part of the island. The informants were purposively selected according to their background, age and gender, and saturation of data was reached after 77 interviews. The rationale of purposive sampling rests on the fact that the researchers, based on their a priori theoretical understanding of the topic, assumed that certain individuals may have important perspectives on the phenomenon in question (Robinson, 2014). Thus, the sample selection considered the backgrounds, age and gender of the informants to ensure that enough diversity was included (Ritchie, Lewis, Nicholls, & Ormston, 2014) within the sample. Overall, the age of the informants ranged from 19–87 and included 43 females and 34 males. Out of the 77 informants, 54 had visited northern Cyprus in the past, while 23 had not.

Participants in the study were assured of their anonymity via the use of pseudo-nyms. Semi-structured interviews were conducted by an experienced member of the research team on a one-to-one basis and face-to-face. The interviews were performed in the comfort of the participants' homes and/or preferred meeting point (e.g. cafeteria). The interviews, which took place from June to November 2017, lasted approximately 45–60 minutes each, with the questions being framed according to the research aim. Specifically, each interview proceeded from a number of 'grand tour' questions (McCracken, 1988) seeking to establish the visitation profile of the informants before moving into the topic of the nature and conditions shaping the encounter with the host community. Each interviewee was further probed if necessary and notes were taken before, during and after the interviews to capture verbal and non-verbal aspects of the interviews. All interviews were performed in Greek and transcribed, following translation from a professional, into English. The transcripts were checked for accuracy and were analyzed using thematic content analysis to illuminate underlying themes in the discussion. Specifically, blocks of verbatim text were copied, reorganized and cross-referenced to allow the identification of thematic categories. Sub-categories also emerged, which were combined with preidentified themes to allow for deeper elaboration on key issues that encourage evidence-based understanding (Hennink, Hutter, & Bailey, 2010).

Findings

As the analysis moved on, it became clear that the visitor-host encounter was conditioned by two factors: (i) the structure of the visit including frequency, intentionality and exchange of benefits between the two parties; and (ii) the nature of the contact prescribed along the degree of the interaction and the type of the exchange between the two parties. Five types of visitor-host encounter were, therefore, identified within the post-conflict context of Cyprus, depicted in Table 17.1. The darker the shade of each box in the figure, the less positive the encounter between the host community and visitors and vice versa.

Specifically, there were informants whose visits to northern Cyprus were purposeful and frequent. The majority of informants under this category argued that

Table 17.1 Types of visitor-host encounters

Structure of visit	Frequent Planned Reciprocal	Frequent Planned Non-reciprocal	Occasional Planned Non-reciprocal	Infrequent Unplanned Potentially reciprocal	No visit
Nature of contact	High degree of interaction, beyond commercial exchanges	Minimal interaction, mostly commercially based	Minimal commercial and/or social exchange	Moderate spontaneous interaction, mostly commercial	No physical or verbal contact

their visiting was driven mostly by personal reasons such as visiting friends. In the words of Anthi (77 years old, Limassol), 'I visit my friends in the north regularly, almost on a weekly basis. I enjoy spending time with them but I also go with my husband . . . we eat in restaurants and buy products that are cheaper there,' indicating that the contact between visitors and hosts is marked by both personal and commercial-based elements. Interestingly, frequent and meaningful contact was noted not only among those born and raised in northern Cyprus prior to the 1974 events, but also among Greek Cypriots of younger ages. Driven initially by curiosity to visit northern Cyprus, younger generations of Greek Cypriots find themselves in an important position to maintain contact with Turkish Cypriots. Evidently, through contact with Turkish Cypriots – whom they never had the opportunity to meet before – they understand their national identity better while possibly improving the potential for reconciliation on the island. The following statements are indicative of these visitors' sentiments of the importance of interacting with Turkish Cypriots.

> I try to visit at least every two weeks . . . if we keep visiting and take part in bi-communal activities we understand each other better and plant the seed for a prosperous future for all the Cypriots.
>
> (Savvas, 29 years old, Nicosia)

> I've visited my father's village many times as I want to know where I come from. . . . I feel that the village is part of my identity and it does not feel like a foreign land to me because I grew up listening to my father's stories of life in the village.
>
> (Eleni, 28 years old, Nicosia)

Such visitations are intentional and characterized by reciprocal benefits beyond commercial exchanges. Within the fragile context of post-conflict destinations, encounters of this kind between visitors and the host community are significant as they may yield positive changes in the perceptions and attitudes of people of conflictual destinations. Evidently, the high degree of interaction between visitors and the host community embraces the potential of travel-induced contact in improving the social relations of divided societies.

Nonetheless, frequency of visitation does not necessarily translate into meaningful contact between Greek Cypriots and Turkish Cypriots. The second category consists of informants whose visits were intentional and frequent, yet not meaningful, as they are driven mostly by commercial exchanges. These visitors cross to the 'other' side for gambling or shopping reasons. As Nicos (24 years old, Larnaca) stated, 'I visit northern Cyprus on a weekly basis to buy cigarettes because they are cheaper.' Andreas (44 years old, Nicosia) also expressed similar views, stating that he visits the casinos in northern Cyprus frequently, as there are no equivalent gambling establishments in southern Cyprus. Thus, the encounters between this group of Greek Cypriots and Turkish Cypriots are mostly commercially driven, as the interaction with the host community is grounded on business exchanges. Consequently, there is little reciprocity of benefits between the two communities as such an encounter – based on economic orientations and lacking any social dimensions – cannot contribute meaningfully to the reconciliation of parties previously in conflict.

The third type of visitor-host encounter identified includes visitors who cross to the 'other' side less frequently in order to visit religious and cultural attractions. For these informants, the visit presents an ethical dilemma – considering that the island's northern part is still occupied by Turkish forces – which they appear to counteract by avoiding commercial exchanges such as buying food or drink from the host community. As Niki (51 years old, Limassol) emphasized, 'I only cross to visit the Apostolos Andreas monastery and other religious and cultural attractions.' Therefore, even though some informants in this category stated that their occasional encounters with Turkish Cypriots are not necessarily negative ones, their behaviour towards the host community remains passively defensive. The encounters between Greek Cypriots and Turkish Cypriots are largely conditioned by the organized form of visitation which reinforces barriers to meaningful contact between visitors and the host community. Greek Cypriots in this category remain passive visitors, observing the sites they intended to visit, albeit not deliberately coming into contact with members of the host community.

Moving on, a fourth category of visitor-host encounter was identified including those informants who visited infrequently and unintentionally. 'I visited one day with family members who arrived from the UK and expressed a desire to see the occupied areas . . . it was an impulsive decision, really' said Elena (29 years old, Paphos). The nature of contact between these visitors and the host community was restricted mostly to commercial-based exchanges and was rather moderate, yielding minimal reciprocity between visitors and the host community. Perhaps the spontaneous nature of the visit limited the potentiality of meaningful encounter between visitors and the host community, as visitors were unaware of the structural factors prescribing their visit.

Last, informants who had purposely never visited northern Cyprus were grouped together in a category describing the lack of contact, either physical or verbal, between visitors and the host community. These non-visitors were deterred from visiting the 'other' side due to nationalistic reasons and/or ethical barriers such as 'refusal to show an ID in my own country' and 'concerns that the visit will grant legitimacy to the administration of Turkish Cypriots.' Strong emotional sentiments dominated the perceptions and attitudes of these informants, consequently inhibiting a potential visit and further solidifying the absence of contact between visitors and hosts in a post-conflict context. The following extracts indicate such strong sentiments that prevent the desire for encounter.

> The current status quo is a violation of human rights and international treaties . . . no other country apart from Turkey recognises them [Turkish Cypriot administration] so why should I recognise them by crossing?
>
> (Panos, 40 years old, Famagusta)

I would feel like a traitor if I crossed and to be honest I feel shamed for the Greek Cypriots who visit and spend their money there . . . it doesn't have to do with Turkish Cypriots personally, I am not a racist.

(Konstantinos, 36 years old, Nicosia)

Discussion and conclusions

Drawing from the post-conflict context of Cyprus, which provides an interesting background for examining the socio-cultural and political factors shaping the visitor-host encounter, the study offers interesting insights. First, findings highlight the influence of the socio-political environment on the nature of the visitor-host encounter, as perceptions and attitudes seem to regulate the degree and nature of contact. Specifically, the study identifies a category of non-visitors, revealing that in post-conflict settings, the rigidity of negative perceptions and attitudes may reinforce people's unwillingness to visit a conflictual destination in the first place. In addition to intensifying animosity, prolonged conflict may also increase perceptions of safety in terms of visiting a hostile outgroup. Indeed, concerns over safety issues surrounding a potential visit were expressed by Greek Cypriots. Evidently, if the visitor-host encounter literature is to be enriched, there needs to be a shift of academic focus from being primarily on evaluations of perceptual and attitudinal change following visitation to post-conflict destinations, to also including examinations of the reasons predisposing and/or inhibiting visitation inclination.

Second, by highlighting the complexity of the visitor-host encounters in post-conflict settings, the study suggests that visitation does not necessarily translate into a close, reciprocal interaction between visitors and the host community. In fact, several types of interaction between visitors and hosts were identified. Within this context, the visitation motives and the frequency and structure of the visit emerge as influential on the nature of the encounter and, subsequently, on the mutuality of the benefits derived from the contact. In the complex environment of post-conflict destinations, passive forms of visitor-host encounters may reinforce negative stereotyping and prejudice. Considering the impacts that the visitor-host encounter may have on the tourist experience and on the host community's perceptions and attitudes towards visitors, hopeful implications may emerge from contact between people in hostile destinations affected by conflict, such as in the case of Cyprus. For instance, confidence-building measures, education programmes and bi-communal activities might narrow the gap in communication, interaction and understanding between hostile groups. Such initiatives may seek ways to encourage willingness to cross to the 'other' side, as well as ensure that a structured environment is provided in which the encounter can take place in a positive, reciprocal manner. In this regard, the perceived safety of the environment in which contact takes places is important in strengthening willingness to (re)visit. Indeed, evidence from the Korean Peninsula indicates that fear of being held hostage in North Korea prevents South Koreans from visiting.

Future research would undoubtedly benefit from comparative studies on the visitor-host encounter between Turkish Cypriot and Greek Cypriots as both visitors and the host community. There is great knowledge to be uncovered from the duality of the visitor-host relationship between members of hostile destinations affected by conflict. Given the varying degrees of contact among people visiting a hostile outgroup, it would be interesting if future research examines different types of encounters within post-conflict destinations such as service encounters occurring in commercial settings and/or social encounters in non-commercial settings, rather than placing all forms of relations between visitors and members of the host community in post-conflict settings under the term 'visitor-host encounters.' Extant literature on the tourism and peace nexus would benefit from investigations of the visitor-host encounter in private, socio-cultural and commercial domains, as new perspectives in the visitor-host relationship need to be developed.

References

Allport, G. W. (1954). *The nature of prejudice*. Oxford: Addison-Wesley.

Alluri, R. M. (2009). *The role of tourism in post-conflict peace-building in Rwanda*. Swisspeace: Bern.

Altinay, L., & Bowen, D. (2006). Politics and tourism interface: The case of Cyprus. *Annals of Tourism Research, 33*(4), 939–956.

Anastasopoulos, P. G. (1992). Tourism and attitude change: Greek tourists visiting Turkey. *Annals of Tourism Research, 19*(4), 629–642.

Askjellerud, S. (2003). The tourist: A messenger of peace? *Annals of Tourism Research, 30*(3), 741–744.

Bryant, R. (2010). The state of utella silences. *The Cyprus Review, 22*(2), 113.

Causevic, S. (2010). Tourism which erases borders: An introspection into Bosnia and Herzegovina. In O. Mouffakir & I. Kelly (Eds.), *Tourism, progress and peace* (pp. 48–64). London: CABI.

Causevic, S., & Lynch, P. (2011). Phoenix tourism: Post-conflict tourism role. *Annals of Tourism Research, 38*(3), 780–800.

Chen, C. C., Lai, Y. H. R., Petrick, J. F., & Lin, Y. H. (2016). Tourism between divided nations: An examination of stereotyping on destination image. *Tourism Management, 55*, 25–36.

Chen, C. M. (2010). Role of tourism in connecting Taiwan and China: Assessing tourists' perceptions of the Kinmen – Xiamen links. *Tourism Management, 31*(3), 421–424.

Cho, M. (2007). A re-examination of tourism and peace: The case of the Mt. Gumgang tourism development on the Korean Peninsula. *Tourism Management, 28*(2), 556–569.

D'Amore, L. J. (1988). Tourism-a vital force for peace. *Tourism Management, 9*(2), 151–154.

De Kadt, E. (1979). Social planning for tourism in the developing countries. *Annals of Tourism Research, 6*(1), 36–48.

Dikomitis, L. (2004). A moving field: Greek Cypriot refugees returning "home". *Durham Anthropology Journal, 12*(1), 7–20.

Dowling, R. K. (1992). Tourism and environmental integration: The journey from idealism to realism. In C. Cooper & A. Lockwood (Eds.), *Progress in tourism, recreation and hospitality management* (pp. 33–46). London: CABI.

Durko, A., & Petrick, J. (2015). The utella project an education initiative to suggest tourism as a means to peace between the United States and Afghanistan. *Journal of Travel Research, 55*(8), 1–13.

European Commission. (2017). *Report from the commission to the council.* Retrieved from 5 May 2018, https://eurlex.europa.eu/legalcontent

Farmaki, A. (2017). The tourism and peace nexus. *Tourism Management, 59,* 528–540.

Fisher, R. J. (2001). Cyprus: The failure of mediation and the escalation of an identity-based conflict to an adversarial impasse. *Journal of Peace Research, 38*(3), 307–326.

Guo, Y., Kim, S. S., Timothy, D. J., & Wang, K. C. (2006). Tourism and reconciliation between Mainland China and Taiwan. *Tourism Management, 27*(5), 997–1005.

Hennink, M., Hutter, I., & Bailey, A. (2010). *Qualitative research methods.* Sage: London.

Higgins-Desbiolles, F. (2003). Reconciliation tourism: Tourism healing divided societies. *Tourism Recreation Research, 28*(3), 35–44.

Isaac, R. K. (2010a). Palestinian tourism in transition: Hope, aspiration, or reality. *The Journal of Tourism and Peace Research, 1*(1), 16–26.

Isaac, R. K. (2010b). Moving from pilgrimage to responsible tourism: The case of Palestine. *Current Issues in Tourism, 13*(6), 579–590.

Kim, S. S., & Prideaux, B. (2003). Tourism, peace, politics and ideology: Impacts of the Mt. Gumgang tour project in the Korean Peninsula. *Tourism Management, 24*(6), 675–685.

Kim, S. S., & Prideaux, B. (2006). An investigation of the relationship between South Korean domestic public opinion, tourism development in North Korea and a role for tourism in promoting peace on the Korean peninsula. *Tourism Management, 27*(1), 124–137.

Kim, S. S., Prideaux, B., & Prideaux, J. (2007). Using tourism to promote peace on the Korean Peninsula. *Annals of Tourism Research, 34*(2), 291–309.

Kim, Y. K., & Crompton, J. L. (1990). Role of tourism in unifying the two Koreas. *Annals of Tourism Research, 17*(3), 353–366.

Krippendorf, J. (1987). *The holiday makers: Understanding the impact of leisure and travel.* Oxford: Butterworth-Heinemann.

Litvin, S. W. (1998). Tourism: The world's peace industry? *Journal of Travel Research, 37*(1), 63–66.

McCracken, G. (1988). *The long interview* (Vol. 13). Thousand Oaks, CA: Sage.

Milman, A., Reichel, A., & Pizam, A. (1990). The impact of tourism on ethnic attitudes: The Israeli-Egyptian case. *Journal of Travel Research, 29*(2), 45–49.

Nyaupane, G. P., Teye, V., & Paris, C. (2008). Innocents abroad: Attitude change toward hosts. *Annals of Tourism Research, 35*(3), 650–667.

Pettigrew, T. F., & Tropp, L. R. (2006). A meta-analytic test of intergroup contact theory. *Journal of Personality and Social Psychology, 90*(5), 751.

Pizam, A., Fleischer, A., & Mansfeld, Y. (2002). Tourism and social change: The case of Israeli ecotourists visiting Jordan. *Journal of Travel Research, 41*(2), 177–184.

Pizam, A., Jafari, J., & Milman, A. (1991). Influence of tourism on attitudes: US students visiting USSR. *Tourism Management, 12*(1), 47–54.

Reisinger, Y., Kozak, M., & Visser, E. (2013). Turkish host gaze at Russian tourists: A cultural perspective. In O. Moufakkir & Y. Reisinger (Eds.), *The host gaze in global tourism* (pp. 47–66). Wallingford: CABI.

Ritchie, J., Lewis, J., Nicholls, C. M., & Ormston, R. (2014). *Qualitative research practice* (4th ed.). Thousand Oaks, CA: Sage.

Robinson, O. C. (2014). Sampling in Interview-based qualitative research: A theoretical and practical guide. *Qualitative Research in Psychology, 11*(1), 25–41.

Salazar, N. B. (2006). Building a "culture of peace" through tourism: Reflexive and analytical notes and queries. *Universitas Humanística, 62*, 319–336.

Scott, J. (2012). Tourism, civil society and peace in Cyprus. *Annals of Tourism Research, 39*(4), 2114–2132.

Selwyn, T., & Karkut, J. (2007). The politics of institution building and European co-operation: Reflections on an EC TEMPUS project on tourism and culture in Bosnia-Herzegovina. In *Tourism and politics: Global frameworks and local realities* (pp. 123–145). Oxford: Elsevier.

Sharpley, R. (2014). Host perceptions of tourism: A review of the research. *Tourism Management, 42*, 37–49.

Smith, V. L. (1977). *Hosts and guests: The anthropology of tourism.* Philadelphia, PA: University of Pennsylvania Press.

Sönmez, S. F., & Apostolopoulos, Y. (2000). Conflict resolution through tourism cooperation? The case of the partitioned island-state of cyprus. *Journal of Travel & Tourism Marketing, 9*(3), 35–48.

Sutton, W. A. (1967). Travel and understanding: Notes on the social structure of touring. *International Journal of Comparative Sociology, 8*, 218.

Tomljenovic, R. (2010). Tourism and intercultural understanding or contact hypothesis revisited. In O. Moufakkir & I. Kelly (Eds.), *Tourism, progress and peace* (pp. 17–34). Oxford: CABI.

Wall, G., & Mathieson, A. (2006). *Tourism: Change, impacts, and opportunities.* London: Pearson Education.

Webster, C., & Timothy, D. J. (2006). Travelling to the "other side": The occupied zone and Greek Cypriot views of crossing the Green Line. *Tourism Geographies, 8*(2), 162–181.

Yu, L. (1997). Travel between politically divided China and Taiwan. *Asia Pacific Journal of Tourism Research, 2*(1), 19–30.

Zhang, J. J. (2013). Borders on the move: Cross-strait tourists' material moments on "the other side" in the midst of rapprochement between China and Taiwan. *Geoforum, 48*, 94–101.

Part IV

Conclusion

18 Reflections and future perspectives on conflict-ridden destinations

Erdinç Çakmak, Rami K. Isaac and Richard Butler

The contributors to this volume represent the diversity of interests examining the effects of various conflicts on tourism and hospitality. In particular, the socio-cultural impact of conflict and its relevance for tourism stakeholders is of interest to scholars, not only in tourism and hospitality, but also in mainstream social sciences including sociology, political science and anthropology, many practitioners of which design and consult in both the public and private sectors. From this point of view, we trust this volume is relevant not only for academic readers but also for policy-makers and managers in conflict situations as they review their strategies. We hope also that this volume will accelerate the growth of the studies in exploring conflict and its resolution in tourism destinations.

While this volume's contributors have ranged widely across topics and places, it is worthwhile to summarize a few thematic elements in detail and highlight further developments and future trends from a comparative perspective. These themes reflect some of the contemporary issues in tourism generally, and we recap them briefly in this concluding chapter.

Conflict as an attraction for visitation

Some concluding ideas have already been outlined in the preceding sections, namely in Chapters 2, 3, 6 and 10, which explore structurally similar matter – conflict as an element of thrill and excitement in mutually enlightening ways. Although visitation for holiday purposes to conflict-ridden destinations is rare and confined to a small number of individuals, personal traits, desires for thrill and risk attract people to these places (Butler & Suntikul, 2017). Heritage is often a contested phenomenon and thus a source of conflict, and travel to and experience of destinations with difficult and often conflicting interpretations of heritage is increasingly common in recent years. Difficult heritage and dark tourism sites attract visitors for varying reasons, including a desire to satisfy their curiosity and to validate if those events really happened (Isaac & Çakmak, 2014). As well, there is often an increase in domestic travel to conflict-affected places since domestic tourists also show interest in narratives and memorials, and wish to commemorate victims. Yet, there are few studies which consider the phenomenon of conflict as a tourist attraction and which draws tourists particularly to a destination. There is a need to determine when a conflict is perceived as an attraction, who may be interested in that and how these tourists engage with the actors and places of conflict.

Conflict as a barrier for visitation

While it serves as a leitmotif in every chapter, the notion that conflict destabilizes a destination and negatively influences tourism and hospitality is foregrounded by the authors of Chapters 8, 9, 11 and 13. These chapters mainly argue that political, social, ecological and urban conflicts influence (inter)national tourists' travel patterns, as tourists avoid pleasure travel to a conflict-affected destination. Regardless of whether a conflict has a high intensity (e.g. terrorist attacks, hurricanes, disease outbreaks, political instability) or a light intensity (e.g. disputes between tourism stakeholders, protests, non-violent events, overtourism), it is likely to cause a disruption to the tourism and hospitality industry by means of reducing potential visitors' perceptions of safety, potentially degrading the infrastructure and possibly influencing the mobility of visitors. The individual enterprises in the tourism and hospitality industries are vulnerable to such events. For example, a social conflict that is non-violent at the beginning can transform into a crisis and damage businesses, specifically small businesses. Therefore, it is necessary for all businesses to understand the relevance and potential implications of a conflict and how to position themselves in the market during the recovery process.

Guardians of tourism during conflict

Chapter 4 takes up the issue of whom tourists trust most in a conflict situation. The increasing complexity of conflicts across the world requires high levels of expertise in travel planning. Conflict is often interpreted differently by several sources (e.g. ministries of foreign affairs, DMOs, tour operators) and travel advisories are provided to potential visitors. Although the perceptions of safety and security by various tourist segments and nationalities have been widely examined, there is less known about whom tourists trust most when they decide to travel to a conflict-affected destination, and who they perceive as their guardians in conflict situations. When a destination's image has been affected (e.g. whether a destination would not be safe or stable), visitors, investors and potential movers need relevant and accurate information. It is crucially important for tourism entrepreneurs to communicate effectively with their potential customers and partners in order to minimize any loss of trade during a conflict. There is also a need for studies exploring strategies for destination governments and DMOs seeking to recover their image during and after a conflict.

Making destinations in conflict areas more resilient

Making destinations better able to deal with the effects of the occurrence and resolution of conflict requires such destinations to become more resilient and the role of destination resilience, comprising community and organizational resilience, in reducing vulnerabilities in (post-conflict) destinations is examined in Chapter 5. Resilient destinations have resilient communities and organizations. A resilient destination, through a strong and united community and relevant organizations, has an appropriate capacity to react to inevitable events, recovers fast and restores its appeal and functions. In this way, tourism businesses at a resilient destination are less affected by these sudden events, but developing destination resilience towards conflicts is not a linear process, and is a multifaceted challenge. It is of paramount importance for conflict-ridden destinations to distinguish clearly which capacities should be maintained and what policies should be developed in order to increase their resilience. In addition, future research needs to highlight also the nexus between economic development and resilience in conflict-affected destinations.

Role of tourism in conflict resolution

The authors of Chapters 7 and 12 explore the role of tourism in conflict resolution. While scholarly consensus and disagreement about the role of tourism in conflict areas are contextually situated throughout this volume, exactly how tourism can contribute to the peace of progress is an ongoing discussion. Those sceptical of tourism's contribution to the peace progress have argued that tourism is not capable of being a direct prevention option of conflict, and may even worsen the underlying causes of conflict. Those heralding tourism as a peace generator have argued that tourism improves mutual understanding, brings people closer together and presents a vital force for peace. However, the role of tourism in conflict resolution has not been studied systematically. Existing research has utilized small and mostly single case studies, and tourism's direct contribution to conflict resolution has not been effectively measured in these studies. For instance, while the Myanmar army signed bilateral ceasefires in 2013 and revealed a desire to bring development to conflict-affected regions (e.g. Kayin State as debriefed in Chapter 7), the same army has been accused of persecuting the Rohingya people from Rakhine State since 2017. According to the United Nations Office for the Coordination of Humanitarian Affairs (2018), more than 700,000 Rohingya people have fled across to border to Bangladesh and another 350,000 to the refugee camps along the border as of November 2018. It is not yet clear how and when state forces and local people should start working together at conflict-ridden destinations with a purpose of improving livelihoods, and at what point tourism could be used for this purpose instead of being propaganda for national discourse.

Discourses and representations in conflict-ridden destinations

While every chapter in this volume has in common a concern with discourse, representation and conflict, the notion of discourse in post-conflict destinations is examined specifically by the authors in Part III. In a recovery process, a conflict-affected destination is often being reconfigured in the light of struggles of identities and stories. State- or municipality-driven stories from the 'top' and resident-driven narratives from the 'bottom' often contest with each other in determining which elements to forget and which to remember, particularly with regard to a difficult past. Here, the reconfiguration of a place, the restructuring of a story and the reconstruction of a preserved heritage have been dominated by such discourses. In most conflict-affected places, such a discourse has not been generated from the collective memory, and consists of and reflects an unequal distribution of knowledge and power. Since tourism is a form of communication in which reality is represented by images, symbols and murals, tourism authorities select preferable narratives from the past. Through this, they do not only reconfigure the structure but also contribute to editing history. From this viewpoint, examining discourses and representations in conflict-affected destinations becomes a matter not only for scholars, but also for global institutions and actors. Some of these include the United Nation World Tourism Organisation, globally affiliated social and political interest groups, cultural entrepreneurs in post-conflict destinations and local residents, survivors and politicians.

Putting it together: a parting comment

The editors feel that this volume faithfully reflects the collage of contemporary issues in the emerging topic of tourism and hospitality in conflict-ridden destinations. Collectively, the contributors of this volume have striven to capture the socio-cultural impact of conflict on tourism and hospitality, co-deployed by stakeholders engaged in creating, consuming and coping practices in conflict-affected places. Although this volume has its own internal logic and many areas of consensus, it does not provide ready-made solutions or universally accepted cutting-edge definitions. Some questions remain just that – questions. We expect this volume to act first as a kaleidoscope of viewpoints on the dynamic subject of tourism and hospitality in conflict-ridden destinations, as the depth and breadth of this emerging topic is explored as scholars discover patterns, linkages and paradigms in their work, and then to sharpen the thoughts and stories in this field. We hope the research exemplars presented in this volume inspire additional inquiry, and encourage readers to contribute in exploring other issues affecting tourism and hospitality in what seems to be a never-ending and constantly changing set of conflict-ridden destinations worldwide.

References

Butler, R., & Suntikul, W. (Eds.). (2017). *Tourism and political change*. Oxford: Goodfellow Publishers Ltd.

Isaac, R. K., & Çakmak, E. (2014). Understanding visitor's motivation at sites of death and disaster: The case of former transit camp Westerbork, the Netherlands. *Current Issues in Tourism, 17*(2), 164–179.

United Nations Office for the Coordination of Humanitarian Affairs (OCHA). (2018). *Rohingya refugee crisis*. Retrieved January 25, 2018, from https://www.unocha.org/rohingya-refugee-crisis

Index

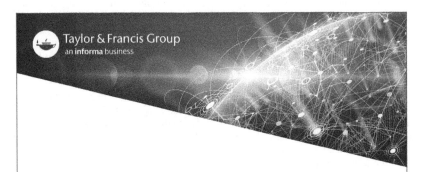